THE CONTENTIOUS PUBLIC SPHERE

Princeton Studies in Contemporary China

Yu Xie, *series editor*

The Contentious Public Sphere, Ya-Wen Lei

The Contentious Public Sphere

Law, Media, and Authoritarian Rule in China

Ya-Wen Lei

PRINCETON UNIVERSITY PRESS

PRINCETON AND OXFORD

Published by Princeton University Press,
41 William Street, Princeton, New Jersey 08540

In the United Kingdom: Princeton University Press,
6 Oxford Street, Woodstock, Oxfordshire OX20 1TR

press.princeton.edu

ISBN 978-0-691-16686-5

Library of Congress Control Number: 2017935147

British Library Cataloging-in-Publication Data is available

This book has been composed in Adobe Text Pro and Gotham

Jacket photograph courtesy of Valery Voennyy / Alamy Stock Photo

Printed on acid-free paper. ∞

Printed in the United States of America

10 9 8 7 6 5 4 3 2 1

To my mom, Shu-Ling Wu

CONTENTS

LIST OF FIGURES AND TABLES

Figures

Tables

ACKNOWLEDGMENTS

This book is the product of a long and unexpected intellectual journey to which many people have contributed. First, during my time at the University of Michigan, Greta Krippner encouraged me to follow my intellectual and sociological passion, rather than worry about what might be fashionable or easily publishable. Her perspective on scholarship, her intellectual resourcefulness, and her sincere personality continuously make her mentorship paramount. She is my lighthouse in a sometimes stormy scholarly sea. Likewise, it would be difficult to overstate the valuable critical intervention of Peggy Somers. Unsatisfied with a dissertation prospectus outlining my plan to write three articles rather than a manuscript, Peggy insisted I reconsider the book format. She pushed me to find a puzzle to be solved and generously helped me outline the entire dissertation. I count her notes on that prospectus among my treasures. Mary Gallagher, Mark Mizruchi, and Yu Xie also posed important and challenging questions that further developed this project. Their teaching, encouragement, criticism, and generous help were priceless. At Michigan, I also benefited tremendously from Daniel Xiaodan Zhou, Alwyn Lim, Byungho Lee, and Hiro Saito. I am so grateful for their friendship and intellectual input.

Harvard's Society of Fellows gave me tremendous freedom and ample resources with which to pursue my work. From their fold, I received encouragement from Amartya Sen; knowledge about the publication process from Noah Feldman; and great academic advice from Matthew Desmond. In addition, Daniela Cammack, Marta Figlerowicz, Abhishek Kaicker, Florian Klinger, Adam Mestyan, Chris Rogan, and Alma Steingart, my dear friends, questioned, criticized, and thus strengthened my book proposal. I also benefited greatly from the kindness and friendship of Alexander Bevilacqua, Ann Ran, and Andrew Strominger. Diana Morse, Kelly Katz, and Yesim Erdmann at the Society of Fellows provided administrative assistance, social support, and genuine warmth.

I benefited from the China sociology group at Harvard, especially from the important questions of Ezra Vogel and Marty Whyte. In the Department of Sociology at Harvard, I also benefited from the administrative assistance of Deborah De Laurell and Suzanne Ogungbadero. Kimberly Hoang and Maggie Frye gave incredibly useful feedback on my writing and even helped me develop a writing schedule. Phillipa Chong assisted in all of these ways, as well as offering emotional support throughout; I thank her especially. I have so much appreciation for Kim Greenwell, my outstanding editor, for her brilliant feedback and dear friendship. I have been working with Kim for years, and her expertise was invaluable as I wrote this manuscript. I also thank my excellent copyeditor Melanie Mallon; my two former editors at the Princeton University Press, Eric Schwartz and Eric Crahan; as well as my current editors Meagan Levinson and Ellen Foos, for their professional handling and assistance. Meagan's excellent work made the publication process much smoother.

As a first-time book author, I was privileged to have seven senior scholars—Yochai Benkler, Edward Greer, Orlando Patterson, Michael Schudson, Paul Starr, Ezra Vogel, and Guobin Yang—to read my book manuscript, six of whom attended a workshop on my book. Their candid criticism and constructive suggestions significantly strengthened the finished product. After working on this project for so many years, I found my enthusiasm rekindled by the participants in that workshop. A special thank you to Michael Schudson—a phenomenal reader and mentor. Michael read my manuscript *twice*. His extremely detailed and helpful criticisms helped transform my work from a dissertation to a book. The generous support of Harvard's Weatherhead Center and Michèle Lamont made my book workshop possible.

I would not have been able to accomplish all that I have without various forms of institutional support. I received funding from the Rackham Graduate School, the Center for Chinese Studies, and the Department of Sociology at the University of Michigan, as well as from the National Science Foundation, the Chiang Ching-Kuo Foundation for International Scholarly Exchange, the Republic of China (ROC) Ministry of Education, and Harvard University's Milton Grant, to name a few funding sources. I am indebted to many more institutions for their provision of fellowships, scholarships, and grants. In addition, I have incorporated materials from three earlier articles: "Freeing the Press," *American Journal of Sociology*; "Contesting Legality in Authoritarian Contexts," *Law and Society Review*; and "The Political Consequences of the Rise of the Internet," *Political Communication*. I thank the journals for permission to use the material here.

I am grateful to many friends in China and Taiwan, including Tianzhao Liu, a Knight-Wallace Fellow at the University of Michigan. How I cherish the many snowy days spent talking with Tianzhao in her cozy apartment about media in China. I learned so much! I thank Lin Wang for his friendship and fieldwork assistance as well as his unfathomable knowledge and wisdom. I am deeply grateful to all my friends and interviewees whom I cannot name due to confidentiality. I was honored and touched to hear their stories and thus bear witness to their lives. The encouragement, support, and assistance from my friends in China continue to motivate me to work harder, always hoping to repay what I have received. Similarly, I would like to thank my friends in Taiwan: I am grateful to Allen Li and Chih-Jou Chen for their friendship and best wishes. I thank M. J. Wang for discussing my ideas and supporting me in innumerable ways.

Most important, I am deeply indebted to my dear family. I dedicate this book to my mom, Shu-Ling Wu, who respects my life choices and provides me with unconditional love. My brave mom raised three daughters on her own in a patriarchal society. Although she's never attended college or studied feminism, she believes in enabling women through the power of education. I owe all my achievements to her constant love and wisdom. I also have the best sisters in the world: Ya-Chun and Ya-Ting. And I thank Ning-Er, my daughter and friend, who imbues my life with pleasure and meaning. I thank my grandma, my brother-in-law Elton, my niece Yu-Chien, my father, and other family members for their love. And I hope my grandpa, who has passed away, knows that I am working hard and love what I do. Lastly, I thank my partner, Adam Mestyan, for everything.

ABBREVIATIONS

ACJA All-China Journalists' Association

BBS bulletin board system

CCP Chinese Communist Party

CNNIC China Internet Network Information Center

CPPCC Chinese People's Political Consultative Conference

EU European Union

ICT information and communication technology

IPO initial public offerings

KMT Kuomintang

LGBT lesbian, gay, bisexual, and transgender

NCFC National Computing and Networking Facility of China

NGO nongovernmental organizations

NPC National People's Congress

PRC People's Republic of China

RTO reverse takeover

SEEC Stock Exchange Executive Council

SOE state-owned enterprise

TASS Telegraph Agency of the Soviet Union

VPN virtual private network

WTO World Trade Organization

1

Introduction

In the early to mid-2000s, something new began to happen in online forums in China. Increasingly, contentious events were capturing widespread public attention, sparking heated discussion and even protests and other forms of collective action. Chinese citizens were coming together not only to converse and debate with one another, but also to challenge a government infamous for censorship and political control. One after another, these contentious events, or what Chinese people began to call "public opinion incidents," came and went, like waves hitting the rocks.

In 2003, for example, Sun Zhigang, a twenty-seven-year-old man in Guangzhou, died in police custody after being wrongly detained and beaten by officers. His death triggered strong criticism, online and off, of the Chinese government. The synergy between media and legal professionals and Chinese netizens (*wangmin*), or Internet users,[1] eventually led to the overhaul of unconstitutional detention regulations.

In 2008, the Chinese government ordered that all new computers be sold with preinstalled content-control software to prevent the viewing of pornography. Chinese netizens accused the state of infringing on their right to free communication, and the Chinese state decided to abandon the policy.

In 2012, the Propaganda Department of Guangdong Province interfered in the publication of *Southern Weekly*'s New Year special editorial. Published by the Southern Media Group based in Guangzhou, *Southern Weekly* is considered one of the most outspoken newspapers in China, despite being affiliated with the Guangdong provincial government. The original editorial, titled "Dream of China and Dream of Constitutionalism," promoted notions of freedom, liberal democracy, and constitutionalism. Guangdong propaganda officers bypassed ordinary editorial practices to impose significant revisions. After journalists disclosed this intervention, intellectuals, lawyers, media professionals, students, entrepreneurs, celebrities, and ordinary citizens protested vigorously against the censorship and voiced support for *Southern Weekly*. The original editorial publicly circulated online, as protesters, explicitly identifying themselves as citizens (*gongmin*), demonstrated outside *Southern Weekly*'s headquarters. Their protest banners and signs unequivocally demanded democracy, constitutionalism, freedom of speech, and freedom of the press.

I give these examples not to suggest the complete victory of public opinion in China. Indeed, the *Southern Weekly* protests ultimately led to the government tightening its control of the Southern Media Group in 2013. My point, rather, is to highlight the novelty and vibrancy of political communication, contention, and participation in and beyond China's public sphere that emerged during this period. I am far from a naïve observer of China's politics; nonetheless, the emergence of a contentious public sphere in China was a revelation to me because it defied the conventional image of political and civic life in an authoritarian country. China is arguably one of the more "politically closed" authoritarian regimes today, as it is one of the few without multiple political parties or national elections (Diamond 2002). Furthermore, international organizations that monitor and rank political freedom, such as Freedom House and Reporters Without Borders, consistently rate China as one of the countries with the least freedom of press and freedom of speech[2] and one of the top "enemies of the Internet."[3]

Authoritarian states, by definition, undermine civil society—the basis on which the public sphere is built—thus conventional wisdom tells us that the conditions for political life and a public sphere in such contexts are likely to be quite bleak and suffocating (Habermas 1996, 369). Yet, when I looked at what was going on in China, I saw lively political discussion, contention, and engagement—in short, the emergence of a vibrant public sphere, against all apparent odds. Moreover, this public sphere did not look much different from the one I'd grown up with in Taiwan, a young liberal democracy, or the one in the United States, where I have been living for more than a decade—an ostensibly advanced liberal democracy. These seeming similarities deeply perplexed me. Common indices used by social scientists to measure levels of freedom and to classify political regimes, such as Freedom House's Freedom in the World Index, suggest that civil and political liberties have remained static in China since the 1989 Tiananmen incident, but such indices fail to capture a profound political, social, and cultural transformation that has occurred in the absence of regime change.

When I say that a nationwide contentious public sphere has emerged in China, I am referring to an unruly sphere capable of generating issues and agendas not set by the Chinese state, as opposed to a sphere mostly orchestrated and constrained by said state. Over time, China's contentious public sphere has been increasingly recognized by the Chinese state as a force to be reckoned and negotiated with. Starting around 2010, official media of the Chinese Communist Party (CCP), such as the *People's Daily*, began to warn of a threatening public sphere mediated by cell phones, the Internet, and even some unruly voices within state-controlled media.[4] The state's awareness of these developments is precisely why I am careful not to overstate the stability or permanence of the newly emerged contentious public sphere. Indeed, this provocative public arena has encountered serious opposition and setbacks, particularly since 2013. Seeing the rise of such a sphere as a threat to national security and an indication of ideological struggle between the West and China, the Chinese state has taken comprehensive and combative measures to contain it. These measures include enhancing censorship and surveillance, attacking key actors, upgrading propaganda, and asserting China's cyber-sovereignty. The scale and intensity of crackdowns on public opinion leaders, lawyers, journalists, activists, nongovernmental organizations (NGOs), and media are immense.

The Book's Central Questions and Arguments

In this book I aim to demonstrate as well as understand these political, social, and cultural transformations. How can we explain the formation and development of China's contentious public sphere, particularly in light of ongoing state control and repression? How did a political culture of contention emerge and extend to various social groups? And how durable is China's emergent and contested public sphere? I argue that the rise of China's contentious public sphere was an unintended consequence of the Chinese state's campaign of authoritarian modernization. The government desperately needed to modernize in the aftermath of the Cultural Revolution. To do so, the state institutionalized the double-edged instruments of modern law, marketized media, and the Internet. It sought to utilize but also contain these instruments, recognizing the potential risk each posed of empowering professionals and citizens and destabilizing political control. Nonetheless, the state's choices set in motion complex and interconnected processes beyond its control. Building legal and media institutions and adopting information technologies, paired with political fragmentation and marketization, increased the capabilities of citizens and professionals, encouraged the formation of multiple overlapping social networks of collaboration, engendered widespread legal and rights consciousness, and created a space for contentious politics. Through everyday practices and the production of so-called public opinion incidents (*yulun shijian*), media and legal professionals, public opinion leaders, activists, NGOs, and netizens translated individual grievances into collective contention—and in so doing, facilitated the rise of a contentious public sphere.

The future of this sphere remains unclear. Inadequate institutional protection means the state can still use the law, media, and information technologies for punishment, surveillance, and propaganda. How different political and social forces will work together—in creative, possibly even unexpected ways—over the years to come, in a changing global context, will shape the adversarial public space and determine its future.

My perspective departs from that of most research on the public sphere in that I accentuate and trace the connection between multiple institutional processes—the building of legal and media institutions and the adoption of information technologies—as well as the relationship between these processes and a broader historical and global context of modernization. Studies of the public sphere in different contexts tend to focus on the role of the media—mostly a specific type of media, such as television and, increasingly, the Internet—in mediating the public experience (e.g., Calhoun and Yang 2007; Dahlgren 1995; Papacharissi 2002; Shirky 2011). Few studies consider institutional processes in the legal field or the connections between different institutional processes. After studying this issue for more than a decade, however, I have become convinced that to understand China's contentious public sphere, one has to weave together analytical strands usually kept separate by scholars in different disciplines, and then situate them in relation to China's modernization in a global context. I argue that the oft-neglected connections between different institutional processes—namely, the development of a legal system, the marketization of media, and the adoption of information technologies—are key to understanding China's contentious public sphere. These connections explain how contentious culture and practices emerged and spread across social groups and boundaries. Understanding the broader historical and global context of China's modernization is also crucial to understanding how various actors—from the Chinese state to political elites and ordinary citizens—participated in these institutional processes.

Briefly, there are four major components to my argument. The first two concern China's modernization project and its constituent institutional processes, as well as their effects on the contentious public sphere. The final two components concern the mechanisms and conditions that have mediated boundary transgressions and the connections between institutional processes.

CHINA'S MODERNIZATION PROJECT AND THE AUTHORITARIAN DILEMMA OF MODERNIZATION

Situating the development of China's contentious public sphere in relation to the Chinese state's post–Cultural Revolution project of modernization is critical. Although Jürgen Habermas's *Structural Transformation of the Public Sphere*, analyzing the development of the classical bourgeois public sphere

in Europe, offers little discussion of the state, several schola
pointed out the need to examine the state's role in the devel
public sphere, especially the role of the state beyond suppression
Schudson 1994). In Paul Starr's book on the creation of media communica
in the United States, he argues that the developmental path of the American
media and public sphere was shaped by cumulative and branching "constitutive
choices," by which Starr means "choices that create the material and institutional framework of fields of human activity" (Starr 2004, 1–2). His narrative
shows that the state was a key player in making these constitutive choices—an
argument highly relevant to the Chinese context.

The Chinese state likewise made constitutive choices, which must be understood in relation to the Chinese state's pursuit of modernization in a global
context. In J. P. Nettl and Roland Robertson's work on globalization, they argue
that societies engaged in modernization often compare themselves with other
societies. Using Meiji Japan as an example, Nettl and Robertson show that
"latecomers" to the project of modernization tend to encounter difficulties
deciding which images of modernity should guide them and where they should
look for inspiration. These difficulties are further intertwined with issues related to national identity (Nettl and Robertson 1966; Robertson 1992). In the
case of China, globalization provides a critical context that has influenced the
state's understanding of modernity and how it has acted to achieve that end—
especially the state's adoption of and engagement with ideas, institutions, and
cultures from elsewhere. Modernization in China was a defensive reaction to
imperialism, initiated by nationalist elites to preserve the Qing dynasty state.
Following a series of military defeats by the West and Japan, intellectuals and
officials within China began to see their country as a latecomer to development, and they started looking to the West and Japan as major reference points.
At first, modernization focused on learning Western science, technology, and
education, but it eventually extended to include the adoption of Western legal
and political institutions (Zarrow 2016).

China's pursuit of modernization, despite being interrupted by revolutions,
regime changes, wars, and other upheavals, has continued in the People's Republic of China (PRC) era. Pursuit of socialist industrialization and elimina-
tion of exploitation and poverty were written into the preamble of the PRC's
first constitution, enacted in 1954. China amended its constitution in 1982.
The amended preamble makes clear the nation's most critical task: to "concentrate its effort on socialist modernization along the road of Chinese-style
socialism"; in addition, the Chinese people are enlisted to "develop socialist
democracy, improve the socialist legal system, and work hard and self-reliantly
to modernize industry, agriculture, national defense, and science and technology step by step to turn China into a socialist country with a high level of
culture and democracy." Like China's modernization projects in the late Qing

and republican periods, the PRC's modernization project has also involved interacting with and even partially adopting ideas and institutions from other parts of the world, particularly the Soviet Union and increasingly the West, such as modern law that acknowledges the concept of rights. In addition, in the PRC state's pursuit of political and economic goals, it has had to open itself to certain transnational institutions. For instance, to profit from international trade, the Chinese state subjected itself to the rules of the World Trade Organization (WTO) when building domestic institutions (Bhattasali, Li, and Martin 2004; DeWoskin 2001; Lee 2003; Lin 2004; Pangestu and Mrongowius 2004; Wang 2001; Zhao 2008).

Despite influence from the West and transnational institutions, however, PRC's modernization project is clearly still very much an authoritarian one (Atabaki and Zürcher 2004; Gel'man 2016). The project's goals include a high level of socioeconomic development through rapid economic growth, as well as improved efficacy of governance through legal and political institution building—but all under the political monopoly of the CCP. And the ultimate goal of pursuing modernization and developing what leaders have termed "socialism with Chinese characteristics" is to strengthen the CCP's legitimacy and secure its authoritarian rule.

Yet the Chinese state's authoritarian modernization project has encountered what I call an "authoritarian dilemma of modernization." On the one hand, the state has to build economic, legal, and political institutions to pursue socioeconomic development. The state also needs capable professionals and citizens to make institutions work, produce economic growth, and ultimately achieve the goal of modernization. These capable agents need to be educated and have knowledge, information, and even some autonomy to participate in the tasks designated by the state. For instance, to have a functioning legal institution, the state needs capable legal professionals as well as citizens who have at least some basic legal knowledge. To collect information about governmental problems on the ground, the state must create institutions to inform citizens about what they should understand as "problems" as well as enable citizens to communicate with the state or media (Lorentzen 2014).

On the other hand, institution building and the creation of capable agents can be politically risky. When the state attempts to emulate successful examples of development, it tends to look to those found in liberal democracies. Adopting institutional designs associated with liberal democracies, even selectively, can have undesirable consequences for the maintenance of political monopoly. In addition, expansion of capability enlarges citizens' freedom to choose among different ways of living (Sen 2008). When agents become more capable, the state has more difficulty controlling their thinking and actions. Capable agents can identify loopholes in institutions and use knowledge, information, technology, institutions, and other resources for their own ends. They can participate in and influence the state-initiated modernization project in ways that potentially contradict the state's interests (Starr 2004). In addition, political elites, such as legal and media professionals, can promote their own versions of modernity that compete with the state's version, often challenging the state's ideal political and social order in the process. Of course, while expanding individual capability, the state can always seek to minimize such negative consequences, but the outcome remains uncertain. A vast literature debates the various political consequences of modernization, especially the relationship between modernization and democratization (Inglehart and Welzel 2005; Inglehart and Welzel 2010; Lipset 1959; Przeworski and Limongi 1997; Welzel 2006; Welzel and Inglehart 2008). I discuss my findings in relation to this literature in the concluding chapter.

MEDIA AND LAW AS DOUBLE-EDGED SWORDS

The Chinese state's institution building in the media and legal fields demonstrates the state's authoritarian dilemma of modernization. As part of the PRC state's authoritarian modernization project, building media and legal institutions had profound consequences for the development of China's contentious public sphere. The state wanted to use media and the law to achieve its goals, but it was unable to prevent other actors from using the same tools to achieve other purposes. Understanding how this happened requires considering the double-edged nature of media and the law—specifically, in what ways and under what conditions do these institutions serve alternately as tools of empowerment and emancipation or as tools of control and suppression?

Many studies have pointed to the media influence on the development of the public sphere. In the Western context, scholars have repeatedly argued that economic power has entrenched media institutions, contributing to depoliticized public communication and politically alienated citizens (Boggs 2000; Bourdieu 2001). Yet research also suggests that when the media is able to mediate the discussion of fundamental societal problems, it can help to produce a more critical political culture and facilitate an effective public sphere (Gurevitch and Blumler 1990; Habermas 1989, 1996, 2006; Peters 2008). In the Chinese context, scholars have studied the political consequences of the state's media policy. In the past, newspapers in China were fully subsidized by the state and expected to serve as mouthpieces of state propaganda. Faced with financial difficulty, the Chinese state began to substantially withdraw funding for the media starting in 1992, forcing newspapers to rely on advertising and sales to survive. Media marketization became an integral part of the state's economic reform agenda. As a result of this process, newspapers remain state agencies responsible for propaganda, but they are also now market actors that must attract readers to survive. Scholars have studied the political implications of this process, yet most studies have not found the expected liberalizing effects (Hassid 2008; Lee 2000; Zhao 1998, 2004, 2008).

In a similar vein, existing studies also consider whether and how information communication technologies (ICTs), especially the Internet, can positively or negatively affect the public sphere (Benkler 2006; Shirky 2011; Dahlgren 2000; Dahlgren 2005; Downey and Fenton 2003; Papacharissi 2002; Sunstein 2007). Technocrats in China embraced ICTs to pursue modernization despite the potential political risks (Tai 2006). Some scholars argue that opening the country to the Internet has had democratic effects (Lei 2011; Tai 2006, 289; Tang 2005, 87, 98; Yang 2009; Zheng 2008), but others find no democratizing consequences, contending that the Internet has remained primarily a playground for entertainment and is still under the control of the state (Kluver et al. 2010; Peters 2002; Yang 2009, 10). Still other, middle-ground arguments reflect ambivalence about the Internet's impact (Zhao 2008; Zhou 2006).

In addition to the media, I emphasize the role of legal institutions in the development of the public sphere. The law is rarely discussed in the literature, but it must be incorporated into analysis of China's contentious public sphere for two reasons. First, while the media can reach various social groups, the law can provide a culturally integrative interface under certain conditions. As Habermas (1996, 353–54) points out, law provides a common cultural medium and language for citizens to use in identifying and talking about problems across different spheres of life. To be sure, Habermas's statement depends on many factors, such as the existence of a legal tradition and state efforts to diffuse law to citizens. In many authoritarian countries, legal principles and texts remain unknown to citizens and irrelevant to everyday life. Yet when law does penetrate society, it can serve as a common cultural medium.

Second, although the law is an instrument of domination, it can also be a symbolic resource for challenging the state's power (Bourdieu 1987; Bourdieu and Wacquant 1992, 112; Bourdieu 1994), and this has critical implications for explaining how resistance, contention, and opposition are possible in a politically restrictive environment. Given its institutional characteristics, the law is a resource that can be used against the state. Using codified law to govern is a form of symbolic domination through which the state imposes a common set of coercive norms (Bourdieu 1987; Bourdieu and Wacquant 1992, 112; Bourdieu 1994). The dilemma facing the state is that it cannot reap the benefits of this domination without at least appearing to subject itself to the order of law (Bourdieu 1987; Bourdieu 1994). Existing studies show that when authoritarian states begin to use the law to govern the populace and to recognize citizens' rights, citizens respond by learning how to mobilize the law themselves to negotiate and contend with the state (Lee 2007; Moustafa 2007; O'Brien and Li 2006). Furthermore, law's cultural characteristic as a plastic medium enables actors to develop alternative discourse and thus facilitates political contention

(Balkin 2009; Somers 1993). Legal reasoning is often indeterminate because the processes of fact finding, applying legal doctrines, and interpreting law are rife with opportunities for innovation and contestation (Balkin 2009). Citizens are not necessarily bound by the state's interpretation of legal texts or principles. Of course, whether ordinary citizens are able to use the law as a resource against the state hinges on many factors, particularly support from legal professionals.

INSTITUTIONS, INDIVIDUALS, NETWORKS, AND CIVIL POWER

Another major component of my argument is that the linkage between different institutional processes in China's modernization project played a key role in the development of China's nationwide public sphere and the formation of "the public." I argue that the *conjunction* of institutional processes in the legal and media fields not only led to individual transformation and empowerment but also gave rise to crosscutting, boundary-crossing social networks, which helped to spread contentious culture and practices across social groups. Collaboration across media and legal professionals, market mechanisms, and ICTs aided the creation of overlapping social networks. In short, sociologically speaking, institution and network mechanisms contributed to the social bases and formation of "the public" as a collective social entity.

The current literature suggests that a thriving public sphere depends on a favorable organization of citizenry (Calhoun 1993, 276). Habermas (1996, 369) contends that without a supportive civil society, the public sphere cannot discipline the political authority. In addition, the capacities of a public to identify, interpret, and present society-wide problems are rooted in "the voluntary associations of civic society and [are] embedded in liberal patterns of political culture and socialization" (Habermas 1996, 359). In Habermas's (1989) narrative, the conjugal family that emerged in the transition to capitalism produced rational agents who believed in the autonomy of the market and their own independence, while also coming to value the noninstrumental aspects of life (Habermas 1989, 46).[5] Other scholars focus on how socialization in voluntary associations produces capable agents. For instance, generalizing from social histories in Europe, Geoff Eley (1992, 296–97) points out that voluntary associations were key sites in and through which people expressed opinions, formed identity, and developed a political culture.

Together, the literature I discuss above underscores the need to explain how a public emerged in China. The Chinese state uses a technique of "divide and rule" to prevent social groups from joining and potentially becoming organized social or political forces (Perry 2007). Any explanation of the emergent public sphere thus needs to address the constituent processes of identify formation, capability development, politicization, and the establishment of social relations among individuals and within and between social groups (Calhoun 1992; Dahlgren 1995, 2005; Fraser 1990).

Drawing from the sociological literature on networks and institutions, I analyze the coevolution of individuals, networks, and institutions to understand the emergence of a public (Owen-Smith and Powell 2008; Padgett and Powell 2012a, 2012b). Specifically, my analysis highlights the connections and forms of feedback between three processes: (1) the development of legal and media institutions, (2) the transformation of individuals, and (3) the emergence and overlapping of multiple networks. I contend that these coeval processes led to the genesis and expansion of a public by breaking down existing boundaries. Essentially, through tracing the coevolution of individuals, networks, and institutions, I am able to explain the development of China's contentious public sphere and link historical processes that unfolded at and across multiple levels.

FRAGMENTED AND ADAPTIVE AUTHORITARIANISM

The final component of my argument concerns the conditions for the formation of crosscutting social networks and political contention. I argue that the fragmentation of the Chinese state opened a space for various actors to form overlapping social networks and to use the law and the media for contention. This argument builds on the fragmented authoritarianism model of Chinese politics. Instead of seeing the state as a monolithic entity, the fragmented authoritarianism model notes that government agencies across levels and localities may have different interests and political goals. The complex and sometimes conflicting relationships between government agencies shape bargaining and negotiation between levels and sectors and can influence policy implementation (Lieberthal 1992). In fact, each state agency often has its own problems with which it must cope. As such, research in this area sees the fragmented nature of China's political regime as a weakness of the state. Political fragmentation can open a space for policy entrepreneurs, such as peripheral local government officials and media, to participate in and influence politics (Mertha 2009). The fragmentation of the Chinese state has thus made implementing its modernization project uncertain.

Nonetheless, the Chinese state has been adapting itself to address the problem of fragmentation. As Sebastian Heilmann and Elizabeth J. Perry (2011) argue, the Chinese state's adaptive governance explains how the CCP has managed to endure in a drastically changing environment when many other regimes have failed. They contend that the CCP's long revolution contributed to "guerrilla-style policy-making," characterized by continual learning, experimentation, and transformation to cope with uncertainty and challenge. While Heilmann and Perry focus on policy adaptation, other scholars highlight the

Chinese state's adaptability in making formal and informal institutions (Nathan 2003; Tsai 2006). The bottom line is that Chinese state agencies are able to troubleshoot continuously and respond to individual problems.

But the Chinese state's adaptability can also increase fragmentation along temporal and ideological dimensions. Top leaders in the Chinese state initiate adaptations to address various problems at different points of time, often coming up with new ad hoc policies, theories, and practices, without formally repudiating or revising previous ones. As a result, contradictory policies, theories, and practices can be enacted, creating opportunities for capable agents to exploit such contradictions to pursue their own agendas. In short, I argue that the Chinese state's fragmentation and adaptivity have influenced the development of China's contentious public sphere by creating or closing opportunity structures available to various political and social actors.

A Note on Data and Research Methods

Analyzing the development of China's contentious public sphere has been a daunting task. Given my training in sociology, I was well aware of the limitation of relying on a single research method or a single source of data. As such, I have employed multiple methods of analysis and triangulated various types of data. This strategy enabled me to gain a broader picture of the development of the contentious public sphere, while also helping me to understand various components of the historical process and their relationships to one another. Since most of my empirical chapters have their own distinct data sources and research methods, I describe data sources and research methods in detail in an appendix. Here, I briefly describe how I analyzed various data sources and what I gained from such analysis.

Newspapers: I analyzed the content of national and local newspapers published in China between 1949 and 2015 across localities. Newspapers analysis was particularly helpful in terms of detecting trends over time, such as patterns in reports on public opinion and the growth of rights discourse in China. By analyzing newspapers in different localities and different types of newspapers, I was also able to identify variation in news reports and moments of divergence between official discourse and alternative discourse.

Yearbooks, laws and regulations, and other official documents: I examined volumes of the *China Journalism Yearbook*, published between 1983 and 2014; the *Law Yearbook of China* for the years 1987–2014; gazetteers published by local governments; and Party Congress reports. Reading through these materials helped me to understand the Chinese state's modernization project and institutional processes in the media and legal fields. I also analyzed top Chinese leaders' speeches and writings to understand their rationales when making constitutive choices.

Interview data: Between 2009 and 2016 in China and in the United States, I conducted more than 160 in-depth interviews with ordinary citizens and informants, including media and legal professionals, local and central government officials, legal and communication studies scholars, public opinion leaders, grievants, and activists. Qualitative analysis of interview data allowed me to understand the thinking, decisions, and actions of actors who have participated in China's modernization project and shaped China's contentious public sphere. Interview data also helped me to uncover the formation of social relations between different actors.

Online text in Internet forums and social media data: I extracted textual data from web pages of online discussion forums in China from October 2007 to 2010, analyzing them both qualitatively and quantitatively. I drew on such analysis to understand the formation of contentious events, or public opinion incidents, as case studies. I also extracted data from Chinese social media, or Weibo. I drew on techniques of content analysis and social network analysis to identify the political orientation of and connections between public opinion leaders in China.

Survey data: I employed statistical techniques to analyze the 2002 Asian Barometer Survey, the 2008 Asian Barometer Survey, the 2003 AsiaBarometer Survey, 2006 AsiaBarometer Survey,[6] the 2005–2008 World Values Surveys, and the 2008 China Survey conducted by Texas A&M University. Because most of these data sets were nationally representative, they allowed me to succinctly describe the demographic background, social networks, political attitudes, and political behavior of Chinese netizens. My statistical analysis is complemented by my findings from in-depth interviews and analysis of online texts and social media data.

In short, the combination of multiple research methods and analysis of various data helped me to trace and understand the multifaceted and multilevel processes that have shaped the development of China's contentious public sphere. In my writing, I have put a heavy emphasis on evidence and chosen a more detached, impersonal voice to let the evidence speak for itself.

Chapter Outlines

The chapters of the book systematically establish the empirical phenomenon to be explained, and then outline the multistage processes that constitute my explanation. In chapter 2, the first empirical chapter, I marshal evidence to establish my starting point: the rise of a nationwide contentious public sphere in China, a development I trace to the mid-2000s. Then, in chapter 3, I situate and explain the Chinese state's turn to the law and rights as part of the state's authoritarian modernization project, as well as the rise of legal and rights consciousness in a longer historical context. In chapter 4, I detail how the state's use of media to disseminate law and report on certain local problems, paired with political fragmentation and the marketization of the press, provided conditions for certain media and legal professionals to build networks and collaborate. Such collaboration pushed the boundaries of critical news reporting and expanded the concept of rights beyond socioeconomic issues. In chapter 5, I show how the Chinese state's regulation of the press market unexpectedly elevated the importance of Internet companies as news providers and facilitators of public opinion, while also amplifying the influence of politicized, proliberal media and legal professionals. In chapter 6, I then demonstrate how critical culture and practices were extended from legal and media professionals to ordinary citizens through the diffusion of the Internet. I also demonstrate the rise of an opinionated, critical, and politically active online public, whose everyday practices and participation in public opinion incidents contributed to the rise of China's contentious public sphere. Finally, in chapter 7, I discuss how the Chinese state, particularly the Xi Jinping leadership, has strategically responded to a rising contentious public sphere in China. Throughout, I highlight the novelty and significance of these developments. The emergence of a contentious public sphere in China is a remarkable event—one that warrants further investigation precisely because its future remains so unclear.

2

The Rise of a Nationwide Contentious Public Sphere

When talking about my research, I always receive varied responses, generally depending on people's familiarity with or relation to China. People savvy about the Internet in China, especially younger generations, tend to accept my premise that a nationwide contentious public sphere has emerged. They see this proposition as self-evident. Others are more skeptical. People less familiar with China usually question whether a nationwide contentious public sphere really exists and point to the Chinese government's reputation for censorship and suppression. Conversely, people knowledgeable about Chinese history and less taken with the purported novelty of the so-called Internet age counter that a nationwide contentious public sphere is not that new. These interlocuters cite instances of public contention, in particular the Hundred Flowers Campaign in 1956, the Cultural Revolution between 1966 and 1976, the Tiananmen incident in 1976, the Democracy Wall movement started on Xidan Wall between 1978 and 1979, and the Tiananmen incident in 1989. I am pushed to clarify whether I'm saying there was no contentious public sphere in the past or in what specific ways the sphere I'm identifying differs from those in the past. Such questions have been invaluable; they have helped me tremendously to clarify my ideas and define the parameters of my arguments over the years. As Merton (1959, xiii) usefully reminds us, one should ensure the existence of a fact before trying to explain it; too often social-scientific explanations are provided for "things that never were." I would add that it is equally critical to delineate and characterize a fact before trying to account for it. Therefore, my primary aim in this chapter is to establish *as* an empirical fact the rise of a nationwide contentious public sphere in China and to describe the scope and characteristics of this phenomenon. I do this through tracing the historical trajectory of public opinion in China.

Because the concept of public opinion is crucial to the study of the public sphere, I explain here how I conceptualize public opinion and connect it to the notion of public sphere. As communication studies scholar Vincent Price (1992) points out, there is no generally accepted definition of public opinion. Two major conceptions of it exist. The first, favored by political scientists in the United States, equates public opinion with aggregated political attitudes or individual opinions. Scholars who adopt this conception study public opinion by analyzing public opinion polls. Jürgen Habermas (1989) calls this a social-psychological conception of public opinion.[1] The second conception frames public opinion as a collective, supraindividual phenomenon and emphasizes its discursive and communicative nature. Habermas's conception of public opinion falls in this category, as "publicly expressed opinion" or "public discourse" rather than aggregated political attitudes or individual opinions. His conception relates to his theorization of the normative role of the public sphere in deepening formal democracy.

I adopt a Habermasian conception of public opinion for two reasons. First, this conceptualization is rooted in the literature of the public sphere, and my book is a study of the public sphere. In *Between Facts and Norms*, Habermas (1996, 360) writes, "The public sphere can best be described as a network for communicating information and points of view (i.e., opinion expressing affirmative or negative attitudes); the streams of communication are, in the process, filtered and synthesized in such a way that they coalesce into bundles of topically specified *public* opinions" (emphasis in original). In other words, the public sphere is a critical venue where public opinion forms through a communicative process. The formation of public opinion is a process that requires public expression, discussion, and communication; a simple aggregation of attitudes or opinions cannot turn privately expressed individual attitudes or opinions into *public* opinion. As Habermas (1996, 362) puts it, "Public opinion is not representative in the statistical sense. It is not an aggregate of individually gathered, privately expressed opinions held by isolated persons. Hence it must not be confused with survey results. Public opinion polls provide a certain reflection of 'public opinion' only if they have been preceded by a focused public debate and a corresponding opinion-formation in a mobilized public sphere."

Second, a Habermasian conception of public opinion fits well with the Chinese context. Scholars of the history of public opinion in China use the term "public opinion" in ways that resemble Habermas's conceptualization. The famous Chinese writer and linguist Lin Yutang published *A History of the Press and Public Opinion in China* in 1936, narrating the history of public opinion from the Han dynasty to the republican era in the early twentieth century. By "public opinion" Lin meant publicly expressed opinion or public discourse. Reflecting on the transition from imperial rule to a republican form of government in China, Lin stated, "All changes of form of government are futile, unless there is a growth in the power of public opinion, able to bring the government to act in accordance with its dictates" (1936, 115). It is public utterance, expression, and formation that makes opinion powerful. Academic institutes and market organizations conduct surveys to collect political attitudes and individual opinions in China (Thornton 2011), but such aggregated attitudes and opinions do not actually have strong political influence in China, as they often do in liberal democracies, mainly because of the absence of meaningful elections. In comparison, publicly expressed opinion and criticism in China, when spread widely, can tarnish the state's legitimacy, lead to social instability, and impose pressure on the state. It is important, then, to keep my specific conception of public opinion in mind when reading this chapter and the rest of the book.

Since patterns of public opinion can indicate characteristics of the public sphere, I study changing patterns of public opinion to demonstrate the rise of a nationwide contentious public sphere in China. Although Lin Yutang (1936) lamented the dormancy of public opinion in the country, seventy-some years after the publication of Lin's book, public opinion appears to be changing dramatically in China, despite continued authoritarian rule. Many studies have indicated a rise of public opinion and even the emergence of a public sphere—networks of information, points of view, and public opinion (Habermas 1996)—in the country, especially following the popularization of the Internet, before the Chinese state began its intensive crackdowns in 2013. For instance, Yang (2009) points out the emergence of a discursive space of and for citizens online, where Chinese citizens actively discuss public affairs. In a similar vein, Qian and Bandurski (2010) argue that a public sphere is emerging in China, and Xiao (2010) suggests that Chinese authorities have become more responsive to web-based public opinion.

Studies that focus on the role of the Internet tend to take the rise of public opinion in China as given and frame that rise as something new. Such presumptions encounter two challenges. The first challenge is empirical: one can reasonably question whether there really was a rise of public opinion in China, given the Chinese government's long-standing reputation for censorship and suppression. The second challenge concerns the novelty of the development—is public opinion really something new in China? There have arguably been many instances of public contention in the country's history. In what ways, then, is the purported recent rise of public opinion new and/or different from previous forms of public contestation? In his 1996 book *Mass Politics in the People's Republic*, Alan Liu (1996) argues that uninstitutionalized public opinion has existed in China ever since the inception of the Communist regime, eventually growing powerful enough to thwart Mao Zedong's policies and programs. He also contends that the CCP's post-Mao reforms were shaped less by Deng Xiaoping than by public opinion. How should Liu's work be understood in relation to recent studies declaring the supposedly unprecedented rise of public opinion in the Internet age?

In this chapter I aim to address these challenges and questions, as well as gauge how public opinion has been affected by the Chinese state's sweeping attacks on the Internet and various actors, such as lawyers and journalists, since 2013 (Yuen 2015). Tracing the historical patterns of public opinion in PRC is a formidable task given the compounded difficulty of finding direct measurement and longitudinal data. Examining reports regarding public opinion in the *People's Daily* as well as interview data related to that coverage provides one way to access and assess historical patterns of this otherwise elusive phenomenon.

The *People's Daily* as a Window for Understanding Public Opinion

The *People's Daily* is the mouthpiece of the CCP's Central Committee, a political organ comprising top leaders in China. The *People's Daily* editorial board manages news production but is supervised regularly by the Department of Propaganda. The department ensures that *People's Daily* articles correctly report the view of the central leadership and comply with their instructions. When getting the message right has been particularly important, top Chinese leaders have even written pieces in the *People's Daily* themselves. As such, articles in the newspaper report the CCP's policies and represent party attitudes toward domestic and international issues. Indeed, the major political function of the *People's Daily* is to disseminate policies and the central leadership's views to all of officialdom and other media, which then reprint or broadcast *People's Daily* articles and the central leadership's views more broadly. In short, the *People's Daily* is the most authoritative form of media in China (Wu 1994).

People's Daily coverage of public opinion provides a window through which we can trace its historical trajectory. The news production of the paper is guided by the fundamental principle of party journalism and, more specifically, the idea of the "mass line" (Zhao 1998, 24–25). The concept of "mass line" is best explicated by Mao Zedong in his essay "Some Questions Concerning Methods of Leadership":

> In all the practical work of our Party, all correct leadership is necessarily "from the masses, to the masses." This means: take the ideas of the masses (scattered and unsystematic ideas) and concentrate them (through study turn them into concentrated and systematic ideas), then go to the masses and propagate and explain these ideas until the masses embrace them as their own. (cited in Howard 1988, 21)

Political communication via mass line journalism thus involves both top-down and bottom-up communication. News media's role is to collect and reflect public opinion, specifically public concern, at the grassroots, thereby facilitating the party-state's decision making. Mass line journalism also requires that news media inform Chinese citizens about how the party-state is addressing public concerns. As the most authoritative national newspaper representing the voices of the central leadership, the role of *People's Daily* is to inform other media and party-state agencies of the central leadership's attitude toward public opinion. Far from reporting on *all* public opinion, however, the *People's Daily* tends to be very selective and cautious in practice—it reports only on public opinion deemed worthy of the central leadership's attention. Therefore, the newspaper's level of coverage or lack thereof of public opinion reveals much about the extent to which, and how, the central party-state perceives and assesses that opinion. In this way, *People's Daily* coverage enables one to trace the historical pattern of public opinion.

Of course, the point can be made that *People's Daily* coverage may well provide a skewed or inaccurate reading of both the extent and the nature of public opinion in China; neither the newspaper nor the central party-state are by any means infallible in assessing the Chinese public. Nonetheless, I would argue that this problem is mitigated by the length of my study. As my interviewees emphasize, when the Chinese state makes a mistake, it can adjust its strategy according to a corrected evaluation. In other words, though the state may "get it wrong" in certain instances, its assessment of and reactions to public opinion should tend toward accuracy over the long run. If I were examining public opinion only at specific moments, then relying solely on *People's Daily* coverage might, indeed, bias the findings. But as my goal is to study the development of public opinion between 1949 and 2015, analysis of *People's Daily*'s coverage, supplemented by interviews with informants, can still help trace such long-term development.

To look specifically at the newspaper's coverage of public opinion, I collected articles with titles containing "public opinion" (*yulun, yuqing,* or *minyi*) published between 1949 and 2015 (see the appendix for detailed information). I first looked at the source of the opinion in each article; because articles in the *People's Daily* engage with viewpoints from outside China as well as from within, identifying where a particular opinion originated is necessary. When I found an article engaging with public opinion within Mainland China, I coded the article in relation to two themes. The first theme concerns how the *People's Daily* covers the opinion—is the coverage positive or negative? By positive coverage, I mean an article that covers a specific public opinion favorably, such as by praising or encouraging the viewpoint, even if the opinion reveals problems or contains criticism of the state. By negative coverage, I mean an article that covers a public opinion unfavorably, such as by criticizing the opinion or expressing the need to change it. I tried to categorize each article as either positive or negative. If I did not have adequate information to decide, I coded the article as "not applicable." The second theme I used to code articles was whether an article on public opinion mentions the Internet or Internet users.

I also analyzed in-depth interviews with journalists and editors at the *People's Daily*, as well as with propaganda officials (see table A2.1 in the appendix for the distribution of interviewees). I tried to select interviewees from different generations to get a better sense of how the *People's Daily* covered public opinion over time, and to infer the historical patterns of public opinion from that coverage.

Public Opinion as Covered in the *People's Daily*

I identify six different periods and patterns of domestic public opinion between 1949 and 2015: Low Visibility (1949–1986); Outburst (1987–June 1989); Setback and Suppression (July 1989–1997); Contained Growth (1998–2005); Rising Contention (2006–2012) ; and Fluctuation (2013–2015). I discuss each in turn.

LOW VISIBILITY (1949–1986)

Today, when the Chinese government, media, or people mention the notion of public opinion, they are referring primarily to domestic public discourse. This was not the case until the late 1980s, however, when the *People's Daily* began to report regularly on domestic public opinion. Figure 2.1 compares the numbers of articles addressing public opinion in Mainland China, Hong Kong, Macao, Taiwan, and elsewhere, by year. Although the notion of public opinion occurred frequently in the *People's Daily* from 1949 to the late 1980s, those articles mentioning it were reporting on public opinion outside China rather than within. During this period, the *People's Daily* often reported on outside public opinion that either criticized the enemies of the CCP or supported the CCP and its allies. For example, the *People's Daily* frequently provided coverage when and if public opinion around the world denounced the United States and its foreign policies, such as the U.S. involvement in the Korean War.[2] Conversely, before the deterioration of Sino-Soviet relations in the late 1950s, the *People's Daily* was quick to report when public opinion in other countries offered praise of the Soviet Union.[3] Similarly, the newspaper regularly featured stories about public opinion in other countries that supported China, its leaders, and their policies.[4] For example, in 1954, the *People's Daily* presented articles reporting that public opinion in Sweden, Uruguay, and several Asian countries was calling for the restoration of China's legitimate rights at the United Nations.[5] My interviewees pointed out that frequent coverage of this

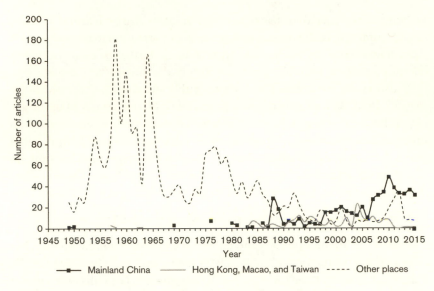

2.1. Coverage of public opinion in *People's Daily*, raw numbers, 1949–2015.

particular foreign opinion reflected the UN's refusal to recognize the PRC as the legitimate representative of China until 1971. To bolster PRC's legitimacy, the Chinese government drew on foreign public opinion that supported China or acknowledged China as a legitimate member in international communities.

Equivalent coverage of public opinion *within* China was extremely rare during this same period. My interviewees pointed out that, in general, the *People's Daily* coverage of foreign versus domestic public opinion serves two very different purposes. Coverage of foreign public opinion focuses on praise of China or the CCP, thus strengthening China's international legitimacy. In contrast, coverage of domestic public opinion focuses on important social problems or criticisms of the party-state's policies and rule. The latter practice may seem surprising, but it is crucial to recognize how the central leadership uses the *People's Daily* to give clear signals to party-state agencies and other news media about the central state's attitudes toward these problems or criticisms.

Between 1949 and the late 1980s, domestic public opinion was reported only on a few occasions in the *People's Daily*—during the Cultural Revolution and in response to the 1976 Tiananmen incident—and in both instances, the purpose of the coverage was to denounce the public opinion. During the Cultural Revolution, articles in the *People's Daily* stressed the need to combat counterrevolutionary public opinion.[6] Then, in 1976, after the death of Premier Zou Enlai, people gathered in Tiananmen Square, protesting against the Gang of Four, the political faction that came to prominence during the Cultural Revolution. The central government criticized the protests as counterrevolutionary and suppressed them immediately. After the incident, several articles in the *People's Daily* emphasized the government's determination to fight against both counterrevolutionary public opinion and the capitalist enemy, particularly Deng Xiaoping.[7]

But again, such references to domestic public opinion were extremely rare until the late 1980s, particularly when compared with the *People's Daily* much more frequent coverage of public opinion in other countries. My interview data suggest that the newspaper's general indifference to domestic public opinion before the late 1980s can be linked to the relatively few instances of widespread public criticism that were *not* orchestrated or authorized by the Chinese state. In other words, the state was sufficiently effective during this period at either suppressing or directing domestic public opinion that the government was under little pressure to report or address it at all. This is not to say that public contention, protests, and movements within China were absent during this period—far from it; most notably, in addition to the Tiananmen incident in 1976, there was the Hundred Flowers Campaign in 1956 and the Democracy Wall movement between 1978 and 1979. Yet these events were relatively short lived, and public contention became neither routine nor widespread, especially after the government suppressed the unrest. In essence, the data suggest that the state deemed little domestic public opinion sufficiently influential or strong to warrant acknowledgment from 1949 to 1986.

OUTBURST (1987–JUNE 1989)

With the unfolding of China's economic reform in the 1980s, the *People's Daily* reporting of domestic public opinion changed drastically. In figure 2.2, I plotted the percentages of all *People's Daily* articles, by year, that covered public opinion in (1) Mainland China; (2) Hong Kong, Macao, and Taiwan; and (3) other places. Figure 2.2 shows that reporting of domestic public opinion in the *People's Daily* began to increase, while articles pertaining to public opinion outside China gradually declined after 1986. In 1988, one year before the 1989 Tiananmen democratic movement, the percentage of reports alluding to domestic public opinion reached a peak and surpassed, for the first time, the percentage of reports on foreign public opinion. This change reveals the rising importance of domestic public opinion. The surge at the time was mainly triggered by problems such as severe corruption and inflation accompanying the economic reform initiated after the Cultural Revolution (1966–1976). In December 1986, students of the University of Science and Technology of China organized movements protesting this corruption and demanding democratization. The student movements quickly spread from Hefei to Beijing, Shanghai, Guangzhou, Tianjin, and other major cities. In addition to such student activism, concern about rocketing inflation and criticism of economic reform was

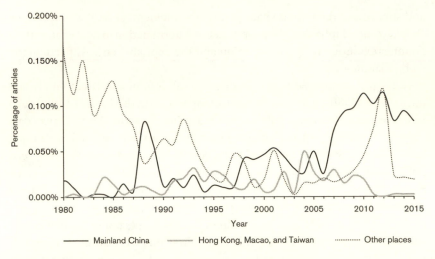

2.2. Coverage of public opinion in *People's Daily*, percentages, 1980–2015.

increasingly widespread among Chinese people. My interviewees pointed out that, compared with the previous period, domestic public opinion from 1987 to early 1989 was not only more prevalent but also more spontaneous in the sense that it was generated from the bottom-up. Analysis of interview data suggests that this surge in discontent prompted the central state to engage with public opinion—and it did so through the *People's Daily*.

Coverage of public opinion in the *People's Daily* not only increased but also changed around 1987. Figure 2.3 shows the amount of positive and negative stories about public opinion in the *People's Daily* by year. In figure 2.4, I plotted the percentages of positive coverage versus negative coverage in all *People Daily* articles by year. As figure 2.3 shows, on the few occasions when public opinion was addressed before 1980, the *People's Daily* framed it unfavorably. The articles during this period demonstrate that the state considered public opinion at the time to be "counterrevolutionary" and problematic.[8] In the early 1980s, however, a new trend emerged, as articles in the newspaper began not only to cover domestic public opinion, but also to cover it favorably.

My interviewees suggested that central party-state leaders recognized increasing public concerns about economic reform and believed that addressing these concerns was necessary to carry out the reform agenda. Additionally, party-state leaders did not view public concerns at that point as oppositional to or threatening of the CCP's rule. In 1987 in the Thirteenth Party Congress report, Zhao Ziyang, then general secretary, formalized an affirmative approach to rising public opinion, reframing it as a necessary and useful check on political power. The state's new goal was to understand and address public concerns. An in-depth reading of articles in the *People's Daily* between 1987 and the 1989

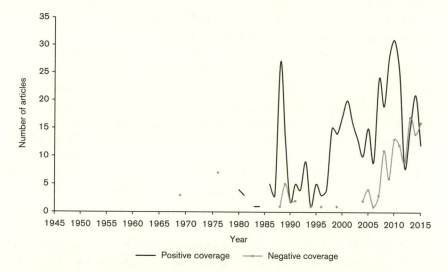

2.3. *People's Daily* positive and negative coverage of domestic public opinion, raw numbers, 1949–2015.

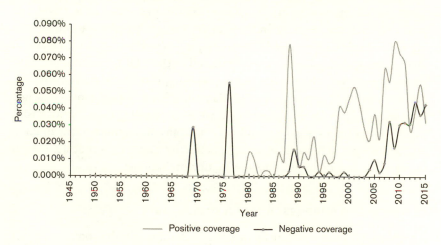

2.4. *People's Daily* positive and negative coverage of domestic public opinion, percentages, 1949–2015.

Tiananmen democratic movement reveals that CCP leaders not only acknowledged the diversity of public opinion, but also endorsed the right of citizens to speak out about problems. Many articles in the *People's Daily* between 1987 and 1989 explicitly addressed how Chinese newspapers investigated and reported citizens' complaints and problems, thereby enunciating public opinion on behalf of citizens. These articles also emphasized that government agencies should acknowledge and actively address public criticism rather than ignoring problems or attempting to repress public opinion.[9]

The *People's Daily*'s positive coverage of how public opinion helped food safety issues on March 4, 1988, illustrates the affirmative approach to public opinion of both state and newspaper. In 1988, two companies in Shaanxi sold industrial oil as edible oil, causing the intoxication of several consumers and an influx of complaints. At first, the relevant local government agencies were reluctant to tackle the problem, even though they were in charge of food safety issues and aware of the incident. After the *People's Daily* and *Shaanxi Daily* disclosed the food safety issue on behalf of citizens, the State Council of the central government and the Shaanxi provincial government intervened in the investigation process. These interventions prompted related local government agencies to fulfill their administrative obligation. Public opinion mediated by newspapers thus operated as a check on political power and held local government agencies accountable.[10] This is just one of many similar instances illustrating the *People's Daily* positive coverage of public opinion and the Chinese state's novel, affirmative approach to handling the concerns of the people.

The *People's Daily*'s increasing and increasingly positive coverage of domestic public opinion from 1987 to June 1989 shows a rise in the amount of public opinion not perceived by the Chinese state as oppositional or threatening to CCP rule. Unfortunately, these trends—in public opinion itself and in the government response—were interrupted by the 1989 Tiananmen incident. Again, as with the public contention of previous protests and movements, the grievances that generated the 1989 Tiananmen democratic movement lost national visibility soon after the protests were suppressed, so swift and decisive was the government response. And as a result, any momentum public opinion might have gained toward becoming an effective check on political power in the years leading up to 1989 was lost in June of that year.

SETBACK AND SUPPRESSION (JULY 1989–1997)

After the 1989 Tiananmen incident, articles alluding to public opinion largely declined for almost a decade, as figures 2.1 and 2.2 show, indicating the intense setback of domestic public opinion. Interview data suggest that the Chinese state's harsh crackdown on democratic movements and the silencing of public criticism were extremely effective. Furthermore, the state's attitude now changed. As figure 2.3 shows, the Chinese government and the *People's Daily* became increasingly hostile to public opinion after the 1989 Tiananmen incident. The new central leadership reviled the previous leadership's approach toward public opinion. After June 10, 1989, the *People's Daily* published a series of articles condemning wrongful public opinion in Chinese society and emphasizing the need for the Chinese state to contain and guide the views of the people. These articles also criticized Zhao Ziyang's approach to public opinion, accusing of Zhao of instigating instability and, ultimately, contributing to the Tiananmen protests.[11]

Articles in the *People's Daily* during this period often pointed out the double-edged nature of public opinion and the necessity of controlling its more treacherous aspects. As the reports framed it, when public opinion operates properly, it can contribute to the solidarity and progress of the nation. When it is not controlled, however, the reports suggested, public opinion can lead to conflicts, sociopolitical instability, and even the disintegration of the nation. Therefore, as mediators of public opinion, news organizations should cover only the positive aspects of Chinese society and avoid inciting unrest over sensitive issues. Most important, it was argued, news organizations should shape public opinion according to the instructions of the Department of Propaganda.[12]

Between 1993 and 1997 the *People's Daily* published articles that covered public opinion only occasionally and unfavorably, touting instead the government's success in shifting collective opinion. For instance, on June 14, 1994, the newspaper reported Henan's laudable experience based on an interview with Li Changchun. Li was then secretary of the Henan Provincial Party Committee and would later become a member of the Politburo Standing Committee and one of the top leaders in charge of propaganda in 2002. According to Li, the local government and media in Henan enacted the principle of promoting stability, solidarity, and positive propaganda when they engaged with public opinion. Poverty was a serious public concern in Henan at the time, and Li believed that public criticism could instigate discontent. Under his leadership, local newspapers, TV stations, and radio stations in Henan emphasized the possibility of progress by highlighting heroic, propagandistic images of CCP members combating challenges and triumphing under difficult circumstances rather than portraying poverty as a problem. Li contended that this strategy helped to shift public opinion in a more positive direction in Henan.[13]

CONTAINED GROWTH (1998–2005)

As figures 2.1 and 2.2 demonstrate, reports on domestic public opinion began to increase again around 1998, following a decade of decline after the 1989 Tiananmen democratic movement. Unlike the period immediately prior to that Tiananmen incident, however, the uptick in domestic public opinion starting in 1998 was not just a short-lived outburst. Rather, the number of reports on domestic public opinion remained high after its takeoff in 1998, although there was some fluctuation. From 1999 onward, the number and percentage of articles on domestic public opinion per year rose steadily higher, in general, than the number and percentage of articles on foreign public opinion.

My analysis of articles in the *People's Daily* and of interview data suggests that the increasing salience of public opinion between 1998 and 2005 was driven by social problems and discontent that had accumulated in the process of economic reform. Peasants and workers were the two most important groups of grievants and producers of public opinion. In 1994, the central government introduced new fiscal reforms. Specifically, tax reform redistributed a large portion of fiscal revenues from local governments to the central government but did not reduce the former's responsibilities in terms of providing public goods. As a result, local government officials were motivated to exploit peasants, mostly through land grabbing and illegal taxation (Man 2011; Wang 1997). Not surprisingly, the process fueled an upsurge in complaints from peasants. Along with peasant resistance, labor disputes also soared during this period, mostly in response to the restructuring of state-owned enterprises (SOEs). Starting in 1997, the central government accelerated its restructuring of SOEs, leading to millions of job losses and sparking labor protests (Gallagher 2005a; Lee 2007).

From 1998 to 2005, reports on public opinion in the *People's Daily* were also characterized by an increase in positive coverage of public opinion, reflecting the Chinese state's shift, once again, toward an affirmative approach. Even though the central government still often sought to suppress public opinion and had criticized Zhao Ziyang's affirmative approach in the decade after the Tiananmen democratic movement, when it found itself faced with rising public concerns in 1998, it returned to Zhao's affirmative strategy of trying to understand and address the concerns. As figure 2.3 demonstrates, the amount of negative coverage of public opinion decreased slightly in this period from that of the previous four years, whereas the amount of positive coverage of public opinion drastically increased. And this time, the rise of positive coverage lasted longer than it had in the 1980s. Essentially, *People's Daily* articles on public opinion during this period demonstrate the rise of the collective voice and the central party-state's willingness to take the public's views into consideration.

Consider, for example, two instances of positive coverage—that is, instances in which the *People's Daily* acknowledged public concerns and signaled the central government's endorsement of an affirmative response. On December 16, 1998, the *People's Daily* published an article titled "Paying Attention to the Supervision of Public Opinion and Improving the Cadre-People Relationship." The article began with the fact that the *People's Daily* received thousands of letters from readers concerned about corrupt officials and cadres at the local level. Readers complained that many local officials not only violated the party-state's law and policies but also damaged people's interests. These unscrupulous local officials taxed and fined peasants illegally, took bribes from citizens and businesses, intervened in court decisions, embezzled public funds, sold state assets to benefit themselves, and infringed on the rights of SOE employees. The article emphasized that leaders of local governments should accept the supervision of the people and address public concerns. After stating the importance of public opinion in primarily abstract terms, the article illustrated the idea using the concrete case of a local party cadre in a poor village in Chaoyang County who embezzled more than 700,000 RMB (renminbi, the PRC currency) from peasants. Fed up, the peasants collectively reported the problems to the *Liaoning Daily*. Despite resistance and intervention from the local government, journalists at the *Liaoning Daily* diligently investigated the cadre's illegal behavior and eventually published an investigative report. The report was then picked up by the provincial judicial organization, which prosecuted the unscrupulous local cadre. The *People's Daily* praised the *Liaoning Daily*'s recognition of public opinion as a check on political power and lauded the paper's role in helping resolve social conflicts.[14]

Another *People's Daily* article, this time in 1999, entitled "Cadres Investigated Public Opinion about Problems to Search for Solutions," reflected the government's increasing recognition of public opinion as something that needed to be understood and addressed. The article reported that the local government in Datong, Shanxi, had created many channels through which citizens could contact news media and government agencies to express their opinions. Datong faced severe unemployment problems given the large-scale layoff of workers from the local SOEs during the transition to a market economy. Social tensions accompanying this economic restructuring increased pressures on the local government. To address escalating conflicts, the Datong government encouraged citizens to voice their opinions to news media and government agencies. In so doing, the local government increased both its awareness of public opinion and, it hoped, its ability to handle such opinions before problems became intractable.[15]

The growing and increasingly positive coverage of public opinion in the *People's Daily* between 1998 and 2005 indicates the rise of public opinion as well as its relative containment by the state. This was the first time in the PRC's history that the central government chose to acknowledge and respond regularly to public opinion. My interviewees emphasized that the *People's Daily* received many complaints from citizens; only when the journalists there considered a certain public opinion to be widely held and strongly felt would they be more likely to report on it. Given this tendency toward selectivity, the newspaper's increasing coverage of public opinion is a telling indicator of the perceived potential influence of the people's voice.

Additionally, my interviewees pointed out that the decreasing negative coverage and increasing positive coverage of public opinion in *People's Daily* indicate the perceived contained nature of public opinion. By "contained" I mean that the central party-state did not feel that public opinion was out of its control. As my interviewees emphasized, the central state felt confident that public opinion, while gaining strength, did not directly question state plans, threaten the authority of the central government, or risk instigating large-scale protests. As one interviewee explained:

> One of the reasons that leaders in the central government did not consider public opinion threatening was that public opinion was mediated by media—which were ultimately controlled by the government. The leaders believed that as long as they can rein in the media, they can benefit from public opinion without losing control of it. In fact, this is the period where marketized newspapers expanded drastically. Marketized newspapers played a key role in collecting and reporting public opinion. (July 2014, Beijing)

This quotation shows that the central government's confidence was closely related to the role of state-controlled media, especially marketized newspapers, in mediating public opinion. Precisely because of the perceived contained nature of the public opinion, the central party-state moved to acknowledge such opinion and respond to it affirmatively. In so doing, the Chinese state was able to monitor local problems, address public concern, and boost its own image and popularity, without worrying that its affirmative attitude would lead to an unmanageable situation.

RISING CONTENTION (2006–2012)

As figures 2.1 and 2.2 show, domestic public opinion continued to grow post-2005 and received increasing attention from the *People's Daily*. Two new developments emerged in this period. The first concerned the actors whom the Chinese government regarded as the most relevant in producing public opinion. I plotted in figure 2.5 the number of articles on public opinion that mentioned the Internet or Internet users, showing that the continuing growth of public opinion was associated with the rise of the Internet.

The second new trend, as figure 2.4 shows, is that the percentage of negative coverage of public opinion in all the *People's Daily* articles rose drastically in 2008 and has remained high ever since. Analysis of interview data suggests that this rise in negative coverage of public opinion was motivated by the central leadership's belief that public viewpoints had become problematic and now threatened social stability and the CCP's legitimacy. The *People's Daily* criticized or even stigmatized public opinion in news reports to make clear the central government's attitudes. My interviewees explained to me that it is important for the *People's Daily* to cover, rather than simply ignore, public criticism because the newspaper is the mouthpiece of the central party-state and thus needs to convey the state's stance to other party-state agencies and media.

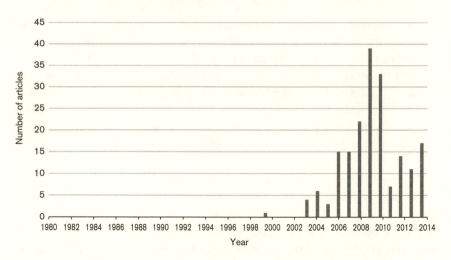

2.5. *People's Daily* reports on public opinion mentioning the Internet or Internet users, 1980–2015.

An article published on May 11, 2010, illustrates such negative coverage of public opinion. The article begins by stating that the Internet has become a major space in which collective views are generated and amplified, and that surging public opinion has, in fact, become an increasingly negative influence on the harmony of Chinese society. The article then proposes that the government should fight for, rather than abandon, the battleground of public opinion to inhibit the diffusion of wrongful discourse and viewpoints. Specifically, the article suggests that first, the government should guide the formation of public opinion by disseminating an official response whenever a potentially high-profile event occurs; and second, the government should accelerate the lawmaking process to regulate online speech more effectively and establish a system to monitor and more quickly react to public opinion incidents.

Yet, as figures 2.3 and 2.4 show, while the *People's Daily* increased its negative coverage of public opinion, it *also* increased its positive coverage. The percentage per year of positive coverage of public opinion in all the *People's Daily* articles reached a peak in 2009. Figures 2.3 and 2.4 reveal that the 2006–2012 period is the *only* time in the PRC's history when positive and negative coverage of public opinion both increased *simultaneously*. My interview data suggest that, in this period, the Chinese state attempted—often in a somewhat contradictory manner—to both control and denounce public opinion, but also to acknowledge it as an independent and influential force to be reckoned with. In fact, several media professionals from local newspapers and the Internet sector pointed out this seemingly contradictory strategy to me and described the phenomenon as paradoxical. As one editor at the online news service NetEase put it,

> Since public opinion became contentious and unruly, the government has made the harshest attack on public opinion since 2005, but paradoxically, public opinion has continued to grow. The government is, to [a] certain extent, forced to compromise and really see public opinion as a force. This is very different from what happened in the past. The government tended to and actually was able to have more consistent attitudes towards public opinion in the past. Now public opinion is no longer something [over which] it could have complete control. (June 2011, Beijing)

Other interviewees pointed out that propaganda officials tried to avoid alternating too quickly between encouraging and denouncing public opinion, as it was recognized that doing so would be politically unwise and confusing. For example, explicitly encouraging supervision of the local government but discouraging the supervision of the central government could damage the latter's reputation. Furthermore, propaganda officials at the central level wanted to give clear signals to news media, government officials, and citizens. Positive coverage of public opinion is characterized by toleration of criticism and negative reports, whereas negative coverage tends to avoid or discredit criticism. Thus, when the *People's Daily* pursued a strategy of both encouraging and discouraging public opinion within the same period, it risked appearing incoherent and inconsistent.

Analysis of in-depth interview data helps illuminate why such a paradoxical strategy nonetheless resulted. One propaganda official mentioned that the rise of public opinion in the post-2005 period was unexpected and had presented the government with a dilemma. In the previous period, 1998–2005, the *People's Daily* had covered public opinion favorably but only did so because public opinion was not seen then as threatening to CCP rule. In comparison, in the post-2005 period, the central state regarded criticism from the people as both threatening and influential and decided that it could not afford to simply disregard or denounce it. My interviewees explained that the positive coverage of public opinion by the *People's Daily* in the post-2005 period was reluctant, almost a bowing to pressure. Criticism from the people was very strong and justifiable according to the Chinese state's own rhetoric. Therefore, even though government officials saw public opinion as deviating from the government efforts to control it, they still needed to acknowledge and respond to it in a seemingly positive manner lest the government appear hypocritical and unscrupulous.

FLUCTUATION (2013–2015)

Data between 2013 and 2015, albeit limited, allow me to provide some preliminary sense of the patterns during the Xi leadership. Two new developments stand out. First, as figures 2.2 and 2.3 show, both the number and the percentage of articles reporting on domestic public opinion per year have declined since 2013. Presumably, this is the result of the Chinese state's intensified crackdowns on the Internet, which began in 2013. Despite this suppression, however, coverage of public opinion between 2013 and 2015 was still significantly higher than that between 1998 and 2005, suggesting that considerably more opinions were circulating between 2013 and 2015 than in the pre-2005 period. But the long-term effects of the crackdowns remain to be seen. Second, as figures 2.3 and 2.4 show, the *People's Daily* significantly decreased its positive coverage of public opinion and increased its negative coverage. The number and percentage of articles per year with negative coverage of public opinion surpassed the amount of positive coverage in 2013 and in 2015. Indeed, state hostility toward public opinion reached new heights, surpassing even that seen in the aftermath of the 1989 Tiananmen incident. This trend reveals that the Chinese state under the Xi leadership has felt extremely threatened and infuriated by public opinion seen as unruly. Arguably, the Hu-Wen leadership responded to public opinion more affirmatively in an effort to show that the Chinese state was not corrupt or hypocritical, even though the state did feel threatened by public criticism. In comparison, the Xi leadership has waged anticorruption campaigns against government officials to generate public support and seems less hesitant to use harsh methods to deal with unruly public opinion.

People's Daily articles and my interviews with journalists at the *People's Daily* suggest that the fear and fury of the Chinese state under the Xi leadership is related to a surge of so-called public opinion incidents (*yulun shijian*)—contentious events that capture the public's attention. From the perspective of the Chinese state, these incidents are far from being spontaneous and are usually organized by a group of actors. Several *People's Daily* articles that cover specific public opinion incidents from 2013 to 2015 describe the common mechanism that leads to such events occurring as well as the consequences when they do. According to these articles, various kinds of grievants (e.g., peasants, workers, etc.) tend to mobilize public support to address their grievance in the name of "rights defense" (*weiquan*), or claiming and defending rights. Statements about such grievances however, are sometimes not based on truth or facts. These grievants are often aided by a group of intermediary actors (*zhong jian ren*) with skillful publicity strategies, particularly rights defense lawyers, journalists, scholars, public opinion leaders, experienced petitioners, and activists. Grievants and intermediary actors often use media, particularly social media, to broadcast grievance and mobilize widespread support in the name of public interest and citizens' rights. Since netizens tend to be radical and emotional, they are easily influenced and mobilized by grievants and intermediary actors to produce contention. In other words, though netizens' engage in spontaneous expression and contention online, they are actually being manipulated by intermediary actors. After winning public support, the grievants, together with intermediary actors and the public, impose pressure on the government. And contention online sometimes spreads offline because the intermediary actors are good at organizing protests, often in front of government buildings. The government is then forced to respond to public opinion, address the grievance, and appease the public.[16]

People's Daily articles further criticize public opinion incidents for imposing enormous social costs. The articles frame such situations as not only undermining normal institutional process and giving people incentive to speak out in public, but also eroding the government's credibility and escalating social tensions. The alternative interpretation, of course, is that public opinion incidents are concerning for the Chinese state because they enable an emergent coalition of actors to use the Internet and an emergent discourse of rights to break geographic, social, and cultural boundaries; mobilize contention; and confront the state online and off. In other words, such incidents have suddenly made clear to the CCP that the state no longer has a monopoly on the capacity to mobilize the masses. The CCP finds this quite alarming.

From a Contained to a Contentious Public Sphere

Based on the above longitudinal analysis, I argue that, beginning in 1998, China has seen the emergence of what began as a contained public sphere that has become, since 2005, a nationwide contentious public sphere. The growth of public opinion between 1998 and 2005 as well as its regular presence has critical implications, indicating the rise of an emergent public sphere as both a space and a force in Chinese society, despite ongoing containment efforts by the state. Before 1998, public opinion generally erupted only when collective actions were mobilized, as shown by the Tiananmen incident in 1976 and the Democracy Wall movement between 1978 and 1979. Such outbursts of public opinion lost their power and visibility at the national level once the collective actions ended or were suppressed. Therefore, such outbursts of public opinion constituted a short-lived public sphere at most. Today, in contrast, public opinion is no longer directly tied to large-scale collective actions, suggesting that the Chinese people no longer have to mobilize extraordinary resources to express their concerns and to have their voices heard by the Chinese government.

I argue that the continuing, drastic growth and unruliness of public opinion in the post-2005 period indicate the shift from a contained to a contentious public sphere. Since around 1998, public opinion has been regularly produced and circulated, and as indicated by *People's Daily* coverage, it has also been considered important and influential by the central Chinese state. From 1998 to 2005, however, public opinion was still relatively contained in the sense that the central government did not consider it threatening and oppositional to its authoritarian rule. The central government's confidence was rooted in its control of the media, which played a critical role in mediating the formation of public opinion. As such, the central state was able to take advantage of the symbolic and practical benefits of public opinion without worrying too much about its negative consequences. The public sphere was thus relatively contained.

In comparison, as my interviewees pointed out, the development of public opinion in the post-2005 period moved beyond the Chinese state's control. The state acknowledged the rise of public opinion as a now unruly force, capable of generating contentions and agendas not set by the central government. The result was a seemingly paradoxical state response between 2006 and 2012: on the one hand, the state considered public opinion threatening and thus sought to strengthen its control over it; but on the other hand, because public opinion was seen as so influential, the central state could no longer afford simply to restrict it and now needed to acknowledge and engage with it. This indicates a more contentious nationwide public sphere. And, indeed, this was confirmed by the state itself beginning in 2011, when the notion of "two public spheres" (*liange yulun chang*) began to appear in the *People's Daily*. The concept referred to the traditional state-controlled public sphere as well as an emerging public sphere not contained by the former.[17] Crucial to note, however, is that the rise of a nationwide contentious public sphere does not guarantee its durability. As I have shown, the Chinese state under the Xi leadership has responded to public opinion in very hostile ways, which have already led to a moderate decline in its expression.

Conclusion: A Qualitatively New Sphere

In this chapter I have traced the historical patterns of domestic public opinion in China. Whereas existing studies tend to relate the rise of public opinion to the introduction and popularity of the Internet in China (e.g., Xiao 2010; Yang 2009), I have shown that neither public opinion nor public contention is necessarily new to the Chinese context. Public opinion became salient in the late 1980s in response to problems associated with economic reform, but this growth of public opinion was interrupted by the 1989 Tiananmen incident. After a decade of post-Tiananmen decline, public opinion began to rise again around 1998, thanks to the key role of state-controlled marketized newspapers in facilitating the formation of public opinion—a theme that I explore further in chapter 4. In this sense, my findings align with Liu's argument that there is a history of public opinion in China. At the same time, I also argue that the continuing growth of public opinion in the post-2005 period—a phenomenon certainly facilitated by the Internet—signals something qualitatively new, as public opinion has become increasingly unruly and capable of escaping state control to set the public agenda, at least occasionally. I thus agree with Qian and Bandurski (2010) that a public sphere is newly emergent in China; furthermore, I have shown that while this sphere was relatively contained between 1998 and 2005, it has developed into a more contentious public sphere in the post-2005 period.

In *Mass Politics in the People's Republic of China*, Liu attempts to show that "there has been public opinion in the PRC since the 1950s, albeit of the uninstitutionalized kind" (Liu 1996, 223). By public opinion, Liu (1996, 5) is referring to "the people's response to controversial state policies that affect their daily lives" and "mobilized public opinion in the form of a social movement." He names the former "general public opinion" and the latter "specific public opinion." Unfortunately, he does not define what he means by "institutionalized." To demonstrate his claim about the existence of public opinion, Liu describes throughout the book how different social groups, particularly peasants, workers, and college students, have resisted government policies. Liu (1996, 224) also argues that public opinion and political culture in China were characterized by what he calls occasionalism and sectionalism. Occasionalism means every group or actor maximizes its, his, or her short-term interests only when there is an opportunity. Sectionalism means every group interacts with the state independently of other groups.

While I agree with Liu that public opinion is not new in China, I caution against reading his work as establishing the existence of public opinion as a consistently influential social force. The public opinion Liu identifies from Mao's era to the mid-1990s was either sporadic or short lived. As such, it did not constitute a constantly present public sphere. As I have shown, public opinion did not really establish a stable and influential presence in China until around 1998, when it demonstrated the ability to provoke recognition by and response from the Chinese state. Furthermore, Liu's description of public opinion as characterized by occasionalism, sectionalism, and political culture does not capture what has happened in the post-2005 period—namely, a surge of public opinion incidents characterized by the frequent participation of various social groups who are at least loosely unified by the concepts of rights and citizens.

As I have shown, the recent rise of the contentious public sphere in the post-2005 period is actually connected to multiple factors: economic reform initiated in the aftermath of the Cultural Revolution, political innovation in the late 1980s, the 1989 Tiananmen democratic movement, marketization of state-controlled media, the introduction and popularization of the Internet, and the rise of the concept of rights and citizens. In the following chapters, I explain the rise of the nationwide contentious public sphere in the post-2005 period by tracing its historical development in relation to the above factors since the end of the Cultural Revolution.

3

The Chinese State's Turn to Law and Rights

I began this book by telling three stories about the rise of the nationwide contentious public sphere in China: the death of Sun Zhigang and its effect on the overhaul of detention regulation in 2003; the public outrage against the state's use of software to restrict Internet access in 2009, seen as infringement of the right to freely communicate; and protests against the violation of freedom of the press by the Chinese government in its censorship of *Southern Weekly* in 2013. The three stories share a critical similarity—the central theme of law and rights.

The paramount importance of law and rights to the contentious public sphere is also demonstrated by the Chinese state's anxiety about the prevalence of public opinion incidents, as well as by their connection to the law and rights. As I discuss in chapter 2, public opinion incidents are often triggered by the motivation to mobilize public support to address grievance. Such incidents often involve the participation of various kinds of actors, from intermediary actors—such as rights defense lawyers, journalists, scholars, public opinion leaders, and activists—to grievants and ordinary Chinese Internet users. As various *People's Daily* articles have noted, public opinion incidents are usually mobilized in the name of citizens, public interests, and rights defense.[1] Recent studies also show that issues related to the law, particularly citizens' rights protection, government's illegal practices, and various legal disputes, are among the most widely discussed topics online (Li, Chen, and Chang 2014; Ru, Lu, and Li 2011). Asserting and defending citizens' rights in accordance with the law is thus a defining, if still evolving, part of the political culture of China's contentious public sphere.

This development is absolutely astonishing given that the very concept of rights was not introduced to China from the West until the late nineteenth century, in the Qing dynasty. At the turn of the twentieth century, the concept of rights was only circulated among the very top political elites (Jin and Liu 1999; Liu 1994), but by the post-2005 period, the concept of rights was already widespread across social groups, including even among peasants and others with little education (O'Brien and Li 2006; Yu 2011). Recall, too, that China was essentially "lawless" in the aftermath of the Cultural Revolution, with prosecutors' offices and courts essentially smashed by the Gang of Four (Wang 2010, 5).[2] But by the post-2005 period, the law had moved to the forefront of China's political culture.

Most interesting is that the authoritarian Chinese state—infamous for disrespecting citizens' rights—actively disseminated law to its populace, informed Chinese people about their rights, and transformed them into active legal subjects. Research shows that the Chinese state's effort to disseminate law and improve Chinese people's legal and rights consciousness has been hugely successful (Gallagher 2006; Goldman 2005). Indeed, representative survey data suggest that Chinese people's legal consciousness has only strengthened over time. Despite the country being virtually "lawless" in 1976 and still governed today by an authoritarian state, Chinese people increasingly demand that the state follow the law. In the 2006 Chinese General Social Survey, 33.0 percent of Chinese respondents disagreed that the government could disregard the law for policy considerations. The rate of disagreement rose to 55.2 percent in the 2008 Asian Barometer Survey. By comparison, only 33.5, 36.4, 42.6, and 53.2 percent of respondents in Thailand, Singapore, Vietnam, and Cambodia, respectively, disagreed with the idea of the government disregarding the law to handle difficult situations. Among the nine countries in the 2005–2008 Asian Barometer Survey, only Taiwan (68.1%), Indonesia (68.4%), and the Philippines (60.7%) expressed a higher disagreement with this idea than did China.

To be sure, the protection of rights remains very weak in China. According to the Rule of Law Index, compiled by the World Justice Project in 2014, China ranked ninety-sixth out of ninety-nine countries (percentile rank: 3%) in its protection of fundamental rights, and seventy-sixth (percentile rank: 23%) in its rule of law in general. Yet, the 2014 Rule of Law Index reveals an aspect of China's rule of law that is often neglected by media and scholarly work— the Chinese state's extraordinary campaign of law dissemination. In the same World Justice Project report, China ranked sixteenth (percentile rank: 84%) in how well its laws are publicized and made accessible to citizens—higher than Germany, the United States, and many other liberal democracies, not to mention all other authoritarian countries.

What characterizes the status of rule of law in China today is the enormous disparity between the government's efforts to diffuse law as an idea and its (in) action to enforce law and protect rights on the ground. A simple calculation reveals the extent of this disparity. Each country included in the 2014 World Justice Project has one score ranging between 0 (lowest score) and 1.00 (highest score) for how laws are publicized and accessible to citizens and another score for how fundamental rights are protected. China scores 0.69 and 0.31 in these two aspects, respectively. Subtracting the score that measures how laws are publicized and accessible to citizens from the score that measures how protected fundamental rights are for each country, China ranks first out of the 99 countries included in the Rule of Law Index—in other words, the distance between these two scores is largest for China. In many authoritarian countries, such as Vietnam and Cambodia, protection of fundamental rights is, if nothing else, commensurate with the extent to which laws are publicized and accessible to citizens. In fact, more than two-thirds of the ninety-nine countries listed in the 2014 Rule of Law Index have higher scores in rights protection than in publicity and accessibility of legal information.

The enormous disparity between the Chinese state's efforts to diffuse law and its efforts to protect rights, combined with increased legal and rights consciousness among Chinese people, has led to rising individual and collective contention as well as public opinion incidents based on rights defense. To illuminate the contentious culture and practices based on the law and rights, I address the following questions in this chapter: Why would an authoritarian state that does not seem serious about protecting citizens' rights endeavor in the first place to disseminate law and legal knowledge to citizens and inform them of their rights? Did Chinese leaders not anticipate that Chinese citizens might, once informed about the law and their rights, then use this knowledge against the government itself? To the extent that this outcome was anticipated, why did the Chinese state still go forward with the campaign to disseminate law to the public? To what extent did the state attempt to temper the *kinds* of rights it promoted over time? Ultimately, I argue that answering these questions helps us understand why and how law and rights became a critical part of China's political culture and a central theme in China's contentious public sphere. First, I briefly situate the PRC government's turn to law and rights, as well as the rise of legal and rights consciousness, in a longer historical context. Then I trace how a series of problems that emerged following the Cultural Revolution motivated the government's turn to law and rights, as well as its campaign to transform Chinese people into legal subjects. Finally, I describe law dissemination on the ground and its consequences. Because this chapter serves to explain the rise of China's contentious public sphere in the post-2005 period, I focus primarily on developments in China's legal system before the mid-2000s.

Modernization of the Chinese Legal System since the Late Qing Period

Although situating the current rise of law and rights in a longer historical context is necessary, the purpose here is modest—I aim only to provide sufficient background information to highlight the novelty and implications of recent developments in the PRC. Contrary to the conventional wisdom that law was neither highly developed nor important in Imperial China, it actually had a long-standing, substantial presence during this period (Alford 1997). For more than two thousand years, Imperial China had a sophisticated legal system influenced by both Confucian and legalist perspectives (Chen 1993; Chen 2008). Confucian thinking emphasized the role of customs, mores, virtues, and norms, as well as internal cultivation through moral education, in achieving a harmonious social and political order; the law's role was to remove those individuals who could not participate in society harmoniously. In comparison, legalist thinking emphasized using publicly promulgated and codified law to induce deference and to punish wrongdoers, including government officials, to achieve a desirable social and political order. The imperial legal system developed an impressive codified law and a multilevel court system (Chen 2008; Peerenboom 2002). Nonetheless, both Confucian and legalist thinkers viewed the legal system as an imperial instrument of governance to secure the emperor's rule and to maintain social order. To wit, the imperial legal system was used primarily to handle criminal cases, and the emperor himself was exempt, subject only to the mandate of heaven. As such, the imperial legal system did nothing to protect individuals against an overarching state. Even when the system punished government officials, the purpose was simply to secure the emperor's rule. Such a legal system reflected the hierarchical and paternalistic social and political order in Chinese society (Chen 1993; Chen 2008; Peerenboom 2002).

Following the Qing Empire's defeat by the United Kingdom in the First Opium War, between 1839 and 1842, the Chinese legal system began to transform drastically as it became increasingly influenced by modern Western political and legal institutions, especially those in continental Europe. A series of military defeats by the West and Japan, as well as the failure of China's self-strengthening movement (1861–1895), which was focused on learning Western science and technology, convinced political elites and eventually the emperors and the empress dowager of the need for profound political and legal reform (Han 2009; Jin and Liu 1999; Li 2014). Ruling elites in the late Qing thus began modernizing China's legal system and decided to build a constitutional monarchy (Chang 1989). This legal system modernization—a process legal scholar Chen Jianfu described as "the wholesale Westernization of Chinese law"—continued into the republican era, and under the PRC (Chen 2008, 23).

Of course, this process of Westernization does not mean that the imperial legal system has completely lost its influence on the current Chinese legal system or that Chinese and Western legal systems have no significant differences. Rather, the point is that the restructuring of the traditional Chinese legal system was profoundly shaped by an effort to emulate Western or Westernized legal institutions. Further, the significance of this influence is only underscored by the already long-standing history and uniqueness of the traditional Chinese legal system.

The most important aspects of legal change since the late Qing period for the development of China's contentious public sphere are the adoption of the concept of rights from the West, the enactment of constitutions, and the continuing redefinition of the relationship between individuals and the state. These aspects are closely intertwined because writing constitutions involves engaging with the concept of rights and defining the relationship between citizens and government. To be sure, the concept of rights in China meant not so much protecting individuals against the state as strengthening the nation and the regime's legitimacy (Han 2009; Jin and Liu 1999; Li 2014; Peerenboom 2002). The Outline of Imperial Constitution (*qinding xianfa dagang*), the first constitution in Chinese history, was enacted in 1908 to establish a constitutional monarchy. Borrowing from Japan's Meiji Constitution, the Outline of Imperial Constitution acknowledged the rights of "subjects of the empire" (*chenmin*), such as freedom of speech, freedom of association, and property rights, but sovereignty rested with the "divine emperor" instead of Chinese people. After the 1911 Revolution, it took the Republic of China (ROC) thirty-five years to enact its constitution, although the government came up with several related documents and constitutional drafts between 1912 and 1946. All these documents, drafts, and the ROC Constitution declared that the country's sovereignty rested with the people and acknowledged the people's rights. After the PRC was established, it enacted its first constitution in 1954, which also acknowledged fundamental rights. Instead of using the term "people's rights" (*renmin zhi quanli*), however, as the ROC Constitution had, the PRC Constitution referred to "citizens' rights" (*gongmin quanli*). Compared with the term "people" (*renmin*), "citizen" (*gongmin*) in Chinese has a much stronger connotation associated with the concept of public (*gong*), which is often used by Chinese people to contrast with the concept of private (*si*).

Still, the dissemination of modern law and the concept of rights was not a priority for the Chinese state until the PRC initiated its economic reform in 1978. During the ROC period, China was divided by warlords and devastated by Japan's invasion and the Chinese Civil War. The Nationalist (Kuomintang, or KMT) government mainly focused on building modern legal institutions, particularly making legal codes and establishing the judiciary and the legal profession. As Chen Jianfu notes, "the KMT law and legal institutions were far from reaching the Chinese people and had no substantial impact on the society at large" (Chen 2008, 37).

Then, the modernization of the Chinese legal system encountered serious setbacks under Mao's rule. Influenced by the Soviet model as well as by Marxist theories, the law under Mao was politicized and used as a terrorizing instrument for class struggle (Chen 2008). Just three years after the enactment of the 1954 constitution, Mao initiated the antirightist movement in 1957, explicitly designed to wipe out "bourgeois rightist" thinking and intensify the reeducation of rightists. During this movement, a considerable proportion of lawyers were labeled as "rightists" and physically and politically attacked. The Chinese state not only ceased its efforts to make codified law, but abolished the Ministry of Justice and the institution of the bar—something not reestablished until 1979. The situation worsened during the Cultural Revolution, as many law schools, courts, and prosecutors' offices were closed (Baker 1981).

The Chinese state also revised the PRC Constitution in 1975 during the Cultural Revolution. The number of clauses addressing the protection of citizens' rights decreased in the new version; for instance, the clause on "all citizens equal before the law" was deleted, as was the clause declaring citizens' right to demand compensation from the state for infringement of their rights. The right of the accused to a legal defense and a public trial, previously inscribed in the 1954 constitution, was also taken out (Baum 1986). In addition, the 1975 constitution was characterized by its endorsement of mass line politics. It promulgated that the state would allow the masses to speak out freely, air views fully, hold great debates, and produce large-character posters in support of socialist revolution and ongoing CCP rule. Moreover, the 1975 constitution stipulated that the mass line must be applied in trials; in major counter-revolutionary criminal cases, the masses should be mobilized for discussion and criticism. In short, the concept of rights and the effort to modernize the Chinese legal system were seriously eroded under Mao's rule.

What this historical context helps to highlight is the contemporary salience of the law and rights in China's contentious public sphere, and the truly remarkable institutional and cultural transformation represented by that salience today. The modernization and Westernization of the Chinese legal system since the late Qing period laid a critical institutional foundation for the rise of China's contentious public sphere, providing new ways for Chinese people to think about their relations with one another and with the state. Nonetheless, modern law and the concept of rights were not widely circulated among citizens and were even attacked under Mao's rule. In the following section, I turn to how the Chinese state in the post-Mao era returned to the law and rights, and how modern law and the concept of rights traveled beyond the circle of ruling elites and intellectuals.

Legitimacy Crisis after the Cultural Revolution

As British political scientist Colin Hay (1999, 317) argues, crisis should be conceptualized as not only "a moment of fragmentation, dislocation or destruction," but also as "a moment of decisive intervention." In the process of narrating a structural crisis, a disaggregated state is reconstituted as a more unified and centralized agency, the central project of which is to restructure itself to address the crisis. With the end of the Cultural Revolution, social and political orders were both jeopardized, and economic failure imperiled the legitimacy of the state. During the critical period from October 1976 to 1981, leaders of the CCP constructed a narrative of the crisis acceptable to the core leadership—a narrative organized around the principles of stability (*anding*), unity (*tuanjie*), and, importantly, modernization (*xiandaihua*).

The first component of the narrative is the presence of a crisis. Although the Gang of Four—the most prominent political faction during the Cultural Revolution—was smashed by the CCP leaders, a crisis still existed in the form of unstable leadership, a disrupted social order, and a plunging national economy. Yu Qiuli, the vice prime minister, summarized the perceived precarious scenario well in October 1977, when he charged that the Gang of Four had usurped political power, sabotaged production, and damaged the national economy. As a result, the national economy was on the verge of collapse. Meanwhile, the CCP lost its great leaders Chairman Mao and Premier Zhou Enlai in 1976. Everybody was anxious about the fate of the party and the nation, as well as unsure how to deal with the declining national economy.[3] In a critical party resolution, CCP elites admitted that party organizations at all levels were either partially or entirely paralyzed because of the pervasive class struggle during the Cultural Revolution.[4] Deng Xiaoping emphasized the negative consequences of the crisis on Chinese people's material life as well as China's economic and scientific development, modernization, and power as a nation.[5] Ye Jianying, the chairman of the Standing Committee of the National People's Congress (NPC), in his speech celebrating the thirty anniversary of the PRC's founding, described the Cultural Revolution as a period of havoc, division, and bloody terror, framing it as the most severe setback in the PRC's history. It became a consensus among CCP elites in 1981 that the Cultural Revolution was a period of domestic turmoil that resulted in the most severe catastrophe to ever beset the party-state and the Chinese people.[6] The editorial of the *People's Daily* in 1978 explicitly framed the crisis as a threat to the PRC's legitimacy and rule.[7]

The second component of the collective narrative concerned the cause of the crisis and why this nasty, brutal, and nationwide "war of all against all" could not have been prevented or rectified at an earlier stage. Appraising cause was a necessary but formidable task. Proposing effective solutions rested on a valid causal analysis, but a causal analysis inevitably required imputing blame and considering whether the crisis was inherent to the nature of socialism. At first, the Hua Guofeng government attempted to eschew the question of what caused the Cultural Revolution and who should bear political responsibility, lest any blame or repercussions fall on Hua himself. At the central working conference that aimed to prepare for the Third Plenary Session of the Eleventh Central Committee in 1978, Hua instructed party elites to discuss economic issues only. Nevertheless, the meeting deviated from Hua's plan, with influential party elites demanding to discuss the Cultural Revolution. They asserted that without addressing critical historical and political issues, it would be difficult to consolidate party members and the nation, not to mention concentrating on the task of achieving economic development and modernization. Hua could not reject this request (Cheng, Wang, and Li 2008, 165–70).

CCP leaders took almost five years from the end of the Cultural Revolution to negotiate a consensus on its causes. Eventually, they decided to follow a precedent established in 1945, forming and documenting their consensus through a highly formal format. In 1981, they adopted the "Resolution on Certain Questions in the History of Our Party since the Founding of the PRC" (the 1981 Resolution) at the CCP Central Committee.[8] This treatment of sensitive historical issues was a powerful expression and an indication of consensus and unified CCP leadership (Hu 1999, 32).

Party leaders concluded that the calamity of the Cultural Revolution resulted from a convergence of leadership errors and complex social, political, and historical conditions. Importantly, the crisis was caused not by the nature of socialism, but by theories and practices that deviated from Marxism-Leninism and from Mao Zedong's earlier thinking—thinking from which Mao himself was thought to have mistakenly strayed. According to the 1981 Resolution, the direct cause of the Cultural Revolution was Mao's erroneous appraisal of class relationships and the political situation in China. Mao asserted that the contradiction between the proletariat and the bourgeoisie remained the principal contradiction, so there was a need for class struggle against the revisionist line, that is, a continued revolution. Nevertheless, party elites contended that such a revolution had neither economic nor political basis because the exploiters as a class were eliminated after China's socialist transformation. They also agreed that the counterrevolutionary forces capitalized on Mao's "left error" and expanded class struggle to an extreme.

Importantly, the 1981 Resolution identified two critical structural conditions as indirect causes of the Cultural Revolution. The first condition was China's short history as a socialist nation. Owing to inadequate experience and misunderstanding of socialist theories, Chinese people waged class struggle in situations where class struggle did not exist. Then, when dealing with actual class struggle under new conditions, Chinese people were inclined to address those issues with an outdated strategy of mass mobilization. Therefore, class struggle tended to be waged at a large scale, dividing a unified party leadership and nation. The second condition was weak institutionalization. Party elites believed that because of the long-lasting effects of feudalism, China had failed to institutionalize inner-party and nationwide democracy. It had also failed to build legal institutions. Weak institutionalization had led to the overconcentration of power, the arbitrary "rule of man," and the rise of the cult of personality. Few individuals were able to replace collective leadership and abolish the constitution and the law (Hu 1999, 90, 113).

The third component of the narrative concerned the solution to the crisis. In the Third Plenary Session of the Eleventh Central Committee in late 1978, CCP leaders agreed that the solutions were to resume the disrupted task of achieving *socialist modernization*, particularly *economic development*, as well as to secure long-term *stability* and *unity*. Economic development was perceived by CCP elites as the only way to secure CCP rule, and stability and unity were seen as indispensable conditions for realizing economic development (Hu 1999, 11).[9] The leaders agreed that only by restructuring the state and economy, and more particularly, by building an advanced legal system, could they remove the structural conditions that had produced the crisis. In an interview with Italian journalist Oriana Fallaci, when asked how to avoid tragedies like the Cultural Revolution, Deng Xiaoping (1994, 348) responded that the issue should be addressed by restructuring institutions, especially establishing socialist democracy and socialist legal institutions. In CCP leaders' effort to learn from the Cultural Revolution, they rediscovered the instrumental utility of the law, seeing it now as an institutionalized instrument to achieve stability, unity, and modernization—that is, an instrument to rescue and strengthen the legitimacy of the CCP (Deng 1994, 189, 381).[10] This solution was actually similar to how the Qing state had reacted to the crisis situation in the late Qing period.

In 1978 a new constitution was enacted, reinstating some of the rights that had been removed from the 1954 constitution. It also restored the public security organs, prosecutors' offices, and people's courts, which had been partly smashed by the Gang of Four. The 1978 constitution was then overhauled in 1982 to reflect party elites' consensus regarding the 1981 Resolution.

Post–Cultural Revolution: The Instrumentality of Law

Although party leaders did not develop a systematic theory of law, important party documents and speeches reveal that when they initiated China's legal reform, top CCP leaders defined the nature of law as a partial substitute for class struggle and a practical instrument to achieve stability, unity, and modernization. Class struggle had been the dominant symbolic structure in China before the end of the Cultural Revolution. Accordingly, CCP leaders rectified the "left errors" of the Cultural Revolution and the Hua Guofeng leadership by redefining the relationship between class struggle/class relationship and the law. During the Cultural Revolution, class struggle and class relationship trumped law because Mao emphasized the continued existence of class struggle. As Mao's secretary Hu Qiaomu (1999, 113) recalled, "various fundamental principles in the constitution and law became useless." Slogans of class struggle created by Mao conveyed the dominant symbolic structure to the Chinese people and guided their practice. Gao Xingjian, a Chinese-born Nobel laureate in literature, comments on the slogans when recalling his experience in the Cultural Revolution:

> I admit that I was like a gambler and a mobster. It was because I needed to oppose against repression. But whose slogans did people use to oppose repression? Those were Mao's slogans. Those who repressed others and those who opposed repression used exactly the same language. Were you able to resist using Mao's slogans? Those slogans as such were violence. They were naked violence and the most fascist violence. . . . If you didn't participate in the struggle, you would be singled out immediately. Objectively, everyone was a ruffian. You were either a victim or a mobster. You were not able to play any other role.[11]

In the aftermath of the revolution, CCP leaders tried to solve the problem of "overapplication of class struggle" by adjusting the jurisdiction of the two sets of symbolic structures. Drawing on Mao's talk in 1957 to correct Mao's own mistake, party elites emphasized the need to distinguish between two types of contradictions: those between the enemy and the people, and those among the people themselves. According to CCP leaders, law governs both types, whereas class struggle is only applicable to contradictions between the enemy and the people (Deng 1994, 175). CCP leaders thus sought to rectify the injustices of misplaced class struggle *through* the law. Reformist leader Hu Yaobang led the state's response to petitions demanding redress for prosecution during the Cultural Revolution. CCP leaders pointed out that although China could not relax class struggle against a small handful of counterrevolutionary members and criminals who did, indeed, attempt to undermine socialist modernization, such struggle should be conducted in accordance with the procedures prescribed by the constitution and the law.[12] Those parts of the 1978 constitution now deemed to have overemphasized class struggle came under new scrutiny. Article 43, for example, accorded rights to "speak out freely, air their views fully, hold great debates and write big-character posters," and was used to legitimize practices of class struggle during the Cultural Revolution. Similarly, Article 34 authorized the formation of revolutionary committees. Given the articles strong association with the Cultural Revolution, both were removed or revised.

Nonetheless, the CCP leadership's return to law should not be read as the complete subordination of class struggle to the legal system. Instead, the symbolic structure of class relationship still constrains how law is applied when a class struggle is initiated. According to reform architect Deng Xiaoping (1994, 266–67), the CCP does not extend the freedoms of speech, press, assembly, or association to counterrevolutionary members. Similarly, when clarifying the difference between "socialist democracy" and the "bourgeois democracy," Hu Qiaomu (1999, 143), the main drafter of many important party documents, emphasized that "socialist democracy" does not allow enemies to have freedom. When dealing with enemies, the CCP should not only punish them according to the law, but also inform the Chinese people that the conflict constitutes class struggle (Hu 1999, 199–200).

Chinese leaders defined law as not only a partial substitute for class struggle, but also a practical instrument to achieve stability, unity, and modernization. As Williams Alford (1990, 1999) states, CCP leaders regard law as a "tool of state administration," instead of an end itself. This conception of law reflects Deng's pragmatic thinking. The 1981 Resolution is clear on the instrumental value of law: "We must turn the socialist legal system into a powerful weapon for protecting the rights of the people, ensuring order in production, work and other activities, punishing criminals and cracking down on disruptive activities of class enemies."[13]

Law's purpose as a weapon to maintain stability and unity was accentuated most by party leaders at the critical moment of establishing China's legal institutions. In one of his important talks in 1980, Deng (1994, 253) asserted that party cadres and members should "learn to use and master the weapon of law" to combat criminals, as being benevolent to criminals would merely damage the interests of the people and the undertaking of socialist modernization. Deng further instructed that the state should enact laws and regulations to secure stability and unity. Specifically, the state should use law to require mediation before strikes, demand permission for demonstrations, outlaw connections between individuals across organizational units or regions, and prohibit illegal organizations and publications (Deng 1994, 271). Through emphasizing the role of law in maintaining stability and unity, party leaders distanced the socialist legal system from the views of both leftists and rightists. Indeed, party elites accused both camps of producing dissent and unrest. They particularly condemned participants in the 1978–1979 Democracy Wall movement for mistakenly promoting bourgeois democracy and demanding freedom of speech. Party leaders' crackdown on this democratic movement and their use of the category of counterrevolutionary crime to punish dissidents demonstrated the leaders' conception of law as a weapon to maintain social order.

At the same time, CCP leaders' goal of developing the economy also required that they emphasize the law's role as an instrument to enable and advance the "commodity economy," later termed the "socialist market economy" by Deng Xiaoping. To enable this transition from a socialist planned economy to a socialist market economy, and to join the global market economy, the party-state enacted civil laws—the general part of private law—and economic laws to delineate properties, while also governing market transactions. In an important talk in 1978, Deng urged the government to accelerate lawmaking so that economic activities could be conducted in accordance with the law. In the realm of the economy, Deng especially pointed out the need to enact civil law, labor law, and law on foreign investments (Deng 1994, 146–47). Deng was very concerned with whether Chinese laws would be able to attract foreign investors (Deng 1993, 79–80).

How foreign investment influenced lawmaking in China can be seen from an interview with Jiang Ping, a prominent law professor who participated in constructing some of these laws. According to Professor Jiang, foreign investors did not want to invest in China in 1978, and they expressed a great deal of concern regarding what kinds of rights they would have and whether/how those rights would be protected. Chairman Ye Jianying of the NPC Standing Committee was very anxious about this. As a result, China looked extensively to foreign laws during its own lawmaking process, to assure foreigners that their rights would be protected under Chinese law.[14]

The urgent need for foreign capital and the influence of the global economy on China's domestic legislation is also illustrated in the enactment of the Law on Chinese-Foreign Equity Joint Ventures (1979) and the Administrative Litigation Law (1989). The former was passed within only three years of the end of the Cultural Revolution and around seven months after the decision to pursue economic reform. Distinct from its counterparts in other countries, the Law on Chinese-Foreign Equity Joint Ventures set not an upper limit, but a *lower* limit, or floor, for the proportion of foreign investment in joint ventures, signifying that China welcomed and needed foreign investment. The Administrative Litigation Law is widely considered by scholars within and outside China to be a progressive piece of legislation, as it enables Chinese people to sue the authoritarian state (Peerenboom 2002; Pei 1997, 398). Nonetheless, the real impetus behind the law's passage was, in fact, its consideration of foreigners. As one core participant in the lawmaking process recalled, this legislation encountered tremendous opposition from the leftists in the party-state for ideological reasons, and from party elites who worried about the negative consequences of this law on policy implementation and economic development. Local government officials in many provinces sent hundreds of letters to the central government, asking it to cease the legislative process. Despite such opposition, CCP top leaders insisted on passing the Administrative Litigation Law, as they believed it would be very difficult to attract foreign investment without administrative litigation.[15]

The importance of law to the Chinese state's efforts to build a market economy was manifested by the rising number of economy-related laws. As

Minster Deng Liqun, of the Department of Propaganda, said at a law dissemination conference in 1985, more than half of the laws enacted between 1978 and 1985 in China concerned the economy.[16] It should be noted that the Tiananmen incident in 1989 did not halt the state-led economic reform or legal institution building, though it did contribute to CCP leaders' insistence on the party's monopolistic control of political power. After a couple years of economic expansion, economic and political problems, particularly inflation and corruption, became salient. These problems triggered the 1989 Tiananmen democratic movement. Political turmoil and the opposition to economic reform of leftists inside the party-state complicated things, making the path of economic reform very uncertain.[17] The situation changed, however, after Deng Xiaoping's Southern Tour in 1992, during which Deng coined the term "socialist market economy" and decisively announced the plan to accelerate China's economic reform.

In the mid-1990s, the NPC finally passed several laws concerning ordinary Chinese citizens' economic life, particularly in the commodity, labor, and real estate markets. Important statutes and regulations, such as the Law on Protection of Consumer Rights and Interests (1993), the Product Quality Law (1993), the Corporation Law (1993), the Labor Law (1994), the Law on Urban Real Estate Administration (1994), and the Law on Township Enterprises (1996), acknowledge Chinese citizens' rights as real estate owners, as consumers to purchase qualified products and services, as labor providers to receive remunerations, and as business owners. In short, after Deng's Southern Tour, China sped up its lawmaking. Since the mid-1990s onward, rights have been embodied in concrete laws that thoroughly infiltrate and govern citizens' economic lives, instead of remaining an abstract concept at the level of the constitution. The principle of "ruling the country in accordance with the law" (*yifa zhiguo*) was endorsed by the Fifteenth Party Congress in 1997 and added to the constitution in 1999. The completion of this infrastructure was critical for China's subsequent accession to the World Trade Organization (WTO) in 2001.

The 1980s: Law and the Supervision of Governance

The Chinese state's continuing emphasis on the law and its effort to ensure the law's penetration throughout society also stemmed from the daunting issue of governance. Numerous governance problems were engendered by China's economic reform and the Chinese state's endeavor since the 1980s to solve such problems by establishing supervisory institutions (*jiandu jizhi*). A legal scholar who participated in China's legal reform and advised several top CCP leaders emphasized to me the importance of understanding the Chinese state's turn to law in a broader context of building supervisory institutions to keep power—especially power at the local level—in check:

It is true that building a market economy motivated Chinese leaders to establish legal institutions. But what is often neglected by scholars and China
watchers is the fact that Chinese leaders at the central government—from
Deng to Zhao, Jiang, and Hu—needed to establish supervisory institutions
to curb power and maintain CCP's legitimacy. As Chinese leaders rejected
checks and balances in liberal democracies, they needed to come up with
some alternatives. Zhao Ziyang stressed the role of law, media, and citizens
in constraining political and economic power. Although the CCP purged
Zhao and set aside Zhao's political reform agenda after the Tiananmen incident, Zhao's successors continued to recognize the importance of law as a
supervisory institution and the necessity to mobilize media and the masses
to supervise local officials and businesses. (Interview, June 2011, Beijing)

Indeed, despite their different views on political reform, Chinese leaders in
the central government in the 1980s were greatly concerned with the social
conflict and instability that was and could be generated by the abuse of political
power and the collusion of political and economic power. They believed that
law, along with other supervisory institutions, could help identify and solve
problems before local problems escalated into large-scale conflicts.

After initiating economic reform, Chinese leaders soon recognized the
urgency of developing supervisory institutions to check political power and
manage political, social, and market order. Although the economic reform
seemed to address the state's legitimacy crisis in the aftermath of the Cultural
Revolution, the transition to a market economy brought with it tremendous
problems. China's political system, already characterized by overconcentration of power, became a bed of corruption as government officials were able
to parlay political power into money in the market. Corrupt local officials
and market actors sought to capitalize unduly from the transition. In the late
1980s, popular perception of corruption grew drastically. The direct cause of
the problem was China's dual-track system—the coexistence of the planning
system and the emerging product market. Government officials in charge of
resource allocation in the planning system could profit enormously from selling in-plan resources in the market, taking advantage of the gap between the
plan price and the market price (Dittmer and Liu 2006; Gong 1993; Li 2002,
497; Lieberthal 1992). Corruption and inflation reinforced one another and
led to public outrage, eventually triggering the 1989 Tiananmen democratic
movement (Zhao 2001). Figure 3.1 shows the scale of corruption problems
after China's economic reform. The *People's Daily* had many articles with titles
containing "corruption" (*fubai* or *tanwu*) when the PRC was first founded, but
reports at that time associated corruption with the previous KMT regime and
capitalism. Then, between the early 1950s and the late 1970s, the *People's Daily*
had almost no articles with titles referring to corruption. The situation changed

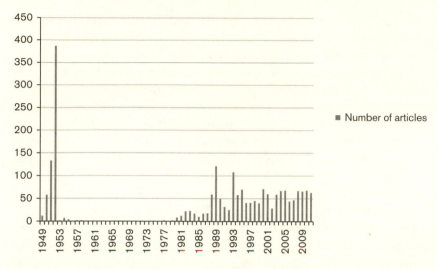

3.1. *People's Daily* articles with titles referencing "corruption" (*fubai* or *tanwu*), 1949–2012.

after China's economic reform. Since then, issues related to corruption have become a frequent feature in the *People's Daily*.

Public concern about corruption in the late 1980s worried the Chinese leadership because it undermined CCP's legitimacy and sociopolitical stability. Widespread corruption also gave left-wing CCP members an excuse to oppose the reform.[18] Facing corruption and economic disorder, CCP reformist ruling elites formulated a detailed and progressive political reform proposal in the Thirteenth Party Congress in 1987 (Deng 1993, 176–77; Zhao et al. 2009). This unprecedented political reform program promoted separating the party from the state, decentralizing political power, reforming government organizations and the cadre system, improving legal institutions, and establishing institutions to facilitate societal negotiation and dialogue.

Importantly, Zhao Ziyang highlighted the concept of supervision, especially legal supervision (*falu jiandu*), democratic supervision (*minzhu jiandu*), and supervision by public opinion (*yulun jiandu*) in his Thirteenth Party Congress report. The report argued that because law serves as the standard of supervision, the government should speed up the lawmaking process. Party-state agencies, news media, and the masses—actors both outside and within the party-state—should oversee state and business actors in accordance with the law, ensuring that it is both followed and enforced. In addition, media should facilitate citizens' efforts to exercise this right of supervision.[19] Zhao saw citizens' oversight of political and economic power as a critical form of political participation and an important element of the rule of law and socialist democracy. He stressed the importance of protecting citizens' liberties and political rights, particularly freedom of speech, the press, assembly, association, and demonstration.[20] In the Third Plenary Session of the Thirteenth Central Committee in 1988, Zhao emphasized again the importance of supervision within the party-state as well as mass supervision. He contended that law and socialist democracy—exemplified by the political participation of citizens—could help to "resolve conflict at the grassroots level and nip them in the bud."[21]

The results of pilot anticorruption programs in several localities between 1987 and 1989 reassured the central government of the critical role of citizens in overseeing local problems, strengthening law enforcement, and addressing conflicts. After the Thirteenth Party Congress in 1987, the Political Reform Office of the CCP Central Committee guided several local governments (at different levels) to examine the effect of various anticorruption intervention programs. The office believed that corruption in China was rooted in insufficient regulation of administrative and market behavior. Criticizing the efficacy of conventional anticorruption programs based on mass political movements, the office concluded that supervision—particularly mass supervision (*qunzhong jiandu*)—and publicity (*gongkai*) were two keys to addressing the problem. The office proposed that the Chinese state mobilize the masses to oversee administrative and market behavior according to law, because relying on the government would be insufficient. To enable mass supervision, the government should publicize laws and regulations, letting people know their rights. The office found that corruption became less rampant in localities where local government distributed pamphlets giving clear information about the law and rights. The office also proposed that the government publicize the outcome of supervision.[22] In essence, the office still recognized the importance of mass line (*qunzhong luxian*), but now it emphasized that mass supervision be grounded in law. The findings and suggestions of the Political Reform Office reaffirmed Zhao Ziyang's contention that mass supervision and open information could help to solve problems and conflicts at an early stage.[23]

Although Zhao Ziyang was purged after the 1989 Tiananmen incident, the Chinese leadership continued to see supervisory institutions, particularly law, as solutions to address governance problems and to maintain social stability. Zhao's idea of using law and other supervisory institutions to "resolve conflict at the grassroots level and nip them in the bud"[24] remains a dominant logic in Chinese officialdom. In fact, on August 22, 1989, about two and a half months after the June 4 Tiananmen incident, the *People's Daily* published—on the front page, no less—a speech titled "The Communist Party Must Accept Supervision." The speech had been delivered by Deng Xiaoping in 1957. According to one of my interviewees who worked for the *People's Daily*, this was an attempt to carry on part of Zhao's reform by anchoring the agenda in Deng's words.[25] Deng's speech identified three kinds of supervision: by party organizations, by the masses, and by the democratic parties and democrats without party affiliation. Deng argued that supervision would ensure the party was better informed about problems. He also contended that mass supervision would give the public plenty of opportunity to air their views, offer suggestions, and express their anger, thus minimizing not only social instability but also demands for more formal democracy. The day after the *People's Daily* published Deng's 1957 talk, an article titled "Supervision of the Communist Party Is a Major Issue for Building the Party" appeared on the front page of the *People's Daily*.[26] Two days later, the paper published yet another article on supervision: "Supervision: A Major Problem of Party Building." Framing supervisory institutions as Deng's legacy, the article elaborated on the significance of supervision. The author stated that mass supervision in accordance with the law would help leaders acquire information from the masses, improve policy making, and address problems before they became intractable—all of which would contribute to social stability. The article also dismissed concerns among some party members that supervision could lead to social instability.[27]

The Chinese leadership's continuing emphasis on supervisory institutions, particularly legal supervision and mass supervision, after the 1989 Tiananmen incident mainly stemmed from the expanding and diversifying problems that had accumulated during the reform process as well as anxiousness to discover and address problems at the earliest opportunity. The central government's concern about being unaware of local problems was reflected in "The CCP Central Committee's Decision on Strengthening the Ties with the Mass and the People," which was ratified in the Sixth Plenary Session of the Thirteenth Central Committee in 1990. The decision instructed that cadres should make friends with workers, peasants, intellectuals, and other people who dared to speak up about local situations, so that the government could learn more about people's genuine opinions and discover emerging problems. In the early 1990s, the central government also required party-state agencies and public organizations to assist mass supervision in accordance with the law so that the party-state could learn of problems and address them as soon as possible.[28] Meanwhile, the central government asked the NPC to speed up the lawmaking process to enable mass supervision.[29] Jiang Zemin's two Party Congress reports also reflect the leadership's emphasis on supervisory institutions. In his Fourteenth Party Congress report in 1992, Jiang highlighted the importance of legal supervision and supervision by public opinion, as well as the need to develop comprehensive supervisory institutions. Jiang advanced his theory of supervision in the Fifteenth Party Congress in 1997. He asserted that the CCP should integrate supervision within the party as well as legal supervision, mass supervision, and supervision by public opinion to ensure that the constitution and laws are implemented and that power is not abused.

In sum, mobilizing law, the masses, and the media to keep political and economic power—particularly political power at the local level—in check has been the central government's solution to emerging governance problems since the late 1980s. Though at first, the Chinese central state used supervisory institutions mainly to address corruption, the state saw supervision as a solution to ensure the implementation of law in general and to create a desired market, social, and political order. As such, not only state actors but also nonstate actors, particularly those in business, became objects of supervision. And yet, despite the Chinese state's continuing emphasis on supervisory institutions, the leaderships before and after the 1989 Tiananmen incident had different understandings of supervision's role. Although Zhao Ziyang did not embrace liberal democracy in the 1980s, he considered the protection of political rights indispensable to establishing various forms of supervision. As such, during his leadership, the National People's Congress proposed to enact the Press Law (*xinwen fa*).[30] While Chinese leaders after the Tiananmen incident continued to embrace the notion of supervision, they abandoned the lawmaking agenda.

The 1990s: Law and Conflict Resolution

Chinese leadership sees law not only as a supervisory institution to help identify and address problems at an early stage, but also as a conflict-resolution institution capable of maintaining social stability when crises emerge. The government has increasingly emphasized the function of legal institutions in conflict resolution since the mid-1990s, when threats of social conflicts and instability began to loom large. Recognizing how China's reform drastically restructured the distribution of wealth and resources, in the Second Plenary Session of the Fourteenth Central Committee in 1993, Jiang Zemin warned of the consequences on social stability of increasing conflicts and stressed the need to mobilize the law to address such conflicts. Jiang's worry was not unfounded. The central government's fiscal reform in 1994 largely lowered the local government's share of fiscal revenues, motivating local government officials to exploit peasants, mostly through illegal taxation and land seizure (Cai 2010; Man 2011; O'Brien and Li 2006; Tong and Lei 2014; Wang 1997). The process fueled a surge in resistance, protests, and collective petitioning. Labor disputes also increased immensely after the government introduced a labor contract system in 1995 and accelerated the restructuring of SOEs. The process led to millions of job losses and soaring labor protests (Gallagher 2005a, 2005b; Lee 2007). As social conflicts and protests rose drastically from the mid-1990s onward, Jiang, in his Fifteenth Party Congress report in 1997, pointed to the urgency of using the law to tackle the conflicts and thereby avoid instability.

My interviews with officials in the Ministry of Justice and scholars at the Central Party School of the CCP help explain why the central leadership considered law to be such a critical means to address social conflicts and maintain stability.[31] Basically, what worried the central leadership was collective action or mass incidents (*quntixing shijian*), which often brought together people with similar interests, mostly peasants and workers, and threatened to disrupt public order. After investigating many mass incidents in the 1990s, the central government found that because participants in such incidents knew very little about the law, they appealed to noninstitutional channels to resolve their problems. The central government believed that if provided with more legal knowledge and shown how to use legal institutions, unruly citizens would be less likely to go to the streets; conflicts would also be less likely to become systematic, political, and oppositional. As an official in the Ministry of Justice put it, "The central leadership sees law as a safety valve [*an quan fa*] for social order. Since legal process is characterized by order, it can resolve disordered conflicts and lower the level of confrontation."[32] Based on this understanding, the central government focused on making substantive laws in areas where problems could arise, particularly around labor issues. The government also required the Ministry of Justice to disseminate legal knowledge to citizens and strengthen institutions that help resolve conflicts at the grassroots level, such as legal-aid programs.[33]

The Central Government's Law Dissemination Strategies: From Obeying Law to Asserting Rights

For Chinese leaders, whether the "weapon of law" was able to build a market economy, monitor political and economic power, or address social conflicts ultimately depended on how well information about the law was disseminated and accepted by the Chinese populace. This prerequisite was a daunting task, particularly in the 1980s, considering China's huge population and territory, low literacy rate,[34] and the previous demolition of the law during the Cultural Revolution. The general unfamiliarity with the law among the Chinese populace was manifest in an emergent category deemed "legal illiterates" (*famang*)—those who did not know law and/or lacked any sense of legality. This term first appeared in the *People's Daily* in October 1979. It was used to talk about how peasants without legal knowledge were empowered through learning about the newly enacted criminal law.[35] Another *People's Daily* article, in December 1979, advocated using education to reduce the number of legal illiterates. The author pointed out that the rise of the Gang of Four had led to a huge number of legal illiterates in China. The old generation did not study law, while the young generation, who grew up in a lawless situation, never heard of the law and lacked a sense of legality.[36] The term "legal illiterates" became increasingly popular from 1979 onward. In 1988, Peng Zeng, chairman of the NPC Standing Committee, also pointed out that the efficacy of mass supervision would ultimately rest on legal education. Considering many Chinese people had little to no legal knowledge, Peng stressed the importance of disseminating law to Chinese citizens, especially law relevant to everyday life.[37] This phenomenon of "legal illiteracy" reflected the difficulty that Chinese leaders faced in attempting to "deliver law to people."

Leaders in the central state decided on China's return to law, rebuilt the nation's legal institutions, and initiated the law dissemination campaigns; however, the media played the most important role in truly making law and the concept of rights part of the public discourse and imagination. The Chinese state demanded—and continues to demand—that the media disseminate law as part of their propaganda work. Peng told journalists in 1984 that helping people know, understand, and abide by law is, in fact, media's mission.[38] Indeed, the five-year law dissemination campaigns since 1985 had been jointly supervised by the Department of Propaganda and the Ministry of Justice. The former is the highest party organ that administers ideology, enforces censorship, and regulates media. The Department of Propaganda has repeatedly demanded that media disseminate law in innovative ways to capture the audience's attention and effectively place law in the hands of the populace. Studies of Chinese people's legal consciousness based on survey data show that the media (TV, newspapers, and radio) are the primary means through which Chinese people know and understand law. In fact, the media's significance is much higher than any other activities organized by the government via law dissemination campaigns, and higher than information received from acquaintances or from legal education at school (Zhao 2006; Zheng 2007).[39]

In the following sections, I discuss the kinds of messages about law the Chinese central state intended to disseminate to its populace. At first, the government focused on addressing the chaos following the Cultural Revolution, and the party-state stressed "knowing law and abiding by law." But eventually, discourse about law shifted to rights protection, which turned out to be an even more effective means of spreading law to Chinese people.

EDUCATING CITIZENS IN OBEDIENCE: THE LATE 1970S TO THE MID-1980S

Soon after CCP leaders decided to return to the law, its dissemination became an imperative, because CCP leaders thought that Chinese society was still in turmoil.[40] It was often reported that the country was still in a state of chaos following the Cultural Revolution, thanks to serious crimes and the 1978–1979 Xidan Wall (Democracy Wall) democratic movement.[41] Chinese leaders believed that only when the majority of people were familiar with and spontaneously obeyed the law, and when cadres understood and could enforce the law, would the desired social order and stability be attained. Chinese leaders thus stressed the importance of educating people to be disciplined and obedient to the law. For instance, at the Eighth National People's Judicial Working

Conference in 1978, party leaders urged that courts at all levels should regularly disseminate law and strengthen legal education to prevent illegal behavior and crime.[42] Deng Xiaoping (1993, 267) stated that the essence of rule by law is that everybody understands, obeys, and safeguards the law. And the key to attaining this lies in legal education, which should begin with toddlers and extend to the entire society (Deng 1993, 163). The CCP general secretary Hu Yaobang endorsed the same view.[43] The importance of education to create disciplined and law-abiding citizens was later written in Article 24 of the 1982 PRC Constitution: "The state strengthens the building of a socialist society with an advanced culture and ideology by promoting education in high ideals, ethics, general knowledge, discipline and legality."

To ensure the societal penetration of law, the Chinese government stressed the necessity of suppressing crimes and spreading details about harsh punishment to the public as part of legal education. This practice of publicizing crimes and imposing stigma reflected Chinese leaders' conception of law as an instrument to maintain stability. In 1979, the party-state proposed a strategy called "comprehensive governance" (*zhonghe zhili*) to maintain social security and order. The party-state demanded that police and judicial agencies punish criminals who destroy social order as harshly and swiftly as possible. This policy was adopted formally in the 1983 anticrime (*yanda*) Strike Hard campaign. The party-state also required all organizations to publicize the law, particularly criminal law. It demanded that courts disseminate law by announcing sentences in the form of mass gatherings. The purpose was to induce deterrence.[44] This form of law dissemination, reminiscent of mass mobilization during the Cultural Revolution, was widely practiced in the 1983–1985 anticrime campaign.[45] As Liu Fuzhi (1998, 179–80), the minister of public security in 1983–1985, recalled, Deng had insisted that mass mobilization was an indispensable means to crack down on criminal activities and a critical form of legal education, despite the CCP's promise of no more mass mobilization, as well as disagreement inside the party.

The policy of the central government was executed by local governments. According to *People's Daily* reports and local gazetteers, governments in both rural and urban areas actively spread the law beginning in late 1978. They aimed to inform citizens and cadres of the law, and to ensure their compliance with it. Local police offices, courts, and other agencies held diverse law dissemination campaigns in government, party organizations, schools, factories, people's communes, streets, and so on. These law dissemination campaigns, along with media reports, often aimed to create the norm that "abiding law is honorable; breaking law is shameful."[46]

While the central government continued to enact laws, officials sensed a continuing lack of legal knowledge among citizens. To increase the law's penetrative reach into society, the central government decided to initiate a social engineering project that would mobilize the entire society to accelerate the spread of law. In June 1985, the Propaganda Department and the Ministry of Justice jointly announced a five-year plan of disseminating law. This plan detailed methods, steps, and organization for circulating information about the law. The law dissemination campaign aimed to acquaint citizens with basic knowledge of the law within five years, so that each citizen would know and abide by the law.[47]

DISCOURSE OF RIGHTS

Although ensuring that citizens' knew and obeyed the law was the main focus when the central government began to rebuild China's legal institutions, the focus of legal dissemination eventually shifted. Gradually, the discourse of protecting rights became increasingly widespread in both legal dissemination campaigns and other occasions when law was mentioned to the public. I show this trend in figure 3.2, which plots the numbers of the *People's Daily* articles with "rights" and "abiding by law" in the title, each year from 1949 to 2010.[48] Since the title of a newspaper article usually reveals its main thrust and contains important information to grab readers' attention, how often "rights" and "abiding by law" appear in newspaper titles indicates the visibility of the two discourses in the public forum.[49] Figure 3.2 indicates that the discourse of knowing and abiding by law has slightly increased since 1985, when the law

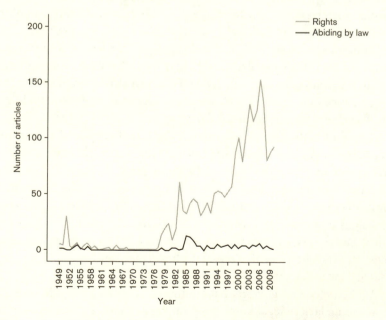

3.2. Number of *People's Daily* articles with "rights" or "abiding by law" in the title, 1949–2010.

dissemination campaign was initiated, but then gradually declined. Although this discourse did not totally disappear, its visibility remained very limited. In comparison, the discourse of rights, not originally part of the main focus of the early law dissemination programs, became highly visible in the late 1980s and then climbed drastically around 1998.

I also analyzed eleven comparable local newspapers across localities in the same ways. Figure 3.3 plots the number of articles with "rights" and "abiding by law" in the title each year from 2000 to 2010. The figure shows that, in general, the discourse of rights gained prominence over time, while the discourse of knowing and abiding by law remained sporadic over time across types of newspaper and geographic areas. Importantly, the discourse of rights expanded in the mid-2000s in most of the local newspapers I examined.

To be sure, the concept of rights was not entirely novel in the PRC. Before the Cultural Revolution, the language of rights was used in the PRC's first constitution (1954) and in the Marriage Law (1950). But generally speaking, the concept of rights was foreign to most Chinese people and had little meaning in their everyday lives. The question, then, is why the discourse of rights became so dominant with the development of China's legal system. First, there had been calls since the mid-1980s to fix problems in law dissemination campaigns and to use the discourse of rights, rather than the discourse of abiding by law, to disseminate law inside the party-state. For instance, an article in the *People's Daily* written by a law professor, Kong Qingming, in 1985 criticized the discourse of obeying law as reflecting an outdated concept of law rooted in China's feudal and patriarchal tradition, in which an individual had absolute obedience to authority but no rights, and in which law was a synonym of punishment and vice. Kong contended that this outdated concept of law made law seem irrelevant to Chinese people's lives as long as they were not breaking it. Citing the PRC's constitution, Kong argued against this outdated concept and for raising Chinese people's rights consciousness and disseminating law from the perspective of rights protection instead. He believed that a concept of law centered on rights would provide citizens with incentives to understand and engage with the law.[50]

Another *People's Daily* article published in 1988 also stated that local law dissemination campaigns overemphasized the discourse of obeying law and citizens' obligations, without advocating citizens' rights and raising their rights consciousness. The author argued that legal education and law dissemination campaigns should discard the concept of law based on Chinese feudalism, which aimed only to govern the populace. Instead, the government should raise Chinese people's law and rights consciousness so that people would know how to use the weapon of law to protect their own rights.[51] Similar reflection on the law dissemination campaigns appeared in academic journals starting in the late 1980s. Scholars proposed deepening law dissemination through raising

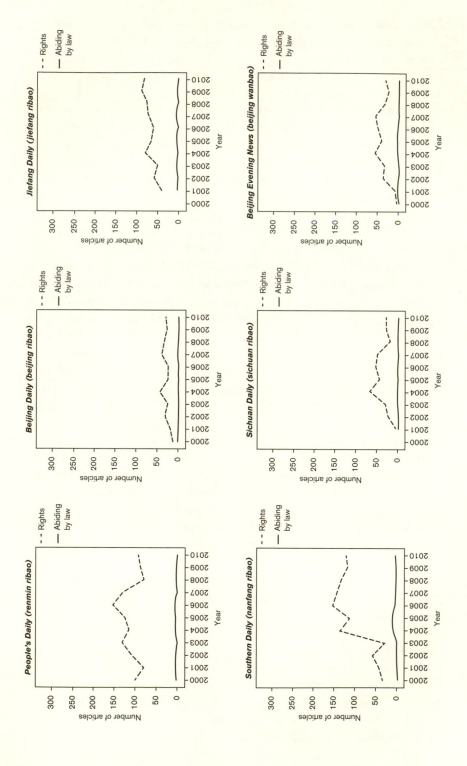

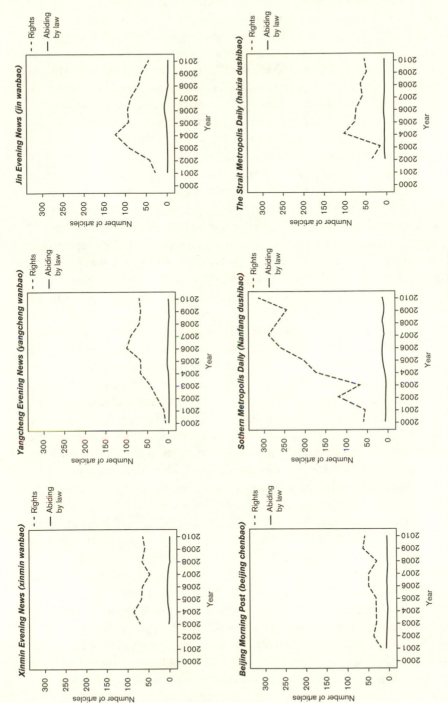

3.3. Number of articles with "rights" and "abiding by law" in the titles of twelve newspapers, 2000–2010.

rights consciousness. Some articles even anticipated and addressed potential state concerns regarding citizens who might develop a rights consciousness *too* strongly; these articles suggested the government should not worry about rising rights consciousness among citizens because such citizens would only be more rational and respectful of law (Cheng and Zhang 1988; Zhou 1999).

The second, more important factor leading to the prevalence of the discourse of rights was the enactment of laws closely related to ordinary citizens' economic lives that relied on the language of rights. Most of these laws did not come into existence until the mid-1990s. From the mid-1990s onward, rights have been embodied in concrete laws that thoroughly infiltrate and govern citizens' economic lives, instead of remaining an abstract concept at the level of the constitution. Of course, it took time for these laws to be disseminated from the central government to ordinary citizens and to be practiced by these citizens. The role of law as an instrument to advance the economy also became salient in law dissemination campaigns with the deepening of economic reform. When reporting to the NPC Standing Committee in 1986 on the implementation of the five-year plan, the minister of justice, Zou Yu, still talked about the need to combine the law dissemination campaigns with the "comprehensive governance" program to prevent crime, but he accentuated the link between law dissemination campaigns' effects on citizens' material lives and their participation in the commodity economy. Tian Jiyun, the vice chairman of the NPC Standing Committee, further associated law dissemination with citizens' rights and the development of the market economy. In his talk to journalists on law dissemination in 1993, Tian said that journalists should diffuse law to the public so that citizens would be able to protect their own rights in the market economy.[52] The Department of Propaganda and the Ministry of Justice increased the visibility of rights in their plans. With the second five-year law dissemination plans, which went into effect in 1991, the central government began emphasizing that it expected ordinary citizens to use law and to exercise their rights in accordance with law.

To trace the development of the discourse of rights in China, I analyzed articles in the *People's Daily* with rights (*quanli, qunyi*, or *weiquan*) in the title and examined the kinds of rights each article addressed during the period 1949–2010. In table 3.1, I present the five categories of rights that appear with the highest frequency. These results reflect the Chinese state's logics of using law to develop the market economy, address governance problems, and solve social conflicts. Between 1949 and 1976, few articles mentioned rights. Among the forty-four articles that did mention them, 34.09 percent addressed civil and political rights, and 29.55 percent addressed the rights of women and youth. These articles were all published before the Cultural Revolution. Articles about civil and political rights mostly dealt with citizens' rights to participate in politics and the protection of civil liberties.[53] Articles that addressed the rights of women and youth tended to emphasize the superiority of communism over capitalism in protecting the rights of these groups.[54] With China's unfolding economic reform, the number of articles addressing rights increased between 1977 and 1989, with the government beginning to deal with the rights involved in doing business. Meanwhile, the Chinese state still emphasized the rights of women and youth. Civil and political rights remained a critical agenda during this period because of Chinese leaders' decision to initiate political reform.

In the post-Tiananmen era, however, the categories of rights emphasized in the *People's Daily* changed. This shift demonstrates the Chinese state's decision to accelerate economic reform. Between 1990 and 1997, the number of articles that addressed consumer rights rose tremendously. Articles on consumer rights often framed protection of those rights as critical to building an ordered socialist market economy.[55] Articles on consumer rights also described mass supervision in accordance with law as key to ensuring business actors' compliance with the law.[56] Issues related to labor rights were also on the rise. Since 1998, labor rights, particularly issues related to the mass layoff of SOE employees and labor disputes of migrant workers, became the most important issues in rights protection. Many *People's Daily* articles considered protection of labor rights as critical to addressing rising social conflicts and maintaining social stability.[57] *People's Daily* articles also mentioned that the protection of labor rights rests on supervision of multiple parties. Government agencies, labor units, and laborers should all oversee whether business actors are in compliance with the law.[58] Although protection of peasants' rights was not among the top five important categories between 1990 and 1997, peasants' rights has become the fourth most important issue since 1998. Articles that addressed peasants' rights often alluded to the necessity for peasants to oversee local government officials.[59]

My analysis thus reveals three general patterns from 1949 to 2010. First, the Chinese state has constantly emphasized protecting the rights of women and youth since 1949, despite the enormous social and economic change in China. Second, rights related to the economic lives of ordinary citizens—particularly labor rights, consumer rights, and to a lesser extent, peasant rights—contributed to the drastic rise of the discourse of rights since the late 1990s. By disseminating law closely related to ordinary citizens' economic lives, the Chinese government attempted to establish an ordered market economy, keep state and business actors in check, and address social conflicts.

Third, whereas the Chinese state stressed civil and political rights before the 1989 Tiananmen democratic movement, the importance of civil and political rights has declined since 1990, despite the rise of the discourse of rights in general. The government's law dissemination programs did not target the diffusion of knowledge about political and civil rights. As an official at the Ministry of Justice explained frankly to me, this was the central government's intentional decision to avoid the possibility that law dissemination would aid prodemocratic movements. The focus of law dissemination was on issues related to ordinary citizens' material interests in their daily lives. These issues, unlike issues directly related to political and civil rights, were seen as relatively remote from the constitution, political regime, and responsibility of the central

TABLE 3.1. Categories of rights and interests in *People's Daily*, 1949–2010

Years: 1949–1976		
Categories of rights and interests	Numbers of articles	Percentage
Civil and political rights	15	34.09
Women and youth	13	29.55
Labor rights	6	13.64
Right to education	2	4.55
Peasants	1	2.27
Others	7	15.91
Total	44	100
Years: 1977–1989		
Categories of rights and interests	Numbers of articles	Percentage
Women and youth	49	14.54
Civil and political rights	47	13.95
Business	33	9.79
Peasants	28	8.31
Labor rights	23	6.82
Others	157	46.59
Total	337	100
Years: 1990–1997		
Categories of rights and interests	Numbers of articles	Percentage
Consumer rights	68	19.94
Women and youth	60	17.60
Labor rights	42	12.32
Business	34	9.97
Civil and political rights	33	9.68
Others	104	30.50
Total	341	100
Years: 1998–2003		
Categories of rights and interests	Numbers of articles	Percentage
Labor rights	90	17.51
Consumer rights	87	16.93
Women and youth	87	16.93
Peasants	31	6.03
Civil and political rights	30	5.84
Others	189	36.77
Total	514	100

TABLE 3.1. (*continued*)

Years: 2004–2010		
Categories of rights and interests	Numbers of articles	Percentage
Labor rights	282	35.03
Consumer rights	108	13.42
Women and youth	78	9.69
Peasants	43	5.34
Civil and political rights	42	5.22
Others	252	31.30
Total	805	100

Note: Any rights other than labor rights, consumer rights, women and youth's rights, peasant rights, or civil and political rights are categorized as "Others" and did not come up as often as the other five categories of rights. Examples include intellectual property rights, rights to collective culture, environmental protection rights, rights to health care, and so forth.

government. By focusing on rights related to the economy, the central government hoped to benefit from legal institutions, while minimizing political risk.[60]

Law Dissemination on the Ground: TV Programs, Newspaper Reports, Legal Aid, and the Rise of Legal and Rights Consciousness

Having examined how the central state intended to disseminate legal knowledge, I now turn to what kind of legal information ordinary citizens have received in their daily lives from TV and newspapers. As noted, the Chinese state began its first national law dissemination campaign in 1985. In the same year, Shanghai Television had China's very first legal TV show, *Law and Morality (falu yu daode)*. Through reporting on legal cases and interviewing legal experts, the program aimed to disseminate legal knowledge (Liu 2014). Since the 1990s, legal programs have become the third most popular category of TV programs, following news and entertainment (Li 2007). In 1994, China Central Television had its first legal program *Social Longitude and Latitude (shehui jingwei)*. The program told stories about court cases to educate audiences on law (Huang 1999). In 1999, China Central Television began to broadcast *Legal Report (jinri shuofa)*, which became one of the most famous TV programs in China. Over time, China Central Television and local TV stations developed several legal programs. More than three hundred provincial and city legal TV programs aired in China in 2014. Twenty TV stations have daily legal programs, all of which generally have high ratings (Gao and Liu 2012; Li 2007; Liu 2014).

Most legal TV programs in China use the case study storytelling format. Through specific cases, the programs vividly depict how a protagonist encounters and then pursues a legal problem, all the way to the final outcome. For each case, the hosts of the programs, as well as legal experts, usually discuss relevant legal issues to educate the audience. Though civil and administrative cases are sometimes covered, criminal cases are the most popular, and reporting tends to be detailed and sensational. Audiences are left with the impression that law exists and functions primarily to punish criminals (Gao and Liu 2012). Such legal TV programs also sometimes discuss cases in which peasants, workers, and consumers encounter legal problems and pursue "rights defense" activities.

Some legal TV programs have a more complex format, featuring multiple components. For instance, Zhengzhou Television's one-hour daily flagship program, *Zhengzhou Legal Program* (*zhengzhou fazhi baodao*), includes several features, from "prosecutors' notebook," "judges talk about cases, and "news on the spot" to "rights defense" (Liu 2014). Nanjing Television's flagship legal program, *Talking about Law on the Spot* (*fazhi xianchang*), is another example. The program began in 2000 and has been among the top five most popular TV programs in Nanjing. The show has several parts. In one section, judges analyze court cases to disseminate legal knowledge. In another part, lawyers use concrete cases to discuss and teach rights defense. The program focuses on ordinary citizens' legal problems and disputes. One of the main aims is to provide legal aid and information to citizens, especially "the disadvantaged" or vulnerable groups such as low-income families and unemployed workers (Wu 2012).

Other programs focus on a variety of civil cases, ranging from divorce and inheritance issues to wage disputes, product defects, violation of labor contracts, and so forth. For example, Tianjin Television has had a legal program called *Court Today* (*jinri kaiting*) since 2006. Using a mock court format, *Court Today* features plaintiffs and defendants debating fiercely over civil disputes, while judges analyze and adjudicate the disputes using plain language. The program dramatizes the emotional and moral dimensions of law to capture the audience's attention and make legal reasoning less boring. Many of the programs in this format emphasize how to do rights defense.[61]

Some producers and reporters of such legal TV programs see them as a means not only to disseminate legal knowledge but also to provide legal aid. They often work with rights defense lawyers to assist the disadvantaged, particularly migrant workers (Ruan 2014). Indeed, "disadvantaged" viewers are extremely appreciative of such programs. Research shows that TV is the main channel through which peasants acquire legal knowledge and seek legal aid. In a survey conducted in a village in Jiansu Suining, 62.5 percent of the peasants reported that they frequently watch TV legal programs, while 29.2 percent reported that they watch legal programs occasionally. In short, peasants' level of exposure to legal TV programs is impressive. These viewers are particularly interested in legal information related to their lives, such as state land acquisition, housing demolition, social security, rights defense, corruption, issues related to taxes and levies, village elections, and democracy (Wang, Bao, and Dong 2015). Research also shows that the main audience of *Legal Report*, arguably the most popular legal TV program in China, are citizens who need to restore their own rights, particularly workers (Niu 2012).

Legal stories and issues are also featured in Chinese newspapers, particularly those marketized for general readers, specialized to provide legal information, or targeted for workers or peasants. Similar to TV programs, Chinese newspapers tell stories and provide dramatic details about crimes that catch readers' attention. In such coverage, editors and journalists often ask lawyers or legal scholars to comment on the stories (Song 2009). In addition, newspapers report often on everyday citizens' legal disputes. Many newspapers have special columns, for example, that allow readers to share their own rights defense problems and seek advice. The papers usually work with rights defense lawyers to come up with solutions. Editors and journalists see such columns as both a form of legal aid and a way to disseminate legal knowledge (Chen 2013). This format is well received by readers, as evidenced by the numerous daily inquiries from readers that such newspapers receive (Peng 2008). Not surprisingly, research shows that columns designed to help peasants assert and protect their rights are popular among peasants (Wu 2008). Some newspapers, particularly newspapers for workers and specialized legal newspapers, even have weekly editions specifically devoted to rights defense. In these weekly editions, newspapers often invite lawyers, judges, and legal scholars to provide legal analysis and suggest dispute resolution and litigation strategies (Yang 2006).

As the above analysis shows, the themes of rights defense and legal aid are salient in TV legal programs and legal reports in newspapers. Media professionals who produce legal programs or reports see one aspect of their job as providing legal aid and working with lawyers, while rights defense lawyers see themselves as providing a public service. This shows the influence of the institution of legal aid on law dissemination and the effort to put the law and rights into practice. Starting in 1994, the Ministry of Justice began to develop the institution of legal aid to provide legal service to people who could not otherwise afford it. Since 1996, lawyers have been providing legal aid, and the state has begun to build legal-aid centers (Liebman 1999). In 2003, the State Council passed the Regulation on Legal Aid. Gao Zhen, the chief officer in charge of legal aid at the Ministry of Justice, recognized that Chinese media and lawyers made extraordinary efforts to help publicize and build the institution of legal aid (Gao 2004).[62] By 2008, legal-aid stations had already been established in many rural areas in mid- and eastern China (Gao and Jia 2008). Despite building many such legal-aid centers and stations, however, the state still relies heavily on private lawyers, rather than state-related personnel, to provide this public service (e.g., private lawyers provided 99.6% of legal aid in Beijing in 2013; Yang and Chen 2015). Some private rights defense lawyers have even begun to form legal-aid NGOs, which provide legal education and legal aid to the disadvantaged, particularly migrant workers (Wang 2011).

The efforts of the Chinese state, media, and lawyers to disseminate law and the concept of rights has led to an incredible rise in legal and rights consciousness among citizens, as evidenced by studies of different social groups. Kevin O'Brien and Li Lianjing found what they called "rightful resistance" among peasants in rural China as early as 1994. They observed that local cadres were struggling to deal with unruly and contentious peasants who had enthusiastically embraced law as a means to assert their rights to protest, topple village leaders, and demand accountability (O'Brien and Li 2006). Li Fan's research identified two waves of peasant resistance based on law and rights since the 1990s. The first wave was triggered by corruption and illegal levies. The second wave, which became particularly salient after the turn of the twentieth century, was fueled by land disputes with local governments, cadres' corruption, environmental pollution, and village election problems. Villagers protested, petitioned, and sued the local government to restore their rights (Li F. 2011). Ching Kwan Lee's study from the mid-1990s to early 2000s found contentious workers who mobilized laws to go to the streets and the courts to fight for their rights (2007). Shi Yunqing (2015) describes how more than ten thousand urban dwellers whose housing complex had been demolished by the local government in the process of urban expansion filed collective lawsuits against the government. Shi's study powerfully shows that these urban dwellers had developed an identity as citizens rather than as mere "subjects of the empire" or property owners. Chinese citizens are increasingly willing to sue the government and confront the state in order to realize their rights as protected by the constitution. These studies, along with numerous media reports on rights defense activities all show that the Chinese state has successfully "placed the law in the hands of the masses of people" within three decades of the end of the Cultural Revolution. Chinese people have become more cognizant of and contentious about their rights.

Conclusion: Modernization and the Ascent of Law and Rights

In this chapter, I have tried to situate and explain the Chinese state's turn to law and rights as well as the rise of legal and rights consciousness in a long historical context. The change in China's legal and political institutions and political culture is truly remarkable when we consider it in relation to the past 150 years. The Chinese state's approach to law has important continuities from traditional Chinese legal thinking. For example, the Chinese state's law dissemination strategies resemble the legalist thinking that law should be publicized to and known by people in order to shape their behavior. Likewise, the tendency of Chinese TV and newspapers to focus on criminal law continues a long-standing preoccupation that can be traced to the traditional Chinese legal system. Nevertheless, we can also see the growing influence of the West. It is fair to say that the Chinese state's turn to law and rights, as well as the current rise of legal and rights consciousness, is the outcome of modernization and Westernization of the traditional Chinese legal system. The process began in the late Qing period as a way for the Chinese state to address its crisis. Although the process was interrupted under Mao's rule, it resumed in the aftermath of the Cultural Revolution, when the Chinese state encountered another crisis situation. The rise of legal and rights consciousness and the growing contentious practices of asserting and defending rights show how the crisis situation led to modernization and institutional change, and how institutional change spurred remarkable cultural change.

The specificity of the Chinese context, however, should not be downplayed. Though the influence of other legal systems is clear, Chinese people's understandings of rights and the relationship between the state and individuals is still different from how rights and this relationship are understood elsewhere. I acknowledge the complexity and contingency of culture. My claim, rather, is that both traditional Chinese and Western institutions and thoughts have influenced the country's current legal institutions and political culture, as well as how people make sense of rights and their relationship with the state. As such, I do not agree with one-sided claims that recognize only the influence from traditional Chinese culture or from the West. For instance, Perry (2008) argues that the current Chinese conception of "rights" significantly differs from the Anglo-American tradition. According to Perry, the Chinese conception of rights was highly influenced by Mencius thinking, which emphasizes socioeconomic security over other aspects of life. In addition, from Perry's perspective, rights are a state-authorized mechanism more concerned with strengthening the state than with providing protection to individuals. As such, "popular demands for the exercise of political rights are perhaps better seen as an affirmation of—rather than an affront to—state power." Accordingly, Perry argues that Chinese people have, at most, a form of "rules consciousness" but not "rights consciousness" (Perry 2008, 46–47).

I agree with Perry that Chinese people demand socioeconomic security in their exercise of rights, but as studies show (O'Brien and Li 2006; Shi 2015), peasants and urban dwellers clearly see political rights as a condition to protect their socioeconomic security. Moreover, though the state has its own rationale for adopting and disseminating the concept of rights, it cannot completely control how Chinese people understand rights and define their relationship with the state. Chinese people have their own agency. In the imperial legal system, the state was not subject to law, but recent studies have shown again and again how Chinese people mobilize laws and the concept of rights to hold the state legally accountable, despite its reluctance and resistance (Li F. 2011; O'Brien and Li 2006; Shi 2015). It is thus difficult to deny that such redefining of the relationship between individuals and the state was influenced by Western institutions and conceptions of rights.

The question remains as to why the Chinese state decided to disseminate legal and rights-based knowledge at all, given the risk that Chinese people might use this knowledge against the party-state itself. Importantly, Chinese leaders did anticipate and even debated the potential drawbacks of building legal institutions and diffusing law. As I pointed out earlier, many officials were concerned about the enactment of the Administrative Litigation Law, the rise of rights consciousness, and the mobilization of law and the masses to oversee the government. Nonetheless, pragmatic Chinese leaders in the central government determined that the benefit of having legal institutions and legally empowered citizens outweighed the potential negative consequences. Legal institutions and educated legal subjects could help the central leadership build a market economy, monitor political and economic power at the local level, and address social conflicts. The Chinese state also took measures to avoid the negative consequences. Though Chinese leaders in the central government mentioned political and civil rights in their speeches and in important documents, actual law dissemination campaigns were careful to focus on economic rights and specific substantive laws, rather than on political and civil rights and their relation to the constitution. As I demonstrate in the rest of the book, however, this strategy was not without unintended consequences. In fact, there was actually a clear endeavor to reveal more about the public than just the purely private dimensions of law and rights. Such efforts have led to continuous rethinking and reconfiguration of the relations between individuals and the state as well as relations among individuals, clearly influencing how people think about the notions of the public and citizens. In the following chapters, I describe the actors and social networks that have played a key role in this process.

4

Critical News Reporting and Legal-Media Collaborative Networks

The Chinese central state attempted to avoid the negative implications of law dissemination programs, especially after the 1989 democratic movement, by focusing on economic rights, downplaying political and civil rights and their relation to the constitution. Nevertheless, the actual law dissemination process did not unfold completely according to the central state's plans. Although the Chinese state was generally able to control media, in the mid-2000s local commercial-oriented newspapers in some localities—particularly in Guangzhou and to a lesser degree in Beijing—were increasingly willing and able to produce critical news reports, that is, reports identifying fundamental societal problems, analyzing their causes, and searching for solutions (Habermas 1989, 1996, 2006).[1] These critical news reports aimed to discuss fundamental societal problems in China. They diffused ideas about the state's infringement of rights, judicial independence, civil society and political participation, and constitutionalism—topics not welcomed by the Department of Propaganda. Importantly, these critical news reports also attempted to uncover public dimensions of law and rights—dimensions related to the relationship between individuals and the state and the communal relationship among individuals. As such, such critical news reporting went beyond private disputes between individuals. The rise of such news reports is pivotal because that shift enabled the emergence of a broader critical political culture (Habermas 1989, 1996, 2006). Furthermore, in the process of producing critical news reports, important collaborative networks formed that would facilitate the rise of China's contentious public sphere.

Let me give an example of such critical news reporting. Every spring, delegates of the National People's Congress (NPC) and the National Committee of the Chinese People's Political Consultative Conference (CPPCC) have annual meetings in Beijing. The meetings are two of the most symbolically important political events on China's political calendar, as the Chinese government essentially seizes these opportunities to stage a show of democracy for the whole world. Delegates from across China and media from around the world gather in Beijing to participate in or report on the two meetings. The high levels of national and international visibility also make the meetings key opportunities for Chinese people to pursue political agendas and gain attention for particular issues. On March 1, 2010, just a few days before the meetings were scheduled to take place, thirteen local newspapers across eleven Chinese provinces collectively published an editorial calling for the People's Congress and the CPPCC to end China's notorious *hukou* (household registration) system. Hukou, introduced during the Maoist era to prevent Chinese people, particularly rural residents, from moving freely, had long been controversial. The editorial pointed out that the system was unconstitutional and fostered inequality:

> China has suffered from the hukou system for so long. We believe people are born free and should have the right to move and migrate freely, but citizens are still troubled by the bad policies that were born in the era of the planned economy and that have been existing unsuitably for decades. Citizens' concerns cannot be addressed without reform. . . .
>
> In accordance with the Constitution, PRC's citizens are equal before the law, the state shall respect and protect human rights, and freedom of citizens is inviolable. The right to move and migrate is an inseparable part of human rights and personal freedom. This is a fundamental right endowed by the Constitution. Nevertheless, the current hukou system has led to inequality between urban and rural residents and restricted Chinese citizens' freedom of movement. It obviously contradicts the Constitution. As we all know, no laws, administrative regulations, and local regulations can violate the Constitution. This is the legal ground to accelerate the hukou system reform.[2]

The joint editorial was reprinted by major news websites soon after it was published and quickly turned into a lightning rod. Not surprisingly, the Department of Propaganda swiftly censored the editorial. Zhang Hong, the vice chief editor of the *Economic Observer*, was removed from his post for his critical role in organizing the collective action. The publication of the joint editorial, however, reveals that some Chinese newspapers and journalists were willing to mobilize law and rights—in this case, the PRC Constitution, civil rights, and human rights—to expose societal problems and demand reform from the state, notwithstanding their knowledge that such action could be censored and repressed.

In this chapter, I show how the Chinese government's law dissemination programs, described in chapter 3, converged with the unfolding process of media marketization, the transformation of media and legal professionals, and the country's fragmented political structure to facilitate the rise of critical news reporting in some localities in China in the mid-2000s. This story is essentially about the unintended consequences of the law dissemination programs described in chapter 3. The central state's shift to law as a new mode of domination, and especially its use of the media to disseminate law, created a bridge between the legal and media fields as well as connections between legal and media professionals. Unlike the Chinese state's usual efforts to prevent connections across organizations to forestall the rise of competing political power (Deng 1994, 271), this institutional intersection created a novel and critical condition for the formation of collaborative networks across the legal and media fields. These networks played a key role not only in the production of critical news reports, but also in the formation of social networks and, ultimately, a contentious public sphere in China.

In what follows, I first demonstrate the rise of critical news reporting in the mid-2000s. Next, I describe how media marketization—a process that accelerated starting in the early 1990s—reshaped the political, economic, and professional environment in which Chinese newspapers were embedded. After briefly describing a parallel process in the transformation of the legal profession, I then show how the national process of media marketization and law dissemination programs unfolded differently in localities with dissimilar political and market conditions. In some localities, particularly Guangzhou, the confluence of law dissemination programs and media marketization created opportunities for critical news reporting and led to the rise of such reporting in the mid-2000s.

The Rise of Critical News Reporting in the Mid-2000s

ANALYZING CRITICAL NEWS REPORTS

To assess and explain the rise of critical news reporting in Guangzhou, I analyzed news reports published by six comparable newspapers in Guangzhou, Beijing, and Shanghai as listed in table 4.1. These newspapers are all local, commercially oriented, nonspecialized newspapers (i.e., *dushibao* and *wanbo*) that attempt to attract urban readers. As table 4.1 shows, half of the newspapers were not even established until at least the late 1990s.

As I have stated, critical news reports are those that identify fundamental societal problems, analyze their causes, and search for solutions. To determine what constitutes fundamental societal problems and thus critical news reports,

TABLE 4.1. Selected newspapers

Newspaper	Locality	Year founded
Southern Metropolis Daily (nanfang dushibao)	Guangzhou	1997
Yangcheng Evening News (yangcheng wanbao)	Guangzhou	1957
Beijing Times (jinghua shibao)	Beijing	2001
Beijing Evening News (beijing wanbao)	Beijing	1958
Shanghai Morning Post (xinwen chenbao)	Shanghai	1999
Xinmin Evening News (xinmin wanbao)	Shanghai	1929

I inductively developed a six-dimensional scheme based on fifty-eight in-depth interviews with journalists. In other words, I used the inductive definitions of journalists themselves. I asked them to name five important societal problems, as well as potential solutions to these problems, that journalists should cover if given a context of no governmental censorship or pressure. I combined similar responses into categories and then selected the categories that were mentioned by at least 40 percent of the subjects, as 40 percent reflected a relatively high level of consensus. Their answers are captured as six categories listed in table 4.2.

The first dimension is *unconstitutionality*. Since the government wants citizens to comply with laws unconditionally, news reports that allude to unconstitutionality remind readers of the danger of taking law's legitimacy for granted. The second dimension is *the state's infringement of rights*. There was a consensus among my interviewees that many serious problems in China are caused by government infringement of citizen rights. This dimension concerns the extent to which newspapers point out when government agencies are, in fact, the cause of societal problems. The third dimension is *judicial independence*, or the notion that the judiciary must be separate from other institutions of government. Many interviewees considered judicial independence—or more accurately, the lack thereof—to be the most fundamental problem in China's legal system. The fourth dimension is *civil society and political participation*. Over half of my interviewees argued that many societal problems in China are caused by citizens' lack of de facto political rights to oversee the party-state and to participate in politics. To address fundamental societal problems, they identified broadening civil society and citizens' rights to political participation as key. The fifth dimension is the *rights of disadvantaged groups*. Increasing inequality is a serious problem in China, occurring in every critical aspect of life. News items that frame such inequality in terms of the rights of disadvantaged groups, instead of as individual anecdotes, emphasize the social importance of said issues. The sixth dimension is *crony capitalism*, the collusion of power and money that endangers the country.

TABLE 4.2. Dimensions and keywords for content analysis

Dimension	Keywords
Unconstitutionality	违宪 恶法 宪法审查 法律审查
The state's infringement of rights	侵害公民 侵害民众 侵害人民 损害公民 损害民众 损害人民 漠视公民 漠视民众 漠视人民
Judicial independence	法院 独立 司法 审判
Civil society and political participation	公民社会 公民参与 公众参与 政治参与
Rights of disadvantaged groups	弱势群体 权利 边缘群体 边缘人群 权益
Crony capitalism	权贵 权力资本 官商 利益集团

I developed this analytical scheme in 2011, but I received unexpected confirmation of its validity in 2013 when the Chinese government came up with its "seven don't mention list," also known as the "number nine document," which was distributed to party-state agencies. In it, the Department of Propaganda listed seven politically sensitive topics that should be avoided in public discussion. The state asserted that the seven topics were based on Western ideology and thus detrimental to Communist ideology. As such, the state prohibited party-state agencies from promoting the seven topics and banned the media from covering them. The topics were: constitutionalism, universal values, freedom of the press, civil society and citizen rights, the CCP's historical mistakes, crony capitalism, and judicial independence. The similarities between my six-dimensional scheme and the "seven don't mention list" are striking.

The six dimensions I have identified reveal the deep connection between critical news reporting and the public dimensions of law and rights. The dimensions of constitutionality, the state's infringement of rights, judicial independence, civil society and political participation, and crony capitalism are all related to the relationship between individuals and the state, particularly the limitation of the state's power and the rights of individuals to oversee the state's power and to influence its decisions. The dimensions of civil society and political participation and the rights of disadvantaged groups relate to the communal relationship of individuals as members of a polity—how individuals as citizens can and should build a civil society as well as how and why individuals should care about the rights of disadvantaged and vulnerable groups. As I show in chapter 6, these public dimensions of law and rights contributed to the emergence of a contentious *public* sphere because they enabled various actors, ranging from opinion leaders to ordinary citizens, to reflect on what constitutes the public and the nature of public events.

After identifying these six dimensions, I categorized as a "critical news report" any report retrieved from WiseNews, a professional news database, that dealt substantively with one of these issues. I first used the keywords listed in table 4.2 for the preliminary selection of news reports. These keywords are common terms used to describe and discuss issues related to the six dimensions outlined above. Next, I decided whether one of the six dimensions was the major theme in each article in the domestic context. Finally, to capture the intensity of critical news reports, I also identified those reports that suggested the *central* government should be or is responsible for problems. Previous literature argues that resistance in China is limited in that resisters usually target their criticism at local, rather than central, levels of government (Lee 2007; O'Brien and Li 2006; O'Brien 1996). My interview data similarly reveal that criticism of the central government is very politically risky; thus journalists tend to avoid blaming the central government, even when they view it as responsible for the local government's problems and institutional defects. This corresponds with research on censorship in China indicating that the Chinese state is less likely to tolerate criticism of the central, as opposed to the local, government (Lorentzen 2014). As such, criticism of the central government, when and if it appears, qualifies as a particularly intense form of critical news reporting.

CRITICAL NEWS REPORTING IN GUANGZHOU, BEIJING, AND SHANGHAI, 2000–2006

To show change over time, figure 4.1 presents the percentage of critical news reports for each newspaper per year in 2000–2006. To calculate these percentages, I counted the number of critical news reports that the newspaper published in a given year and divided that number by the *total* number of news reports the same paper printed that year. Focus on this period illustrates the rise of critical news reports in the mid-2000s and is also appropriate given that half the newspapers were not established until the late 1990s or early 2000s. Because the news archive that I used does not include news reports produced by the *Beijing Times*, the *Shanghai Morning Post*, or the *Xinmin Evening News* for 2000–2002, I present their percentages of critical news reports for 2003–2006 only. Figure 4.1 shows that, in the early 2000s, the percentages of critical news reports were still very low. In the mid-2000s, however, there was a rise in critical news reports in Guangzhou and Beijing, especially from 2003 onward, the year when the Sun Zhigang case occurred. This timing corresponds to the expansion of rights discourse in the mid-2000s, as demonstrated in chapter 3. Figure 4.1 also indicates that the rise of critical news reporting was uneven across localities: it was more salient in Guangzhou than in Beijing, and critical news reporting remained very limited in Shanghai in the mid-2000s.

Next, let us consider variation across localities from 2003 to 2006, as critical news reporting became more salient. In addition to the six selected local newspapers, I also include analysis of the *People's Daily*. As the central party-state's

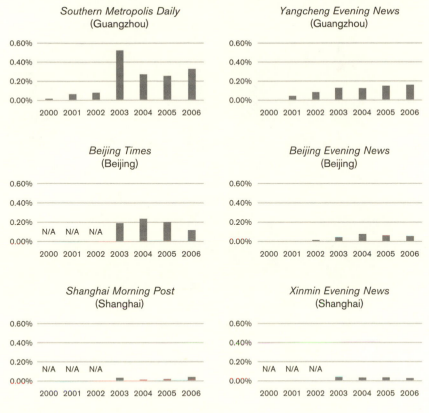

4.1. Percentage of critical news reports, 2000–2006.

official newspaper, the *People's Daily* serves as the yardstick of dominant official discourse. Analysis of its content helps us understand when and how critical reports depart from official discourse. Figure 4.2 presents the percentage of critical news reports printed by each newspaper (out of their respective total numbers of news reports) for the whole 2003–2006 period. Figure 4.3 shows the percentage of critical news reports grouped by city, with the *People's Daily* percentage for comparison. Figure 4.4 shows the same but organized by the dimensions of the reports. These figures illustrate several findings. First, among the newspapers that I analyzed, the *Southern Metropolis Daily* had the highest percentage of critical news reports. Second, considerable disparity existed between newspapers in different localities. Among the three cities, Guangzhou and Shanghai had the highest and lowest percentage of critical news reports, respectively, while Beijing was in the middle. This disparity is striking given that all the selected local newspapers aim to attract a similar readership in the most prosperous areas in China. Third, the *People's Daily*, the central party-state's mouthpiece, did report on some critical issues. This created space for

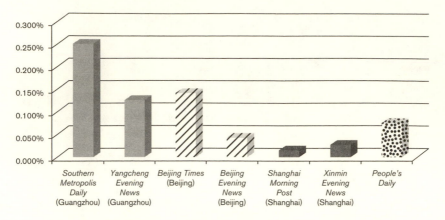

4.2. Percentage of critical news reports, by newspaper, 2003–2006.

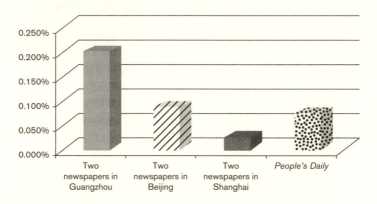

4.3. Percentage of critical news reports, by city, 2003–2006.

local newspapers to adopt similar framings and produce critical news reports. On average, the selected newspapers in Guangzhou and Beijing had a higher percentage of critical news reports than the *People's Daily* did, even though the local newspapers did not have the political privilege of the latter. In contrast, the selected newspapers in Shanghai did not take advantage of the space created by the *People's Daily*.

I also identified critical news reports that suggested central government responsibility for identified problems (see figure 4.5); this is a particularly intense form of critical news reporting. For example, an article published by *Southern Metropolis Daily* on October 16, 2006, discussed several cases in which local governments infringed on citizens' rights by confiscating land. While the article criticized the local governments for violating law, it also blamed the central government for asking local governments to be

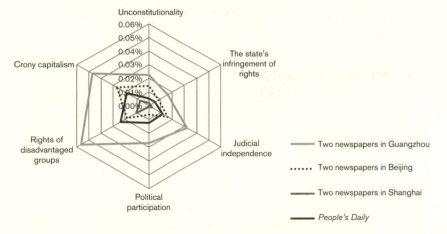

4.4. Percentage of critical news reports, by dimension and city, 2003–2006.

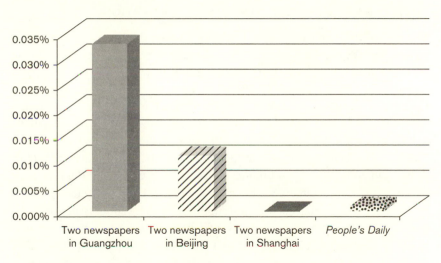

4.5. Percentage of critical news reports suggesting central government responsibility, by city, 2003–2006.

responsible for more and more public provision without allocating them adequate fiscal revenues. The article argued that the structural conditions determined by the central government motivated local governments to confiscate land illegally to gain revenues. My analysis reveals that, on average, the two newspapers in Guangzhou had the highest percentage of such critical news reports, directly implicating the central government. The two newspapers in Beijing had the second highest percentage, while the two newspapers in

Shanghai and the *People's Daily* had hardly any reports that challenged the central government.

Embeddedness of Newspapers between Market and State

Having established the rise of critical news reporting and the uneven occurrence of this phenomenon, I now turn to how media marketization, a nationwide process that began to accelerate in the early 1990s, reshaped the political, economic, and professional environment in which Chinese newspapers were embedded. The national process of marketization was an important condition for journalists to produce critical news reports and uncover public dimensions of law and rights. Since my purpose is to explain the rise of critical news reporting in the mid-2000s, I do not cover the post-2005 period in this chapter.

FROM THE SOVIET MODEL TO MEDIA MARKETIZATION

It is helpful to begin by briefly considering the development of the Chinese press before the unfolding of marketization in the early 1990s. Journalism in the PRC was greatly influenced by the Soviet model of *Pravda* and the Telegraph Agency of the Soviet Union (TASS). *Pravda* was the official newspaper of the Communist Party of the Soviet Union; TASS was the Soviet Union's national news agency. In the 1950s, China sent journalists to Moscow to learn news production from *Pravda* and TASS. Likewise, *Pravda* and TASS sent their journalists to China to share knowledge and advice with journalists there (Xin 2006; Zuo 2008). The Soviet model as practiced in China had the following features: First, newspapers were responsible only to the party instead of to readers. Second, journalists were not supposed to write about issues or problems without the party's approval. As such, reporting on social problems was generally discouraged, if not prohibited. Third, the writing was full of "false, pompous, and empty" language. Fourth, the funding for newspapers came exclusively from the state because they were the state's mouthpieces and instruments for propaganda instead of commodities in the market (Zuo 2008, 55).

From the 1950s onward, there were various attempts to break from the Soviet model. In 1957, Huang Wenyu established the *Yangcheng Evening News* (*yangcheng wanbao*) in Guangzhou, the first evening newspaper in China, in an effort to establish an alternative. Huang emulated newspapers from the ROC period as well as Hong Kong papers, which were more reader oriented, often including supplements that covered a wide variety of subjects. Through the *Yangcheng Evening News*, Huang covertly sought to recover the tradition of Chinese journalism before the PRC—a tradition that Huang saw as devoted to the Chinese nation and people, particularly the disadvantaged and vulnerable people in society (Zuo 2008). Unfortunately, the *Yangcheng Evening News* was closed in 1966 during the Cultural Revolution and did not resume publication until 1980.

The Chinese press developed little and even degenerated significantly between 1949 and 1976. During the Cultural Revolution, many newspapers ceased publication. In fact, only four national and thirty-eight local newspapers operated in the entire country in 1968, leading some scholars to refer to the Cultural Revolution as "the dark age of Chinese journalism" (Zhao 1998, 32).[3] The Third Plenum of the Eleventh Central Committee in 1978 shifted the CCP's focus from class struggle to economic reform. The political climate also shifted in a liberal direction after the end of the Cultural Revolution and remained so until the 1989 Tiananmen incident. In this relatively liberal period, the freedom of the press was the main focus of those in the media field. Reformist officials and journalists attempted to advance press freedom, but progress remained limited to theoretical discussion and institutional design, such as the drafting of the Press Law (*xinwen fa*)—the most fundamental law providing institutional protection for media and journalists. Unfortunately, actual institutionalization of press freedom was interrupted by the 1989 Tiananmen incident (Zhao 1998, 45–47).

In addition to the effort to institutionalize protection of freedom of the press, two other important developments occurred in the media field in the 1980s, both intended to break from the Soviet model of news production. First, reflecting on how some media wrongly aided the Gang of Four during the Cultural Revolution, journalists and reformist officials emphasized that the media should produce truthful news and speak for the people, rather than serving only as mouthpieces of state propaganda. Journalists also sought some degree of professional autonomy from the party-state; those who dared to voice truth and criticism were considered as exemplars. Literary reportage, a genre between literature and journalism, which often uncovers and describes societal problems, became popular among journalists and the broader literary circle in the 1980s (Hu 2008; Qian 2008). Liu Binyan was arguably one of the most influential journalists and writers in this genre in the 1980s. As a journalist at the *People's Daily*, Liu produced many reports and literary pieces that revealed social problems and corruption, establishing a model and an inspiration for a generation of journalists (Qian 2008; Wagner 1986).[4]

Another important development in the 1980s was the establishment of *Southern Weekly* (*nanfang zhoumo*) in Guangzhou in 1984. *Southern Weekly* was the weekly supplement of *Southern Daily* (*nanfang ribao*), the official newspaper of the Guangdong provincial government. Zuo Fang, the founder of *Southern Weekly*, said he was deeply influenced by Huang Wenyu, founder of *Yangcheng Evening News*. *Southern Weekly* attempted to overcome the Soviet model of news production, explore the possibility of marketized newspapers, and reconnect Chinese journalism to its pre-PRC traditions. In its first two years, *Southern Weekly* focused on entertainment news in Hong Kong and Taiwan, given the popularity of their entertainment culture, but after 1986 the paper shifted its focus to social issues and problems in response to reader demand. The paper sought to influence and "enlighten" readers who had at least a middle-school level of education. Although political constraints prevented *Southern Weekly* from covering everything journalists wanted to cover, according to Zuo, the organization at least refused to publish anything untruthful (Zuo 2008). Through its efforts to follow a marketized model and to report on important social issues and problems, *Southern Weekly* set an important precedent for other newspaper organizations that followed.

The relatively liberal period in the 1980s ended with the repression of the 1989 Tiananmen democratic movement. Nonetheless, similar to the developments in the legal field described in chapter 3, the repression of the Tiananmen democratic movement did not completely halt reform in the media field, though it did contribute to CCP leaders' insistence on the party's monopolistic control of political power. After Deng Xiaoping's influential Southern Tour in 1992, the economic reform agenda was reconfirmed. The Fourteenth Party Congress that year further recognized the concept of a socialist market economy and stated its goal of focusing on the development of the country's service industry. Later, the State Planning Commission officially categorized the news industry as part of the service industry. This confirmation of the role of news organizations as market actors accelerated the process of media marketization, which unfolded rapidly after 1992.

In the past, newspapers had mostly been subsidized by the state and expected to serve as mouthpieces of state propaganda. From 1992 onward, however, the state reduced its funding of media, forcing newspapers to rely more and more on advertising and sales to survive. With this new goal of maximizing revenue, newspapers and journalists had to consider consumers' preferences in ways that had previously been unnecessary. At the same time, the demand for news services rose along with the increase in urban dwellers' purchasing power (Zhao Y. 1998, 2000).

With the unfolding of media marketization, new types of newspapers and magazines emerged to satisfy the demands of readers. First, a new form of newspaper—metropolitan dailies (*dushi bao*)—emerged and achieved great popularity among local urban dwellers. The first, *Huaxi Metropolitan Daily* (*huaxi dushi bao*), was established in Chengdu in 1995. The founder of *Huaxi Metropolitan Daily*, Xi Wenju, aimed to produce a newspaper that readers and the government would both like. He hoped the paper would help the government and the people solve their problems. As such, the paper emphasized readability and usefulness, while providing huge amounts of information related to the daily lives of urban residents, such as news about politics, economy, culture, society, technology, sports, and entertainment. Xi Wenju also broadened the coverage of social news, particularly reports on legal cases. At the same time, he still emphasized the role of the paper to disseminate information, law, and policy for the government. He insisted that *Huaxi Metropolitan Daily* follow the party's political principles.[5] This type of metropolitan newspaper quickly spread to other cities in China in the second half of the 1990s and the early 2000s. Similar to evening newspapers, metropolitan dailies are nonspecialized papers that attempt to attract urban readers. Since these two kinds of newspapers became pillars of marketization, I focus in this chapter on the rise of critical news reporting among these and similar general, commercially oriented local newspapers.

Notwithstanding this focus, I should note that media specializing in finance, business, and the economy also emerged with the unfolding of media marketization and the development of the stock and capital markets in China. This specialization was inspired by Western print media such as *Bloomberg Businessweek*, *Fortune*, the *Wall Street Journal*, and the *Financial Times*. *Caijing* magazine is arguably one of the best-known business and economics publication in China. Established in 1998 by the Stock Exchange Executive Council (SEEC),[6] *Caijing* emphasizes its independence from the state as well as from capital and aims to satisfy the public's "right to know." The magazine focuses on issues related to finance and business, public health, corruption, sociopolitical problems, and environmental protection. *Caijing*'s founder, Hu Shuli, stresses that Chinese media should define finance, business, and economic news broadly and consider political and social issues as critical components of such news (Hu 2008). In addition to *Caijing* magazine, several newspapers, such as the *China Business News* (*diyi caijing ribao*), the *21st-Century Business Herald* (*er shi yi shiji jingji baodao*), and the *Economic Observer* (*jingji guancha bao*), also specialize in economic and business reports while covering political and social issues. Different from metropolitan dailies and evening newspapers, which target local general urban readers, newspapers and magazines specializing in finance, business, and the economy target more highly educated readers.

Essentially, although Chinese journalism was deeply influenced by the Soviet model, media marketization led to the growth of print media that aimed to meet the demands of readers. Importantly, the process gave rise to a huge expansion of local newspaper markets (Zhao Y. 1998, 2000). The rising number and income of urban readers convinced many party-state agencies that the newspaper market held tremendous economic potential. As a result, the number of newspapers increased dramatically, from 476 in 1981 to 2,051 in 1998.[7] Numerous local newspapers competed for the same readers, leading to intensely competitive local newspaper markets (Wu 2000). Seeing the dramatic increase in newspapers as a sign of inefficiency and a potential threat to political control, the Chinese state began to merge newspaper organizations into newspaper conglomerates (Zhao Y. 2000). This process of consolidation involved negotiations between different party-state agencies, because the outcome promised to affect various agencies' interests. To secure political control, the Chinese state, in principle, prohibited conglomerates from operating in multiple localities. It also prohibited the entry of foreign capital. By the early 2000s, some newspaper conglomerates had already become the golden geese of their local governments.

THE STATE'S CONTINUING CONTROL OVER THE PRESS

Though Chinese newspapers became newly embedded in the market, they were also still embedded in the state. In short, media marketization did not stop the Chinese state from continuing to control the press and journalists (Esarey 2005; Hassid 2008; Stockmann 2013; Zhao 1998). Newspapers that previously operated within the party-state apparatus are still under pressure to follow the party line. Because newspaper organizations remain part of the party-state, their structure reflects China's complex and fragmented bureaucratic system. In general, each newspaper organization is affiliated with a party-state agency and ranked accordingly within a state-established hierarchy. The rank of a newspaper organization is determined by the rank of the party-state agency with which it is affiliated.

   While the General Administration of Press and Publication, under the State Council, is responsible for drafting and enforcing regulations related to news organizations, the CCP's Department of Propaganda[8] is in charge of ideology and censorship. The propaganda system is structured hierarchically and geographically. The Department of Propaganda is situated at the top of the hierarchy. Each local party-state has its own propaganda department, and each newspaper organization is directly supervised by the propaganda department at the same rank in the same locality. For instance, a newspaper affiliated with the Guangdong provincial party-state is a provincial newspaper, so it is directly supervised by the provincial propaganda department in Guangdong; whereas a newspaper associated with the Guangzhou city party-state is a city newspaper, and thus overseen by the city propaganda department in Guangzhou.

   The propaganda departments at various levels exercise censorship before and after the publication of newspapers, and they delegate their authority to high-level editors who serve as internal censors in the press. The Department of Propaganda determines the topics and events that should or should not be covered. These instructions often employ abstract and vague concepts, such as social stability and national security, and provide few concrete guidelines. The instructions are transmitted to lower-level propaganda departments and then to newspaper organizations through meetings and the circulation of documents. Local propaganda officials have regular meetings with senior editors of local newspapers. Most of the time, lower-level journalists do not have a chance to see the instructions in print; they are simply informed of "the gist of documents" (*wenjian jingshen*) by higher-level editors. Many editors and journalists whom I interviewed emphasized that the instructions of the Department of Propaganda tend to be very vague and flexible, remaining more or less similar over time. Ex-ante censorship influences topic selection and framing of news reports, as well as journalists' earnings. It is not uncommon for unpublished reports to be "shot to death" (*qiangbi*) by internal censors within newspaper organizations. Since part of journalists' earnings depends on the number of published reports they produce, when their pieces are not published, they receive less income (Hassid 2008). Propaganda officials at various levels also conduct ex-post censorship by reviewing published news articles. They can fire or discipline journalists and newspaper organizations in many ways.

To be sure, the state's political control does not mean that journalists are forbidden from reporting on critical social problems, but they encounter risks when they do so. Nonetheless, contradictory political logics make critical news reporting possible. In interviews, many journalists described the Chinese party-state, newspapers, and journalists as having multiple personality disorder (*renge fenlie* or *jingshen fenlie*), as each group acts in self-contradictory ways. My interviewees related this "personality disorder" to the relatively liberal atmosphere of the late 1980s—a period in which Chinese leaders seriously considered political reform. As mentioned in chapter 3, from the 1980s onward, reformist leaders attempted to establish supervisory institutions (*jiandu jizhi*) to address problems accompanying China's economic reform. In 1987, when general secretary Zhao Ziyang reported to the Thirteenth Party Congress, he highlighted the concept of supervision, especially legal supervision (*falu jiandu*), democratic supervision (*minzhu jiandu*), and supervision by public opinion (*yulun jiandu*). He asserted that media should uncover problems to support *yulun jiandu*—basically, the state should recruit the media to serve as watchdogs. Although Zhao was later put under house arrest until his death because he was deemed to have been too lenient with the 1989 Tiananmen protesters, his idea of supervision by public opinion remained popular among his successors. According to my interviewees—including a former central-level propaganda official and a prominent communication scholar and government adviser—top Chinese leaders since 1989 have appealed to the notion of supervision by public opinion as a way to demonstrate that they are democratic and open minded.

Despite this seemingly liberal gesture, my interview data suggest that most government officials at both central and local levels, especially those in the propaganda system, are not actually that enthusiastic about media's watchdog function and can restrict the ability of media to perform this role. Since reports on problems could threaten individual officials' economic and political interests, such reports often trigger retaliation. In addition, my interview data suggest that propaganda officials, especially after the 1989 Tiananmen protests, tend to be the most politically conservative people within the state apparatus. Journalists and propaganda officials consistently told me that despite the notion of supervision by public opinion, the dominant political logic continues to discourage reporting on social problems.

TRANSFORMATION OF THE JOURNALIST PROFESSION

Since media marketization carved out a larger, relatively more flexible space for journalists to think about and practice their craft, the profession of journalism transformed with the unfolding of media marketization, despite the state's continuing control. Scholars have observed important shifting journalist paradigms in the early 2000s (Pan and Chan 2003). An older set of professional norms positioned journalists as mere mouthpieces of the state, but with marketization, reporters increasingly emphasized and committed to journalistic independence—more specifically, to the notion that journalists, not the party-state, should decide standards of newsworthiness (Hassid 2011). Research shows that a considerable group of Chinese journalists admire elite Western media outlets as professional exemplars. As a result, Chinese journalists tend to give lower evaluations to media outlets closely associated with party journalism (e.g., *People's Daily*, *Guangming Daily*, *Xinmin Evening News*) than to elite foreign media and domestic media considered akin to elite foreign media (e.g., *Southern Weekly*, CNN, *New York Times*, BBC, Phoenix TV). Such evaluation is associated with the desire for more liberal arts training in journalism than training in communist propaganda (Pan and Chan 2003).

The political scientist Jonathan Hassid (2011) notes the emergence of different types of journalists. A minority of journalists adhere to the traditional communist model. Seeing themselves as mere mouthpieces of the party, they continue to follow the instructions of propaganda officials and are less likely to be critical of or confront the party. A larger group comprises "workday journalists." Similar to their communist colleagues, workday journalists have weak commitment to journalistic independence. But rather than being motivated by any commitment to communism, they tend to see their jobs as simply a means to make money and are thus reluctant to pursue stories that could jeopardize their employment security. Another considerable group is that of advocacy journalists, who see themselves as spokespersons for citizens. This group is committed to journalistic independence and sees journalism as an important way to bring about social and political change. Because they see themselves as spokespersons for the public, these journalists are more likely to report on social problems, fight for professional autonomy, "educate" the public, help vulnerable groups, and resist the undue intervention of political and market forces.[9]

The emergence of advocacy journalists facilitated the growth of critical news reporting in the mid-2000s. These journalists and the professional paradigm shift they signaled were shaped by traditional norms about Chinese intellectuals as well as journalism in both China and the West. Marketization provided the conditions necessary for journalists to feel able to explore and combine various norms and practices. My interview data suggest that the tendency of Chinese journalists to see themselves as advocates of the people and agents of social and political change was also influenced by knowledge of the traditional role of Chinese intellectuals and the founding history of Chinese journalism. In Imperial China, Chinese intellectuals usually aimed to become part of the state as "scholar-officials" (*shi daifu*) by passing imperial examinations. There was a norm of "worrying about the nation and the people" (*youguo youmin*) among intellectuals and scholar-officials. My interviewees who see themselves as spokespersons of the people and agents of social change drew comparisons between their role and that of these traditional scholar-officials. Citing the writing of Zhang Zai, a Song dynasty scholar, several interviewees said journalists should "establish the heart and mind for Heaven and Earth, and secure the life for the people" (*wei tiandi li xin, wei shengmin li ming*). Some interviewees also connected their practices to the history of the modern Chinese press since the late Qing period. They emphasized that the Chinese press was established to bring about social and political change and to strengthen the Chinese nation in the Qing dynasty. Indeed, similar to the establishment of the modern Chinese legal system, the development of journalism in China was related to the defeats by the West and Japan as well as the decision of Chinese scholar-officials and intellectuals to pursue modernization. Some reformist officials and intellectuals saw building a modern press as a means to strengthen the Chinese nation (Lin 1936). In sum, the role of traditional Chinese intellectuals and the early history of the modern Chinese press were important to advocacy journalists in China, especially those born between the 1950s and the 1970s—the cohorts that contributed to the rise of critical news reporting.

The commitment of advocacy journalists to journalistic independence and their norms of "good journalism" have been influenced by journalism in both China and the West. My interviewees talked about wanting to continue the tradition of good journalism in China. They pointed to certain newspapers in the late Qing and ROC periods, such as *Shun Pao*, and to Chinese journalists in the 1980s as setting important examples and establishing the fight against political intervention. The interviewees also acknowledged the influence of Western journalism on their practices. They were familiar with elite Western media. Some told me that Hu Shuli, the founder of *Caijing* magazine, played an important role in disseminating knowledge and information about American journalism among Chinese journalists. Hu had spent a couple months observing journalism in the United States after receiving a fellowship from the Minnesota-based World Press Institute in 1987, and she turned her observations into a book titled *Behind the Scenes at American Newspapers* (*meiguo baoye jianwen lu*) in 1991. The book was popular among Chinese journalists.

But it was primarily in the workplace itself, not in schools or departments of journalism, that advocacy journalists formed their identities and views about journalism between the late 1990s and the mid-2000s. According to my interviews, a considerable percentage of advocacy journalists who contributed to the rise in critical news reporting had not majored in journalism. Many of them had actually majored in Chinese literature or law and had received no journalism education at school. Even those who did major in journalism found little inspiring about such education in Chinese colleges or universities, which tended to emphasize party journalism. Even journalism education abroad did not contribute much to the transformation of the journalist profession between the early 1990s and the mid-2000s. In fact, very few advocacy journalists studied abroad, although the number who went to the United States as visiting scholars began to increase in the early 2000s. Most of the advocacy journalists I interviewed emphasized that their work environment, colleagues, and work experiences greatly influenced how they thought about and practiced journalism. Junior journalists tended to have apprentice relationships with senior journalists in their news organizations, viewing them as their teachers and role models. Senior journalists born in the 1950s and 1960s tended to appreciate the relatively liberal atmosphere in the 1980s. Professional associations, particularly the All-China Journalists' Association (ACJA), did not contribute to the emergence of advocacy journalists or to the shift in professional paradigm because the ACJA is actually run by the Department of Propaganda as an instrument for political control (Hassid 2011).

A Parallel Transformation of the Legal Profession

From the beginning of China's economic reform to the mid-2000s, the legal profession underwent a parallel transformation to that of the media and journalism. This change—particularly the emergence of legal professionals who advocate for the public interest—provided a vital condition for collaboration between media and legal professionals, which in turn fostered the rise of critical news reporting.

Similar to developments in the media field, the growth of a private sector in the field of law triggered the transformation and diversification of the legal profession. In the past, lawyers had been simply state civil servants. With the unfolding of economic and legal reforms, however, the legal service market emerged and expanded, contributing to the rise of partnership law firms.

Though some lawyers sought to increase their business opportunities by establishing clientelist relations with government agencies, particularly with the Ministry of Justice and its local counterparts, the expanding legal service market primarily decreased lawyers' economic dependence on the government (Liu and Halliday 2011; Peerenboom 2002). Law school education also shaped the identity of the legal profession. As legal education improved, legal professionals' ability to interpret and apply law did likewise. This, in turn, strengthened lawyers' identities as independent professionals serving clients in a legal market. In addition, China passed the Lawyers Law in 1996, which stipulates lawyers' rights and obligations. Although the Lawyers Law authorizes the Ministry of Justice to assess potential attorneys' qualifications, issue certificates to lawyers and law firms, and conduct annual reviews, one of the main purposes of the Lawyers Law is to promote the independence of the legal profession (Peerenboom 2002). The expanding legal service market, along with the improvement of legal education, the enactment of the Lawyers Law, and the establishment of bar associations, gave the legal profession a higher level and sense of autonomy, even though the Chinese government continued to oversee the legal profession through the Ministry of Justice and bar associations. As a result, many legal professionals no longer viewed themselves as servants of the state.

The most critical development of the legal profession in terms of its influence on critical news reporting has been the emergence of lawyers who see themselves as advocates of the public interest. Although most legal professionals are still focused on making money, some have begun to see themselves as guardians of citizens' rights, as indicated by the rise in public interest and rights defense lawyers who advocate for concerns broader than those of their immediate clients. Although these attorneys have diverse visions and goals, they tend to help disadvantaged groups realize their rights while also promoting public interests (Fu and Cullen 2008).

The institutionalization of legal aid played a critical role in the emergence and growth of this group of lawyers. As noted in chapter 3, the Ministry of Justice established the institution of legal aid to provide legal services to people who could not otherwise afford it. Still, given the limited resources of the government, lawyers at private law firms have been the most important providers of legal aid. According to Liebman (1999), as well as interviewees who have been working as public interest and rights defense lawyers since the late 1990s, attorneys began to provide legal aid and establish legal-aid centers to help vulnerable groups, particularly migrant workers, in the late 1990s. Many of these lawyers had grown up in villages and thus understood what life was like at the "bottom" of society. They often worked in small firms in major cities (Fu and Cullen 2008). Influenced by both their legal education and their personal background, they decided to provide legal aid even though it offered no financial benefits. Some of the public interest and rights defense lawyers I interviewed were affiliated with law schools as lecturers or were researchers at the legal-aid centers of law schools. These academic lawyers were usually interested in public law, particularly constitutional and administrative law, which deals with citizens' fundamental rights and the relationship between the state and individuals.

In the beginning, public interest and rights defense lawyers focused on providing consultation, disseminating legal knowledge, and handling individual cases. Their funding came from four main sources: revenues from handling ordinary cases, subsidies from the government, donations from large law firms, and grants from international organizations, such as the Ford Foundation. Because public interest and rights defense lawyers were exposed to similar cases, some of them came to recognize the severity of systemic problems and broadened their activities to participate in the process of lawmaking. A few, especially frustrated with the system and the government, even became radical and aimed to bring about social and political change (Fu and Cullen 2011). To push police, prosecutors, and judges to handle cases properly, some of these lawyers sought public attention through the media. They also used lawsuits as a means to achieve their larger goals.

How Local Conditions Moderated Collaboration and Critical News Reporting

The national process of media marketization and the transformation of the media and legal professions unfolded differently in localities with dissimilar political and market conditions, leading to varied levels of critical news reporting in Guangzhou, Beijing, and Shanghai. The main purpose here is to demonstrate how media and legal collaboration and the rise of critical news reporting were possible given the limited freedom of the press in China. Since I aim to explain the rise of critical news reporting in the mid-2000s, I do not cover the development of critical news reporting beyond that period.

GUANGZHOU: ROBUST COLLABORATION BETWEEN MEDIA AND LEGAL PROFESSIONALS

The market and political environment in which newspapers were embedded in Guangzhou was relatively fragmented compared with the city's counterparts in Beijing and Shanghai (Huang and Zeng 2011). As the capital of Guangdong Province, Guangzhou was well known for its intensely competitive newspaper market. This competitive market was due, in part, to Guangdong being the first to undergo China's economic reform. In 1994, the Administration of Press and Publication came up with criteria for establishing newspaper conglomerates.

Considering newspapers in Guangzhou highly competent, the administration approved three conglomerates in the city in the late 1990s: the Guangzhou Daily News Group, the Southern Media Group, and the Yangcheng Evening News Group. These organizations were the first three newspaper conglomerates in China, with each owning multiple newspapers. In 2005, the World Association of Newspapers included five from Guangzhou in its list of the top one hundred daily newspapers in the world in terms of circulation. No other city in China had as many newspapers on the list. The Guangzhou Daily News Group's *Guangzhou Daily*, the Southern Media Group's *Southern Metropolis Daily*, and the Yangcheng Evening News Group's *Yangcheng Evening News* ranked twenty-fifth, twenty-ninth, and thirty-third in the world, respectively.[10] This shows the intense competition in the newspaper market in Guangzhou in the mid-2000s.

In addition to a very competitive market, newspapers in Guangdong were situated in a relatively fragmented political structure. Since Guangzhou is the provincial capital of Guangdong Province, both provincial and city party-state agencies are located there, including the provincial and city propaganda departments. The three newspaper conglomerates are part of the local party-state. The Guangzhou Daily News Group is affiliated with the CCP Guangzhou Municipal Committee, while the Southern Media Group and the Yangcheng Evening News Group are affiliated with the CCP Guangdong Provincial Committee.

The complex bureaucratic system in Guangzhou diminished the capacity of the central Department of Propaganda to produce coherent censorship standards. The provincial and city party-states in Guangzhou are both state actors and market players. Although provincial and city propaganda departments both belong to the larger propaganda system, they are also part of their own local party-states and thus influenced by local party-state interests. As a result, provincial and city propaganda departments do not necessarily have coherent censorship practices. The problem is due in part to the asymmetrical political and economic relationship between provincial and city party-states. In Guangzhou's newspaper market, the provincial and city newspapers were supposed to compete on a level playing field, but their disparate positions in the official hierarchy motivated the provincial party-state to translate their political power into economic interests. Ultimately, local party-states wanted their newspapers to profit and contribute to their tax revenues, as long as those newspapers did not cause intractable political problems in the process. Consequently, sometimes provincial propaganda departments enforced central party-state censorship standards more flexibly with provincial newspapers. In a similar vein, the official hierarchy also influenced the decision making of newspaper organizations. For instance, since the city propaganda department in Guangzhou had no authority over provincial newspapers, provincial newspapers sometimes made editorial decisions contrary to the interests of the city party-state. As I show below, this contradiction within the complex bureaucratic structure opened up opportunities for journalists.

Since the late 1990s, Chinese people have demanded more and more information about the social problems engendered by the country's transition to a market economy. Though many newspapers were interested in investigating these problems and possible solutions, critical reporting was rare because of government censorship. The highly competitive market for news in Guangzhou, however, forced journalists and newspapers to take consumers' demands more seriously. Intensive market competition also gave public-minded journalists leverage to persuade managerial cadres to take more political risks. The intensifying market demand for critical news reports in Guangzhou also aligned with the increasing tendency among journalists to see themselves as spokespersons for citizens and agents of social change. As one journalist at the *Yangcheng Evening News* recalled:

> Our pursuit of professional ideals was quite consistent with newspapers' pursuit of market profits. Although the managerial cadres were concerned about political risks, they understood that we would lose the market share if we could not satisfy the demands of readers. Ultimately, managerial cadres were faced with tremendous pressure. No other place in China was like Guangzhou—we were competing with the most competitive newspapers in the country. (Interview, June 2011, Guangzhou)

Market logics and emerging professional norms thus worked together to increase the demand for more critical news reports under the conditions of a highly competitive market.

But when Guangzhou journalists attempted to satisfy market demands and enact their professional ideals, they encountered two hurdles. The first difficulty was political risk. Even though party leaders in the central government occasionally encouraged "supervision by public opinion," this was mostly for show and stood in stark contrast to the actual practices of state agencies. Propaganda officials still tended to view critical news reports as a deviation from an important principle—namely, that newspapers should report on the party-state's achievements, not its problems. Furthermore, since critical news reports might affect government officials' political careers and economic interests, government officials and their associates often retaliated against outspoken journalists and newspapers.

The second hurdle that journalists encountered when they decided to produce more critical news reports was a technical one: Guangzhou journalists found that their training was inadequate for analyzing emerging societal problems. This was partly because the unfolding legal reforms were busy transforming myriad societal problems into legal issues. As many of my interviewees pointed out, the best and safest way to frame a phenomenon *as* a problem was to demonstrate its deviation from legal texts or principles. But most journalists knew little about the legal system that was being so rapidly introduced to enable the new market economy, let alone how to use law as an analytical tool or a weapon of self-defense. A former editor in chief at the *Southern Metropolis Daily* described the dire need for legal expertise:

> We found that readers demanded news reports that uncover corruption and other illegal practices, speak on behalf of citizens about their problems, and publicize legal knowledge. Readers became more demanding as they were no longer content with being presented with only facts. Instead, readers expected journalists to discuss and analyze the underlying causes of problems. . . . Law became the yardstick to discuss problems after the legal reform. These demands created new problems for us as we were not legal experts. Traditional investigative reports, albeit still important, became inadequate. (Interview, June 2011, Beijing)

This quotation reflects the enormous need among journalists for legal proficiency to produce critical news reports.

To overcome both political and technical hurdles, journalists began to collaborate with legal professionals. Journalists in the Southern Media Group, including *Southern Metropolis Daily* and *Southern Weekly* reporters, sought assistance from lawyers and legal scholars. Legal experts could not only help journalists investigate and analyze societal problems, they could also assess the political and legal risks that journalists might encounter.[11] As one journalist said, "Lawyers know the art and skill of resistance. They can better calculate the cost of resistance and prepare for battles" (Interview, June 2011, Guangzhou). The *Southern Weekly*'s national reputation and popularity among intellectuals brought the *Southern Metropolis Daily* many collaborators, including nationally renowned legal scholars and lawyers, as well as a small number of open-minded government officials in the legislative and judicial branches. The Southern Media Group's strategy was mimicked by other Guangzhou newspapers, including the *Yangcheng Evening News*. These newspapers successfully collaborated with local legal scholars and lawyers in Guangzhou.

While collaboration between journalists and the legal profession helped the former to address new problems and demands, the relationship also benefited certain legal professionals—specifically, political liberals who were committed to protecting citizens' rights, advocating public interests, advancing a genuine rule of law, and bringing about social, legal, and political change. Public attention and support generated by media helped legal professionals push the government to follow the law. Like journalists, legal professionals were also subject to the arbitrary power of the authoritarian state. When legal professionals pressured the government to follow the law and protect citizens' rights, they ran their own risk of retaliation from government officials. Publicizing the wrongdoing of government officials could prevent such retaliation; thus journalists could help legal professionals protect themselves (Liebman 2005; Liu and Halliday 2011). Furthermore, for legal professionals interested in bringing about social change and advocating for public interests and a genuine rule of law, newspapers provided a powerful medium for their ideas. As a result, legal professionals who identified themselves as guardians of citizens' rights and public interests made natural allies for journalists who saw themselves as spokespersons for the people (i.e., advocacy journalists). They all aimed to help members of the public realize their rights and bring about social change. In short, the collaboration between these two professions was mutually beneficial as it helped actors in both fields pursue their agendas safely and more effectively.

This collaboration wasn't politically implausible, even though the Chinese state had a long-standing "divide and rule" strategy, designed to discourage collaboration across organizations and fields and to prevent the formation of crosscutting social and political forces (Perry 2007). During this period, however, interaction between journalists and those in the legal profession seemed appropriate and acceptable, given that the government was asking journalists to publicize legal knowledge and oversee local problems according to law. In addition, although public interest and rights defense lawyers faced the risk of local government retaliation, some actually received government awards for their provision of legal aid and assistance to vulnerable groups (Fu and Cullen 2011).

In this process of collaboration, advocacy journalists and legal professionals not only pursued their own respective agendas, but also developed a common goal of cultivating civil society—and critical news reporting was seen as an important means of achieving that goal. Actors in both fields also shared an understanding of China's critical historical events and its current problems, which motivated them to pursue sociopolitical and cultural change. The 1989 Tiananmen democratic movement, for example, loomed large in the memories of both groups. As the sociologist Dingxin Zhao (2000) writes, "The movement was suppressed, but people did not forget. Much of Chinese politics since then has centered on the ghost of the movement and its aftermath." Most of my interviewees in the Guangzhou collaborative networks mentioned how much the Tiananmen incident had affected their career choices and linked their professional goals to specific political agendas. These interviewees also alluded to the influence that the CCP's former general secretary Zhao Ziyang had on them. Although Zhao was put under house arrest after the 1989 Tiananmen protests and is still designated as part of the unspoken history of the CCP, his political reform agenda and increasing disenchantment with the Communist regime greatly influenced many journalists and legal professionals in the Guangzhou collaborative networks.

Many of the interviewees also mentioned their admiration of Hu Yaobang, also a former CCP general secretary, in the 1980s, who had been relatively liberal and tolerant of critical voices.

These professionals perceive the current single-party rule as the root of China's problems. Many of them described how they had become disillusioned with the CCP over time and frankly expressed their opposition to it. They sought to advance public interests and the development of a genuine rule of law and civil society in China, which they thought could bring about the country's democratization or at least political liberalization. As they saw it, critical news reporting would help Chinese citizens become politically self-conscious, forcing the government, in turn, to become accountable to its citizens. A journalist at *Southern Metropolis Daily* described the evolving nature of such collaboration:

> The alliance turned out to be like a loosely connected, informal political party. We collaborate because our political views are similar in critical aspects and we want to bring about political, social, and cultural change. Political liberals who highly value citizens' rights and genuine rule of law are much more motivated to cultivate such collaborative relations. There are a variety of ways in which journalists and lawyers can live their lives. Journalists and lawyers who see themselves as wage laborers, or who are fine with the dominant official discourse and practices, are not motivated to do these extra and risky things. They can just follow ordinary routines and live a satisfying life. (Interview, June 2011, Beijing)

Understanding the political nature of this collaboration is important because it reveals why many journalists and legal professionals associated with collaborative networks in Guangzhou saw critical news reports as resistance against CCP's political control and persisted in producing critical news reports despite potential and actual political repression.

The fragmented bureaucratic structure in Guangzhou allowed journalists to collaborate with legal professionals, providing opportunity for resistance. Journalists in Guangzhou figured out how to utilize the "cracks" in the bureaucratic structure in two ways. First, journalists at some provincial newspapers exploited the political power of their organization's place in the official hierarchy to produce critical news reports. These journalists usually avoided directly criticizing the central government, the Communist regime, or the Guangdong provincial party-state. What they produced instead were reports targeting their criticism at local party-state agencies with no authority over the Guangdong provincial newspapers, such as lower-level governments in Guangdong or local governments outside Guangdong. Then, within these articles, journalists found ways to include suggestions that problems were not just local but systemic. As a journalist at the *Southern Metropolis Daily* explained:

When writing a critical news report, we often write in a tone that sounds as if we were the central government. We criticize local governments and individual officials for breaking the law. Of course, we know that the central government should be held accountable as well, so we do try very hard to suggest to readers that many societal problems in China are systemically rooted in China's institutions and political regime. (Interview, June 2011, Guangzhou)

The Southern Media Group, including *Southern Metropolis Daily*, was well known for using its political position in the government hierarchy to produce such critical news reports.

Of course, managerial cadres of newspaper organizations still faced pressure from provincial propaganda officials responsible to the central Department of Propaganda. These cadres often needed to convince provincial propaganda officials that the economic return of their reports for the provincial party-state would outweigh the political costs. And provincial propaganda officials sometimes turned a blind eye to critical news reporting if they estimated that reports would not lead to intervention from central propaganda officials.

The second way in which journalists exploited the fragmented political structure was to produce critical news reports based on articles already published elsewhere. In Guangzhou, *Southern Metropolis Daily*'s outspoken reporting provided cover for other local newspapers when it published critical reports, as these reports could usually be reprinted without sanction. A journalist at *Yangcheng Evening News* confirmed the benefits of this strategy:

If *Southern Metropolis Daily* has already reported on a problem, we can continue to report it, given that the news is already released and we are not the first newspaper to stir up trouble. The existence of multilevel newspaper organizations and government agencies in a city actually benefits all of the parties involved. (Interview, June 2011, Guangzhou)

Indeed, as the provincial propaganda department has authority over the city propaganda department and is the highest censorship authority in Guangzhou, once provincial newspapers report on certain problems, journalists at other newspapers in Guangzhou could then assume that those reports had already passed the censorship at the provincial level. As such, a follow-up was less likely to be questioned by either city or provincial propaganda officials. Furthermore, the strong market competition in Guangzhou pushed journalists and newspapers to seize on such opportunities created by other newspaper organizations.

The combination of a relatively competitive newspaper market and fragmented political structure in Guangzhou made it possible for journalists to collaborate with legal professionals and, in turn, produce critical news reports.

By allying with legal professionals, journalists in Guangzhou gained valuable resources for such reporting. Legal professionals assisted journalists in three ways that were not mutually exclusive. First, they provided expert advice, answering journalists' questions. Second, some legal professionals actually wrote articles for newspapers when asked to do so by journalists. Third, legal professionals assisted journalists with news topic selection, investigation, and framing. Many reporters pointed out in their interviews that lawyers were among the most knowledgeable critics of social problems. Lawyers' inter- actions with citizens across strata and localities made them critical commen- tators on many social issues. As such, lawyers were able to provide journalists with suggestions for news topics and analyses. In some instances, lawyers even sent their employees to help journalists investigate stories. These various forms of assistance greatly aided critical news reporting.

One important consequence of these alliances was that journalists were able to broaden the "gray area" of reporting. Although certain topics remained strictly forbidden in China, a gray area did exist (Lin 2008), and legal profes- sionals were particularly adept at working within this space by articulating potentially sensitive problems using language acceptable to the central gov- ernment. A lawyer who worked with the *Southern Metropolis Daily* explained:

> We know how to frame problems properly in accordance with law. There is an old Chinese proverb, "Set your own spear against your own shield." It means that we refute somebody with his or her own argument. If we want to criticize the government and uncover problems, we need to frame the problems according to the official language, that is, law. But that does not mean that we accept the official ideology. We actually use the official language to challenge the official ideology. (Interview, June 2011, Beijing)

Thanks to the contributions of legal experts, critical news reporting tended to have broader claims and deeper critiques. In short, precisely because legal professionals were experts in the government's new form of symbolic domi- nation, they were also uniquely situated to turn that symbolic order into an instrument of resistance.

In addition to providing resources for critical news reporting, collabora- tion between the two professions also empowered journalists to decrease their own self-censorship. As a journalist at the *Yangcheng Evening News* explained,

> The real power of censorship and political control lies in its inducing fear and self-censorship. After my colleagues and I worked with lawyers, we know we are righteous. . . . We become much more confident and less constrained by censorship. (Interview, June 2011, Guangzhou)

Compelling journalists to self-censor was one of the most effective means through which the government enforced censorship; thus, when journalists gained new confidence as a result of their collaboration with the legal profession, it decreased the power of the censorship system.

By collaborating with liberal-leaning legal professionals, journalists in Guangzhou were able to get around some censorship issues and produce more critical reports—an outcome that deviated from and even undermined the original purpose of the government's law dissemination programs. The irony of this outcome was not lost on my interviewees, as one journalist at *Southern Metropolis Daily* explained: "We have been implementing the task of law dissemination as required by the government. We just use this opportunity to diffuse ideas about genuine rule of law and talk about problems in Chinese society" (Interview, June 2011, Guangzhou). Of course, the fragmented field environment and collaboration with legal professionals did not shield Guangzhou newspapers from political repression completely. Critical news reports produced by Guangzhou newspapers could and did trigger repression, and periodic crackdowns and battles between journalists in Guangzhou and regulatory agencies were common. The point, however, is that critical news reporting emerged, and to certain extent persisted, despite the ongoing use of such repressive state tactics.

BEIJING: PARTIAL COLLABORATION BETWEEN MEDIA AND LEGAL PROFESSIONALS

Beijing newspapers were situated in a less fragmented market and political environment than in Guangzhou because of Beijing's less competitive newspaper market (Huang and Zeng 2011; Liu 2010). In the early 2000s, Beijing had four conglomerates: the Guangming Daily News Group, the Economic Daily News Group, the Beijing Daily News Group, and the Beijing Youth Daily News Group. But the Economic Daily News Group did not publish newspapers targeting general city residents, and the news groups and newspapers in Beijing were not as highly developed or capable as those in Guangzhou.

Further, the Beijing newspaper market was not as competitive as the market in Guangzhou, yet newspapers in both localities were embedded in a relatively fragmented political structure. Because Beijing is a municipality and the national capital, both national and provincial party-state agencies reside there. Many central party-state agencies publish newspapers, such as the Communist Youth League's influential *China Youth Daily*, which are directly supervised by the Department of Propaganda.

The bureaucratic structure in Beijing created two problems for censorship. First, central-level newspapers did not necessarily follow the instructions of the Department of Propaganda. Since these newspapers were affiliated with state agencies of the same rank as the Department of Propaganda in the official hierarchy, journalists for these newspapers did not always feel subordinate to the central department. In some situations, their boss could be more politically powerful than the department head. This was different from the relationship between newspapers and propaganda departments at lower levels, since those lower-level departments can always call on the central Department of Propaganda for support if necessary. Second, central state agencies rank higher in the official hierarchy than municipal propaganda departments, so central newspapers in Beijing did not necessarily need to even consider the interests of the latter, especially given that, unlike most municipal propaganda departments, Beijing's could not necessarily rely on effective support from the central department. The multilevel government structure thus made censorship inconsistent and avoidable in Beijing.

The ways in which the local market and the political environment shaped critical news reporting in Beijing were closely related to similar processes in Guangzhou but followed a different pattern. Although newspapers in Guangzhou were often targets of repression, they were still relatively successful in several respects. Guangzhou newspapers gained market revenue and earned the respect of readers and journalist communities throughout China. As a result, the strategies and practices of Guangzhou newspapers were often emulated by newspapers in other localities. My interviewees in Beijing said that journalists there, like their counterparts in Guangzhou, adopted the same collaborative practices with legal experts. Yet, Beijing newspapers were not as successful in their efforts to produce critical news reports because of differences in the two cities' local markets and political environments.

The multilevel, fragmented political structure in Beijing did allow local newspapers to produce critical news reports. The main challengers of the censorship order in Beijing were newspapers, such as *China Youth Daily*, affiliated with central party-state agencies. Using their position in the official hierarchy, these central-level newspapers reported on problems in Beijing and elsewhere, even though their reporting could have negative consequences on Beijing and other local governments. A journalist for *China Youth Daily* summed up the problem:

> Central-level newspapers do not have to listen to the Beijing municipal government or local governments in other places, so they sometimes are able to report news that cannot be covered by local newspapers. This is why the Beijing local government has been asking the central government to let them take over newspapers that are directly supervised by the Central Propaganda Department. (Interview, June 2011, Beijing)

Sometimes, when journalists at municipal newspapers encountered censorship problems, they provided materials to journalists at central-level newspapers to get news published. As in Guangzhou, when higher-level newspaper organizations published critical news reports, they provided cover to other newspapers in Beijing, who could reprint these reports without sanction.

But even though journalists in Beijing could take advantage of the fragmented political structure to resist political forces and produce critical news reports, such actions were not as common in Beijing as they were in Guangzhou. Beijing's less competitive market gave newspaper organizations greater power over readers and public-spirited journalists. Journalists in Beijing acknowledged that local newspapers experienced less pressure to satisfy market demands, even though readers there expressed a similar desire to know more about social problems. As a result, the managerial cadres at Beijing newspapers did not see a pressing need for journalists to collaborate with legal or other experts.

The less competitive market was also unfavorable for recruiting public-minded journalists, thus decreasing the chance of collaboration between media and legal professionals. Many journalists committed to citizen advocacy preferred working in an environment where they saw more opportunities to push the boundaries of reporting. Recognizing that the market structure in Beijing gave them less space to do this, many talented and public-minded journalists chose to work for newspapers in Guangzhou instead, as one journalist for the *Beijing Times* described the situation:

> In Beijing, because the market was less competitive than that in Guangzhou, many managerial cadres did not worry too much about market revenues. In this situation, it is difficult for journalists to persuade managerial cadres to take more political risks. Knowing this situation, many public-spirited journalists chose to work in Guangzhou. (Interview, June 2011, Beijing)

Thanks to this self-selection, journalists for local newspapers in Beijing were not as motivated as their Guangzhou counterparts by professional ideals or the desire to advance sociopolitical and cultural change, and they were also less supportive of one another. Furthermore, journalists in Beijing were less likely to actively collaborate with legal professionals to expand the boundaries of critical news reporting.

The market and political conditions in Beijing affected the extent to which journalists there used network mechanisms to produce critical news reports in two related ways. First, the local environment influenced the *scope* of collaboration. Legal professionals did work with journalists, but their role in news production was relatively limited compared with what was taking place in Guangzhou. Legal professionals helped journalists in Beijing analyze social problems, while also writing commentaries on social problems for newspapers, but they did not have much substantive participation in news selection and investigation. As a result, the ability of journalists to work within the gray area of news reporting was much more limited.

Second, the local environment in Beijing affected the *nature* of collaboration. The networks that developed between legal experts and journalists in

Beijing were less politicized than those developed in Guangzhou. Although many interviewees in the Beijing collaborative network saw critical news reports as important to the development of an informed citizenry and the rule of law in China, few of them alluded to critical historical events that motivated them, or to their own efforts to bring about social or political change. Unlike their counterparts in Guangzhou, journalists and legal professionals in the Beijing collaborative network did not share a cohesive political outlook or agenda. As a result, when they perceived considerable political risk, their lower level of enthusiasm and commitment to advancing sociopolitical and cultural change led them to err on the side of political safety.

SHANGHAI: STIFLED COLLABORATION BETWEEN MEDIA AND LEGAL PROFESSIONALS

Newspapers in Shanghai were situated in a less fragmented environment than that of their Guangzhou and Beijing counterparts (Lee, He, and Huang 2007). Similar to the situation in Beijing, the local newspaper market in Shanghai was less competitive than the Guangzhou market (Liu 2010). There were two newspaper conglomerates in Shanghai in the early 2000s: the Wenhui-Xinmin Press Group and the Jiefang Daily News Group. Both organizations were affiliated with the Shanghai municipal party-state.

The local political environment in Shanghai was distinguished by its relatively unified political structure. Unlike Guangzhou and Beijing, a single-level party-state resides in Shanghai. In terms of censorship, the Shanghai municipal propaganda department served as a de facto "local emperor." Because both news groups were affiliated with the Shanghai municipal government, neither could claim higher authority over the Shanghai party-state. As a result, the relationship between newspaper organizations and the Shanghai municipal propaganda department was much less complicated than the various relationships in Guangzhou and Beijing.

Newspapers in Shanghai were also influenced by the collaborative model of critical news reporting in Guangzhou. When considering how to enhance market and professional performance in the early 2000s, journalists in Shanghai looked to other newspaper organizations. As in Guangzhou, Shanghai readers were eager to know more about emerging social problems. Journalists in Shanghai realized that the rule of law, which was intertwined with these problems, was the key to understanding and resolving them, as a journalist for the *Shanghai Morning Post* recalled:

Many problems have occurred in the process of China's economic development. For example, workers cannot get their wages. People without urban dweller status are treated as second-class citizens due to the household registration system. There are various problems, and we realize that every problem is related to unenforced or unjust laws. Things were not like that in the past. Because of the importance of law in everyday life and in official rhetoric, we thought that collaborating with the legal profession, as Guang-zhou journalists do, would be a great idea. (Phone interview, August 2011)

Guangzhou newspapers stood out as examples for newspapers in Shanghai, but journalists in Shanghai had less success in adopting the model.

Shanghai journalists eager to replicate Guangzhou's collaborative practices experienced great difficulty transplanting the model to Shanghai given the less fragmented market and political environment there. Similar to the situation in Beijing, the structure of the newspaper market in Shanghai was not favorable to the adoption of the Guangzhou model. The competition in the Shanghai newspaper market was not as high as in Guangzhou. Many managerial cadres at Shanghai newspapers tended to believe that their newspapers could be profit-able without taking political risks. Furthermore, Shanghai municipal party-state officials did not consider competition between newspapers relevant to them. A senior editor at *Xinmin Evening News* explained the officials' position:

Ultimately, the Shanghai municipal government received the same rev-enues. All of the newspapers were part of the Shanghai government. Competition mattered for newspapers but not the Shanghai government. This is different from what happened in Guangzhou, where the provincial government was competing with the city government for revenues from newspapers. (Interview, June 2014, Shanghai)

As a result of the market structure in Shanghai, managerial cadres of newspaper organizations did not have leverage to negotiate the boundaries of reporting with the Shanghai municipal party-state.

Unlike journalists in Beijing, Shanghai journalists encountered a further obstacle when attempting to adopt the Guangzhou model: concentrated po-litical power. The multilevel government structure in Guangzhou and Beijing created tensions that journalists and legal professionals could exploit to pro-duce critical news reports. In comparison, a single propaganda department directly regulated and monitored every local newspaper in Shanghai, and no newspaper organization was higher than that department in the official hier-archy. When Shanghai propaganda officials determined that news content was inappropriate, they called newspaper organizations directly to issue a warning. Sometimes the officials also notified other newspaper organizations in Shang-hai to prevent them from covering the inappropriate stories. Essentially, the single-level government structure in Shanghai facilitated an extremely effective form of censorship that was much easier to enforce compared with censorship in Beijing and Guangzhou.

The less fragmented political structure in Shanghai also substantially re-stricted collaboration between legal experts and journalists. The legal profes-sion had little opportunity to comment on social problems or to participate in news topic selection, investigation, or framing. To be sure, Shanghai news-papers did invite legal experts to write commentaries, but collaboration often ceased following intervention by the Shanghai propaganda department. A journalist at the *Shanghai Morning Post* was familiar with that experience:

> We did want to have collaboration with legal professionals and public intel-lectuals, but there were a lot of difficulties. Local government officials, es-pecially those in the propaganda department, frown on such collaboration. They call us when they see our reports. Knowing our situation, potential collaborators tend to prefer working with news organizations that give them more freedom. (Phone interview, July 2011)

Apparently, the concentrated political structure not only interrupted ongo-ing collaboration, but also discouraged legal professionals from working with Shanghai newspapers at all.

Although the institutional connections of the legal and media fields created a structural opportunity for critical news reporting in Shanghai, the unfavor-able local environment led to reports that tended to adhere to the original purpose of the law dissemination programs—namely, helping citizens obey the law and strengthening the government's legitimacy.

Instead of producing critical news reports, the institutional connections between the media and legal fields spurred two other kinds of reports in Shang-hai. The first entailed obtaining relevant laws, policies, and court decisions from government officials in charge of legal affairs, then simply disseminating government accounts verbatim. The second kind of report involved happy stories of citizens using the law to combat injustice, and the government pro-tecting citizens' rights. Such stories satisfied the government's demand for "positive" propaganda and law dissemination, as well as superficially meet-ing readers' demands for legal knowledge (Stockmann and Gallagher 2011). Instead of interviewing legal professionals who knew the odds of successful legal mobilization, journalists were pressured into interviewing only those citizens who were lucky enough to experience justice. In the process of pro-ducing both types of reports, journalists in Shanghai did not use the law to reveal fundamental problems in Chinese society; rather, they helped the state to advance its authoritarian political order.

Conclusion: Unintended Consequences of Reform

This chapter continues the narrative started in chapter 3 regarding the Chinese state's turn to law and rights. Following the end of the Cultural Revolution, the

Chinese state initiated a program of legal reform that marshaled the media to diffuse law to citizens, thus replacing the public's existing symbolic structure of class struggle with one framed in terms of laws and rights. Although the Chinese state attempted to avoid the negative consequences of disseminating legal knowledge by focusing on economic rights and issues only, the actual law dissemination processes were more complex and unpredictable than many officials at the central party-state had envisioned because of the increasing complexity of and connection between the legal and media fields.

As the Chinese state relied on media to disseminate legal knowledge, the national process of legal reform and law dissemination programs interacted with the process of media marketization, and the development of both the legal and media fields influenced how ideas about laws and rights were mobilized and diffused to citizens. Both the legal and media profession became more established and diversified with the unfolding of legal reform and media marketization. Market forces aligned with professional norms among journalists, enabling some reporters to pursue their professional ideals when state censorship left readers' demands unsatisfied. Media marketization thus created opportunities for public-spirited, liberal-leaning journalists and legal professionals in key sites to collaborate and pursue their political agenda through critical news reporting.

Scholars often describe Chinese media as successful in propagandizing for the government and pursuing economic benefits (Stockmann and Gallagher 2011) but uninterested in democratic causes (Pan 2010; Zhao 2004). The conventional description is, indeed, applicable to certain Chinese media, as demonstrated by the two selected newspapers in Shanghai. Yet, as I have shown here, journalists in Guangzhou and, to a lesser degree, in Beijing did attempt to produce news reports critical of the existing political structure. Although journalists were closely watched by the state, a more fragmented political and economic environment in certain sites provided opportunities for critical news reporting, while a more unified political and economic environment in other locations did the opposite. The very embeddedness of journalists within the state in some contexts afforded them political power over certain state agencies and opportunities to collaborate with legal professionals. These conditions, in turn, allowed journalists and lawyers to make more boundary-pushing claims. Going beyond the prevailing form of collective resistance, which demands only the implementation of law (Lee 2007; O'Brien and Li 2006), journalists working in amenable contexts mobilized constitutional principles, called for broader civil and political rights, and challenged the legitimacy of law; sometimes they even questioned the central government. The issues covered by critical news reports uncovered public dimensions of law and dealt with the relationships between the state and individuals as well as the communal relationship among individuals.

Nonetheless, the above findings about variation in critical news reporting should not be overinterpreted. Even critical news reports continued to operate within the limit of the constitution, without truly challenging the political monopoly of the CCP. Furthermore, the proportion of critical reports was far below one percent at even the most critical newspaper examined here. This suggests the ongoing adverse effects of China's authoritarian regime on critical news reporting. Despite such limitations, in a context where the state tends to censor news reports that reveal societal problems and even punishes journalists for doing so, even a modest rise in critical news reports was significant, for it disclosed important problems to the public, manifested resistance against censorship and control, and advanced a more critical political culture. The rise of critical news reporting and the formation of collaborative networks between media and legal professionals also helped to facilitate the development of the Internet sector and the subsequent rise of a contentious public sphere in China in the post-2005 period. Beginning in 2003, journalists and lawyers who collaborated in critical news reporting began to use the Internet to increase the influence of their reports and to produce so-called public opinion incidents. In the next chapter, I describe how these collaborative networks extended to the Internet and influenced production of news and online public opinion.

5

Extending Liberalization from the Press to the Internet

In chapter 4, I describe the process of media marketization that unfolded rapidly from 1992 onward and the consequences of this process for the rise of critical news reports and collaborative networks between media and legal professionals in certain localities in China. The most common argument about China's media marketization is that it has not produced significant liberalizing effects in the country (Hassid 2008; Stockmann and Gallagher 2011; Stockmann 2013; Zhao 2008). For instance, Hassid (2008, 414) argues that "increasing economic liberalization of the Chinese media has not resulted in proportional political liberalization." This observation is true when we focus on Chinese newspapers' news production. Indeed, the Chinese state, in general, has maintained firm control over the press.

And yet, the rise of the Internet in China has broadened the media field, and limited liberalization effects in the press sector can "travel" to and be amplified in the Internet sector. As the old Chinese saying goes, a single spark can start a prairie fire (*xingxing zhi huo keyi liaoyuan*). To be sure, from the moment that China connected to the Internet, the Chinese state imposed various controls to minimize what it saw as the negative political consequences of the new online sphere (Harwit and Clark 2001; Tsui 2003; Yang 2009; Zheng 2008), as evidenced by China's low ranking according to measures of Internet freedom.[1] Nevertheless, China's Internet sector was shaped not only by the Chinese party-state, but also by private business actors, ordinary citizens, and public opinion leaders. At the same time, the Chinese state's actions were also constrained by certain global conditions, particularly the international trade framework. The interplay of multiple actors in building the Internet sector rendered the state's control incomplete and uncertain. Many journalists moved from the traditional press to Internet companies. Given the heterogeneity among newspaper organizations in terms of news production, those who effected such a move and gained positions of power in the Internet sector were able to influence online news production and the development and operation of social media.

With the rise of the Internet, Chinese officials, media, and scholars recognize that state-controlled media has become increasingly marginalized in its influence on public opinion. Indeed, the Chinese state's control over media has actually harmed the media's credibility in the Internet age. The Chinese media's declining credibility is confirmed by nationally representative survey data. Analysis of the 2002 and 2008 Asian Barometer Survey (see table 5.1) shows that Chinese people's trust in the central government, local governments, courts, civil service, People's Congress, newspapers, television, and police all declined over time between 2002 and 2008. Indeed, distrust in all social and political institutions in China has increased. Among these institutions, trust in newspapers and televisions dropped the most—from 73.11 percent in 2002 to 42.78 percent in 2008, and from 85.61 percent in 2002 to 50.96 percent in 2008, respectively. Analysis of the 2003 and 2006 AsiaBarometer Survey, as presented in table 5.2, reveals analogous trends.[2] Trust in the central government, local governments, the legal system, People's Congress, media, and the police all dropped over time, while distrust in all institutions rose greatly. Media suffered from the greatest loss of trust, dropping from 71.0 percent in 2003 to 41.2 percent in 2006.

As trust in traditional media declined, more and more Chinese people turned to the Internet to discuss social problems and to criticize the Chinese state (Yang 2009). The Chinese party-state saw this development as a threat to its political monopoly. The State Internet Information Office and the Department of Propaganda accused China's major Internet companies, which provide news service on Internet portals as well as social media services, of failing to comply with state regulations and instructions. Factually speaking, the state's complaints were not ungrounded. Major Internet portals at times reprinted news articles that contradicted the Department of Propaganda (Lei and Zhou 2015). And even when Internet portals appeared to follow the instructions of the department, they often still found ways to imply their disagreement. For example, in the 2013 *Southern Weekly* incident discussed in chapter 1, the propaganda department of Guangdong Province interfered in the publication of *Southern Weekly*'s New Year special editorial, which promoted notions of freedom, liberal democracy, and constitutionalism. The Department of Propaganda instructed major Internet portals to reprint an article published by the *Global Times*, a subsidiary of *People's Daily*, that criticized *Southern Weekly*. Although the top four major Internet portals all reprinted the article, Sina,

TABLE 5.1. Trust in institutions, Asian Barometer Survey

	Trust in the central government		Trust in local government		Trust in courts		Trust in civil service	
Year	2002	2008	2002	2008	2002	2008	2002	2008
A great deal or quite a lot of trust (%)	93.15	87.96	73.96	55.32	71.13	69.77	68.93	49.69
Not very much trust or no trust (%)	1.26	4.94	18.91	37.88	15.99	21.22	19.86	40.05
Don't know or no answer (%)	5.59	7.10	7.13	6.81	12.88	9.00	11.22	10.26

	Trust in parliament		Trust in newspapers		Trust in television		Trust in the police	
Year	2002	2008	2002	2008	2002	2008	2002	2008
A great deal or quite a lot of trust (%)	88.56	82.59	73.11	42.78	85.61	50.96	75.43	67.32
Not very much trust or no trust (%)	1.29	6.39	13.79	44.78	7.85	40.31	18.41	25.93
Don't know or no answer (%)	10.15	10.65	13.10	12.44	6.53	8.73	6.16	6.75

	Our form of government is the best for us.		You can trust people who run our government to do what is right.	
Year	2002	2008	2002	2008
Agree (%)	78.61	74.34	75.43	52.12
Disagree (%)	4.68	2.82	13.29	32.68
Don't know or no answer (%)	16.71	22.83	11.28	15.20

Source: Asian Barometer Survey in China, 2002 and 2008
Note: N = 3,183 in 2002; N = 5,098 in 2008.

NetEase, and Tencent made the unusual move of adding a disclaimer. The disclaimer stated that by reprinting the article, Internet portals were not necessarily indicating their agreement with the expressed viewpoints or statements—in this case, the viewpoints and statements of the *Global Times* article and, in turn, the Department of Propaganda.

In this chapter I examine the connection between the press and the Internet sectors. I discuss how and why the major Internet companies providing news

TABLE 5.2. Trust in institutions, AsiaBarometer Survey

	Trust in central government		Trust in local government		Trust in the legal system		Trust in parliament	
Year	2003	2006	2003	2006	2003	2006	2003	2006
A great deal or quite a lot of trust (%)	90.13	84.70	80.25	59.85	73.88	64.70	81.88	71.25
Not very much trust or no trust (%)	8.88	13.70	18.25	37.85	22.88	34.40	14.88	26.85
Don't know or no answer (%)	1.00	1.60	1.50	2.30	3.25	0.90	3.25	1.90

	Trust in media		Trust in the police	
Year	2003	2006	2003	2006
A great deal or quite a lot of trust (%)	71.00	41.20	70.75	64.40
Not very much trust or no trust (%)	26.50	57.75	27.88	35.00
Don't know or no answer (%)	2.50	1.05	1.38	0.60

Source: AsiaBarometer Survey in China, 2003 and 2006
Note: N = 800 in 2003; N = 2,000 in 2006

service and social media in China became a thorn in the side of the Chinese state, despite the state's efforts to control them. Existing studies of rising public opinion in China tend to focus on how technological properties of the Internet can empower citizens to bring about social change and how the Chinese state has attempted to forestall such change (Hung 2003; Lagerkvist 2005; Lei 2011; McCormick and Liu 2003; Rosen 2010; Shen et al. 2009; Tai 2006; Zheng and Wu 2005; Zheng 2008). Such work tends to pay less attention to the ways in which particular contexts mediate and moderate the technological effects of the Internet. I trace the restructuring of the media field in China, especially the development of the online news market, following the state's decision to connect the country to the Internet. This story is a sequel of sorts to chapter 4's narrative of the rise of critical news reporting. As I demonstrate, preexisting conditions in the newspaper market played a key—but often neglected—role in shaping China's online news market and discursive arena.

Boundary Setting in the Newspaper Market

Understanding the development of China's online news market requires understanding the boundaries already established by the Chinese state in the newspaper market. Although this market was created by the Chinese state, it established geographic and sectoral boundaries to retain political control. As discussed in chapter 4, despite the acceleration of media marketization in China since 1992, the party-state retains control over news media (Lee 2000; Zhao 1998, 2004, 2008). News media are simultaneously market and state actors. Only organizations affiliated with the party-state are allowed to publish newspapers, and most of these organizations are party organs (e.g., local party committees), government bureaucracies, and mass organizations incorporated into the state.[3] One important feature of the press structure is that only party committees are allowed to publish newspapers for general readers. Other organizations can publish only specialized newspapers (e.g., business and law) or newspapers for specific target groups (e.g., peasants, laborers, and youth). The power of local party committees is limited geographically, however, so they tend to publish only local commercial newspapers for local newspaper markets. These papers rarely have cross-regional and cross-sectoral influence. Therefore, even though the state loosened regulations on cross-regional collaboration and operation, marketized newspapers continue to operate, at most, in multiple localities at the local level, or at the national level with a narrow specialization. The central party-state permits no one to publish a national market-oriented daily newspaper for general readers.

This absence is a result of deliberate political decisions. Although news organizations are state actors, they are likely to represent interests of a specific faction inside the CCP. The possibility for national-level media organizations to be used by factions inside the party-state was vividly demonstrated during the 1989 Tiananmen protests. The leadership of the *People's Daily* at the time was associated with the reformist and relatively politically liberal leaders Hu Yaobang and Zhao Ziyang, who were admired by many of the protesters in the 1989 democratic movement. Furthermore, a large proportion of journalists and editors at the *People's Daily* in 1989 were sympathetic to Tiananmen protesters and opposed to the CCP's conservative faction. Tens of journalists and editors held the banners of the *People's Daily* while participating in the protests. They even chanted the slogan, "We did not write the April 26 editorial," explicitly disavowing state intervention (the infamous *People's Daily* April 26 editorial had defined the democratic movement as an antiparty revolt that should be resolutely suppressed). In the aftermath of the 1989 Tiananmen incident, the CCP purged the *People's Daily*, removing many editors and journalists from their posts to ensure the paper would, henceforth, speak as instructed by CCP leaders. The Tiananmen democratic movement confirmed for CCP leaders that giving news media access to a national general public essentially created a de facto oppositional party capable of threatening the CCP's political monopoly.

Local or specialized news organizations were easier to control because they had a limited range of political influence, as one journalist explained:

> There is no commercial daily newspaper for general readers because of the state's policy. Market demand and business interests were strong. Chinese people want to know more about what happens in the country. Local commercial daily newspapers do not satisfy such need. Considering the size of China's population and advertisement market, the press market can definitely accommodate a few national commercial daily newspapers. The government continues to restrict this out of political considerations. In some news media, journalists share similar political orientation. The government is unlikely to allow them to become nationally influential. (Interview, June 2011, Beijing)

In fact, Deng Xiaoping instructed the state to outlaw connections between individuals across organizations and regions, and to prohibit illegal organizations and publications (Deng 1994, 271). The ultimate goal was to avoid the emergence of cross-sectoral and regional forces that could compete with the CCP. Such threats were seen as potentially arising from within as well as from outside the CCP. By establishing and enforcing clear boundaries in China's newspaper market, the state sought to lower the likelihood that newspaper organizations could have undesirable political influence at the national level. Yet, this boundary setting turned out to have unintended consequences for the development of China's online news market.

The Early Internet in China

Before I trace the development of China's online news market—a process profoundly influenced by major Internet companies—I briefly describe the development of the Internet more generally in China, prior to the growth of Internet companies. Compared with traditional mass media, the Internet has the distinct technological property of decentralization: individuals can communicate with many others without needing to access the resources or approval of media owners (Benkler 2006, 11). Given the potential of such a decentralized medium to undermine the power of traditional gatekeepers, the Internet is often perceived as potentially prodemocratic. This view is best exemplified by former U.S. president Bill Clinton's assessment. In a speech in 2000, Clinton said:

> When China joins the WTO, by 2005, it will eliminate tariffs on information technology products, making the tools of communication even cheaper, better, and more widely available. . . . Now, there's no question

China has been trying to crack down on the Internet—good luck. That's sort of like trying to nail Jell-O to the wall. . . . In the knowledge economy, economic innovation and political empowerment, whether anyone likes it or not, will inevitably go hand in hand.[4]

But given the perceived democratizing potential of the Internet, why did the Chinese state decide to adopt this new technology at all? Scholars have suggested that the ideology and beliefs of Chinese political elites—a form of neo-technonationalism—played an important role in shaping this decision, despite its potential political risks. With a scientific mindset that viewed information technology infrastructure as one essential component of the state-building and modernization project, party elites believed that the Internet could be controlled and used as an engine for technological and economic development (Tai 2006, 129).

China began to develop Internet technologies in the 1980s. The main developers were the government and China's academic institutions. In 1986, the Institute of High Energy Physics of the Chinese Academy of Sciences sent out the first e-mail from China to the European Organization for Nuclear Research (CERN), in Geneva. In 1989, supported by the World Bank, the Chinese Academy of Sciences, Peking University, and Tsinghua University began to establish the National Computing and Networking Facility of China (NCFC). After years of development and negotiation with the United States and other countries, China eventually connected the NCFC to the global Internet in 1994.[5]

At first, the bulletin board system (BBS) was the key site for China's online interaction. In 1994, the National Research Center for Intelligent Computing Systems established China's first BBS site, Shuguan BBS. In the beginning, universities were the main actors operating BBS. Tsinghua University established Shuimu Tsinghua in 1995, which was the first and one of the most influential university BBS sites in China. Some individuals, particularly information technology engineers, also established BBS sites. Their experience operating BBS sites helped them form and operate Internet companies later. For instance, Ma Huateng established a BBS site in 1995 before founding Tencent, one of the largest Internet companies in China, in 1998. Similarly, Ding Lei established a BBS site in 1996 before he founded NetEase, another major Internet company, in 1997; and also in 1996, Wang Zhidong established Si Tong Li Fang Forum, which then became Sina.com, also one of the largest Internet companies in China (Peng 2005). In the late 1990s, many influential BBS sites came to exist, such as Xici Hutong, Tianya, MOP (*mao pu*), and Strong Nation Forum (*qiangguo luntan*). BBS sites became critical forums for students and professionals to express their views and form communities (Tian and Wu 2007).

The power of the Internet for disseminating information, fostering communities, and mobilizing collective action could already be seen in the late 1990s, although BBS sites tended to have only hundreds of users. But already, interaction on BBS sites, particularly university BBS sites, had led to a few contentious events, or public opinion incidents, that had sparked offline demonstrations. These public opinion incidents were mostly related to geopolitics and were triggered by grassroots nationalism (Hughes 2007; Wu 2007; Zhong and Yu 2010). In 1996, for example, Tsinghua University began to monitor the speech of users on Shuimu Tsinghua when heated discussion developed about China's sovereignty over the Japanese-occupied but Chinese-claimed Diaoyu Islands. In 1998, anti-Chinese riots in Indonesia led students from Peking University to protest in front of the Indonesian embassy in Beijing. And in 1999, when the United States bombed China's embassy in Belgrade as part of the NATO (North Atlantic Treaty Organization) bombing of Yugoslavia, the news spread through BBS, leading Chinese university students to protest in Beijing, Shanghai, Guangzhou, and Shenyang. In these events, BBS users condemned not only foreign countries but also the Chinese government, because they thought the government should have taken a much tougher stance toward foreign countries. Reacting to public opinion incidents mediated by BBS forums, the Ministry of Information Industry enacted the Management Provisions on Electronic Bulletin Services on the Internet (*hulianwang dianzi gonggao fuwu guanli guiding*) in 2000, obliging users and providers of BBS to abide by the law and maintain national and social stability.[6]

In essence, because universities played a critical role in the development of the Internet in China, university BBS sites were the most important arenas in which online communication and interaction occurred between the mid- to late 1990s. Bulletin board systems established by individuals, however, also began to emerge and prosper, laying important foundations for the development of Internet companies. Faced with the rapid growth of market forces on the Internet, the Chinese government had to consider how to restructure the media field.

Restructuring the Media Field

Not surprisingly, for both economic and political reasons, the Chinese government wanted to make state-controlled news media, rather than private companies, the main beneficiaries of the Internet. Around the late 1990s, the central state attempted to turn state-controlled news media into key players on the Internet. The government expected that China's national news media, specifically the *People's Daily* and Xinhua News Agency, as well as local press conglomerates would flourish online, thereby enabling the state to "seize the commanding heights" of the Internet.[7] Essentially, the state wanted to shape the economic and political order of the emerging online news service sector to align with the existing press market, which was regulated through bureaucratic-level and geographic boundaries. Imposing this same order in the online news market, it was reasoned, would benefit Chinese news media economically and help maintain political control.

Nevertheless, the central state's plans in this arena were affected by the country's simultaneous efforts to join the WTO and integrate itself into the global economy. Trade in telecommunications was one of the most fiercely debated issues in China's WTO negotiations (Wang 2001). The Chinese government agreed to open its telecommunications service sector, including the Internet information service, but refused to do the same with the media sector (DeWoskin 2001; Lee 2003, 12). Importantly, China's plan to join the WTO and open the telecommunications service sector ruled out the possibility that the state could be the sole provider of Internet content service, but this did not mean the state was ready to relinquish its regulatory power (Hsueh 2011). The entrance of nonstate actors, whether foreign or local, in Internet content service threatened to impede the central state's goal of transposing the order it had imposed in the newspaper market onto the emerging online news service sector. A law professor's comments highlight how the WTO created economic and political opportunities for both foreign and local nonstate actors:

> The government knew very early that it was impossible to keep the telecommunications sector closed. One important consequence is that the government cannot control the Internet content providers in the same way as it controls news media through employment and promotion even though the state can still impose censorship and other regulations. . . . The government's decision to join the WTO opened up opportunities for domestic private players. When people talk about WTO's impacts, they mainly consider WTO's benefit for foreign investors. But WTO has some beneficial impacts on local private actors in China because it limits the state's monopolistic power (Interview, June 2011, Beijing).

In an effort to minimize nonstate actors' potentially negative effects on the state's plans for China's online news service, the Chinese government enacted regulations to secure the state's political control and news media's economic advantages. The State Council required Internet news providers to obtain a license to operate a news service, and it retained the right to terminate licenses if Internet news providers did not follow laws and regulations.[8] In the Provisions for the Administration of Internet News Information Services, the State Council Information Office and the Ministry of Information Industry claimed monopoly power for the state to define and produce news information. The provisions defined news information as covering current affairs and politics, including reports and comments on politics, the economy, military affairs, diplomacy, and other public affairs. The provisions also established a distinction between news media and nonnews media among Internet news providers. Although licensed nonnews media can provide Internet news service, they can only reprint news produced by Chinese news media. They are not permitted to collect or produce news themselves. As such, nonnews media must rely on news media—generally state actors—to provide online news service. This distinction aimed to give news media an edge on nonnews media in terms of competition, while also allowing the Chinese state to control news content online. In addition, Internet news providers that were not officially designated as news media were required to have at least ten full-time news editors with working experience in news media. This requirement ensured that Internet news providers were capable of editing and reprinting news according to related laws and regulations.

Furthermore, to prevent foreign capital from controlling Internet news providers, the state prohibited providers from existing in the form of Chinese-foreign joint ventures, Chinese-foreign cooperatives, or wholly foreign-owned entities, although foreign capital was allowed to invest in Internet news providers.[9] Officials in the central state, at least until the mid-2000s, believed that they could control Internet news as long as the central and local states could monitor news media according to the conventional division of labor, and as long as the state could regulate the few private Internet news providers.

The Rise of Domestic Internet Portals

The development of Internet news services, however, did not proceed according to the state's plan, as Internet portals—*not* the websites of state-controlled Chinese news media—became the most popular sites to which netizens flocked to obtain news. Internet portals were first established in China in late 1998 and obtained approval from the state to provide news service in 2000.[10] This was one year before China's WTO accession and was the first time in the PRC's history that nonstate business actors were permitted to provide daily news to nationwide readers. Today, China has four major Internet portals: Sina, Sohu, NetEase, and Tencent, all of which are among the top fifteen most popular websites in China according to April 2015 statistics.[11] The Internet companies that own and operate Internet portals also own and operate social media, such as blogs, Weibo, QQ, and WeChat. Sina, Sohu, NetEase, and Tencent are all publicly traded companies listed on NASDAQ or HKEX. None of the top twenty websites in China were owned by China's domestic news media according to April 2015 statistics.

The Chinese state's boundary setting in the newspaper market inadvertently contributed to the success of Internet portals. Though the absence of national, market-oriented, general-interest daily newspapers helped the Chinese state to control the press, it also created a niche for Internet portals.

Given the significance of text-based content to both newspapers and Internet portals, the latter actively recruited experienced journalists and editors from the press. In doing so, those running Internet portals became cognizant of the fact that the state's restrictions in the press market had created an unsatisfied market demand. Internet portal executives believed that their companies should provide products similar to national commercial daily newspapers to satisfy this demand. Domestic Internet portals eventually developed a business model that was very different from the U.S. company Yahoo's model in the early to mid- 2000s. Yahoo mainly provided a directory of websites to gain advertising revenues. In comparison, Chinese Internet portals provided their own sizable news services and established online discussion forums to attract web traffic in exchange for advertising revenues, regardless of whether they had other important sources of revenue. Chinese Internet portals also integrated instant messengers like QQ (since 1999), blogs (since the mid-2000s), and Weibo (since 2009) to boost web traffic, while also extending their services to mobile phone users. A nationwide online news market linking Internet and mobile phone users and crossing preexisting boundaries in the press market thus emerged. A chief executive at one of the top four Internet portals recalled the process:

> Although Internet portals began to provide news, such development was not planned. We just tried to search for doable business models. With the recruitment of experienced journalists, we recognized the capacity of Internet portals and discovered the role of Internet portals as daily market-oriented newspapers for the general public. In the U.S., Yahoo was perhaps the only influential Internet portal that provides news. People visit websites of news media to read news. But we have four major Internet portals in China and people read news on Internet portals. Internet portals in China benefited very much from the boundaries that the government set in the press market. (Interview, June 2011, Beijing)

The newspaper market organizations did not dominate the emerging online news market, as the Chinese state had anticipated, for several reasons. First, as both state actors in charge of ideology work and business actors in the news market, Chinese newspapers were faced with uncertain and strict constraints on capital and ownership structure. Although media professionals had been calling for clear guidelines regarding newspapers' ownership and governance structure, the Chinese state had not come up with any systematic proposals. As a result, Chinese newspapers experimented with various arrangements to test the state's attitude on a case-by-case basis. Although some news groups were able to access the capital market through reverse takeovers (RTOs)[12] and initial public offerings (IPOs),[13] starting in 1999, many, such as the Southern Media Group, did not succeed, despite doing well in the newspaper market.

In addition, even when some news groups succeeded in establishing or taking over publicly traded companies through RTOs or IPOs, those companies did not and could not become involved in the core business of newspaper organizations, that is, news production, because of its political nature. Most of these public companies focused instead on advertising revenues. As a result, news media still had difficulty amassing the capital needed to strengthen their news production and online news service. Because of inadequate capital and the absence of profitable business models to generate revenues from websites, even successful news media were unenthusiastic about investing in their online news service. By contrast, Internet companies were merely private actors. Thanks to China's WTO accession and its opening up of telecommunications service, Internet companies had a clearer set of rules about ownership structure and corporate governance, despite the Chinese state's continuing regulatory power (Hsueh 2011). With access to the global capital market, Internet portals were able to aggressively recruit talented media professionals and develop better business models.

The second reason newspaper organizations did not capture the online news market is that, although the state did not allow Internet portals to produce news, intense competition among news media in local and specialized press markets gave Internet portals leverage to obtain news without having to pay high license fees. There were only four major Internet portals but thousands of newspapers. Newspaper conglomerates realized that, with the existence of their competitors in the press market, it would only be to the detriment of newspapers to pass up the chance to boost their national visibility on Internet portals. In fact, very few newspapers took legal action against Internet portals even when those portals reprinted news articles without permission. When I sat in on the news editing meetings of several newspapers in Beijing and Guangzhou, I heard a lot of discussion about this practice of unauthorized reprinting. Although journalists and editors at the newspapers complained about such behavior, they only complained informally to the portals because they also recognized that such reprints provided national-level advertising for their newspapers. Additionally, the journalists and editors also found that Internet portals and local newspapers attracted different kinds of advertising. The rise of the former did not lower the latter's revenues from advertisements. Finally, Internet portals can exchange sports and entertainment news for other news from print media. The official definition of news does not prohibit Internet portals from producing sports and entertainment pieces. Producing sports and entertainment news is expensive for media outside major cities, where celebrities live, but relatively easy and inexpensive for Internet portals, which are also located in major cities. Taken together, the above conditions resulted in more collaboration than competition between Internet portals and newspapers in the 2000s. News produced by numerous newspapers was thus centralized by the four major Internet portals and spread to online forums, communities, and social media.

Major domestic Internet portals surpassed not only China's state-controlled news media but also multinational Internet companies in the online news market. Compared with domestic Internet portals, multinational Internet companies, particularly Yahoo, tended to transplant business models that were successful elsewhere, with little consideration of or adaptation to the local context. When Yahoo China's local competitors invested in news services, it did not follow. Reflecting on Yahoo China's failure, one former employee said,

> The executives in the U.S. did not understand the strong demand for news information in China back in 1998. Although Yahoo's business model succeeded in the U.S. and other countries, demand of Chinese users was very different because of China's political condition. When the executives realized this, it was too late for Yahoo to catch up. (Interview, June 2011, Beijing)

Despite initially being the most popular Internet portal in China, Yahoo China lost its readership quickly because of its unfamiliarity with the Chinese context, especially the Chinese press market, and its failure to adapt to conditions there.

In addition to providing products similar to national, commercial daily newspapers, Internet companies operating the top four Internet portals also developed very successful social media, such as online forums, QQ, blogs, Weibo, and WeChat. Together, Internet portals and social media increasingly played an important role in the production of news and public opinion as well as the formation of so-called public opinion incidents beginning around 2003. Recall that public opinion incidents (*gonggong yulun shijian*) are contentious events that capture the public's attention (Xung 2012). The continuing occurrence of public opinion incidents contributed to the rise of a contentious public sphere in China. In the late 1990s, when the BBS was the main venue for online discussion and interaction, public opinion incidents mostly concerned international affairs and reflected nationalist sentiments. With the rise of Internet portals and forums, especially since 2003, public opinion incidents increasingly highlighted domestic issues, in particular the misbehavior of government officials and other large-scale social problems, such as food safety (Zhong and Yu 2010).

Public opinion incidents developed through two common processes. In the first case, a news event covered by newspapers—particularly if covered in a critical way—would become a lightning rod, thanks to reprinting by major Internet portals and heated discussion in online forums and on Weibo. Such discussion would then provoke follow-up coverage and attention from the government. In other public opinion incidents, information would first travel and become amplified through online forums and Weibo, leading to traditional media coverage. Media reports would then be widely disseminated by online news websites, leading, in turn, to more discussion online and the government's attention (Li 2011; Xung 2012). Together, these processes, mediated by Internet portals, online forums, and Weibo, diversified the ways in which news was produced, as actors other than news media came to play an ever larger role in news production.

As I argue in chapter 2, China's contentious public sphere emerged in the mid- to late 2000s—even before Weibo replaced online forums, such as the Tianya Forum, as the most important venue for news discussion and before the rise of WeChat. Nonetheless, the evolution of Weibo and other social media is informative here. Before 2010, online discussion forums were the most important venue for citizens to discuss news and set news agenda. Weibo started in 2009 and has surpassed online forums in popularity since 2010 (Li 2011). The percentage of Chinese Internet users who visit online discussion forums declined from 32.4 percent in 2010 to 19.9 percent in 2014, while the percentage using Weibo rose from 13.8 percent in 2010 to 38.4 percent in 2014. The primary activities of Weibo users include following news (77.2%), following interesting people (75.9%), forwarding information and news (58.3%), and following celebrities (50.8%). The practice of following other Weibo users led to the emergence of public opinion leaders—people who play an important role in the formation of public opinion (Li 2012; Wu, Shen, and Zhou 2014).[14] Despite the evolution of and changing preference for social media, the percentage of Chinese Internet users who read news online remains high, slightly rising from 77.2 percent in 2010 to 80.0 percent in 2014. A considerable proportion of Chinese Internet users also discuss news online. At the end of 2014, 43.8 percent of Internet users in China commented on news online after reading it.[15] The rise of WeChat, a popular mobile text and voice messaging communication service, has gradually supplanted Weibo in terms of shaping the production of news and public opinion. Users of WeChat mainly connect to and chat with people with whom they already share strong ties, such as family and friends, whereas people use Weibo to follow news and people with both strong and weak ties, such as public opinion leaders. But increasingly, news media, celebrity, and public opinion leaders have set up public WeChat accounts in order to connect with users there.[16]

In summary, the Chinese state's decision to adopt the Internet led to the expansion of the media field, but the government's reconstruction of the media field was conditioned by its decision to join the WTO. This reconstruction created opportunities for domestic nonstate actors familiar with Chinese local contexts, specifically Internet companies, to remove the boundaries in the press market set by the state and form a national online news market. In this online news market, Internet portals aggregate news articles produced by news media, and ordinary citizens and public opinion leaders participate in news production through the mediation of social media.

Extending Elite Networks and Cultural Practices from the Newspaper Market to the Online News Market

INTERNET PORTALS

With the expansion of the media field, social networks and the political culture associated with the few bold newspaper organizations famous for critical news reporting spread to Internet portals, the online news market, and online discursive and social spaces. The labor market was an important mechanism through which the influence of specific news media has been extended to Internet portals. Although the latter are not allowed to produce news, they still have room to edit and compile the news, as well as to produce content that is not "news" according to the state's definition. Since the mid-2000s, the major Internet portals have actively recruited journalists to serve as top-level executives and editors—positions responsible for steering the online news service. Despite the expansion of journalism education and the acceleration of media marketization, competent media practitioners were in short supply in the mid-2000s. A former chief executive at NetEase explained the hiring practices to me:

> In the mid-2000s, the top four Internet portals all direly needed well-trained and competent journalists to help develop Internet portals' online news service. We competed to hire journalists with working experience in successful market-oriented newspapers as that would help Internet portals to attract readers. These successful newspapers tended to be those good at producing critical news reports, as critical news reports, instead of reports that completely followed the party line, were what readers wanted to read. (Interview, July 2014, Beijing)

To recruit talented journalists, the major Internet portals turned to the most successful newspapers, especially the Southern Media Group and print media specializing in covering economic, financial, and business-related news, such as the *Economic Observer, Caijing,* and *Oriental Entrepreneur.*

As noted in chapter 4, the Southern Media Group, a press conglomerate belonging to the Guangdong provincial government, was regarded by media practitioners as one of the very few news organizations that attracted and trained competent journalists. The Southern Media Group publishes the outspoken *Southern Metropolis Daily* and *Southern Weekly.* Both newspapers were famous for producing critical and investigative reports, as well as for promoting citizen identity, civil society, rule of law, and constitutionalism. Although state agencies cracked down periodically on the Southern Media Group, its newspapers and journalists were highly valued in the newspaper and labor markets. In addition to the Southern Media Group, print media that specialized in economic, financial, and business-related news were also considered more outspoken and critical by the media profession and elite readers. Star journalists in the Southern Media Group and from a few economic news media thus became highly sought after, as they were considered to have the knowledge and expertise necessary to tap into readers' preferences and the news market. Furthermore, recruiting such individuals was relatively easy. With Internet portals' access to the global capital market, they were able to provide much more competitive packages than print media could. The huge readership of Internet portals and, therefore, the potential social influence was also attractive for ambitious journalists. In the mid-2000s, the Southern Media Group began losing experienced reporters. A large proportion of high-level positions in charge of Internet portal news services were filled by journalists who had previously worked for the Southern Media Group and other relatively critical newspapers. According to a former chief editor at *Southern Weekly* who had been working for the Southern Media Group for two decades, around two hundred employees at Southern Media Group moved to the Internet news sector between the mid-2000s and 2011.

I examined the background of all the editors in chief at the four major Internet portals from the early 2000s to 2015 to demonstrate the influence of outspoken newspapers on major Internet portals.[17] Since editors in chief steer the online news service, they play a critical role in shaping Internet portals' news production. At the top four Internet portals 43 percent of editors in chief had worked in the Southern Media Group, and 57 percent of the editors in chief at the top four Internet portals had worked in news organizations well known for critical news reporting. Three of the five editors in chief at NetEase came from the Southern Media Group. The editor in chief in 2015, Chen Feng, is one of the *Southern Metropolis Daily* journalists who covered the famous Sun Zhigang case in 2003. As I discuss in chapter 1, this case led to the overhaul of China's unconstitutional detention regulations. In addition, one of the five editors in chief at NetEase was a journalist at *China Youth Daily*, a publication well known for its critical news reporting and connection with the leaders of political reform in the late 1980s (Hassid 2008; Tong 2007). Two of the six editors in chief in Sohu came from the Southern Media Group. One of the six was a journalist at the *Economic Observer*, also an outspoken newspaper, while another served as the executive producer of *News Investigation* at China Central Television, a program famous for disclosing societal problems in China. The backgrounds of these editors in chief show that, although only a few Chinese newspapers actively produced critical news reporting, their journalists and editors went on to have a strong influence on Internet portals' news services.

Through the labor market, the social networks, professional ideals, and political orientation associated with news organizations well known for critical news reporting spread to Internet portals. These social networks included lawyers, legal scholars, commentators, and public intellectuals who collaborated with journalists. Reflecting on the loss of employees, a former editor in chief at the Southern Media Group said,

> Owing to the restricted ownership structure, there is weak connection between employees' economic gains and the success of news media. Our employees are willing to work here mainly because of their recognition of our values and professional ideals. Recently, my colleagues and I counted the number of journalists that we lost. A large proportion of executives and high-level editors in the four major Internet portals worked in the Southern Media Group. At first we felt very sad about such loss, but we realize that it is actually a good thing since our journalists spread elsewhere our core values, ideals, and commitments—building a civil society, enhancing citizenship rights, as well as promoting rule of law. Now many of our journalists take leadership in the Internet sector. They are in a better position to influence more citizens. With the spread of our journalists, we have more alliances elsewhere. (Interview, June 2011, Guangzhou)

The journalists who left news media and took leadership positions at Internet portals were aware of the national influence of such portals and the role they served as essentially national daily newspapers for general readers. There was variation in terms of whether Internet portals created a salient political identity, such as a more liberal or critical stance, as well as whether Internet portals formed a formal strategic alliance with liberal-leaning newspapers. But shared among the media professionals who took such leadership positions was a commitment to the idea of the rule of law, a belief in the importance of civil society, and a desire to help society identify problems and search for possible solutions.

This is not to suggest, of course, that actors operating within Internet portals had no political or economic constraints. As the vice executive of one Internet portal put it,

> For me the decision to move from the press to Internet portals was straightforward. I was amazed by the power of the Internet. When recruiting me, my boss showed me the company's web-traffic report. At that time, only China Central Television had that kind of influence. I was thrilled. For media practitioners, acclaims from the small media circle are not as much worth pursuing as social influence. Ultimately, we want to impact public opinion and how people think. We want to help to build a society in which universal values are respected and citizens have genuine rights. This is

indispensable for China's modernization. We attempt to help the society to identify problems and achieve a consensus through providing an information environment where citizens can evaluate competing viewpoints. We know we are an Internet portal with national influence. Of course, we are constrained by the government. The government does use us as a channel to promote official discourse and agendas, but we still have space to pursue our goals. . . . I benefit very much from my previous working experience. I received excellent professional training, while also cultivating friendship with my colleagues, journalists in other news media, and experts in other fields. These resources are precious for me. (Interview, June 2011, Beijing)

Although Internet portals regularly received instructions from state agencies, within the limitations set by the state, media professionals at Internet portals attempted to select news reflecting current problems in China—more specifically, news understood through the lens of citizens' rights. Editors at Internet portals were politically and economically motivated to reprint problem-oriented news, which tended to attract wide readership and trigger discussion, but they also believed that such news deserved public attention and discussion. Moreover, in many high-profile public events since 2003, media professionals at Internet portals worked with those at the outspoken newspapers and with legal professionals to mobilize support from citizens and influence the state's decision making.

This kind of cooperation has led to many public opinion incidents. For instance, in the Sun Zhigang case in 2003, the editor in chief of the *Southern Metropolis Daily* worked closely with editors at Sina to create the initial report. Sina then reprinted the *Southern Metropolis Daily*'s report immediately after it was published, to increase the event's national visibility. The triumph of public opinion in many public opinion incidents may appear to result from the unorganized and spontaneous action of netizens, but the collaboration of legal professionals and media professionals in newspapers and Internet portals actually plays a crucial role in setting the public agenda, framing issues, and mobilizing public opinion. This partly explains why public opinion incidents and critical news reports have clustered around similar concerns and issues since around 2003. In addition to reprinting problem-oriented news reports, some major Internet portals, such as NetEase, have also produced in-depth reports and analyses of various social problems. These Internet portals often invite lawyers, scholars, and freelancers to write commentaries.

OPINION LEADERS ON WEIBO

In addition to the mechanism of the labor market, social media—particularly Weibo—also helped to spread social networks associated with critical news reporting. Before the rise of Weibo in 2010, online forums were the main venue

where citizens expressed their opinion (Lei and Zhou 2015). Internet companies organized online forums according to discussion topics instead of users.
Users did not have straightforward mechanisms to follow other users, nor did
many reveal their offline identities in online forums. As a result, offline social
capital did not play a critical role in online forum interaction. Users built their
credibility and popularity mostly through writing. Online interaction was thus
relatively equal and disconnected from offline social capital. Before the growth
of Weibo, only some bloggers were loosely connected through hyperlinks to
their blogs.

Since then, the connection between Internet users and the role of offline capital in online interaction has changed significantly with the growth
of Weibo, which allows users to form connections by following other users.
Since most Weibo users follow celebrities and people in their offline social
networks,[18] fame and offline social capital largely influence online interaction.
Thanks to their fame, offline social capital, articulation skill, and access to
information, Big Vs—Weibo users whose identities are verified by Weibo
companies and who have a large number of followers[19]—became a distinct
group. The rise of Weibo ultimately led to the formation of extensive social
networks and, importantly, opinion leaders, who occupy central positions in
Weibo networks.

With the rise of Weibo in 2009 and before intensified crackdowns on the
Internet began in 2013, opinion leaders actively disseminated and commented
on facts and viewpoints. Their followers ranged from tens of thousands to
tens of millions. These leaders actively discussed public affairs and influenced
the formation of public opinion, which put pressure on the Chinese party-
state. For example, after the Wenzhou train collision that led to forty deaths
in 2011, the Department of Propaganda prohibited Chinese news media from
producing their own news reports, but many media professionals and opinion
leaders disclosed information about the incident and criticized censorship on
Weibo. Their messages gained wide resonance before being censored (Wang
and Xie 2012). In the 2013 *Southern Weekly* incident, many public opinion
leaders criticized the censorship practices of the propaganda department of
Guangdong Province, leading to protests in Guangzhou. Through forwarding
and commenting one another's posts, opinion leaders constituted tightly connected communities (Li 2012; Wu, Shen, and Zhou 2014).

Given the importance of opinion leaders in shaping public opinion,
scholars of communication studies in China raced to develop techniques that
analyze so-called big data to detect and monitor these leaders. Shen Yang, at
the Tsinghua School of Journalism and Communication, and Zhu Xuqi, at
the University of Science and Technology of China, established the Micro-
blog Communication Index (BCI), the largest online information dataset of
Weibo, WeChat, and app data. Their index takes into consideration Weibo

users' degree of activeness and dissemination. Degree of activeness considers the amount of posts that a Weibo user produces and the originality of his or her posts. Degree of dissemination examines how often a Weibo user forwards and comments on other people's posts, how often his or her posts are liked, as well as how often his or her original posts are commented on and forwarded by others.[20] Using Shen and Zhu's index, Wu Yingnu, Shen Yang, and Zhou Qin (2014) identified the top 207 Weibo opinion leaders in 2013. They found that the group consisted of government officials (4%), lawyers (4%), scholars (21%), media professionals (34%), entrepreneurs (18%), writers (15%), and actors and singers (3%). They also found that opinion leaders focus particularly on topics related to international relations, political issues, freedom of speech, law, and social conflicts. Since January 2015, Shen and Zhu, along with the Global Times Forum, have published a ranking of Weibo opinion leaders.[21] Their ranking is relatively transparent and reliable compared with others because Shen and Zhu's formula, calculation, and part of the data are open to the public.

To provide a more detailed analysis of opinion leaders on Weibo and show their connection with critical news reporting, I examined the background and posts of the top one hundred opinion leaders identified by Shen and Zhu in January 2015.[22] The group consists of party-state officials, mostly policemen and propaganda officials (6%), lawyers and legal scholars (10%), other scholars (14%), media professionals (31%), entrepreneurs (9%), writers (22%), and others (8%). The dominance of media professionals among the top opinion leaders is not surprising as they have abundant connections and sources of information. Before the rise of Weibo, active journalists leaked the results of their investigations anonymously on Internet forums when their investigations were censored. But with the growing popularity of Weibo, media professionals increasingly use their real identities to disclose information, thus giving the information greater credibility. These journalists also publicize the grievances of ordinary citizens. Similar to media professionals, writers also have strong writing skills that enable them to attract readers. The significance of lawyers, scholars, and entrepreneurs on Weibo is less self-evident. Understanding their role as opinion leaders requires an analysis of their political orientations and relationships with the press.

Analyzing posts of opinion leaders, I classified them into the following three categories according to their political orientation: political liberals, political conservatives, and others. By political liberals and political conservatives, I refer to people who agree or disagree, respectively, with constitutionalism and universal values on Weibo. By others, I refer to people who do not express their views on these issues on Weibo. Constitutionalism refers to the principle that the authority of the government derives from and is limited by the constitution. Universal values include protection of human rights, freedom, justice, equality, and so forth. The notions of constitutionalism and universal values are both related to the public dimensions of law, dealing with the relationships of the state and individuals. These two notions have been particularly contested and politicized in China because they are often associated with Western liberal democracy by Chinese opinion leaders, scholars, media, and the Chinese party-state (G. Yang 2013).[23] As I mention in chapter 4, the Department of Propaganda came up with the so-called "seven don't mention list" in 2013, identifying seven politically sensitive topics. Both constitutionalism and universal values were on the list. Although the CCP decided, in the Fourth Plenary Session of the Eighteenth Central Committee in 2014, that China should be ruled in accordance with the constitution, articles in the CCP's official newspapers and magazine make it clear that "ruling the country in accordance with the constitution" fundamentally differs from constitutionalism in that the former insists on the leadership of the CCP while the latter demands the CCP's subordination to law.[24]

My analysis found that, despite the CCP's ideological control and censorship, 58 percent of the top one hundred Weibo opinion leaders at the time were political liberals, while only 15 percent of these leaders were political conservatives. The timing of my analysis (January 2015) was after the Chinese state launched its "purge the Internet" campaign in August 2013 and arrested several opinion leaders, such as Xue Manzi and Wang Gongquan. This was also after the Chinese party-state's effort to use Weibo to create more "positive energy" (Shen and Wu 2014). Presumably, the percentage of political liberals among opinion leaders could have been even higher before the Chinese state's intensified crackdowns. As I show in table 5.3, among the Weibo opinion leaders who come from the legal field, 78 percent are political liberals; among the opinion leaders who are scholars in disciplines other than law, 69 percent are political liberals; and all of the entrepreneur opinion leaders are political liberals. I further examined newspaper databases to trace the connection of the lawyers, scholars, and entrepreneurs on the top one hundred opinion leader list with newspapers famous for critical news reporting. By connection I mean these lawyers, scholars, and entrepreneurs wrote articles for or were interviewed by the outspoken newspapers.[25] With only two exceptions, all the politically liberal lawyers, scholars, and entrepreneurs had working relationships with the outspoken newspapers in China. Many of these lawyers, scholars, and entrepreneurs began to work with the newspapers before the rise of Weibo and even participated in critical news reporting. These opinion leaders' visibility in the newspapers helped them to build reputations and fame beyond their fields, and Weibo only amplified this visibility. The connection between opinion leaders and media well known for critical news reporting also explains why critical news reporting and public opinion incidents converged in terms of their foci.

TABLE 5.3. Percentage of political liberals among opinion leaders

Occupation	Percentage of political liberals in each occupation
Government officials	17
Lawyers and legal scholars	78
Other scholars	69
Media professionals	58
Entrepreneurs	100
Writers	52
Others	25

In figure 5.1, I mapped the connection between the top one hundred Weibo opinion leaders using social network analysis. An edge between two opinion leaders is directional, showing that one opinion leader follows the other on Weibo. White, black, and gray nodes represent political liberals, political conservatives, and others, respectively. Squares, triangles, boxes, diamonds, and circles denote media professionals, lawyers and legal scholars, scholars in nonlaw disciplines, entrepreneurs, and others, respectively. Gray and black edges show "following" across and between people with the same political orientation, respectively. The graph shows that the connections between opinion leaders are highly associated with political orientation. Political liberals and political conservatives are clustered in the upper-left corner and in the lower-right corner, respectively, with others in between. There are denser connections between people with the same political orientation. The mostly connected nodes among the political liberals are a group of lawyers, scholars, entrepreneurs, and media professionals, including Liu Chun, a former editor in chief of Sohu, one of the top four Internet portals. As I have mentioned, many of these lawyers and scholars became known to the public as a result of their respective working relationship with some outspoken newspapers. The graph suggests that Weibo helps to consolidate and expand such social networks and communities. The visualization also shows that "others"—those who did not express their viewpoints on constitutionalism and universal values—tend to have more connections with political liberals than with political conservatives.

The above findings help explain why the Chinese party-state continues its efforts to suppress and co-opt opinion leaders. In a recent speech to the United Front Work Department in May 2014, President Xi Jinping said that the Chinese state should strengthen its relationship with three groups of people to form a "patriotic united front"—people who study abroad, representative people in new media, and entrepreneurs in private sectors. The second group is essentially opinion leaders and some entrepreneurs in private sectors. President Xi pointed out that the Chinese state should establish regular connections

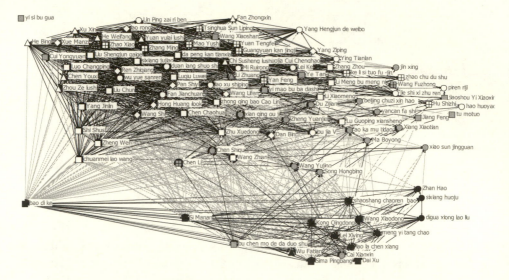

5.1. Networks of Weibo opinion leaders, January 2015.

with opinion leaders and improve the state's online and offline interaction with them so that opinion leaders will help to purge the Internet and spread the "main melody" and "positive energy."[26]

Conclusion: Networks, the Market, and Political Culture

This chapter continues the narrative begun in chapter 4 regarding critical news reporting. In chapter 4, I show that the Chinese state's turn to law as a new mode of domination and its use of media to disseminate law created novel conditions for legal and media professionals to collaborate and produce critical news reporting in localities such as Guangzhou, where political and market conditions were more fragmented. Although outspoken newspapers and critical news reporting remained limited in China, social networks associated with critical news reporting spread to the Internet sector through the labor market and social media, thanks to the Chinese state's decisions to adopt the Internet and join the WTO. The Chinese state's boundary setting in the newspaper market to avoid undesirable political consequences inadvertently helped the major Internet companies to build their online news services and satisfy the demand for national market-oriented daily newspapers. In the end, journalists from the few outspoken newspapers took a considerable proportion of high-level positions in the top Internet companies that provide online news services and operate social media; some lawyers and scholars who collaborated with journalists for critical news reporting became opinion leaders on Weibo. Such processes greatly shaped public opinion incidents starting in 2003. Ironically, although the Department of Propaganda and other party-state agencies conducted propaganda, imposed censorship, and denounced political liberalism, political liberals had more influence on the Internet, even in 2015, after the Chinese state's crackdowns in 2013. The dissemination of liberal discourse and ideology, as well as criticism about social and political problems in China, heightened the Chinese state's concern about major Internet companies' "orientation problems."

Importantly, political liberals would not have become so popular and influential had it not been for the direct and indirect endorsement of Chinese citizens. As I have detailed here, Internet portals made hiring decisions based on their evaluation of whether media professionals could help to attract wider readership. As such, they recruited journalists from successful newspapers in the press market—those famous for critical news reporting. Readers played a crucial role in determining the success of newspapers. In addition, whether Weibo users could become opinion leaders largely depended how often their posts were liked, forwarded, and commented on by other users. How the online space was structured thus partly reveals the political preferences of Chinese citizens, which is the focus of the next chapter.

The findings of this chapter help us reconsider the consequences of the marketization of newspapers that began to unfold rapidly in 1992. As noted in the beginning of this chapter, the most common argument about media marketization is that the process did not result in considerable political liberalization (Hassid 2008; Stockmann and Gallagher 2011; Stockmann 2013; Zhao 2008). Briefly, previous work has focused more on how marketized newspapers in general are outspoken about important social problems (Zhao 2008) and how marketized newspapers directly influence the political attitudes of readers (Stockmann and Gallagher 2011; Stockmann 2013). Based on statistical analysis of surveys conducted in four Chinese cities (Chongqing, Shenyang, Foshan, and Wuxi) in 2005, Stockmann and Gallagher (2011) have shown that exposure to news reporting about labor law–related issues successfully promotes the image of a proworker bias in the law among citizens. They point out that the state was able to achieve its political goal because of the lack of conflicting sources of information and dearth of previous experience with the reformed legal system among citizens. Stockmann and Gallagher contend that, instead of bringing about political liberalization, media marketization turned marketized newspapers into better instruments of state propaganda. Such instruments enhanced the Chinese authoritarian state's legitimacy (Stockmann and Gallagher 2011; Stockmann 2013).

I do not dispute the empirical findings of the above studies, but I argue that their findings should be interpreted with caution. The studies are similar in that they assumed marketized newspapers could bring about political liberalization only through producing critical news reports and influencing their readers. My findings, however, show that the effects of media marketization were even broader. I argue that the limited liberalization effects in the newspaper sector traveled to and were amplified in the Internet sector. This is demonstrated by the fact that Internet portals that provide news services were mostly operated by proliberal media professionals who had previously worked for the few outspoken newspapers. In addition, the collaborative networks formed by proliberal journalists and lawyers in the newspaper sector later developed into networks of public opinion leaders who greatly influenced Internet users and played a crucial role in mobilizing the public and in producing public opinion incidents. Furthermore, critical news reporting and public opinion incidents had increasingly similar foci in the 2000s. Even though media marketization led to only a few outspoken news organizations, liberal and critical voices would not have spread significantly via the Internet had it not been for the social networks and cultural practices developed beforehand through media marketization. In fact, my findings complement Stockmann and Gallagher's work. Their studies were based on data collected in 2005 and did not consider the development of the Internet. As I demonstrate in the beginning of this chapter, based on survey data, Chinese media suffered from enormous loss of trust with the rise of the Internet in the late 2000s. As Stockmann and Gallagher point out, lack of conflicting sources of information partly account for why the Chinese state was able to effectively use marketized newspapers as instruments of state propaganda. With the rise of the Internet sector and the spread of proliberal social networks through the labor market and social media, Chinese people were able to receive more sources of information and different viewpoints.

6

An Emerging Online Public

Thus far, I have been describing the top-down process through which the Chinese state restructured legal and media institutions, as well as the various ways in which party-state agencies, newspaper organizations, Internet companies, media and legal professionals, and opinion leaders shaped this institutional process. Together, the Chinese state and various actors mediating between the state and citizens heavily influenced China's contentious public sphere, but ultimately, the rise of this sphere in the post-2005 period depends on the emergence of a politicized public. My analysis of *People's Daily*'s articles in chapter 2 suggests that a critical and opinionated public emerged with the rise of the Internet in China.

Indeed, around the mid-2000s, newspapers outside China began to report on a new social category in China: netizens. Netizens in China were depicted as a group with a new way of life and socialization. For instance, on December 13, 2003, the *Guardian* wrote:

> As a demographic group, China's netizen population is the first real post-Mao generation. They surf the internet for entertainment, news, job hunting, to send email, text messages and pictures, chat online, play games and sell secondhand items. The internet has become an integral part of China's urban youth culture along with mobile phones, computer games. . . . The loneliness of long hours of study and the strict school system means many turn to the escapism of the web to find friends. The phenomenon of internet friends, known as *wangyou*, is increasingly popular.

Other newspapers reported that Chinese netizens were capable of generating contentious actions. In Singapore, a *Straits Times* article, "Online, China's Protesters Are Too Loud to Ignore," on October 5, 2003, detailed netizens' angry response to a three-day orgy involving hundreds of Japanese tourists and Chinese prostitutes that ended on September 18, 2003, but quickly gained national attention. The date was already a sensitive one, identified by some as an unofficial "national humiliation day" given Japan's invasion of northeast China on September 18, 1931. It was not surprising, therefore, that the event sparked intense controversy; what was surprising was how and where the controversy played out. As the *Straits Times* noted:

> There was no protest at the Japanese Embassy, nor angry mass rallies, as there might have been elsewhere. Instead, tens of thousands of furious Chinese logged on to the Net and vented their anger in chatrooms and on bulletin boards. . . . It's debatable whether the sound and fury of China's online community reflects true public opinion. What is more significant is that netizens have become an immensely influential pressure group that the Chinese authorities have begun taking seriously.

In other instances of online outcry, netizens took on not only unruly foreigners, but also their own government. The *South China Morning Post*, for example, reported a case of netizens venting their fury toward the misbehaving rich and an unresponsive government on May 24, 2004:

> Su Xiuwen, allegedly the relative of an official, became enraged last October when a farm vehicle scratched the side mirror of her BMW. She slapped the farmer, jumped back into her car, and drove over a crowd of 13 farmers, killing the one who damaged her car. Su was handed a suspended sentence after paying compensation to the victims—reportedly due to political intervention. . . . After seeing the story on the website Sina.com, newspapers around the country ran with the news. Resulting chat room traffic and postings complaining about the light sentence and judicial corruption were soon exceeding 180,000 a day on some websites. A national uproar forced the government to reopen the case.

The article concluded that "the internet is fast becoming the tail that is wagging the communist dragon."

This chapter focuses on the emergence of this online public in China and delves into its relationship with the party-state and various intermediary actors (e.g., media outlets, journalists, lawyers, NGOs, public opinion leaders), as well as its interaction with legal and media institutions. I argue that netizens' everyday practices and participation in public opinion incidents facilitated the rise of contentious culture and China's contentious public sphere. Because the late 2000s were critical to the rise of an online public and the contentious public sphere, my analysis focuses mostly on this period. To depict a more comprehensive picture of Chinese netizens, I first draw on statistical data to describe their demographic background, social networks, political attitudes, and political behavior. Next, I describe their everyday practices and participation in public opinion incidents. I then examine the case study of a public opinion incident involving food safety, and show how netizens interacted with the Chinese party-state and various intermediary actors to *make* what happened a "public opinion incident." Finally, I draw on in-depth interviews with ordinary citizens to understand how netizens' everyday practices and participation in public opinion incidents contribute to politicization.

A Brief Description of Netizens in China

In China, people use the term "netizens" (*wangmin*) to denote Internet users. As figure 6.1 shows, the number of Internet users in China grew tremendously over two decades, especially in the late 2000s. By 2016, more than 720 million Chinese people were using the Internet, and the penetration rate—that is, the percentage of Internet users among the entire population—reached 52 percent (figure 6.2). Currently, more than 90 percent of China's netizens use mobile phones to surf the Internet. The demographic characteristics of netizens has changed significantly over time, shifting increasingly away from the educated, and spreading more and more from urban to rural areas. As a result, digital inequality has been decreasing over time, although it still exists. Before 2002, the largest group of netizens was college educated. Between 2002 to 2010, people with high school education constituted the largest group. Since 2011, however, people with middle school education became the largest group of netizens (around 37%). As figure 6.3 shows, since 2011, the percentage of netizens with college education has remained stable (around 10% of Internet users). This demographic change is important to understanding the

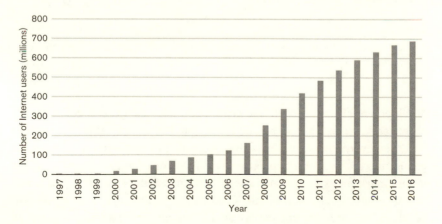

6.1. Number of Internet users in China, 1997–2016. *Source:* China Internet Network Information Center.

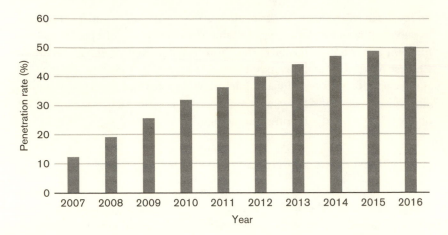

6.2. Penetration rate of Internet use, 2007–2016. *Source:* China Internet Network Information Center.

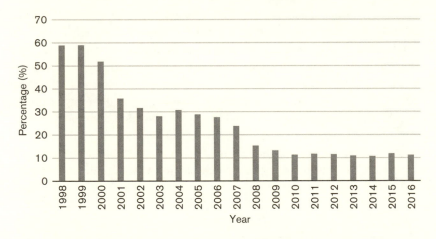

6.3. Percentage of Internet users with college education, 1998–2016. *Source:* China Internet Network Information Center.

development of China's contentious public sphere, for, I argue, demographic characteristics partly account for netizens' practices. Despite this demographic shift, however, other things have not changed: Internet users still tend to be young, and the two most popular activities netizens conduct online are using instant messengers to communicate with friends and reading Internet news.[1]

Since Internet users and China's contentious public sphere grew tremendously in the late 2000s, I focus here on the demographic characteristics, social networks, political attitudes, and political behavior of Chinese netizens during this period. I analyzed three nationally representative survey data sets: the

2008 China Survey, the 2007 China World Value Survey, and the 2008 Asian Barometer Survey. Combining these provides a comprehensive understanding of Chinese netizens and enables me to check the consistency of my findings. The 2008 China Survey was conducted by Texas A&M University. It included respondents eighteen years old and older and found that 12.10 percent of respondents used the Internet. Netizens' average number of years of education was 11.6 years, significantly higher than non-Internet users (7.2 years). Netizens' average age was 31.1 years old, younger than non-Internet users (47.9 years old). Of the interviewed respondents, 6.57 percent (i.e., 54.50% of netizens) read and commented about political issues or national affairs using social media. Of this group of people, 55.34 percent were male. This group's average age was 30.2 years old, younger than other Internet users (31.1 years old) and non-Internet users (47.9 years old), and 37.40 percent of this group had a college education. In comparison, only 33.96 percent and 1.97 percent of other Internet users and non-netizens, respectively, had any college education. The survey thus suggested that netizens, especially the population that used social media to read and write about political issues in the late 2000s, tended to be young and highly educated.

The data also revealed that netizens were more likely than non-netizens to have large social networks; netizens had more daily interaction with people. The main difference in social networks between netizens and non-netizens with similar demographic backgrounds, levels of life satisfaction, and degree of political interests was that netizens tended to have more nonkin in their social networks. They were also more likely to interact with people with political and social resources, such as party-state leaders, lawyers, and journalists (see tables A6.1 and A6.2 in the appendix). These findings confirm theories suggesting that the Internet could facilitate and broaden social interaction (Benkler 2006).

Statistical analysis also shows that netizens, especially those using social media to read about political issues and national affairs, tended to have different expectations and evaluations of Chinese state and society, in comparison with non-netizens, controlling demographic factors like age, education level, and gender (see tables A6.3 through A6.5 in the appendix). Similar to other research that has analyzed the same data set (Tang, Jorba, and Jensen 2012), I found that netizens were less trusting in political institutions. I also found that netizens were more likely to think citizens should oversee the government and more likely to disagree with the Chinese state's main political agenda and ideology. Whereas the Chinese government prioritized social stability above all else, for example, netizens were more likely to disagree with such prioritization, particularly if it meant prohibiting demonstration. Netizens tended to disapprove of one-party rule and to consider improving democracy a critical priority. They also tended to be more politically vocal and active (see tables A6.6 and A6.7 in the appendix). This could be related to the fact that netizens also tended to feel more politically efficacious and actually believed they could influence politics (Tang, Jorba, and Jensen 2012). Rather than keeping silent about grievances and problems, netizens were more likely to discuss political issues and join petitions. They were also more likely to contact government officials, media, and NGOs to express their viewpoints. This finding could partly explain why netizens were more likely to interact with party-state leaders, journalists, and lawyers.

I also analyzed the 2007 China World Value Survey (2007 WVS), the questions of which were designed to systematically examine political beliefs. In the 2007 WVS data set, the target population included adults between the ages of eighteen and seventy. Subjects who responded using the Internet to obtain information in the week prior to taking the survey were coded as netizens. Subjects who did not constitute netizens but reported using newspaper, news broadcasts on radio or TV, printed magazines, or in-depth reports on radio or TV to obtain information were coded as traditional media users. Subjects who were neither netizens nor traditional media users were coded as nonmedia users. The three groups are *mutually exclusive*. It should be noted that *all* the netizens also obtained information from traditional media as well. Descriptive statistics of basic demographic variables of netizens, traditional media users, and nonmedia users is presented in table 6.1. Details regarding the statistical methodology I applied are in the appendix.

I identified three types of respondents in terms of political beliefs: "the contentious," "the conformist," and "the apathetic." The apathetic compose 33.1 percent of the survey sample. People in this group tended to be less opinionated regarding the norms of democracy and unwilling to participate in collective action; they also tended to evaluate the Chinese state very highly.

TABLE 6.1. Descriptive statistics of basic demographic variables

2007 WVS (N = 1,576)	Netizens (11.93%)	Traditional media users (71.57%)	Nonmedia users (16.50%)
	Mean(SD) or %	Mean(SD) or %	Mean(SD) or %
Female	0.48(0.50)	0.51(0.50)	0.64(0.48)
Age	34.98(11.47)	45.38(12.96)	48.07(13.02)
Education			
No formal school	2.13	22.16	54.23
Completed primary school	6.91	28.37	25.77
Completed secondary school (technical, vocational)	25.53	13.30	4.62
Complete secondary school (university preparation)	21.28	33.24	15.38
College degree and above	44.15	2.93	0.00

The apathetic had very few comments on the norms of democracy. In terms of their evaluation of the status quo, they gave fairly *positive* evaluations of concrete institutions, including TV, police, courts, the central government, and the party, but their substantive response rates remained low when they were asked to evaluate *abstract* concepts, such as democracy and human rights protection in China. A large proportion of the apathetic explicitly rejected participation in collective action.

The conformist and the contentious make up 42.4 percent and 24.5 percent of the survey sample, respectively. Unlike the apathetic, the conformist and the contentious were politically opinionated. Both groups tended to support the norms of democracy and express higher willingness to participate in collective action. Despite their similarity, however, the conformist and the contentious differed strikingly in their assessment of political reality. The contentious supported the norms of democracy, had relatively negative evaluations of the party-state and political conditions, and were willing to join collective action. By contrast, the conformists thought highly of the party-state and did not see many problems with human rights protection or democratic conditions in China, although they also supported democracy and said they would like to participate in collective action. I name this group "conformist" because of their attitudes toward the party-state. The evidence demonstrates that even though the contentious and the conformists both supported the norms of democracy and were politically active, they had very different understandings of democracy. The contentious were more likely to look to the government for liberalization or democratization, whereas the conformists were more likely to support the status quo and regard the CCP as representative of democracy.

After identifying these types, I then explored whether they could be predicted by media embeddedness—that is, the means by which respondents engaged with media. I tabulated types of political belief by media embeddedness in table 6.2. At first glance, netizens, traditional media users, and nonmedia users had notably different patterns of political beliefs. Most striking, a majority of netizens, 59.57 percent, fell into the category of the

TABLE 6.2. Type of political belief by media embeddedness

Type of political belief	Media embeddedness			
	Netizens (%)	Traditional media users (%)	Nonmedia users (%)	Total (%)
Contentious	59.57	20.83	14.62	24.43
Conformist	32.98	47.25	30.00	42.70
Apathetic	7.45	31.91	55.38	32.87

contentious, while only 20.83 percent of traditional media users and 14.62 percent of nonmedia users belonged to this group. The results of multinomial logit latent class regression are presented in table A6.11 (appendix). They suggest a statistically significant association between being a netizen and holding specific types of political beliefs. Compared with traditional media users and nonmedia users, netizens were generally more likely to belong to the ranks of the contentious versus the conformist and the apathetic, controlling for other covariates, including gender, age, education, income, employment, occupation, subjective class, party membership, interests in politics, and life satisfaction.

The results of logistic regression regarding participation in collective action are reported in table A6.12 (appendix). Being a netizen versus a traditional media user or a nonmedia user had a higher probability of joining in boycotts or signing a petition, controlling for other factors. Since political beliefs are expected to be related to political action, I incorporated political beliefs into the analysis. The significance and magnitude of coefficients remained fairly stable after political beliefs were added to the model. Accordingly, being a netizen was not only associated with political beliefs, it also increased the likelihood of *actual* participation in collective action as well.

Finally, I analyzed the 2008 Asian Barometer Survey. This survey contains several questions related to perceptions of the Chinese state's legality; this allowed me to examine the relationships between Internet use, perception of the government's legality, and trust in the government and political regime. I present basic descriptive statistics in table A6.13 (appendix). I first examined the relationship between respondents' main source of political information and their perception of the government's legality. I found that respondents whose main source of political information was the Internet were more likely to think that government officials withhold information, that the central government does not always follow the law, and that local government could be corrupt (table A6.14, appendix). In contrast, respondents who relied on television as their main source of political information were less likely to think that the central government does not always abide by law and that government officials at both local and central levels could be corrupt.

I also found that perception of the government's corruption, violation of law, and withholding of information had constant negative effects on trust in all kinds of institutions (table A6.15, appendix). Specifically, when a respondent believed that local or central governments withheld information, violated law, or were corrupt, he or she was less likely to trust the central government, local government, and courts. That respondent was also less likely to believe the current form of government was the best for the Chinese people. The effect of Internet use on trust in political institutions was mainly mediated by perception of the government's legality.

Everyday Practices: Encounters with Grievances and Community Building

I now turn to Chinese netizens' everyday practices between the 1990s and the 2000s. Netizens became highly active soon after China connected to the Internet in 1994. In the 1990s and early 2000s, they used bulletin board system (BBS) forums, newsgroups, mailing lists, and online chat rooms to exchange information and discuss issues related to history, domestic and international affairs, literature, and hobbies, while also building communities. With limited channels of political participation, Chinese netizens found reading and discussion online to be exciting activities (Yang 2009). They were also quick to demonstrate considerable technological and intellectual savviness, in part because the earliest netizens tended to be highly educated elites, as discussed in the previous section.

I argue that airing and encountering grievances and building communities were among the most salient aspects of netizens' activities between the 1990s and the 2000s, and that these two aspects were closely related. As I note in chapter 5, soon after China connected to the Internet, the latter became a venue where netizens nursed and aired nationalistic sentiment and grievances against foreign countries, foreign companies, separatists, and even the Chinese government itself (Hughes 2007; Wu 2007). When geopolitics came to the foreground, netizens were active in voicing support for the Chinese nation. But in addition to participating in nationalism, Chinese netizens were also attentive to an increasingly wide array of problems, grievances, and political issues between the 1990s and the 2000s, such as censorship, discrimination, corruption, protection of vulnerable groups, rights defense, and environmental issues, articulated in terms of their own and other people's experiences (Yang 2009). China's drastic economic and social change as well as the rising legal and rights consciousness among citizens gave rise to these problems and grievances as well as awareness of them, which gradually converged under the umbrella of rights defense, or rights protection, post-2005. Reading about, discussing, and helping to address these grievances became part of netizens' everyday practices. Active netizens, NGOs, rights defense and public interest lawyers, journalists, mass media, and Internet portals helped to accentuate the relevance and importance of these issues to Chinese netizens. The issues also gained resonance because they had clear emotional and moral appeal as well as legal justification. In the process of airing, discussing, and addressing grievances, various communities flourished and overlapped. Here, I discuss examples that illustrate how certain grievances—censorship, discrimination against hepatitis B patients, protection of vulnerable groups, corruption, and environmental problems—became resonant among netizens, connected to rights defense, and facilitative of community building.

Censorship was one of the first types of grievance seized on by netizens. The Internet was seen, ideally, as a space of freedom, yet netizens soon recognized the omnipresence of state power and restrictions on this space in China. The Chinese state swiftly developed control mechanisms after connecting the country to the Internet. As early as 1996, the Chinese government was instructing universities to temporarily shut down popular BBS sites and other controversial forums to contain anti-Japanese discourse and sentiment. In the late 1990s, China set up the famous Great Firewall of China, a series of blocks and filters to prevent netizens from accessing undesirable content and information (Reed 1999). Censorship was not only built directly into the technology, but also imposed through plentiful laws and regulations. The government developed extensive regulations aiming to control Internet content in the early 2000s (Yang 2009). These laws and regulations were implemented by the government's law enforcement agencies and Internet content providers (ICPs). The law enforcement agencies policed netizens' behavior, while the government reviewed ICPs' licenses and imposed liability on them to ensure they would properly censor information.[2]

Early Chinese netizens, however, drew on their high levels of education to devise various strategies to eschew state censorship and control—strategies sociologist Guobin Yang terms "everyday forms of resistance" (Yang 2009, 55). By the late 1990s, Chinese netizens were already adept at bypassing the Great Firewall. Netizens were not necessarily oppositional to the Chinese government, but their frustrations with censorship led them to both creatively circumvent and mock such state practices. Netizens created and remixed linguistic symbols and phrases to avoid censorship. They also produced satirical writings, forms of slang, and images that ridiculed the Chinese government and censorship. Producing and sharing these expressions of resistance forged emotional bonds among netizens—and, indeed, continues to do so today, particularly after the Hu-Wen leadership's "harmonious society" campaign to increase social stability and tighten political control in the mid-2000s (Tang and Yang 2011; Meng 2011; Nordin and Richaud 2014; Wang 2012; Xiao 2011).

Responding to censorship, Chinese netizens also began to assert and demand freedom of expression and freedom to access information based on citizens' rights in the late 1990s and early 2000s; some of them did this through writing petition letters and protesting online (Yang 2009; Zhou 2006). The leadership role undertaken by activists in terms of framing issues, initiating causes, and publicly disseminating relevant legal concepts since the early 2000s should not be overlooked. For instance, a document titled "The Declaration of Internet Citizens' Rights" was circulated and supported by many Chinese netizens and websites in 2002. This document demanded that the Chinese state acknowledge and protect free expression, freedom to access information, and freedom of association on the Internet. The document was jointly drafted by sixteen intellectuals, including prominent writers, constitutional lawyers, journalists, and economists. Some of these intellectuals were later invited by certain outspoken newspapers and Internet portals to serve as commentators. The cause was also supported by NGO activists, especially activists who worked on HIV/AIDS issues, such as Wan Yanhai of the Beijing Aizhixing Institute on Health and Education. Because the websites of HIV/AIDS NGOs were sometimes shut down by the government because of their dissemination of "sensitive" information, these NGOs were very critical of censorship.[3] Far from actually silencing netizens, then, daily censorship made the Internet an important venue where netizens could reconsider and negotiate their relationship with the state.

Another grievance with which Chinese netizens engaged in the early 2000s was discrimination against hepatitis B patients. It began with some hepatitis B patients establishing a website to form a supportive community. They shared their experiences, feelings, and grievances both online and offline. Many of these hepatitis B patients were college graduates who had been denied or removed from government and private employment because of their illness. When they pursued antidiscrimination initiatives, rights defense and public interest lawyers provided the patients with legal aid and helped them to file lawsuits against employment discrimination. Antidiscrimination causes were thus incorporated into rights defense activities. Mass media and Internet portals covered such lawsuits to disseminate legal knowledge and raise legal consciousness. In 2006, for example, rights defense lawyer Li Fangping represented a college graduate filing a lawsuit against the company that had dismissed him solely based on his illness. Widely covered by mass media and Internet portals, the case quickly received the support of netizens online. It was eventually selected by the *Legal Daily* and the All China Lawyers Association as one of the ten most influential lawsuits in 2006 in terms of improving lawmaking and judicial decisions as well as raising legal and rights consciousness, based on the voting of media outlets, legal experts, and netizens. The selection was sponsored and covered by Sina, a major Internet portal in China. This process shows how discrimination against hepatitis B patients became a public agenda through the building of communities and collective efforts of various actors.[4]

Netizens rallied around other disadvantaged or vulnerable groups, calling for the protection of their rights, a salient theme online. Consider, for example, netizens' support for HIV/AIDs patients. In the 1990s, illegal blood collection was rampant in rural Henan and Anhui, where many collection stations failed to screen blood donations. Contaminated blood transfusion practices led to a severe HIV/AIDS epidemic, particularly among peasants (Yu 2012). In the early 2000s, NGOs such as the Beijing Aizhixing Institute on Health and Education were actively involved in disseminating knowledge about HIV/AIDS, addressing discrimination, and helping patients obtain medical treatment and legal compensation (Jia 2011). NGOs relied heavily on the Internet to do this work. The Internet enabled NGOs to connect HIV/AIDS patients with one another and form communities, even though many of the patients were peasants with very limited education. Through websites and popular online forums, NGO activists publicized information about the epidemic and disclosed stories about how poor families in rural China were suffering from HIV/AIDS. Such stories touched many netizens and mobilized them to become volunteers and/ or donors for NGOs. Furthermore, because HIV/AIDS patients encountered many difficulties (e.g., suppression by the local government) in the process of seeking legal compensation, HIV/AIDS NGOs (e.g., the Beijing Yirenping Center and the Beijing Aizhixing Institute) began to work closely with rights defense and public interest lawyers in the mid-2000s. NGOs and lawyers collaborated to provide legal aid, using litigation to both help patients win compensation and publicize the issue. Framing the issue as aiding "the disadvantaged," or vulnerable groups, to seek "rights defense," NGO activists and lawyers were able to render the HIV/AIDS epidemic a public concern. In the process of providing legal aid, HIV/AIDS NGOs also emphasized that HIV/ AIDS patients were only one of many vulnerable groups in society, and they encouraged netizens and lawyers to help other such groups, such as migrants, defend their rights.

Corruption was another issue that captured Chinese netizens' attention (Yang 2009). As noted, growing corruption after China's economic reform led to the 1989 Tiananmen incident. From the mid-1990s onward, the number of petitions in Beijing continued to grow dramatically, and threats of social instability began to loom large (Ji 2005). More and more grievances were being caused by local government officials' corruption and their exploitation of peasants, mostly through illegal taxation and land seizure, as well as infringement of citizens' rights (Cai 2010; Man 2011; O'Brien and Li 2006; Tong and Lei 2014; Wang 1997). Such corrupt practices fueled, in turn, rights defense activities. Starting in the mid-2000s, netizens began to appropriate the official discourse that Chinese people had the right to form public opinion in order to supervise the government. They established "anti-corruption and rights defense" (*fanfu weiquan*) websites to oversee the government. Some rights defense and public interest lawyers served as legal consultants for these websites and provided legal aid. Petitioners and grievants disclosed government officials' corrupt practices on such websites and in other online forums, while also sharing their experiences of "rights defense." Their experiences were sometimes covered by newspapers and Internet portals, triggering widespread discussion. Because most of the grievants were peasants, laid-off workers of state-owned enterprises (SOEs), or migrant workers, anticorruption issues became closely associated with the rights defense of vulnerable groups.

Environmental issues have also been a major grievance for Chinese netizens. Starting in the mid-1990s, environmental NGOs and initiatives, such as the Friends of Nature, Green Earth Volunteers, and Green Camp, began to emerge and promote environmental protection. Many established websites and mailing lists to publicize their causes in the early 2000s. Environmental journalists were important participants in this process. For example, Wang Yongchen, a journalist at China National Radio, founded the Green Earth Volunteers. Along with Zhang Kejia, a journalist at *China Youth Daily*, Wang Yongchen established a salon for environmental journalists in Beijing under the Green Earth Volunteers (Calhoun and Yang 2007).The salon invited environmental experts to give monthly talks to journalists and facilitated information exchange between environmental NGOs and media outlets, with both parties using the Internet to disseminate information and reach other actors.

Beyond NGO activists and journalists, a growing number of ordinary citizens, netizens, legal-aid centers, and lawyers also used the Internet to make environmental protection a critical public issue. In the early 2000s, Chinese people began to complain about pollution in online forums in order to seek assistance. One of the most famous cases was a torts lawsuit filed by 1,721 villagers in Nanping County in Fujian against a chemical plant that produced potassium chlorate in the early 2000s. The chemical plant severely polluted forests and rivers, causing much illness in the village. After failing to obtain assistance from the local government, villagers posted complaints and photos in online forums. College students who participated in the Green Camp, an environmental protection initiative, saw the posts and contacted villagers, offering their help as volunteers. Ultimately, the students submitted an investigative report to the State Environmental Protection Administration (SEPA). The Center for Legal Assistance to Pollution Victims at the China University of Political Science and Law also stepped in to provide legal aid. The center worked with environmental experts, journalists, and lawyers, helping 1,721 villagers to collect evidence and file a torts lawsuit. The court finally instructed the company to cease pollution and compensate the villagers.[5] In this way, environmental protection and rights defense causes went hand in hand. The lawsuit was selected by the *Legal Daily* and All China Lawyers Association as one of the ten most influential lawsuits in 2005 based on the voting of media outlets, legal experts, and netizens. Legal experts considered the lawsuit an excellent demonstration of public rights defense.[6]

In sum, airing and encountering grievances and establishing communities were critical aspects of netizens' everyday practices between the 1990s and 2000s. As grievants of various types sought to claim and defend their rights with the aid of NGOs and rights defense and public interest lawyers, various kind of grievances converged under the umbrella of "rights defense" over time. As I note in chapter 4, state infringement of rights, the rights of disadvantaged groups, and civil society and political participation all constituted important dimensions of critical news reporting. They were recurring themes in netizens' everyday practices. The convergence of critical news reporting and netizens' everyday practices is understandable, considering that rights defense and public interest lawyers and journalists not only contributed to critical news reporting but also actively participated in the framing of grievances online.

Public Opinion Incidents

Chinese netizens' everyday encounters with grievances and community building laid the groundwork for heated contention and, ultimately, public opinion incidents between the late 1990s and the early 2010s. These incidents and the responses to them, furthermore, gave rise to China's contentious public sphere. In the absence of meaningful electoral battlefields and functioning institutions for political participation, the Internet became a major venue for various actors to influence the public agenda. In addition, because the formal institutions that did exist, such as the courts and the People's Congress, had limited capacity to address problems and grievances, many ordinary citizens as well as legal and media professionals, NGO activists, and public opinion leaders were compelled to mobilize public opinion (He, Wang, and Su 2013; Liebman 2011; Liu and Halliday 2011; Yang 2009). Public opinion incidents raised the probability that government agencies would respond to problems and grievances, even though the state's responsiveness was never guaranteed. As a result, it was not uncommon for actors to deliberately attempt to create public opinion incidents and mobilize the public in order to influence political and legal processes (Fu and Cullen 2008; Halliday and Liu 2007; He, Wang, and Su 2013; Liebman 2005; Liu and Halliday 2011; Stern 2011). Whether grievants, netizens, and other actors achieved their immediate goals, public opinion incidents provided a chance for them to contend with official discourse and to negotiate with state actors on important issues.

Scholars of communication studies in China define public opinion incidents as events that capture widespread public attention. In empirical analysis, scholars consider an event that generates more than ten thousand reports on Google and Baidu a public opinion incident (Tang 2015; Zhong and Yu 2010). Studies find that the number of public opinion incidents grew dramatically between the late 1990s and 2000s, particularly in the second half of the 2000s. There were around 160 public opinion incidents between 1998 and 2009 (Zhong and Yu 2010), and around 672 public opinion incidents between 2003 and 2014 (Tang 2015). Although the popularization of Weibo (microblogs) did contribute to this growth, the number of public opinion incidents had already increased greatly before Weibo was released in August 2009. Over time, the production of public opinion incidents has become an important cultural and political practice that puts enormous pressure on the Chinese government (Li, Chen, and Chang 2015).

THE SUBSTANCE OF PUBLIC OPINION INCIDENTS

In the late 1990s, public opinion incidents were primarily related to nationalist concerns and sentiments, but over time, domestic issues and grievances increasingly began to generate such incidents. Zhong and Yu's study (2010) finds that 21.5 percent of the public opinion incidents between 1998 and 2009 were about government officials' corruption and illegal practices; 17.5 percent concerned Chinese people's everyday well-being, particularly in terms of education, health care, housing demolition and relocation, pollution, and food safety; and only 9.0 percent of the incidents were about geopolitics and nationalism. Note that although the above classifications are mutually exclusive, in reality the situation tends to be more complicated. Grievances about housing demolition and relocation, pollution, and food safety are often entangled with government officials' problematic and illegal behavior. In addition, as I show later, how netizens define the nature of an incident can and often does shift over time.

Tang's study (2015) finds that judicial cases, malpractice of individual government officials, and government administrative measures generated a significant proportion of public opinion incidents between 2003 and 2014. The study also finds that 30.7 percent of these incidents were associated with peasants and workers—both groups considered by the online public to be "disadvantaged," or vulnerable, groups. In these incidents, netizens supported and argued for the rights and interests of peasants and workers. Tang argues that public opinion incidents in China are often related to legal institutions, citizens' political participation, and citizens' supervision of the government. Tang's findings are consistent with other studies that find that issues related to law, particularly citizen rights protection, illegal government practices, and legal disputes, have generated the most public opinion incidents (Li, Chen, and Chang 2014; Ru, Lu, and Li 2011). The above studies, as a whole, suggest the salience of law and rights, particularly citizens' rights vis-à-vis the government, in China's public opinion incidents. This is not surprising considering that various types of grievances online converged under the umbrella of "rights defense" or rights protection in the second half of the 2000s.

THE FORMATION OF PUBLIC OPINION INCIDENTS

Public opinion incidents between the late 1990s and the early 2010s usually developed along the following trajectory: First, an event or issue would be exposed by a few mass media outlets and/or by individuals on the Internet. Second, the event or issue would be discussed, interpreted, and amplified by netizens through the mediation of Internet forums, Internet portals, blogs, and/or Weibo. Third, the discussion would lead to wider mass media coverage and heated discussion among a broader public, eventually culminating in a public opinion incident (Li 2011; Tang 2015). In these processes, a variety of actors—mass media outlets, Internet portals, grievants, netizens, journalists, lawyers, NGOs, activists, public intellectuals, and public opinion leaders—worked together to shape public agenda and produce public opinion incidents. At the same time, the government agencies and business actors involved often tried to suppress public opinion incidents. When the government failed to suppress the exposure of an issue or an event, the government would then strive to propagate an official interpretation of the incident and shape it in a desirable direction.

When and how an event or an issue is disclosed is critical to the formation of a public opinion incident. Existing studies suggest that, despite state censorship, mass media outlets were the most important actors that disclosed the information generating public opinion incidents in China. More than 44 percent of public opinion incidents between the 1990s and 2014 came to light thanks to mass media outlets (Tang 2015; Zhong and Yu 2010). This shows the importance of critical news reporting to the growth of public opinion incidents and the contentious public sphere. Although only a few newspapers managed to produce critical news reports, some of these reports were still able to reach a wider audience and exert influence, especially when they were reprinted by Internet portals and aroused the interest of netizens. Studies also show that around 20–30 percent of the public opinion incidents were first exposed by individuals online, mostly in online forums and increasingly in Weibo (Tang 2015; Zhong and Yu 2010). In such scenarios, information was often disclosed by grievants, activists, or journalists who were not able to get their reports published because of censorship. By finding this alternate route, netizens mitigated the negative consequences of censorship and undermined the role of mass media outlets as gatekeepers.

Simply disclosing information and stories, however, did not guarantee that information would reach the public, let alone resonate with it. Internet portals, ordinary netizens, and public opinion leaders played a crucial role in amplifying the influence of an event. When Internet portals reprinted news reporting, an issue or event became more likely to reach the public and generate discussion. Therefore, journalists producing critical news reports sometimes worked with editors in Internet portals to maximize public attention before the government tried to censor their reports. As noted in chapter 5, the social networks and diffusion of culture between outspoken media organizations and major Internal portals increased the possibility that Internet portals would reprint critical news reports. In addition to Internet portals, netizens were also key players in the production of public opinion incidents. Between the late 1990s and the late 2000s, netizens' heated discussions in major online forums brought issues and events into the spotlight. After the rise of Weibo, Chinese netizens shaped the development of public opinion incidents through forwarding and "liking" posts. Over time, Chinese netizens developed a cultural practice called "surrounding gaze" (*weiguan*). Rooted in modern Chinese literature and culture, the term "surrounding gaze" originally referred to the phenomenon of a crowd of people gathering around a public spectacle.[7] Now the term is used to refer to the practice of paying collective attention to and discussing issues and events through the mediation of the Internet to generate collective power and bring about change (Teng 2012).

Finally, public intellectuals and public opinion leaders began to assert influence in the formation of public opinion incidents beginning in the mid-2000s. Between then and the early 2010s, public intellectuals and public opinion leaders used their cultural and social capital to grab netizens' attention, while also providing alternative discourse to compete with official discourse. As noted in chapter 5, some of these figures wrote commentaries for newspapers already known for critical news reporting. As a result, the collaborative social networks connecting public-spirited lawyers and journalists also extended to public intellectuals and public opinion leaders. This connection helped journalists and lawyers pursue their agenda. Before the rise of Weibo, public intellectuals and opinion leaders used blogs to disseminate information and their viewpoints. Weibo gave public opinion leaders enormous leverage to influence the formation of public opinion incidents. As a popular saying about Weibo notes, "If you have more than 10,000 followers, you are like a magazine; if you have more than 100,000 followers, you are like a metropolis daily; if you have more than one million followers, you are like a national newspaper; if you have more than 10 million followers, you are like a TV station."[8] The influence of public opinion leaders was further magnified by the dense connections among the leaders themselves. Public opinion leaders constituted connected communities. Leaders with similar political orientations tended to follow and forward one another's posts. In doing so, public opinion leaders were able to exert considerable influence in making public opinion incidents (Wu, Shen, and Zhou 2014).

Case Study of a Public Opinion Incident: The Sanlu Milk Scandal

To illustrate these interactive processes and the salience of law and rights in public opinion incidents, I discuss here a case study of a specific public opinion incident that received national attention: the Sanlu milk scandal of 2008. I examine how members of an online forum, the Tianya Forum, discussed various problems and ideas about law in relation to the incident.

In September 2008, a news report revealed that several infants suffered from kidney damage after drinking melamine-tainted milk formula produced by the Sanlu Group. According to the official estimate, at least 4 infants died and 860 babies were hospitalized, many from poor families. The Tianya Forum was the most popular, influential, and relatively diverse online discussion forum in China between 2008 and 2010. The forum was established in 1999 and owned and operated by the Hainan Tianya Community Network Technology Company. In 2005, Google and Lenovo invested five million US dollars in the Tianya Community, and by 2010 Tianya had more than 32 million registered users. Compared with other popular online forums, participants in Tianya were more diverse in terms of their political orientation. In 2009, Tianya was identified by the Chinese government as one of the major forums for the development of grassroots public opinion.[9] Research also indicates that the Tianya Forum was the core online communication network regarding public opinion incidents in 2008–2010 (Li 2011). Not surprisingly, given its level of influence, the forum attracted the attention of both the media and the Chinese state. Journalists regularly observed discussion in Tianya to stay abreast of potential news topics. Similarly, both central and local party-state agencies monitored discussion in Tianya regularly to acquire information about public concerns. The government also demanded that Tianya be responsible for censoring online discussion. Tianya hired full-time editors and part-time moderators to do this, but desiring to maximize profits, the forum also sought to create an environment for lively discussion that would attract and retain users and minimize the negative impact of censorship on users' participation.

It is difficult to collect precise demographic data about Tianya users, so I have relied on the estimates of the Tianya Forum itself, which collected self-reported demographic information from users for the purpose of marketing. In 2009, the estimated average age of users in Tianya was twenty-eight years old. About 75 percent of the users were between twenty-three and thirty-five years old. Around 60 percent of users had a bachelor's degree. The average Tianya user was more highly educated than the average Internet user in 2009.[10] The employees of the Tianya Forum reported that a large proportion of Tianya users resided in coastal cities, particularly in Beijing, Guangzhou, and Shanghai.

In short, users in the Tianya Forum were a very special group of Chinese citizens, but their lack of representativeness did not undermine their political influence. Although the media and the Chinese government are fully aware that individuals who read and discuss public affairs in online forums are not representative of the Chinese population, they still take the opinions and influence of these citizens seriously. In an interview, a former central-level propaganda official explained that representativeness is not a really relevant issue for the Chinese party-state. As the official put it, in the end, those who speak up instead of those who keep silent influence other people and bring trouble for the Chinese government.

I qualitatively and quantitatively analyzed online texts produced by Tianya participants between 2008 and 2011. In addition, I analyzed fifteen in-depth interviews with Tianya moderators and participants that I conducted in 2011. To better understand the political and discursive contexts in which the online public formed public opinion, I examined official discourse (texts produced by the *People's Daily* and Xinhua News Agency) and alternative voices such as lawyers, NGOs, victims' parents, and outspoken journalists, based on analysis of news reports and in-depth interviews. Finally, I analyzed how participants in Tianya engaged with official discourse and alternative voices, as well as how they collectively constructed a narrative of events. Please refer to the appendix for detailed information on data and methodology.

POLITICAL CONTEXT

The Sanlu Group was a company jointly owned by the Shijiazhuang city government in the Hebei Province and the New Zealand Fonterra Group. Beginning in March 2008, the Sanlu Group began to receive a growing number of complaints from parents who suspected that their children were becoming sick after consuming Sanlu's milk formula. After several months of internal investigation, on August 1, 2008, the Sanlu Group determined that Sanlu's milk formula, along with that of some other companies, was contaminated with melamine. The next day, Sanlu reported the crisis situation to the Shijiazhuang city government but begged the government to control the story and protect the company from public outrage. Together, Sanlu and the Shijiazhuang government decided to handle the problem quietly. Instead of making the information public and announcing a recall, Sanlu conducted a less extensive trade recall (i.e., recovering products from wholesalers) and explained that it was doing so only to provide better products for the 2008 Beijing Olympics. Although Fonterra, the New Zealand joint owner of Sanlu, began lobbying for a public recall as early as August 2, its suggestion was not adopted in Sanlu's board meetings.[11]

Sanlu wasn't the only actor aware of a problem. Parents of victims also complained to media outlets, but they, too, were unable to "blow the whistle" thanks to multiple layers of censorship. In July 2008, several journalists began to investigate the illness of infants in Hubei, Hunan, and Guangdong, and even considered Sanlu's formula as a possible cause, but the timing of events made whistle blowing extremely difficult. Prior to the opening of the Olympics in August 2008, the central Department of Propaganda was intent on creating a positive image of China. It prohibited news coverage related to domestic food safety problems, as such news would tarnish the country's reputation. Certain newspapers, such as *Southern Weekly*, were thus prohibited from publishing their investigative reports on Sanlu's problems. Censorship also operated at the local level. Both the Sanlu Group and the local government focused on their own interests and silenced whistle blowers. As a large state-owned business, the Sanlu Group was able to mobilize political connections and money to prevent local newspapers in Hubei and Hunan from covering the milk scandal. With its close ties to the Shijiazhuang city government, the Sanlu Group also received assistance from the government to silence the local news media there. These multiple layers of censorship delayed the disclosure of the scandal for almost two months.[12]

Both the New Zealand Fonterra Group and the Chinese press attempted to overcome this censorship. After failing to persuade the Sanlu Group and the Shijiazhuang government, Fonterra reported the scandal to the New Zealand government. Prime Minister Helen Clark decided to bypass the local government and inform the Chinese central government on September 8, but the Chinese central government still did not disclose the information to the public. The scandal was ultimately exposed by the Chinese press. After witnessing the suffering of young victims, some journalists decided to report on the problem. In late August and early September 2008, the *Changjiang Times*, in Wuhan, and the *Lanzhou Morning Post*, in Lanzhou, both reported that several children had developed kidney stones linked to milk formula. Still, the reports did not disclose Sanlu's brand name in order to avoid defamation lawsuits. It was Jian Guangzhou at the *Oriental Morning Post* in Shanghai who, finally, publicly linked Sanlu to the scandal on September 11. On September 16, the General Administration of Quality Supervision, Inspection, and Quarantine finally released its investigative reports, confirming that melamine had been found in baby formula produced by twenty-two Chinese companies. The scandal then turned into a lightning rod for heated discussion and evolved into a public opinion incident.[13]

In an effort to control the crisis, the Department of Propaganda and the State Council Information Office of the central party-state imposed censorship and initiated propaganda work to influence public opinion. They monitored developments closely to adjust their censorship and propaganda practices as needed. The propaganda system first ordered newspapers and online news providers to use news articles written by the *People's Daily* and Xinhua News Agency when reporting on the scandal. The propaganda system also took measures to minimize the negative impact. It instructed that reports on the Sanlu milk scandal were not allowed to appear in the headlines. News media and Internet news providers should not connect the Sanlu milk scandal to other food safety incidents or publish special reports on food safety issues. In addition, news media, Internet news providers, online forums, and blogs should not criticize the party-state—the scandal should simply be defined as the

Sanlu Group's problem. Furthermore, news media, Internet news providers, online forums, and blogs should not disseminate any information that would encourage calls for "rights defense" (*weiquan*) or petitions, as either of these outcomes, it was argued, would threaten social stability. After some of the victims' parents began to mobilize and initiate civil litigations, the propaganda system further prohibited discussion of these actions or the criminal charges imposed on the parents. The Department of Propaganda instructed media to publish reports that focused instead on the government and the health care system's efforts to address the problem. Online forums were similarly required to spread information that praised the party-state and the health care system.[14]

THE MAIN MELODY: THE CONSTRUCTION OF PROBLEMS AND LEGALITY IN OFFICIAL DISCOURSE

News reports written by the *People's Daily* and Xinhua News Agency were consistent with the Department of Propaganda's guidelines. According to official discourse, the Sanlu milk scandal was an isolated food safety incident. Connections to other food safety cases were avoided at all costs, and reports attributed blame to illegal milk farmers and the Sanlu Group specifically. The causal analysis was straightforward: first, market actors disregarded morality in their pursuit of market profits; second, government agencies had failed to adequately regulate and monitor market actors—more specifically, the government had failed to implement existing laws and regulations; and third, those laws and regulations were not comprehensive enough to prohibit various forms of harmful behavior. Official discourse was notably silent regarding the two-month delay before the scandal was disclosed to the public. Among the 161 articles that I analyzed, only one discussed this issue of timing. Instead, official framing emphasized that the Shijiazhuang government had lacked political sensitivity by paying more attention to the interests of business actors than to consumers' health.[15] Key here was the admission of problems with governance only at the *local* level, thus leaving the authority of the central government intact.

In the wake of the Sanlu milk scandal, the State Council classified the incident as the highest-level food safety incident and proposed various solutions, which were then disseminated by the *People's Daily* and Xinhua News Agency. Follow-up reports focused on the implementation of solutions, most of which were law related.

The first solution was free medical treatment. Official discourse emphasized that affected children would receive free medical treatment and examination, with all expenses covered by the government. Importantly, however, while the state highlighted free medical treatment, it simultaneously downplayed issues related to compensation, especially civil litigations. The few reports that touched on the issue of compensation made a point of praising the efforts of the dairy industry to take responsibility and establish a special compensation fund. Those reports also endorsed the fairness of the compensation packages provided by the twenty-two companies that had produced contaminated formula. The *People's Daily* published no reports that discussed civil litigation until March 2009, even though the scandal had broken in September 2008, and many lawyers and parents had attempted to file lawsuits immediately.

When the *People's Daily* finally did address the issue of compensation, it was in a very short piece that documented the conversation between Shen Deyong, the vice president of the Supreme People's Court, and users of the Strong Nation Forum, an online forum affiliated with the *People's Daily*. With the rise of online public opinion, the Strong Nation Forum sometimes invited high-level government officials to communicate with forum users to show the government's responsiveness. One user asked the vice president about the issue of compensation in the Sanlu case and complained that there was insufficient information. The vice president responded that more than 95 percent of the three hundred thousand patients had already accepted the compensation packages provided by the dairy industry, and that Chinese courts were "prepared to accept" civil litigations filed by those parents. The vice president's response obliquely referenced a gatekeeping procedure in Chinese civil procedure law that often drew criticism: the requirement that all cases must first appear before a special division of the court with the discretion to decide whether or not to accept them. Yet, even after the vice president said that Chinese courts were prepared to accept compensation cases, no subsequent article in the *People's Daily* ever reported on civil litigation related to the Sanlu scandal. This striking silence on compensation and civil litigation in the official discourse corresponded with the propaganda system's instructions to discourage any efforts to frame the scandal in terms of rights or the need to defend them.

The official discourse also highlighted punishment in accordance with law as a solution to the scandal. News reports written by the *People's Daily* and Xinhua News Agency stressed that the government would severely punish the actors responsible for the milk scandal. The Intermediate People's Court in Shijiazhuang sentenced three dairy farmers to death for adding melamine to milk and then selling the toxic milk. In addition to the dairy farmers, the court sentenced Tian Wenhua, the general manager of the Sanlu Group, to life in prison. Several other managers in Sanlu were also given sentences of varying lengths. In addition to controlling the judicial investigation, the central government handled the associated administrative responsibilities. Several officials in Shijiazhuang were removed from office, and Li Changjiang, the minister of the General Administration of Quality Supervision, Inspection, and Quarantine, was forced to resign.

The third official solution concerned the party-state's restructuring of the food regulatory regime. News articles reported an intensification of enforcement on the part of several government agencies, particularly the Ministry of the General Administration of Quality Supervision, Inspection, and Quarantine; the Ministry of Health; the State Administration for Industry and Commerce; and the Ministry of Agriculture. Reports also covered efforts to revise and enact existing laws and regulations. These efforts included the enactment of the Regulation on the Supervision and Administration of the Quality and Safety of Dairy and the Food Safety Law. Essentially, news reports conveyed the idea that the appropriate response was for the Chinese government to strengthen its regulation regime and ensure the enforcement of laws and regulations.

Computer-assisted content analysis confirms the Chinese state's emphasis on law in the official discourse. In news reports written by the *People's Daily* and Xinhua News Agency, the term "law" (*falu*) was ranked 16 out of 1,413 terms[16] (percentile rank: 99.99 percent) in terms of frequency. Based on the top one hundred terms that co-occurred most frequently with the term "law," the notion of law in official discourse was characterized by its association with food safety, responsibility, Chinese people, legislation, socialism, and "Chinese characteristics."

The terms "food" (*shipin*) and "safety" (*anquan*) were ranked 7 and 9, respectively. This shows that law was framed as a solution to food safety problems. The term "law" was also connected with responsibility (16, *zeren*) and supervision (12, *jiandu*), as well as with citizens (40, *gongmin*) and people (25, *renmin*). Law correlated strongly with terms regarding legislation (1, *lifa*), particularly legislative draft (4, *caoan*), regulation (7, *fague*), legislative review (11, *shenyi*), People's Congress (15, *renda*), and the Standing Committee of the National People's Congress (19, *quanguo renda changweihui*). This is consistent with my qualitative analysis, as the results of both analyses indicate the critical importance of lawmaking in the government's solution to the Sanlu milk scandal. Compared with terms related to legislation, terms regarding the judiciary, particularly trial (60, *shenpan*) and judiciary (66, *sifa*), were not so highly correlated with the notion of law. This also corresponds to my qualitative analysis and indicates that the Chinese state intentionally downplayed the role of the judiciary in addressing the compensation issue for victims. Finally, law was associated with socialism (8, *shehui zhuyi*) and "Chinese characteristics" (13, *zhongguo tese*). This suggests that official discourse attempted to defend China's legal system in relation to alternative models. As a whole, the results of the co-occurrence analysis suggest that law was framed in official discourse as rules enacted by the government according to socialism in order to supervise and address food safety problems faced by the Chinese people.

ALTERNATIVE VOICES

Despite censorship and propaganda, alternative voices existed beneath the main melody orchestrated by the Chinese party-state. Consistent with research showing that lawyers, media, and citizens attempt to mobilize public opinion in order to influence political and legal processes (Fu and Cullen 2008; Halliday and Liu 2007; He, Wang, and Su 2013; Liebman 2005; Liu and Halliday 2011; Stern 2011; Yang 2009), I found that volunteer lawyers, legal-aid NGOs, parents of victims, and a few relatively outspoken members of the media presented neglected facts and views to the public and mobilized public support. They believed support from the public would help victims get reasonable compensation. Some parents of victims created blogs to share their experience and gain public support.[17] Volunteers with legal-aid NGOs, mostly college students, helped to spread information about legal aid online. Through email communication and offline gatherings, legal aid NGOs were able to mobilize outspoken newspapers to report on compensation issues.[18] And, most important, the articles produced in those newspapers were further circulated in and through major Internet portals, particularly Sina, NetEase, Tencent, and Sohu. Editors of major Internet portals reprinted these candid articles out of professional and business consideration. On the one hand, they wanted to present readers with different perspectives; on the other hand, the editors also believed that reprinting articles published by outspoken news media would boost their websites' popularity and revenues.[19] Since around 80 percent of Chinese Internet users read online news in 2008–2009,[20] Internet portals played an enormous role in helping outspoken newspapers reach a broader audience.

Official and nonofficial discourses both addressed the problem of the Sanlu scandal and the appropriate solutions, but the latter deviated from the party-state narrative in several ways. Whereas official discourse focused on food safety problems, some outspoken newspapers considered the media's collective muteness a problem in itself. These newspapers included *Southern Weekly* in Guangzhou and some business-focused newspapers affiliated with central-level party-state agencies, such as *China Economic Times* and *China Enterprise News*.[21] In articles published in these venues, Sanlu and other businesses were criticized for using money to bribe news media, and the media and an Internet search engine company, Baidu, were accused of complicity in Sanlu's public relation crisis management. Yet, even these outspoken newspapers remained silent about the political conditions that had led to the media's collective muteness.[22]

The largest difference between official discourse and alternative voices centered on compensation issues, especially civil litigation. Because many of the victims came from lower-class families, the Open Constitution Initiative (*gongmeng*), an NGO in Beijing, provided legal aid and organized volunteer lawyers across China immediately after the Sanlu scandal was made public. In addition to the Open Constitution Initiative, several NGOs working on HIV/ AIDS and public health issues, such as the Beijing Aizhixing Institute on Health and Education and the Beijing Yirenping Center, also recruited rights defense and public interest lawyers to help victims. Nevertheless, the lawyers were quickly dissuaded from representing victims by the Beijing Lawyers Association, the Beijing Municipal Bureau of Justice, the judicial bureau in Henan, and the Central Political and Legal Affairs Commission. Despite such efforts at suppression, some lawyers still provided free legal aid and, with the help of liberal-leaning journalists, even publicized the difficulties they and the victims were facing.[23]

Some news articles published by outspoken newspapers did criticize the Chinese government's role in the problematic compensation process. For instance, an article published by *Southern Weekly* on October 2, 2008, reported that collective compensation could reduce individual costs, but that government handling and the marginalization of consumers in the process had led to misunderstanding and tension. A news article published by *Caijing* on October 7, 2008, pointed out that free medication provided by the government was a limited solution that did not cover victims' future medical expenses, parents' loss in wages, or lodging and traveling expenses. *Caijing* also reported that judicial officials in Henan harassed volunteer lawyers to discourage them from representing victims. The article further criticized Chinese courts for their refusal to handle any compensation cases. On April 6, 2009, the *Democracy and Legal System Times* (*minzhu yu fazhi shibao*) reported that a court in Shijiazhuang finally accepted a compensation case after many such cases had been rejected by other Chinese courts via the aforementioned gatekeeping procedure. But the article still predicted little success, given the difficulty that prior victims had collecting evidence and the fact that Sanlu had filed for bankruptcy. *Southern Weekly* also reported that the Shijiazhuang local court accepted compensation cases after the vice president of the Supreme People's Court told Internet users that Chinese courts were prepared to accept compensation cases, but the paper remained pessimistic about the outcome.[24] Nonetheless, *Southern Weekly* did note that the mere filing of litigation by sixty-three victims was an important event that could potentially push legal reform in China.[25]

Another important theme in the alternative voices troubling official discourse was the predominance of the "administrative state" over legislation, the judiciary, and society in general. Some newspaper articles pointed out that when the contamination occurred, businesses reported the problems only to local governments, which then reported them to high-level governments. Citizens were left outside the loop of this administrative process. The central government exercised its administrative power to discipline lower actors and expanded its administrative power through lawmaking. The judiciary and law were thus subordinated to and essentially put at the service of the administrative state. The process was so dominated by administrative logics that citizens were not simply neglected but actually stripped of their right to litigation. The news articles commenting on this suggested that the Chinese state should reform how it governs by giving citizens more power and redistributing power among its administrative, legislative, and judicial components.[26]

Some news articles even reported on how the Chinese party-state used legal institutions as well as criminal and administrative laws to retaliate against victims and NGOs. When these politically sensitive articles were reprinted by online news websites, many Internet users explicitly articulated their surprise that they were able to read such provocative stories. *Southern Metropolis Daily* published an article discussing how the parents of victims were suffering as a result of their efforts to pursue compensation. Because of Sanlu's bankruptcy, victims were unable to receive compensation through civil litigation, as their claims did not have priority over insolvency. The article also revealed government retaliation against victims' parents. Zhao Lianhai, the father of one victim, attempted to organize other parents and was subsequently arrested by the police for "disturbing public order."[27] This article was reprinted by the Internet portal NetEase.[28] Similarly, *Oriental Morning Post*, the newspaper that first disclosed the Sanlu scandal, criticized the party-state for its use of criminal law and the courts to repress parents' pursuing litigation.[29] *Southern Weekly* also reported that the Open Constitution Initiative, the NGO that organized volunteer lawyers to represent victims' families in the Sanlu scandal, was unreasonably accused of violating tax regulations by the Chinese government.[30]

THE TIANYA FORUM AS A COURT OF PUBLIC OPINION

Mechanisms

My analysis of textual data and in-depth interviews with fifteen Tianya users suggests that participants in Tianya made sense of the Sanlu milk scandal, related problems, and the role of law in the scandal using three mechanisms: *cross-temporality*, *cross-locality*, and *problem tracing*. Cross-temporality and cross-locality refer to the processes by which the public in Tianya discussed relevant events across time and localities. These events were usually either absent or peripheral in the official discursive space delimited by the party-state. Places outside China also played a significant role in discussion, as perceptions of institutions and life experiences beyond China were cited as representing alternate realities. As one twenty-two-year-old college student said, "It is impossible for one person to know or remember so many events. What is amazing about Tianya is that people can generate collective wisdom by contributing what they know to the community."[31]

In the process of aggregating cases and finding connections between them, Tianya participants drew connections between the repetitive occurrence of similar individual problems and deeper structural problems. In doing so, the perceived significance of problems increased, and participants clamored to identify underlying causes. I call this process *problem tracing*. Many of the interviewees pointed out that their interaction with other participants and their exposure to various ideas in the Tianya Forum alerted them to linkages between different cases, revealing the structural roots of problems, and enabling them to develop a more holistic understanding of social problems and law. One thirty-five-year-old taxi driver described the transformative process: "I used to see problems as a single dot, but I can connect them into a line and a plane after I knew more and more in Tianya."[32] I turn next to how the public in Tianya used these mechanisms to construct problems associated with the Sanlu scandal.

Problems

Although the Department of Propaganda did not allow the news media and Internet news providers to connect the Sanlu milk scandal with other food safety incidents, this was precisely where discussion in the Tianya Forum began. Once Tianya participants aggregated their collective memory of other food safety incidents, they soon declared that the Sanlu milk scandal was not just about food safety. Instead, participants described the Sanlu milk scandal as the tip of a giant iceberg comprising broader issues related to the safety and quality of products in general.

In the process of connecting the Sanlu milk scandal to other product safety incidents, Tianya participants also probed the causes of these recurring scandals. Like the Chinese government, the participants contended that businesspeople's (im)morality and the government's inadequate supervision were factors, but Tianya participants gave greater weight to the latter. Once they had identified the government's incompetence and regulatory inaction as the main cause of product safety issues, Tianya participants brought even more diverse cases into the discussion; for instance, the Wuwang Club fire and the Wenchuan earthquake in 2008 were cited as further illustrations of government failure. In the Wuwang Club fire incident, individuals who operated the night club failed to follow fire prevention regulations. When the fire began, many people were unable to escape as there were no adequate exits from the building. The participants in Tianya expressed anger and suspicion regarding the absence of government intervention before the fire incident. In the case of the Wenchuan earthquake, thousands of children lost their lives when inferior school buildings collapsed. Similar to the situation in the Wuwang Club fire, the government's inaction in Wenchuan before the earthquake was believed by the participants to have contributed to the loss of lives. In short, by expanding their discussions to include this wider range of concrete cases, participants in the Tianya Forum redefined the Sanlu milk scandal as a case that spoke more broadly to how government regulatory failure threatened life and health.

Having made this connection, the public in the Tianya Forum then asked another question: What explained the government's continual regulatory failures, especially its failure to regulate business actors? Not surprisingly, this question was not considered in official discourse. In the news written by the *People's Daily* and Xinhua News Agency, the government's regulatory failure was seen as an explanation for food safety issues, but it was not framed as a phenomenon requiring explanation itself. In contrast, discussion in Tianya framed the government's regulatory failure as a problem that needed to be explained and addressed. The consensus in Tianya was that government agencies did not have adequate incentive to enhance or implement regulations because they had a vested interest in protecting actors who violated laws or regulations. Many participants expressed their belief in and fury with the existence of extensive networks connecting government agencies and business actors. For instance, one participant commented,

> The institution in China combines political privilege and capitalism. . . . Companies can be exempted from quality examination as long as they bribe government agencies. . . . Government and business actors are so unified.[33]

The online public's belief in the collusion of power and money relied on and reinforced a dichotomy that classifies Chinese people into two antagonistic categories: the privileged (i.e., those within networks of power and collusion) and the disadvantaged (i.e., those outside networks of power and collusion). The discussion was thus expanded from the government's regulatory failure in a single instance to the much deeper problem of the collusion between political power and money. Once again, through the mechanism of problem tracing, the identified cause of the problem became a problem in itself.

Participants in the Tianya Forum then suggested that the government's monopoly over political power explained the prevalent collusion of power and money, since the government's political monopoly deprived people of their right to hold the government accountable. The participants stated that, in light of the government's failure to oversee its own actions and those of business actors, intervention from citizens was necessary. And yet, such intervention remained impossible as long as the government prevented citizens from exercising their political rights. "We will not be able to address food safety issues unless every citizen has rights to care about and strengthen food safety," said one participant.[34] Many participants expressed the opinion that China, like other countries, should have independent NGOs to help consumers obtain trustworthy information. They voiced frustration with the government's continuing grip on NGOs within the country. As one participant put it,

> Why can't we organize NGOs? Does that violate Chinese laws? NGOs can help consumers to hold businesses accountable.... Ultimately, the government is afraid that NGOs would subvert the state power.[35]

Participants also talked about not being able to express their fury or to influence the government's decision making by organizing and joining large-scale protests. As participants continued to discuss the causes of food safety problems, the issues at stake stretched beyond food safety to the Chinese state's political monopoly and citizens' lack of political rights.

The public in Tianya also discussed government control of institutions that could help citizens oversee the government, particularly media. Although a few outspoken newspapers identified the media's collective muteness as a problem in itself, they did not publicly criticize the state's censorship. Tianya participants, in contrast, had no problem condemning both Chinese media and the government for covering up the scandal and impinging on citizens' right to be informed. Stories about how the government restricted media coverage of Severe Acute Respiratory Syndrome (SARS) in 2003 were linked by Tianya participants to the media's early silence on the Sanlu milk scandal. The Tianya public criticized the government's restricting freedom of speech and controlling media, while certain Chinese media were praised for their coverage of the milk scandal, and news reports from these outlets were disseminated within the forum.

Considering diverse forms of restrictions on citizens' rights, many participants in the Tianya Forum concluded that the various problems associated with the Sanlu milk scandal were ultimately rooted in the political regime. Again and again, participants asserted, "The problem is about the regime." The Sanlu milk scandal was understood by the online public as a case demonstrating "how the political regime has facilitated the privileged to harm the disadvantaged."[36] In other words, the online public collectively situated the Sanlu milk scandal in relation to cases across time and locality, while also linking the problem to deep-rooted structural issues. Through such processes, the problem eventually escalated from a specific food safety incident to a more generalized pronouncement about China's political regime.

Law

Next, I move to discourse related to law in Tianya, which was intertwined with other aspects of the Sanlu milk scandal. Here, I focus specifically on how participants framed and understood legal norms, legal institutions, and legal ideologies when these topics came up in their discussions. Tianya participants saw the government's continual regulatory failures as the direct cause of the Sanlu milk scandal. Furthermore, they argued that the regulatory failures evidenced in Sanlu and other food safety scandals resulted not so much from insufficient laws and regulations but from inadequate enforcement of these laws. There was a strong consensus among participants in the Tianya Forum on this point, and many participants noted that this failure eroded the credibility of the Chinese government. As one participant commented,

> The government made a lot of laws. . . . but the truth is that half of the laws are never implemented. This tendency has greatly weakened the authority of law.[37]

The insufficient enforcement of law led the Tianya public to reflect much more broadly on the nature and legitimacy of legal authority in China. Many participants expressed the belief that not just law enforcement, but the operation of legal institutions in general was biased because legal norms and legal institutions were essentially government instruments used to achieve government goals.

Tianya participants cited many concrete cases to contend that the Chinese government tarnished the independence of the courts to achieve its goals. First, participants claimed that courts were often used to find scapegoats for powerful actors, such as when the Shijiazhuang Intermediate People's Court's sentenced three dairy farmers to death but gave managers at Sanlu prison sentences of varying lengths. The disparity of these penalties was viewed by the Tianya public as a noxious effort on the part of the government to hide the truth and to scapegoat the least powerful actors. As one participant noted, "Not surprising at all. I already knew that people without power and money will turn out to be scapegoats and be punished severely by the court."[38] Many participants also argued that the government disregarded judicial independence and procedural requirements in criminal trials. The incident reinforced participants' belief that the privileged—those within networks of power and money—would always benefit from the government's regulatory failures, while those outside such networks would take the blame and receive harsh sentences from the court.

Second, Tianya participants claimed that the courts intentionally discouraged and even disabled the disadvantaged from pursuing compensation. Although official discourse avoided the subject of compensation and civil litigation, the alternative accounts produced by victims' parents, lawyers, and outspoken newspapers circulated and were featured prominently in Tianya Forum discussions. Participants complained that many parents of sick children were unable to obtain fair compensation because Chinese courts simply used their discretionary power to refuse to accept the cases. They also criticized the Chinese government for harassing lawyers who represented victims. Participants in Tianya identified these as common methods used by the Chinese government to maintain "social stability" and force victims to accept unreasonable compensation, thus benefiting business interests. Echoing the critiques voiced by volunteer lawyers, many participants in Tianya thought that victims' parents only accepted the unreasonable packages proposed by the dairy indus-try given the complete absence of other meaningful choices. One participant commented, "I feel totally weird. Why don't victims file lawsuits against the evil business? It is because the emperor said no."[39] The famous McDonald's coffee case (*Liebeck v. McDonald's Restaurants*, 1994) in the United States—in which the plaintiff received substantial compensatory and punitive damages—was cited by a number of online participants to emphasize the contrasting failure of Chinese courts to protect the rights of Chinese people.

Third, the Tianya public argued that the Chinese party-state used the courts to punish victims when they attempted to restore their rights. In the Sanlu milk scandal, Zhao Lianhai, the father of one of the victims, organized other parents of sick children to pursue compensation. Although Zhao was careful to avoid criticizing the Chinese government, he was charged with disturb-ing social order and given a two-and-a-half-year prison sentence. "Zhao is a father, husband, and citizen of the Republic who is imprisoned because of his pursuit of rights. His fate is our fate," one participant contended.[40] Considering Zhao's situation and similar stories involving Chinese citizens who pursued their rights, many participants concluded that the Chinese state illegitimately used law and the courts to punish rightful resisters. Significantly, criticism online led to protests offline. Around twelve Tianya participants actually went to the People's Court in the Daxing District of Beijing in November 2010, dur-ing Zhao's trial, and even organized fundraising activities for Zhao's family.[41]

Participants in Tianya also contended that the government used not only the courts but the lawmaking process in general as an instrument to serve its goals. In the midst of the Sanlu milk scandal, the central government set a maximum limit of 1 mg/kg and 2.5 mg/kg for melamine in powdered baby formula and in other dairy products, respectively, as there were no limits specified before. Far from pacifying public fury, the move provoked wide-spread criticism. This time, participants pointed to regulations on melamine in the United States, Hong Kong, Taiwan, New Zealand, and the European Union (EU). Most participants argued that, in comparison with standards elsewhere, the Chinese standard was unreasonably favorable to milk produc-ers; moreover, they linked this standard to malicious intent. For example, one participant stated, "Law is an instrument of the ruling class. Now businesses can add toxic materials to milk legally. This is Chinese law—very Chinese."[42] Many participants argued that the government had simply legalized previously illegal practices to protect businesses.

The Tianya public was particularly infuriated by the differences in how the tainted milk crisis was handled in China versus Taiwan. Because polluted pow-dered milk was also exported from China to Taiwan, the Taiwanese govern-ment initiated administrative measures to deal with the problem. At first, the Department of Health in Taiwan determined that all polluted dairy products had to be recalled, but it later changed its policy, raising the legally acceptable limit of melamine from zero to 2.5mg/kg. The policy shift provoked strong public criticism and ultimately led to the resignation of the minister of the Department of Health and a return to the original zero-tolerance standard. Participants in Tianya found it ironic that a government official in the ROC stepped down because of problems originating from the PRC. They asserted that differences between the two political regimes explained why ROC government officials were held responsible for problematic regulations, while PRC officials were not. By comparing lawmaking processes and the substance of regulations across localities, the public in Tianya compiled and shared evidence that supported an understanding of law as serving only the interests of the Chinese government and those with connections to the government.

Recognizing that the Chinese government used law as an instrument to achieve its ends, Tianya participants concluded that "rule of law with Chinese characteristics"—a phrase coined by the Chinese government to justify differences between legal systems in China and in other countries—was essentially the absence of rule of law and an opposition to justice, citizens' rights, and conscience. Although the Chinese government encourages people to use law as a weapon to protect their interests (Gallagher 2006), Tianya participants contested this rhetoric and argued that law is actually an instrument for the government. Participants juxtaposed "rule of law with Chinese characteristics" with rule of law elsewhere and used the latter as a normative standard to measure the former. From the Taiwanese case, the participants saw the critical role of law in holding the government accountable, as well as the role of democratic elections in empowering citizens. Some participants also praised the legal system in Japan and argued that Japan's democratic constitutionalism explained the strength of the Japanese legal system. The American case was also mentioned frequently in discussions to demonstrate how legal institutions could and should protect citizens' rights. Certain participants argued that if the Sanlu case had occurred in the United States, lawyers for the victims would have been able to file and win lawsuits. The online public connected the political regime in China to what they saw as the country's relative lack of rule of law and concluded that law in China would remain ineffective and unjust as long as the current political regime remained the same.

I turn now to the results of computer-assisted content analysis about the conception of law. Law was central in the discursive space of the Tianya Forum. The term "law" (*falu*) was ranked number 39 out of 2,615 terms (percentile rank: 98.5%). The top one hundred terms associated most frequently with law in the Tianya Forum show that, while the notions of law in official discourse and in Tianya were both strongly connected to terms regarding responsibility (2, *zeren*), Chinese people (14, *renmin*; 30, *baixing*), and citizens (41, *gongmin*), the notion of law in Tianya was uniquely linked to citizens' rights, the moral quality of law, problems associated with law, and a wide range of institutions and places outside China. Although the notion of law frequently co-occurred with "people" and "citizens" in official discourse, the concept of rights did not. In contrast, rights (5, *quanli*) was one of the terms that co-occurred with law most frequently in Tianya, especially political rights (*zhengzhi quanli*) and citizens' rights (*gongmin quanli*). This suggests that, for the Tianya public, the meaning of law centered on law's protection of rights. In addition to rights, the notion of law in Tianya was related to normative values, particularly equality (28, *pingdeng*), freedom (38, *ziyou*), fairness (78, *gongping*), independence (84, *duli*), and justice (91, *zhengyi*). As such, law was expected by Tianya participants to conform to these normative values. Notably, the co-occurrence analysis reveals that none of these values was among the one hundred most frequent terms that co-occurred with the term "law" in official discourse. The notion of law in Tianya was also characterized by its relationship with terms that reference law's negative associations, specifically violence (23, *baoli*), power (29, *quanli*), money (74, *qian*), corruption (55, *fubai*; 60, *tanwu*), and corrupted officials (97, *tanguan*). Again, these terms did not appear in the top one hundred terms in official discourse.

Furthermore, whereas the official notion of law emphasized only legislation, the online public's notion of law associated it with aspects of multiple institutions, such as legislation (9, *lifa*), government (25, *zhengfu*), democracy (26, *minzhu*), courts (33, *fayuan*), court decisions (27, *panjue*), judiciary (20, *sifa*), judges (15, *faguan*), police (77, *jingcha*), People's Congress (24, *renda*), cadres (51, *ganbu*), and procedure (59, *chengxu*). This suggests that the public situated law in relation to a wide range of institutions, the operation of which could, in turn, influence how the public evaluated the law in general.

Lastly, the notion of law in Tianya was also connected by the public to specific places outside China, especially the United States (65), Taiwan (66), and the United Kingdom (68). The term "law" frequently occurred with the term "Mainland China" (59, *dalu*), which is used by Chinese people when they are referring to the relationship between the PRC, Taiwan, Hong Kong, and Macao. The above findings indicate that participants in Tianya considered and appraised law and the legal system in China through comparisons with other contexts. By contrast, none of the above terms appeared in the one hundred most frequent terms that co-occurred with the term "law" in official discourse.

MULTIPARTY NEGOTIATION

My analysis shows that various actors participated in and negotiated the construction of problems and legality in the Sanlu scandal. The party-state's official discourse constructed problems narrowly, downplaying the Sanlu scandal as an isolated food safety incident. The legality constructed in official discourse is a top-down imposed and paternalistic order carefully orchestrated by the party-state. According to this narrative, the benevolent state knows exactly what the problems are and what is best for citizens. Under such legality, the purpose of law is to create the kind of social, economic, and social order desirable for the state. What is missing from the official discourse, however, is any kind of participatory role for nonstate actors, such as citizens and lawyers, to help shape legal norms, choose the kind of legal institutions they want to use, and oversee the implementation of law. Indeed, if anything, the underlying message of the official discourse is that citizens and lawyers' nonorchestrated participation in the legal system could undermine social stability, especially in a crisis situation.

My analysis also finds that the Chinese state attempted to defend China's legal system in relation to alternative models by developing the concept of "rule of law with Chinese characteristics." Consistent with what scholars call "authoritarian rule of law" (Rajah 2012), "rule by law" (Ginsburg and Moustafa 2008), or "a thin theory of rule of law" (Peerenboom 2002, 3), the legality that emerged in the official discourse stressed the formal and instrumental aspects of law and argued that the government is limited by law. Although citizens' rights do exist, their fulfillment ultimately depends on the consent of the state.

As for the media, although state-controlled outlets tend to report on the positive rather than negative aspects of the legal system (Stockmann and Gallagher 2011), a few state-controlled but still outspoken newspapers dare to cover voices excluded from the official narrative. Consistent with studies on migrant wage claimants and legal professionals (Fu and Cullen 2008; He, Wang, and Su 2013; Liu and Halliday 2011), I find that lawyers, disputants, and NGOs attempted to mobilize public opinion through their connection with outspoken newspapers. The alternative discourse produced by lawyers, NGOs, disputants, and outspoken newspapers provided the public in Tianya with different views and information about the Sanlu scandal. They drew connections to problems that were not mentioned in the official discourse. The understanding of legality that emerged from these alternative voices offered a critique of the top-down imposed legal order, in which legal norms and legal institutions, particularly the courts, served the administrative state and in which citizens and lawyers could be excluded at the will of the state.

The discussion in Tianya was essentially an adjudication of various actors and narratives. The party-state propaganda system failed to present a convincing case to the public in Tianya, while the voices of lawyers, victim's parents, and outspoken journalists offered increasingly resonant alternative accounts. Using mechanisms I have identified as cross-temporality, cross-locality, and problem tracing, the online public highlighted the Sanlu scandal's connections with other cases and framed it as indicative of fundamental problems rooted in China's authoritarian regime. The legal ideology among Tianya participants surprisingly resonates with the legal ideology of liberal-leaning lawyers in China (Halliday and Liu 2007) and the common conception of the rule of law in Western liberal democracies (Tamanaha 2004). Similar to liberal-leaning lawyers, participants in Tianya criticized the state for harassing lawyers and tarnishing judicial independence, while also calling for restrictions on state power and procedural justice, as well as greater protection of citizens' rights. Similar to the common conception of the rule of law in liberal democracies, Tianya participants drew a connection between rights, democracy, and the rule of law. This public expressed a belief that law should protect rights—including civil and political rights—and achieve certain normative qualities; and it assessed China's legal system in relation to various institutions and political regimes within and beyond China. The Tianya public also considered the democratic process essential to ensuring that law had proper content and was fairly and effectively applied. Although the Chinese state accentuates the uniqueness and supremacy of "rule of law with Chinese characteristics," for many participants in Tianya, the deviation of the Chinese legal system from their normative ideals and their perceptions of the rule of law in other countries was unjustified.

Politicization of Netizens

The Sanlu milk scandal is just one of hundreds of public opinion incidents that netizens witnessed or participated in between the late 1990s and the early 2010s. Next, I turn to how these contentious experiences, as well as netizens' everyday practices on the Internet, contributed to netizens' politicization. Such analysis helps to unpack the statistical association that I identified in the beginning of this chapter. To do this, I draw on fifty in-depth interviews with ordinary citizens. The distribution of these subjects is depicted in table 6.3. Subjects were selected according to Internet use and social class. To tease out the effect of online experience, I included non-netizens as a comparison group. As political contention in China is often mobilized along class lines (Cai 2010; Lee 2007; O'Brien and Li 2006), position in social structure could presumably influence politicization at the individual level; therefore, I recruited netizens and non-netizens within each social class. I conducted interviews with ordinary citizens in Chongqing in 2011.[43] Each interview lasted about an hour and a half. To increase the possibility that interviewees would reveal their political views, I spent twenty minutes chatting with them informally before beginning the actual interview, to put them at ease and to make the interviews less awkward. Second, following William Gamson's (1992) strategy in *Talking Politics*, I used specific, concrete issues related to food safety, land grabbing, and labor disputes to elicit responses. These issues were selected because they affect the daily lives of ordinary citizens; even citizens with low levels of education can talk a lot about these issues. Furthermore, these issues

TABLE 6.3. Interview subjects in Chongqing

	Netizens	Non-netizens
Peasants	8	5
Working class	9	5
Middle class	9	5
College students	9	0
Total	35	15

are not considered intrinsically politically sensitive in light of common sense understandings of politics in China. Conversation about these concrete issues thus provided a more natural and neutral entry point for me to discuss more abstract topics later.

Each interview was organized around a set of open-ended questions. I discussed food safety, land grabbing, and labor dispute issues with interviewees in that order. I would first talk about the issue briefly, then I would ask interviewees to express their viewpoints on the issue, particularly what they thought about the severity of issue and the cause of the problem, as well as which categories of actors they associated with it—for example, local governments, the central government, courts, businesses, and/or citizens. When interviewees made any judgments, I asked them to explain the criteria and rationale according to which they made those judgments. I also asked interviewees how they accessed information about the issue. Furthermore, I asked if any persons or media were especially influential in terms of helping them gain knowledge or understanding of the issue and why.

After discussing food safety, land grabbing, and labor disputes, I asked interviewees to discuss the similarities and differences among the issues. I also asked interviewees to reflect on whether their views of these problems and the associated actors had changed over time. Then, I moved discussion from these specific issues to more general issues in China, such as conflicts and divisions in China and how interviewees evaluated the government. Lastly, I asked a series of questions about media use, selection of media, and various forms of political participation. I asked subjects to reflect on whether and how media and Internet use shaped their understandings and practices.

I found three salient similarities across all subjects. First, all interviewees perceived problems in China. Among the three issues, food safety and land grabbing problems were considered the most rampant, while labor disputes were seen as becoming less severe. Second, resonating with research that suggests rising legal and rights consciousness among Chinese citizens (Gallagher 2005b; Gallagher 2006; Lee 2007; Lorentzen and Scoggins 2015; O'Brien and Li 2006), I found that interviewees with different backgrounds used the same

cultural discourse—that of laws and rights—to think about and discuss problems, thanks to the Chinese state's dissemination of legal knowledge. When
interviewees made a negative judgment about a specific actor in the interviews,
the negative judgment was usually about the unlawfulness of that actor. This
finding is consistent with my statistical analysis, which suggests that the perception of the government's legality influences trust in the Chinese government.
Interviewees were generally knowledgeable about law, especially law related to
their interests. For example, even subjects without secondary education and access to the Internet knew their rights under labor laws well. Third, interviewees
tended to think that major conflicts and divisions in China did not exist between
different groups of Chinese people per se but were more salient between the
Chinese state and Chinese people. Social inequality was a recurring theme that
interviewees brought up in relation to social conflict and division. Interestingly,
however, many interviewees mentioned that rising social inequality had created tension in China not because of the inequality itself, but because of the
problematic connection between the wealthy elite and the state.

There were, however, critical differences between netizens and non-
netizens with similar socioeconomic backgrounds. First, netizens were more
likely than non-netizens to perceive problems as severe. This is because non-
netizens were less cognizant of problems beyond their local contexts. When
discussing the three issues (food safety, land grabbing, and labor disputes) in
the interviews, non-netizens often mentioned local cases. In contrast, netizens
alluded to many high-profile cases across localities and public opinion incidents. With access to abundant information through major Internet portals and
social media, netizens were familiar with a variety of problems across social
groups and aspects of life.

Second, although both groups invoked the language of laws and rights to
discuss problems, and perceived a significant gap between law on the books
and law in action, the ways in which the two groups understood laws and rights
differed greatly in two important respects. Non-netizens cared about laws and
rights to the extent that these were closely related to their own material or
personal interests, whereas netizens were more likely to demand rights beyond
their material or personal interests, particularly in the case of political rights.
Netizens were more inclined to claim their rights as citizens to participate
in public affairs, even though the government does not allow the exercise of
such rights. Understanding news and expressing opinion were minimal forms
of political participation for them. Netizens were also more likely to see the
lack of de facto civil and political rights as the fundamental cause of problems
in China, as it prevented citizens from using institutionalized channels to hold
the government responsible.

The two groups also differed in terms of whether they took the legitimacy
of law for granted. Non-netizens tended to accept whatever is written in the

law, whereas netizens recognized that law is also an instrument for domination, and thus, consistency is required between laws and rights. Many netizens mentioned that using unjust laws to govern the populace violated the principle of rule of law. In short, although non-netizens and netizens shared the same cultural medium, netizens employed higher standards to identify problems and make judgments.

Third, although both non-netizens and netizens identified the main conflict and division in China as that between the state and Chinese people, the two groups perceived different levels of conflict and related to the conflict in different ways. Non-netizens were more likely to think that conflict and division existed at the local level. They also tended to have a bifurcated view of state legitimacy, seeing the central leaders as benevolent but local officials as corrupted (Lee 2007, 21; Li 2004; O'Brien and Li 2006). As such, only local government and officials were understood by non-netizens as in conflict with Chinese people. In addition, non-netizens are less likely to see themselves as victims in the conflict unless they or their family members personally encountered problems. In comparison, netizens were more likely to think that conflict and division existed at the national level. They tended to regard problems as systemic and to blame state agencies at all levels. This finding aligns with my statistical analysis, which finds that netizens tend to have less trust in the central party-state and regime. Finally, my analysis of interview data also finds that netizens are more inclined to identify themselves as victims suffering from the loss of rights even when they may not be directly involved in specific issues. This identification motivates netizens to contest official discourse online and support other citizens when there is an opportunity.

I pushed interviewees to reflect on the origins of their cultural schemes—how and where they gained their understanding of the world and how to make sense of it. The results revealed that netizens and non-netizens rely on very different sources of information to understand the concepts of law and rights. Non-netizens mostly mentioned learning about laws and rights from TV and local newspapers. Many non-netizens said that local newspapers contain useful information about their rights, and they discuss these issues with family, friends, and colleagues. In general, non-netizens did not question the credibility or value of mass media, even though some did mention that media based in Hong Kong have higher credibility.

In contrast to non-netizens, netizens generally perceived mass media in China as unreliable, and they stated that public opinion leaders and only a very few outspoken domestic newspapers influence how they think about laws and rights. Many netizens mentioned receiving recommendations regarding specific opinion leaders and newspapers from their friends and teachers. Although netizens may not necessarily agree with the concrete opinions of media or opinion leaders, they generally appreciate the analytic frameworks that emphasize citizenship rights, rule of law, and citizen participation. They told me that it is not so much specific information or facts, but rather the alternative analytic framework that has influenced them the most in the long term. My interviewees thought the alternative framework promoted by outspoken newspapers and opinion leaders was distinct from the dominant framework promoted by the Chinese state. Opinion leaders, in particular legal scholars, lawyers, and journalists, have a huge influence on college students through social media such as Weibo. And although debates exist between rightist and leftist intellectuals (Zhao 2008), my interview data did not find that debates defined in such terms had a noticeable influence on ordinary citizens. Essentially, the response of interviewees suggests that elite social networks in and beyond the media field have influenced how netizens understand laws and rights. But while acknowledging the influence of opinion leaders and outspoken newspapers, my interviewees in the netizen group emphasized that such influence was mediated by and intertwined with complex long-term living experiences and personal biographies.

The cultural medium that citizens use to make sense of news and problems, as well as the amount of problem-oriented news and information to which citizens are exposed, influence citizens' evaluation practices in the process of reading and discussing news. Compared with netizens, non-netizens are exposed to less problem-oriented news and information, and they use a lower standard to judge the various actors involved in problems. Generally, when non-netizens have negative perceptions of the local government and officials, it is linked to their own personal experiences and/or the experiences of their family and friends. As a result, non-netizens are more likely to view problems as individual and local, and they are less likely to establish connections with citizens beyond their local contexts.

Netizens, on the other hand, are exposed to a variety of problems and use a higher standard to make their judgments. Despite variation within netizens as a group, most of them told me that various problems in China have the same roots. As netizens are repetitively exposed to numerous problems online across localities and over time, they begin to see the structural roots of problems and, therefore, expand their targets of blaming. Many interviewees in the netizen group cited the recurrence of similar problems over time and the co-occurrence of problems in every locality in China. They pointed to a central government that was reluctant to tackle problems and even indifferent to local government's suppression of victims and whistle blowers. Some interviewees even saw the central state's indifference to such suppression and its "inaction" on many problems as proof of its implication in those problems. As a result, netizens blame state agencies at all levels, and relate the cause of problems to citizens' lack of political rights and the state's lack of accountability. Many of my interviewees said that problems were caused by unchecked political power and the lack of motivation among leaders to take citizens seriously. These interview data help us to understand why Internet use is statistically associated with less trust and more dissatisfaction with the central government and the regime in general. In essence, the aggregation of problems online leads to new understandings about the nature of problems and a tendency to see citizens and the state as opposed to one another—and, significantly, this effect holds despite the ongoing censorship of news and information online.

In fact, my analysis of interview data reveals that the aggregation of various problems in the online discursive arena occurs despite the state's censorship practices, which sometimes allow criticism of local problems (King, Pan, and Roberts 2013; Lorentzen 2014). The key objective of such practices is to censor criticism of the central government, the Communist regime, and any information that might instigate collective action. As such, critical news reports that uncover local problems can still pass the censors as long as such reports do not directly criticize the central state or cause social instability. Under the new Internet conditions, the aggregation of news revealing problems in certain localities and with specific government agencies can still generate negative perceptions of the central party-state and the regime because such stories enable citizens to see the connections between such problems and events. The key is that censorship practices only focus on individual issues and news but cannot control how Chinese people might connect and interpret the news items they consume.

Similar to research showing that online engagement shapes identity formation (Dahlgren 2000; Yang 2009), I find that reading and discussing problem-oriented news and information through the lens of citizenship rights also strengthens citizen identity. In interviews, netizens explained why they think they are similar to and connected with other citizens. First, they all encounter problems and exclusion in their daily lives. Second, while problems may manifest differently, citizens share a common cause: the state's infringement on or failure to protect rights. Third, interviewees believed that ordinary citizens' lack of connection to state agencies makes them susceptible to problems and more likely to suffer from exclusion. Many netizens also alluded to how citizen identity motivates them to voice their opinions, even though they know the limitation of public opinion in China. Several interviewees pointed out that the public has limited attention and capacity to react to all the problems in China. Additionally, there is no adequate institution to force state agencies to deal with these problems. Even though government agencies do tackle some problems, they mostly do so in an ad hoc manner, rather than addressing problems systemically. Furthermore, the public has limited capacity to oversee how the government addresses problems in the long run because of restrictions on political and social organizations. Still, identifying themselves as citizens with rights and responsibilities to demand change motivates netizens to contest official discourse online, support other citizens, and exercise their rights over the government.

Conclusion: Laws, Rights, and the Rise of an Active Online Public

In this chapter, I have analyzed various data to demonstrate and understand the rise of an opinionated, critical, and politically active online public, whose everyday practices and participation in public opinion incidents contributed to the rise of China's contentious public sphere. How and why were Chinese netizens capable of exerting political influence? The first factor is netizens' demographic background in the early years. In the 1990s, the highly generated wave of early Chinese netizens developed innovative political and cultural practices and formed burgeoning communities in online forums. Certain online communities evolved into environmental and antidiscrimination NGOs later, while some early active netizens became NGO activists or even public opinion leaders. Such early developments laid an important foundation for the contentious public sphere by providing cultural scripts and repertoires as well as social capital for future action and collaboration (Swidler 1986).

The second factor is the increasing embeddedness of Chinese netizens in larger discursive and social networks. Two trends between the late 1990s and the early 2010s are noteworthy. First, the size of the online public had been expanding dramatically, while the average education of netizens had been declining. Habermas's (1989) work suggests that such expansion and demographic shift could have led to the rise of the masses or a less critical public. This potential negative consequence, I argue, was mitigated by the second trend—the increasing influence of actors mediating between citizens and the state. Between the late 1990s and the early 2010s, legal and media professionals, NGO activists, public intellectuals, public opinion leaders, Internet portals, and outspoken newspapers played an increasingly important role in producing alternative discourse to compete with official discourse in steering the public agenda. They developed strategies and repertoires about how to collectively produce a public opinion incident. Although these actors often worked on different issues (e.g., environmental protection, antidiscrimination, etc.) and had various forms of expertise, the majority devoted themselves to the agenda of promoting rights protection and advancing what they called a "genuine" rule of law. Furthermore, these intermediary actors endeavored to reach the public and build a civil society. Had it not for been for these intermediary actors, a considerable proportion of netizens likely would not have extended their attention to issues beyond geopolitics and nationalism, which was the major issue that led to public opinion incidents after China initially connected to the Internet. The concerted effort of intermediary actors and the increasing embeddedness of Chinese netizens in broader discursive and social networks strengthened ordinary netizens' capacity, drawing them into efforts to influence politics and to shape public agenda.

The interconnection between the online public and intermediary actors as well as the overlap of discursive and social networks explains how issue-specific public spheres were connected and grew into a more general contentious public sphere. In their article, sociologists Craig Calhoun and Guobin Yang demonstrate the rise of what they call "a green public sphere" in China, which involves the participation of netizens, NGOs, and different media in environmental issues. Calhoun and Yang call for exploring "the sources and consequences of potential synergies between different issue-specific public spheres" (Calhoun and Yang 2007, 230). As analysis in this chapter shows, the cultural medium of laws and rights played a significant role in relating different issues. Almost all specific issues discussed by netizens and intermediary actors were connected to rights defense, rights protection, or citizens' rights over time. In addition, rights defense and public interest lawyers were involved in almost every kind of grievance. They provided legal aid and worked with media professionals to publicize grievances, key events, and cases of litigation. They also collaborated with various kinds of NGOs. Essentially, the cultural medium of laws and rights as well as legal and media professionals significantly contributed to the connection of a variety of issue-specific public spheres and publics. Such connection made a kind of synergy between different actors possible, leading to powerful mobilization related to public opinion incidents and putting the state under enormous pressure.

Finally, it is also meaningful to consider how various information communication technologies led to the growth of China's online public. The few outspoken newspapers played a critical role in producing alternative discourse that competed with official discourse and established cross-cutting elite networks. Internet forums provided a space for netizens to build communities, evaluate various discourses, and develop their own critiques and cultural repertoires. Weibo contributed to the expansion of elite networks and the emergence of public opinion leaders, while also connecting opinion leaders to ordinary citizens. Before the rise of WeChat, China already had an active online public.

7

The Chinese State Strikes Back

The days when the Chinese state could easily control information and public opinion have now passed . . . or have they? As I have shown in previous chapters, with the rise of a contentious public sphere, Chinese people now have greater access to, and ability to discuss, information the state would prefer to keep out of public discussion. What is more, the Chinese public has even begun to ridicule and bargain with the Chinese state. As history has shown, however, one should never underestimate a state well known for its exceptional capacity to adapt to new situations and challenges. Indeed, some scholars of Chinese politics believe this adaptive capacity explains the resilience of the CCP regime (Nathan 2003; Yang 2004). How, then, has the Chinese state responded to the country's growing contentious public sphere? And to what extent and in what ways has the state's response reshaped that sphere?

The Hu-Wen leadership was the first to have to cope with the emergent public sphere, a responsibility that has since been taken up and intensified under President Xi's leadership. Although there has been some continuity between the two leaderships, the discontinuity is striking as well. I focus on the Xi leadership's techniques and their consequences in this chapter, but first, it is useful to compare the rationalities of rule underpinning both administrations as it helps to make sense of why the Xi regime has been so aggressive in its attempt to curb the contentious public sphere.

From Social Stability to National Security

Whereas the Hu-Wen and Xi leaderships are similar in their attempt to contain the contentious public sphere, the Hu-Wen leadership had a relatively more open and responsive approach toward that sphere. Maintaining social stability has been a central concern for the Chinese state since the 1989 Tiananmen democratic movement. The secretary of the Central Political and Legal Affairs Commission Qiao Shi declared in 1990 that maintaining stability should be the paramount long-term political task for the CCP.[1] Under President Jiang Zemin's reign, the Chinese state established the Leading Group of Maintaining Social Stability in the 1990s, building the institutional infrastructure for stability maintenance (Lin 2012). A striking rise of domestic tensions, particularly protests, under the Hu-Wen rule led to Hu's announcement of the "harmonious society" agenda in 2004, which identified the maintenance of social stability as paramount (Guo and Guo 2008).[2] The Hu-Wen leadership was undoubtedly unaccustomed to and deeply uncomfortable with the rising critical voices in China. The revolutionary uprisings of the Arab Spring starting in December 2010 further reaffirmed to the leadership the danger of media, particularly social media, in facilitating protests and collective actions. The Chinese state raised the level of censorship and surveillance in the second half of Hu-Wen's leadership and strengthened its efforts to "manage" public opinion and maintain a "harmonious" society. As the cases of the Sanlu milk scandal and the Wenchuan earthquake in 2008 demonstrate, activists who attempted to mobilize the public were detained or sentenced from time to time (Lei and Zhou 2015; Menefee and Nordtveit 2012; G. Yang 2013). The Chinese state under Hu-Wen also continued to meddle in personnel appointments and editorial decisions of newspapers and retaliated against outspoken journalists and media in order to control news production (Hassid 2008).[3]

Yet, alongside such efforts to maintain social stability and to contain the contentious public sphere, the Hu-Wen leadership was relatively liberal in other respects. The concepts of informing the public of important events and allowing the public to discuss important problems were first raised by General Secretary Zhao Ziyang in the Thirteenth National Congress of the CCP in 1987 as part of Zhao's political reform agenda. But President Hu Jintao first put forth the language of "right to know, right to participate, right to express, and right to oversee the government" in the National Congress of the CCP in 2007.[4] In 2008, the Hu-Wen leadership further enacted the Regulation on the Disclosure of Government Information (*xinxi gongkai tiaoli*) to improve the government's transparency. This regulation acknowledges the right of citizens to request information from the government. The Hu-Wen leadership was also surprisingly responsive to public opinion when faced with a surge of public opinion incidents. When misfeasance of government officials was revealed in such incidents, the Hu-Wen administration was quick to respond to public outcry by punishing the officials (Hassid 2015).

In comparison, the Xi leadership considers the management of public opinion a question of not only social stability but also ideological struggle and national security. The Chinese state under Xi has seen the rise of the contentious public sphere as a more serious threat and has thus reacted to it more aggressively than did its predecessor. In an important speech at the National Propaganda and Ideology Work Conference in August 2013, President Xi described the current moment as one in which many historically critical struggles are unfolding; he further framed the Internet as a key site of such struggles and an ideological battlefield.[5] This talk soon became the major guideline for the state to govern public opinion. But what exactly were the historical struggles to which Xi referred? And why was the Internet identified as such a key battlefield? In the *People's Daily*, Professor Han Qingxiang of the CCP Central Party School explained that these struggles include not only struggles for capital, market, and territory, as well as struggles against separatism and corruption, but also ideological struggles and public opinion struggles. Han further pointed out that ideological battles have been waged by Western forces to sabotage the CCP. The West has disseminated ideologies of constitutionalism, neoliberalism, historical nihilism, and universal values to undermine the core values of socialism. The purpose is to encourage Chinese people to admire the West and use its values to criticize the CCP. Han emphasized that such ideological struggles are mainly fought on the Internet, as manifested by the circulation of online information and opinion seeking to tarnish the CCP; thus, the Internet has become a battlefield for national security.[6]

President Xi's own writing on the breakdown of the Soviet Union also sheds light on how and why ideological struggles and battles over public opinion have become defined as so critical to national security, the continued existence of the CCP, and the unity of the Chinese nation. Xi argues that the repudiation of Lenin, Stalin, the Communist Party of the Soviet Union, and the history of the nation derailed party organizations and the military, eventually leading to the collapse of the Soviet Union. From those experiences, Xi emphasizes the importance of defending the CCP and its vision of socialism with Chinese characteristics. Xi has also recognized the danger of allowing people to negate the history of the PRC, particularly the oft-criticized Mao period. He warns that public criticism of the prereform period can eventually cause the negation of the CCP as a whole and the disintegration of the Chinese nation.[7] Xi's concerns about ideological struggles and the dissolution of the Chinese nation explain why he coined the term the "Chinese dream" to promote the agenda of rejuvenating the Chinese nation (Wang 2014).

After Xi's talk at the National Propaganda and Ideology Work Conference in 2013, major government officials in charge of the Internet, media, and propaganda soon echoed Xi's agenda and made the management of online public opinion a top priority. That same year, Lu Wei, the head of the Cyberspace Administration of China, announced that management of online public opinion has become the most critical part of the state's ideological work because of its impact on national security. He also instructed state agencies and media to propagate the concept of the "Chinese dream" and socialism with Chinese characteristics to win ideological struggles.[8] In a similar vein, Li Congjun, the president of the Xinhua News Agency—one of the Chinese state's three major mouthpieces—also identified the Internet as a key battle-field and emphasized the importance of ensuring a strong state presence in the online public sphere.[9]

The official media Xinhua News Agency and certain prominent propaganda officials even talked about the need to "purify" the online public sphere in 2013, noting that a considerable proportion of Chinese netizens were believed to have joined the wrong side in the ideological battles. Propaganda officials classified Chinese netizens into three groups: red, black, and gray. The red group includes patriotic netizens supportive of the Chinese state; the black group includes those critical of the Chinese state; and the gray group refers to the silent majority. According to propaganda officials, the voice of the red group has little resonance in the online discursive arena, while the black group controls the Internet and new media, setting the agenda, and producing public opinion incidents. Officials talked about the need to crack down on the black group and turn those in the gray group into members of the red group, thereby taming the contentious public sphere.[10]

A talk by Xi at the National Party School Work Conference in April 2016 suggests that this system of classification actually came from Xi himself. He said that he mentioned this classification in one of his previous talks. He restated that ideological and public spheres in China have three main zones (*sange didai*). The CCP must defend the "red zone" (*hongse didai*), use its sword to attack the "black zone" (*heise didai*), and turn the "gray zone" (*huise didai*) into a red one. For Xi, the existence of the black zone is related to China's silence in the global ideological battlefield. Xi further pointed out that the CCP has been addressing three major problems for Chinese people and the Chinese nation: being invaded, being hungry, and being criticized. The three problems are caused by China's backwardness, poverty, and silence, respectively. Xi claimed that the CCP has solved the first two problems successfully. Now the CCP must fight for a say in the international arena to address the nation's lack of discursive power.[11] In this way, Xi linked the existence of critical voices and a contentious public sphere in China to the country's relative lack of discursive hegemonic power internationally.

The Chinese State's Effort to Contain the Contentious Public Sphere

I have shown that the Chinese state under the Xi leadership has seen the rise of a contentious public sphere in China as a national security issue and the result of ideological struggles between the West and China. Now I turn to how the Chinese state under the Xi leadership has attempted to contain the contentious public sphere.

CONSOLIDATING THE CHINESE LEVIATHAN

Scholars of Chinese politics have pointed out that complex and sometimes conflicting intrastate relationships shape bargaining and negotiation between different state agencies and can influence policy implementation. It is not uncommon for the central government, for example, to encounter problems when asking local governments to implement its policies. As such, scholars of Chinese politics see the fragmented nature of China's political regime as a weakness of the state (Lieberthal 1992; Mertha 2009). And as I demonstrate in chapter 4, it was precisely such intrastate tensions and disjunctures that opened up space for critical news reporting. The Chinese state, in other words, may be a powerful Leviathan, but it is an internally fragmented one.

The Xi leadership perfectly recognizes the fact that fragmented state agencies weaken the Chinese state's ability to regulate the Internet, media, and public opinion effectively. Wang Xiujun, the deputy head of the Cyberspace Administration of China, describes the problem of Internet governance and regulation in China as "having nine dragons to tame the floods" (*jiolong zhishui*). Despite having "nine dragons"—or rather, precisely *because* there are so many state agencies governing the Internet—the Chinese state is unable to regulate the Internet effectively.[12] Xi addressed this problem of state fragmentation in the Third Plenary Session of the Eighteenth Central Committee in 2013, saying that with the popularization of social media like Weibo and WeChat, the Chinese state has faced unprecedented challenges regarding how to regulate the Internet, guide public opinion, and ensure social stability and national security. Xi then pointed out that the structural weakness of the Chinese state led to unsuccessful regulation. Specifically, since too many state agencies were involved in the regulation of the Internet, and the function of these agencies often overlapped, the division of labor and distribution of responsibility among agencies was unclear. For Xi, this structural problem ultimately resulted in contradictory policies and practices and ineffective regulation.[13]

Xi's solution has been to consolidate administrative and regulatory power. Since 2000, when Internet news began to emerge in China, the State Council Information Office has been responsible for governing Internet news and websites.[14] There are many problems with this arrangement. First, the State Council Information Office is mainly in charge of organizing news conferences and publicizing news related to China to other countries. In other words, the office has little expertise in governing the Internet. Moreover, in addition to the State Council Information Office, at least fifteen other party-state agencies have some degree of administrative power over Internet regulation.[15] In

2006, all of these agencies formalized a coordination program concerning Internet governance and formed the National Internet Governance Coordination Group, whose office was located in the Ministry of Information Industry. The coordination program enacted an extremely complicated system for the responsibility, collaboration, and coordination of the sixteen agencies. The Department of Propaganda was in charge of coordinating ideology work at the macro level. The State Council Information Office was responsible for concrete ideology work. The Ministry of Public Security was in command of information monitoring and law enforcement. The Ministry of State Security was in control of monitoring online information regarding national safety. And a number of state agencies had power to approve licenses for Internet-related business.[16]

In May 2011, the Hu-Wen leadership established the State Internet Information Office as a specialized state agency in charge of Internet regulation. The head of the State Council Information Office had a joint appointment as the head of the State Internet Information Office.[17] Despite this arrangement, two problems remained. First, the head of the State Internet Information Office was not able to concentrate on Internet governance because of his other appointment. Second, the State Internet Information Office still had very limited authority. Although it was authorized by the State Council to coordinate relevant state agencies,[18] the main law enforcement organization was actually the Ministry of Public Security. Furthermore, even after the establishment of the State Internet Information Office, state agencies still referred to the above-mentioned complicated coordination program in their exercise of administrative power.

To improve regulatory efficacy, Xi consolidated party-state agencies. On the party side, the Xi leadership established the Central Leading Group for Cyberspace Affairs under the CCP's Central Committee in February 2014. The work is seen as so important that the group is headed by General Secretary Xi. The CCP also established the Office of the Central Leading Group for Cyberspace Affairs, which is in charge of the daily operation of the group.[19] Provincial-level leading groups and offices were also formed to implement policies and regulations at the local level. On the state side, the Xi leadership restructured the State Internet Information Office and replaced it with the Cyberspace Administration of China. The Cyberspace Administration of China and the party's Office of the Central Leading Group for Cyberspace Affairs have the same office and are mostly operated by the same personnel. To clarify the division of labor among state agencies, the State Council announced that it had made the Cyberspace Administration of China responsible for managing the content of online information and implementing relevant laws and regulations. The Cyberspace Administration of China thus gained considerable administrative power from the Ministry of Public Security.[20] In addition, the

Cybersecurity Law (Article 8) designates the Cyberspace Administration of China as the paramount regulator of cybersecurity.

Finally, in order to ensure the coordination of multiple party-state agencies, Xi appointed Lu Wei as the head of the Office of the Central Leading Group for Cyberspace Affairs, the director of the Cyberspace Administration of China, the deputy head of the Department of Propaganda, and the deputy head of the State Council Information Office. In so doing, Xi concentrated the administrative power for Internet governance and regulation in Lu Wei, whom Xi oversaw directly. In recognition of his enormous power, the *New York Times* dubbed Lu Wei "China's web doorkeeper."[21] Xi also established the National Security Commission under the CCP's Central Committee and served as the chairman of the commission in December 2013, directly taking the leadership for national security affairs, including cybersecurity. After Xi completed the task of consolidating party-state agencies, Chinese media praised him for ending the "nine dragons" problem.[22] Although Lu Wei was removed from his positions in 2016, the Internet governance structure remains the same.

UPGRADING TECHNIQUES OF SURVEILLANCE AND CENSORSHIP

The Chinese state under the Xi leadership has also upgraded its techniques of surveillance and censorship. First, the Chinese state has continued to expand its capacity to monitor public opinion. Since 2008, the People's Daily Online, a subsidiary company owned by the *People's Daily*, began to provide public opinion analysis for party-state organs under the auspices of the Department of Propaganda. It also publishes an internal weekly magazine called *Online Public Opinion* (Tsai 2016). Over time, and with the rise of big data science, other media organizations, universities, and private companies have also set up labs to monitor and analyze public opinion, leading to the emergence of an industry that provides general and customized public opinion reports to party-state agencies at various levels, as well as to business actors. Public opinion monitoring and analysis services are lucrative. According to a public financial report published by the People's Daily Online, its own online monitoring service brought in 2.69 million RBM in 2015.[23] The rise of a public opinion monitoring and analysis service industry has also brought profits to developers of public opinion monitoring and analysis software. In an interview, one developer told me that public opinion monitoring software companies are very excited about the business prospects associated with cloud computing and big data and the government's emphasis on these technologies.[24]

Providers of public opinion monitoring and analysis services employ public opinion analysts to do the hard work of collecting and analyzing public opinion, with the aid of public opinion monitoring and analysis software. Public opinion analysts collect and sample online discourse and media reports, set keywords to identify important events, and conduct quantitative and qualitative analysis. In addition to analyzing public opinion, public opinion analysts also forecast the development of public opinion. When public opinion analysts identify potential public opinion incidents, they send alerts to their customers and advise them on how to deal with those incidents strategically. With the increasing influence of public opinion leaders, public opinion analysts also identify and monitor public opinion leaders closely for the government. For instance, public opinion analysts at the People's Daily Online identified three hundred opinion leaders and submitted the list to the Department of Propaganda in 2013 (Tsai 2016). According to the estimation of the Ministry of Industry and Information Technology in December 2013, there was a demand for around 1.5 to 2 million public opinion analysts in China.[25]

The Chinese government recognized the need for well-trained public opinion analysts in order to obtain high-quality public opinion monitoring services. The Chinese state under Xi officially recognized online public opinion analysts as a new profession in 2013. The Ministry of Industry and Information Technology is in charge of training, testing, and certifying public opinion analysts. These analysts are expected to possess knowledge ranging from theories of public opinion to Internet regulation, statistics, big data analysis and information forecast, sampling methods, Internet technology, case analysis, and strategic response to public opinion. The Ministry of Industry and Information Technology plans to train one hundred thousand public opinion analysts per year to satisfy the demand.[26] According to my interviewees who participated in the training, most of the trainees have government background and already have some knowledge about how to deal with public opinion. They mostly work for local governments, SOEs, and official media. Their main motivation for training is to obtain a certificate because they believe such qualifications will help them raise their salary and get promoted. Trainers include but are not limited to officials at the Ministry of Industry and Information Technology, senior public opinion analysts at the People's Daily Online and the Xinhua News Agency, developers of public opinion monitoring software, local public security cadres, and professors of communication studies from prominent universities. Like companies that develop public opinion monitoring software, these trainers emphasize the need to keep up with new technological development, particularly cloud computing and big data science.[27] In sum, the Chinese state under the Xi leadership has attempted to make sure that China has enough qualified public opinion analysts in the era of cloud computing and big data surveillance.

In addition to training public opinion analysts, the Xi leadership has also expanded censorship and surveillance in response to concerns about cybersecurity. Scholars of the Internet often liken it to a double-edged sword that can be used to advance both freedom and control (MacKinnon 2012)—an opinion that Xi seems to share. In his talk at the Cyberspace Affairs Work Conference in April 2016, Xi said information technologies are "double-edged swords" (*shuang ren jian*): while they can benefit people and society, they can be used to undermine individual and public interests, like subverting the government, promoting separatism, and spreading terrorism. For Xi, the drawback of the Internet mainly comes from the fact that information circulated online can greatly shape people's values and how they view their society.[28] And with so many enemies in the world ostensibly seeking to undermine the PRC, it is easy to see how the Internet becomes framed as a site of ideological struggle and national security.

Several events suggest that the Chinese state under Xi has upgraded the scale and technologies of censorship and surveillance. First, the government began to block Gmail in 2014. Although Google ended its search engine service in China in 2010 because of censorship and ethical issues, users were still able to use Gmail in China. Many Gmail users in China consider Gmail safer than the e-mail service provided by Chinese companies because they think the latter are too beholden to the Chinese government, which can easily ask such companies to provide information about e-mail accounts and exchange.[29] Since December 2014, Gmail service has been severely disrupted (Yuen 2015). *Global Times*, a subsidiary newspaper owned by *People's Daily*, suggests that newly discovered security concerns might have led the Chinese government to block Gmail. The newspaper urged Chinese users to accept the fact that Gmail is blocked in China.[30]

Second, China has upgraded its Great Firewall and intensified suppression of virtual private networks (VPNs) since 2015. China's Great Firewall helps the Chinese state to filter and block undesirable information flow. VPNs are a circumvention tool that enables users to bypass the Great Firewall. According to a research report conducted in 2014 by GlobalWebIndex, a market research firm headquartered in London, China has 90 million VPN users.[31] Since January 2015, major commercial VPN providers have reported that their service has been severely disrupted by the Chinese government. The attacks have been conducted with unprecedentedly sophisticated technologies (Yuen 2015). Wen Ku, the head of the Department of Communications Development of the Ministry of Industry and Information, acknowledged the blocking of VPNs. He asserted that Internet companies should follow Chinese law and respect China's cyber-sovereignty. He also stated that the Chinese government would continue to regulate unlawful information according to Chinese law and adjust regulatory polices as needed.[32]

Third, China enacted the Counterterrorism Law (*fan kongbu zhuyi fa*) in December 2015, justifying certain controversial surveillance measures. One important measure is real-name registration. There have been debates in China since the early 2000s about whether China should adopt real-name registration for Internet service. Whereas supporters believe real-name registration can help to maintain legal and social order, opponents argue it can infringe on citizens' privacy and freedom of speech. In March 2012, the top four Internet companies began to implement Weibo real-name registration, as per the Chinese state's request, but the legal justification for the request was vague. In 2015, the Cyberspace Administration of China announced that the Chinese state would begin to establish real-name registration, sparking criticism among Chinese netizens (Liao 2015). But the passage of the Counterterrorism Law unexpectedly closed the space for debate by providing the legal foundation for such registration. Article 21 of the law stipulates that providers of telecommunications and Internet services are required to check the identity of their customers and shall not provide service to those who decline to provide identity information.

The Counterterrorism Law also includes the so-called backdoor provision. As the Apple-FBI encryption dispute in the United States in 2016 shows, backdoor access enables bypassing normal authentication to access a computer, cell phone, program, or network (Nasser et al. 2015). Article 18 of the Chinese Counterterrorism Law requires providers of telecommunications and Internet services to provide the government with technical assistance, including backdoor access and decryption. The purpose is to prevent and investigate terrorist activities. Furthermore, the Counterterrorism Law also obliges providers of telecommunications and Internet services to censor information about terrorism. Article 19 of the law requires providers of telecommunications and Internet services to monitor information and take security measures to prevent dissemination of information about terrorism. In fact, the measures related to real-name registration, technical assistance, and information monitoring were already covered by the Decision on Strengthening Online Information Protection (*quanguo renda changweihui guanyu jiaqiang wangluo xinxi baohu de jueding*), which was issued by the NPC Standing Committee in December 2012. But now these measures are authorized by law—a higher order of legal norms.

Finally, the Chinese state introduced a draft Cybersecurity Law in July 2015.[33] The NPC Standing Committee completed the lawmaking process in November 2016.[34] The paramount importance of cybersecurity is demonstrated by Xi's talk at the first meeting of the Central Leading Group for Cyberspace Affairs in February 2014. Xi firmly asserted, "Without cybersecurity, there is no national security; without informatization, there is no modernization."[35] The lawmaking material publicized by the Standing Committee reveals two primary motivations for enacting the Cybersecurity Law. The first motivation is to keep up with lawmaking elsewhere in order to compete with other global powers and cope with increasing cyberattacks. In 2013, the EU enacted the Network and Information Security Directive as the first EU-wide legislation on cybersecurity.[36] Japan adopted the Cybersecurity Basic Act in 2014,[37] and in 2015, the United States passed the Cybersecurity Information Sharing Act.[38]

These lawmaking processes have spurred China to catch up and to assert its own cyber-sovereignty. The second motivation is to strengthen the Chinese state's capacity to maintain social stability and national security.

The Cybersecurity Law requires the government to establish cybersecurity monitoring and alert systems as well as emergency response measures (Article 51). It also gives relevant state agencies, particularly the Cyberspace Administration of China (Article 8), enormous administrative power. Basically the Cybersecurity Law legalizes the surveillance, censorship, and social stability maintenance practices in which the Chinese state is already engaged. Under the Cybersecurity Law, state agencies can establish security standards for network equipment and products and decide whether certain network equipment and products meet with those standards (Article 23). To investigate crime and protect national security, the government can oblige network operators to provide support and assistance (Article 28). The Cyberspace Administration of China and other relevant state agencies also have the authority to monitor information and request that network operators delete information and stop the dissemination of illegal information (Article 47). The above two articles are similar to Articles 18 and 19 of the Counterterrorism Law, respectively. In addition, the State Council has the authority to restrict Internet connections and telecommunication to cope with social security incidents (Article 58). In fact, the Chinese state has already been using this strategy to prevent and end protests and other collective actions. Now the Cybersecurity Law intends to make such controversial practices unambiguously legal.

The Cybersecurity Law imposes massive responsibility on network operators, including but not limited to providers of telecommunications and Internet content services. Network operators are required to collect information about users' identity and implement real-name registration (Article 24). This corresponds to Article 21 of the Counterterrorism Law. Network operators are also obliged to store their data in China unless in exceptional circumstances. In addition, network operators have to monitor content of information, delete illegal information, and stop disseminating such information. These obligations are ensured by legal liability. In sum, the making of the Cybersecurity Law and the Counterterrorism Law shows the Xi leadership's efforts to legalize censorship and surveillance practices while creating the impression that the Chinese state operates in accordance with law. In this way, law has become an important tool within the Chinese state's system of surveillance and censorship.

ATTACKING THE BLACK ZONE

At the same time that the Chinese state has been restructuring party-state agencies and upgrading techniques of surveillance and censorship, it has also begun to intensify active suppression. As noted earlier, President Xi identified the Internet as a battlefield for ideological control and national security at the National Propaganda and Ideology Work Conference in August 2013. After this talk, the Chinese state began to strengthen crackdowns on the so-called black zone, in reference to the color-coded classification of Chinese netizens described above.

On August 10, 2013, the director of the Cyberspace Administration of China, Lu Wei, organized a forum to converse with a dozen Big Vs—Weibo users with a large number of followers.[39] Lu Wei said that Big Vs should take social responsibility to spread "positive energy." He then declared that he and the Big Vs at the forum achieved a consensus about "seven bottom lines": obeying laws and regulations, promoting socialism, protecting national interests, respecting citizens' rights and interests, maintaining social order, honoring morality, and ensuring truthfulness of information. The forum was broadcast on China Central Television and widely reported by print and digital media, apparently staged to signal the Chinese state's will to tighten its control of speech.

In late August 2013, about ten days after the forum, the Ministry of Public Security escalated its attacks on illegal activities online, particularly online rumors. Xue Manzi, one of the Big Vs who had attended the forum, was suddenly arrested for soliciting a prostitute. He appeared on China Central Television once again, but this time he was handcuffed, confessing publicly and renouncing his dissemination of negative emotion and speech on Weibo. In addition to Xue Manzi, many other Internet users were arrested across China and accused of spreading rumors and disturbing social order. Statistics publicized by the Ministry of Public Security shed some light on the scale of the crackdowns. In November 2013, the Ministry of Public Security announced that the ministry had effectively cracked down on thirty-four thousand cases since June 2013.[40] And at the end of 2014, the ministry declared that between 2012 and 2014, the Chinese public security organs initiated more than ten anti-Internet-related crime campaigns, cracked down on three hundred thousand cases, and arrested six hundred thousand suspects.[41]

The crackdowns were significantly facilitated by a judicial interpretation. Since there were doubts about how to apply criminal law to online behavior, in September 2013, the Supreme People's Court and the Supreme People's Procuratorate jointly issued a judicial interpretation that addressed how Internet use could constitute crimes, such as defamation, picking quarrels and provoking trouble, extortion, and illegal operation of business. The first two crimes are particularly relevant to online expression and information dissemination. According to the judicial interpretation, Internet users can be charged with defamation if online rumors they produce are viewed by five thousand Internet users or reposted more than five hundred times. Internet users can be charged with picking quarrels and provoking trouble if they use the Internet to berate or harass others and seriously undermine social order. In addition, if

Internet users knowingly disseminate false information and seriously undermine public order, they can also be charged with the crime of picking quarrels and provoking trouble.[42] This judicial interpretation thus provides the legal support needed to punish Internet users.

A glance at some court decisions can help demonstrate what kinds of behavior were punished harshly in the crackdowns. As police and prosecutors have large discretionary power, only a proportion of criminal cases were sent to criminal courts. In November 2013, the Supreme People's Court required all courts in China to publicize their decisions on the website Judicial Opinions of China, starting on January 1, 2014. And though many courts have not publicized their decisions, some courts did. I searched cases in first-instance criminal courts that drew on the above-mentioned judicial interpretation to adjudicate cases of defamation or picking quarrels and provoking trouble. Although I only found sixteen such cases between 2014 and 2015, the content of these court decisions provide a window onto who was punished and why. Not surprisingly, all the defendants in the sixteen cases were found guilty. In each case, the charge alleges criticism of some entity or person—whether local government (nine cases, 56.25%), the central government (two cases, 12.50%), SOEs (two cases, 12.50%), journalists at the Xinhua News Agency (one case, 6.25%), or private persons (two cases, 12.50%). The majority of the cases I found involved dissemination of information denouncing local officials or cadres for their wrongdoings—corruption, illegal land taking, manipulating village elections, illegal law enforcement, and so forth. These categories of wrongdoing often cause protests and collective actions in China (O'Brien and Li 2006). What's particularly interesting is that in these cases, the defendants were *not* the most common type of netizens—that is, relatively highly educated middle class or young college students (Lei and Zhou 2015); instead, they were mostly peasants and villagers who have no higher education (most had only junior high school education) but who were using social media to address their grievances and to complain about the illegal behavior of local government officials. Some of these defendants had a record of petitioning against local governments.

Consider a few typical cases. In one case, villagers in Fujian Shaoan County had a dispute with their township government because of a land development project. The villagers claimed that the land belonged to them and thus required compensation. They then obstructed construction in order to impose pressure on the township government. When township officials and police came to the construction site, a confrontation between villagers and officials occurred. One villager, Huang, made a video, in which he accused a local cadre of beating villagers. He uploaded the video to Youku, a Chinese video website, where it was viewed 41,574 times and generated twenty-eight comments. Fujian Shaoan County People's Court determined that the accusation in the video was not only untruthful but caused consequential societal negative impacts. Huang was given a one-year prison sentence for picking quarrels and provoking trouble.[43]

In another case, a peasant in Anhui had conflicts with the head of a police station at his village because of local election issues. He videotaped the police's law enforcement process during the election. In the video, he accused the head of the police station of being corrupt and protective of local violence. He then uploaded the video to Youku, where it was viewed 32,434 times. The peasant was sentenced one year for picking quarrels and provoking trouble.[44] In Shaanxi, a peasant, Zhou, posted three messages in online forums, accusing a former propaganda official of illegally selling the government's land and occupying villagers' land. The posts were seen more than five thousand times. The court decided that Zhou's behavior constituted defamation and gave him a one-year prison sentence with two years of probation.[45]

Finally, in Guangxi, villagers in one village had petitioned against their local governments for ten years in relation to eviction compensation issues. When Wei represented other villages in their petitions to Beijing, she was put in labor camps for around three years for disrupting public order. She continued to petition in Beijing after she was released from labor camps. One day, she had a meeting with a journalist at Boxun, an overseas Chinese community website. During the meeting, Wei and another petitioner made a video in which they described how they were tortured by cadres in a Guangxi labor camp. She then uploaded the video to Boxun, where it was watched more than five thousand times. She also wrote nine articles for Boxun, all of which were viewed more than five thousand times. Wei was sentenced to two years in prison for defamation.[46]

As discussed in chapters 5 and 6, people in China have increasingly begun to disclose their grievances online to mobilize public support and hopefully find redress. Such self-help can trigger public opinion incidents when grievances are broadcast by media professionals and public opinion leaders. The above court cases suggest that grievants who try to mobilize public opinion, particularly those having disputes with local governments, can be harshly punished after the crackdowns that began in 2013. Crackdown on "illegal" use of the Internet has thus become a powerful tool for punishing grievants and maintaining stability.

In addition to grievants and petitioners, the Chinese state has deliberately targeted social networks connecting public opinion leaders, rights defense lawyers (*weiquan* lawyers),[47] journalists, NGOs, and activists by arresting and stigmatizing key figures and cracking down on NGOs. In 2012, before President Xi assumed office, one article published by the *People's Daily* already identified five dangerous categories of people in China—rights defense lawyers, followers of underground religion, political dissidents, public opinion leaders, and "the disadvantaged," or vulnerable groups (*ruoshi qunti*).[48] In China, the term "the disadvantaged" is used to refer to people who have difficulty living their lives, such as migrant workers, peasants, unemployed workers, and petitioners. During the Cultural Revolution, Mao identified "five black categories" as enemies of the state and people. Commentators thus called the five problematic groups identified by the *People's Daily* "the new five black categories."[49] According to the *People's Daily* article, the five categories of people are manipulated and used by the United States to destabilize China from within. The United States, the *People's Daily* alleged, uses Internet freedom as a slogan to promote liberal democracy, while using these five groups of people to subvert the Chinese government. Of course, the article did not specify what exactly these five categories of people are doing or why their behavior is so wrong and dangerous.

Another *People's Daily* article reveals why the Chinese state considers "the five black categories" dangerous. The article was published in July 2015, after the Chinese police cracked down on a group of rights defense lawyers, their legal assistants, petitioners, and public opinion leaders. These people were arrested for inciting subversion of state power. Commentators argue this is the largest crackdown on lawyers since the end of the Cultural Revolution.[50] The *People's Daily* article asserts that the arrested people all belong to the "rights defense circle." The article describes their "wrong doings" as follows:

> A concerted operation organized and overseen by the Ministry of Public Security has smashed a suspected major criminal syndicate with the Beijing Fengrui Law Firm as its platform, which since July 2012 has organized and planned uproars around more than forty sensitive incidents, gravely disrupting social order. A suspected major crime syndicate has been uncovered that was composed of rights defense lawyers, helping hands and petitioners acting in collusion, which was tightly organized, extensive and had a rigorous division of labor. The seamy inside is emerging of how, while proclaiming to be for "rights defense," "justice" and the "public interest," it in fact gravely disrupted social order and attempted to achieve its sinister ends.[51]

The article explains that the government is furious and anxious about the prevalence of nationwide public opinion incidents, in which judges, police, and local government officials are criticized and put under unwarranted public scrutiny and pressure.

The *People's Daily* article traces the pattern by which nationwide public opinion incidents came to exist. According to the article, members of the "rights defense circle" were mostly critical of the party and the government, while also being unsatisfied with social reality. They called one another "citizens" and were proud of being put in detention by the government. They gathered frequently to discuss their plans and used WeChat, QQ, and telegram messengers to coordinate their action. When "sensitive events" occurred, rights defense lawyers and petitioners often rushed to the scene. They photographed and videotaped events, using WeChat and foreign websites to disseminate information. Public opinion leaders, particularly Big Vs, then came in to comment on events and forward information, imposing enormous pressure on local governments. In addition, when courts adjudicated cases, rights defense lawyers often openly confronted and expressed their opposition to the court. They also organized petitioners to protest outside the procuratorial, judicial, and public security buildings. The *People's Daily* article argues that the "rights defense circle" people cooperated and took action both online and offline; in so doing, the members of the rights defense circle turned common events into nationwide public opinion incidents and turned "sensitive events" into political events. The article asserts that, through their manipulation of public attention and opinion, the rights defense circle was able to produce outcomes beyond what they would have been able to achieve through normal legal procedures. The article condemns such behavior as not only disrupting public order and polluting online space, but also negatively influencing how the public and netizens think about the government, thus seriously undermining the government's credibility and image. The article appeared in major Internet news portals in China. China Central Television's news channel also reported the government's victorious crackdown on the "rights defense circle."

Clearly, the Chinese state is greatly concerned with this capacity and practice among citizens to turn individual local grievances into nationwide public opinion incidents. Among the "new black five categories," "the disadvantaged," political dissidents, and followers of underground religion are often grievants. Rights defense lawyers and public opinion leaders, along with journalists and NGO activists play a crucial role in making public opinion incidents, given their professional expertise and extensive social networks. The state's intensified crackdowns on these intermediary actors since 2013 suggest that the more likely an intermediary actor is able to reach the public and produce nationwide public opinion incidents, the more likely he or she will be the target of a crackdown.

Consider, for example, the seven founders of the New Citizen Movement, which aims to promote constitutionalism and build a civil society. All of the founders are public opinion leaders, activists, and/or rights defense lawyers. Among them, Xu Zhiyong and Teng Biao are both rights defense lawyers and were the key figures in the 2003 Sun Zhigang case, arguably one of the earliest and most important nationwide public opinion incidents. They were also the founders of the Open Constitution Initiative, a legal-aid NGO that played a key role in helping victims demand compensation in the Sanlu milk scandal. The founders of the New Citizen Movement are definitely among the most capable actors who can and would like to produce public opinion incidents. Since 2013, at least six of the seven founders have been the subject of government crackdown campaigns. Xu Zhiyong was convicted of gathering crowds to disrupt public order and sentenced to four years in prison in 2014.[52] Teng Biao is currently in exile. Wang Gongquan, an entrepreneur and a public opinion leader, was arrested in September 2013 for gathering crowds to disrupt public order and then released in January 2014 after he confessed.[53] Li Xungbing, a rights defense lawyer, was barred from leaving China in December 2015.[54] Li Fangping, also a rights defense lawyer, was taken by the police in March 2016.[55]

The case of Pu Ziqiang also shows how the Chinese government is hostile to key figures in public opinion incidents. As a famous rights defense lawyer and public opinion leader, Pu Ziqiang defended journalists (e.g., editors at *Southern Metropolis Daily*), dissidents (e.g., the artist Ai Weiwei), and "the disadvantaged" in criminal trials. Several of the cases that Pu represented, such as the 2012 Ren Jianyu case, became lightning rods.[56] Pu was arrested in 2014 and indicted in 2015 for using the Internet to incite ethnic hatred, insult people in public, and disrupt public order.[57] He was sentenced to three years in prison and put on probation in December 2015.[58]

China Central Television's staging of public confessions since 2013 further demonstrates the Chinese state's intention to stigmatize and intimidate people with influence in China's contentious public sphere. In these televised confessions, people are presented to a nationwide audience and compelled to criticize themselves and apologize for their "wrongdoings," all before any kind of judicial proceeding. Chinese newspapers and Internet portals then broadly report on the confessions to ensure that they receive public attention. Commentators analogize such televised confessions with public parades in which people were shackled and put in trucks during the Cultural Revolution and anticrime campaigns. Looking at media reports and information on news websites, I found that twenty-two people confessed on China Central Television between August 2013 and January 2016. Eighteen of the twenty-two (81.8%) were rights defense lawyers, activists, journalists, or Internet celebrities. Specifically, four (18.2%) were rights defense lawyers. Five were Big Vs with a record of allegedly trying to produce public opinion incidents (22.7%); six (27.3%) were journalists; one was a Swedish activist working for a legal-aid NGO (4.5%); one (4.5%) sold censored books in Hong Kong (4.5%); and one (4.5%) was a grassroots activist supportive of rights defense causes. In sum, the attack on what the Chinese government calls the "black zone" has focused on individuals who play a major role in forming nationwide public opinion incidents. To counter such incidents, China Central Television has staged nationwide spectacles of public shaming.

The Chinese state has also tightened its grip on organizations that might provide resources for the "black zone," or the "new black five categories," particularly news organizations, Internet portals, and NGOs. First, the Chinese state has increased control over critical news reporting, emphasized the role of media as the party's mouthpiece, and purged "problematic" news organizations.

To be sure, these measures were common in the Hu-Wen era, but the Chinese state under Xi has attempted to strengthen them. As I describe in chapter 4, journalists in China try to take advantage of the fragmented structure of the party-state agencies to produce critical news reports. For example, local newspapers produce critical reports about problems in other localities to circumvent censorship conducted by their own local governments; national newspapers that specialize in one area, such as business, cover problems in areas that are governed by other state agencies to bypass censorship. To address this problem, the General Office of the CCP and the Department of Propaganda began, in 2005, to prohibit cross-locality and cross-industry critical news reporting.[59] Then, in 2014, to further control critical reporting, the State Administration of Press, Publication, Radio, Film and Television (SAPPRFT) announced that journalists are not allowed to conduct critical news reporting unless they receive approval from their organizations. In addition, journalists are allowed to focus on only one industry or area; they are prohibited from reporting on news in other industries or areas. Faced with criticism about such restrictions, officials of the SAPPRFT insisted that these measures are for the protection of ordinary citizens because some journalists threaten victims to disclose "negative information" about them in order to demand "hush money."[60]

In 2014, the SAPPRFT also came up with the Rules on the Management of Information from Professional Activities of News Employees (*xinwen congye renyuan zhiwu xingwei xinxi guanli banfa*; hereafter, the Rules) to regulate media professionals.[61] As discussed in chapters 4 and 5, to counteract censorship, Chinese journalists sometimes provide the results of their investigations to other domestic media or foreign media; other times they share information on Internet forums anonymously or use their Weibo or WeChat accounts to spread information. Now the Rules require news organizations to sign confidentiality agreements with media professionals prohibiting such behavior. The Rules also require news organizations and media professionals to regulate their practices about information sharing and disclosure according to the State Secret Protection Law (*baoshou guojia mimi fa*) and the Labor Contract Law (*laodong hetong fa*). As critical news reporting and leaked results of news investigations often lead to heated online discussion, the above regulations constitute another state effort to prevent the formation of public opinion incidents.

The state's increasing control over media organizations is also shown by President Xi's foremost emphasis on the media's absolute loyalty toward the party. On the morning of February 19, 2016, Xi made high-profile visits to the Chinese state's three major mouthpieces: the *People's Daily*, the Xinhua News Agency, and China Central Television. China Central Television welcomed Xi with a sign that read: "Central Television's family name is the party. Absolutely loyal." That afternoon, Xi gave a speech at the party's News and Public Opinion Work Conference, in which he said, "The media operated by the Party and the government are the propaganda front line of the Party and the government. As such, they must have the Party as their family name. The Party's media must show the Party's will, reflect the Party's assertion, and safeguard the central Party's authority and the Party's unity."[62]

Although it has been always the case that Chinese media must follow the party line, it is still unusual for Chinese top leaders to state this fact so blatantly. Demanding that the media "have the Party as their last name" risks being interpreted as revealing the irrelevance or insignificance of the people in the state's estimation. I searched *People's Daily*'s electronic archive. Before Xi's speech in 2016, only one article mentioned that the media must have the party as their family name. This instance occurred in 1990, around one year after the 1989 Tiananmen incident. The timing was understandable. In addition, that article was based on discussion among party newspapers' chief editors, it was not citing the speech or writing of a top leader.[63] In fact, President Xi's slogan "media must have the Party as their family name" stands in sharp contrast with President Hu Jintao's slogan of "putting people first" (*yi ren wei ben*). Hu visited the *People's Daily* in 2008 and gave an important speech during his visit. He said that the essential of news work is "putting people first." He also emphasized the necessity of connecting the party's assertion to the people's will.[64] Xi's top-level emphasis on the party line suggests his deep concern with the possibility that Chinese media could be used to aid the black zone.

After Xi's speech on February 19, 2016, Ren Zhiqiang, a CCP member, real estate tycoon, and Big V, with 38 million followers, used Weibo to criticize the idea that media should serve the party. He wrote: "When has the people's government become the Party's government? Are we having two opposing camps now? When media all have their family name and do not represent people's interests, people will be abandoned and forgotten!" On February 28, 2016, the Cyberspace Administration of China instructed Sina and Tencent, two major Internet companies operating Weibo, to close Ren Zhiqiang's Weibo accounts because Ren "constantly disseminated illegal information and had very bad impacts."[65] In May, the CCP decided to discipline its maverick member and put Ren Zhiqiang on one-year probation. According to the party's decision, Ren Zhiqiang openly expressed opinion that violated the party's principles. It was made clear that Ren could be expelled from the party if his speech crossed the line again. The news about Ren's censure received wide coverage in major media and Internet news portals.[66] Given that the party has 85 million members while Ren has 38 million Weibo followers, it is no wonder the party is worried about Ren's influence. His case reveals the Chinese state's determination to curb the black zone and demand absolute loyalty to the party.

Of course, the attack on the black zone includes crackdowns on media organizations with strong connections to that zone. The Southern Group, which is famous for producing critical news reports, is considered a troublemaker by the Chinese state given the former's ideological orientation and established history of producing critical news reports. Under the Hu-Wen regime, the Chinese state purged the Southern Group to strengthen its control. In April 2012, the deputy head of the propaganda department of Guangdong Province, Yang Jian, was appointed as the party secretary of the Southern Group. Another propaganda official, Zhang Dongmin, was appointed as the chief editor of the group. These appointments were meant to ensure the propaganda system's direct control over the news production process. But Yang Xingfeng, a Southern Group veteran, still remained as the director of the Southern Group after the purge. Yang Xingfeng was, however, eventually removed from his position in March 2013. As mentioned in chapter 1, journalists at *Southern Weekly* openly resisted censorship imposed by Tou Zhen, the head of the propaganda department of Guangdong Province. Their resistance led to protests against censorship and restriction of freedom of the press, as well as a nationwide public opinion incident in January 2013. The public demanded Tou Zhen's resignation. About two months after this event, the Chinese state removed Yang Xingfeng, the Southern Group veteran, from his position as the director and appointed Yang Jian, the party secretary of the group and a former top propaganda official, in his place.[67] In so doing, the propaganda system achieved the highest-level control of the Southern Group. My interviewee, who was a Southern Group veteran, told me this was the very first time an outsider of the group has served as its director.[68] In 2015, Tou Zhen was promoted by the Chinese state as the deputy head of the Department of Propaganda at the central government.[69]

The Chinese state's attack on the black zone has also involved tightening regulations on Internet news providers when their "slack" implementation of censorship is deemed to have contributed to the formation of public opinion incidents. In February 2015, the Cyberspace Administration of China summoned the executive chiefs of NetEase. NetEase distinguishes itself from other Internet portals by emphasizing its provision of "news with a stance."[70] Officials of the Cyberspace Administration of China pointed out that NetEase's news service had severe "orientation problems" (*daoxiang wenti*), deviating from principles and ideology under socialism. NetEase was also accused of illegally reprinting news information as well as disseminating pornography and rumors. The officials demanded that NetEase correct its problems and strengthen its internal regulation or have its online news service terminated by the state. The Cyberspace Administration of China officials emphasized that online news providers should conform to the correct orientation, protect national and public interests, and actively disseminate "positive energy."[71] In April 2015, the executive chiefs of Sina were also summoned by the Cyberspace Administration of China and given a similar warning.[72] On April 28, 2015, the Cyberspace Administration of China enacted a new regulation that aims to strengthen the state's control over Internet news providers by formally institutionalizing the office's oversight practices and its ability to summon and discipline Internet news providers. This regulation is applied not only to news websites but also to mobile news service, blogs, Weibo, instant messengers, and WeChat, since news is also spread through these channels. Failure to comply with this regulation can lead to the withdrawal of licenses.[73]

Finally, the attack on the black zone has also targeted NGOs, many of which are alleged to have provided assistance to "the disadvantaged" and been involved in "rights defense" activism and public opinion incidents. Some NGOs have also received funding from outside China (Spires 2012). Although local governments often have to rely on NGOs to provide social services (Spires 2011), NGOs' organizational form and financial sources have made them increasingly suspicious to the Chinese state. Given that the Chinese state intends to attack the rights defense circle and the black zone, there is no convincing and logical reason why the Chinese state would *not* target NGOs, particularly those central to the rights defense circle.

In 2015, the Chinese state cracked down on the Beijing Yirenping Center and several labor NGOs in Guangdong. The Beijing Yirenping Center is a high-profiled NGO mainly involved in issues related to discrimination against people infected with hepatitis B and HIV/AIDS as well as people with disabilities. The birth of the Beijing Yirenping Center itself is deeply intertwined with the history of the contentious public sphere. As noted in chapter 6, antidiscrimination against hepatitis B patients was a salient issue in China's online forums in the early 2000s (Yang 2009). The most influential online website supporting hepatitis B patients in China was formed in 2001. The website established a forum dedicated to hepatitis B patients' rights and interests in 2003, with Lu Jun as the forum's operator. In November 2003, netizens associated with the forum collected 1,611 signatures, requesting that the NPC Standing Committee review the constitutionality of regulations that discriminated against hepatitis B patients. The collective action led to considerable legal change.[74] In 2006, Lu Jun and other forum participants formed the Beijing Yirenping Center. The center provides legal education, health education, and legal-aid service, while also collaborating with rights defense and public interest lawyers to file several high-profile public interest litigations in China.[75] The center's legal consultant Li Fangping is one of the cofounders of the New Citizen Movement. This shows the deep connection between the center and some of the country's most prominent rights defense and public interest lawyers. In an interview conducted by *Southern Weekly*, Lu Jun said his strategy was to file antidiscrimination lawsuits against big enterprises and multinational companies, then use media coverage to maximize the visibility and impact of the cases. Lu Jun noticed that cases covered by media were more likely to receive fair handling by the court.[76] In 2008, when the Sanlu milk scandal occurred, the center played a major role in recruiting and coordinating volunteer lawyers and worked closely with the Open Constitution Initiative, a legal NGO.[77] It seems reasonable to conclude that the center's close ties with key rights defense lawyers, its contacts with "the disadvantaged," and its publicity strategies made it a target for state action.

In 2012, the Beijing Yirenping Center began to undertake projects regarding gender equality, thus establishing connections with feminist activists.[78] In March 2015, Chinese police arrested and accused five feminist activists who planned to distribute anti-sexual-harassment fliers on International Women's Day of picking quarrels and provoking trouble. Some of the feminist activists worked with the Beijing Yirenping Center on LGBT (lesbian, gay, bisexual, and transgender) issues. While the center was demanding that the government release the activists, the police raided the center's Beijing office. In June 2015, the police arrested two staff members working at the center's Zhengzhou office, accusing them of illegally operating a business.[79] The center's founder, Lu Jun, is currently in exile.

The Chinese state's crackdown on labor NGOs in 2015 follows a similar logic as that which led to the clampdown on the Beijing Yirenping Center, but labor NGOs are perceived as even more dangerous by the Chinese state because they have the potential to organize large-scale strikes. Such risk has increased with the slowing down of China's economy. Recent studies of strikes and labor protests in China show that labor NGO activists behind the scenes have played a crucial role in the mobilization of collective action. Labor NGO activists have not only disseminated knowledge about law and policy but also coached workers about all kinds of contention strategies, even though these activists did not show up at protests or strikes (Chen 2015; Leung 2015). In April 2014, workers in a Taiwanese footwear factory in Dongguan, a city in the Guangdong Province, had a ten-day strike demanding their employer pay full social security and housing fund contributions. It is estimated that around thirty thousand workers went on strike. Workers spread information and photos using social media and instant messenger platforms. The strike was largely covered by media outside Mainland China. During the strike, the police raided the office of a labor NGO, the Shenzhen Chunfeng Labor Disputes Services Center, and detained two activists (Chen 2015). Under the pressure, the Shenzhen Chunfeng Labor Disputes Services Center decided not to accept foreign funding.[80]

From December 2014 to April 2015, workers in another footwear factory, belonging to the Lide company in Guangdong, initiated three waves of big strikes. Workers began to demand that the company pay its social insurance contributions when they heard that the factory could be moved to another place. Mounting pressure forced the company to reach an agreement with its workers. This time, the Chinese state intensified its crackdown. In December 2015, police in Guangzhou detained and then formally arrested seven labor NGO activists, charging them with gathering crowds to disturb public order or, in some cases, embezzlement. The main target was Zeng Feiyang, of the Panyu Workers Center, the labor NGO that worked with the employees of the Lide company. The Chinese state then adopted a similar media strategy as that used after the police cracked down on a group of rights defense lawyers in July 2015. On December 23, 2015, the *People's Daily* published a long report accusing Zeng of accepting foreign funding, manipulating strikes, and escalating conflicts between employers and employees in the name of rights defense. The article criticized Zeng and his members for operating illegal organizations and participating in more than ten strikes in the Pearl River Delta area. It asserted that, in every incident, Zeng asked workers to use Weibo and WeChat to broadcast the strikes and disclose information to foreign media to enlarge the strikes' impact. The article condemned Zeng's behavior as crossing the line. It was reprinted by other newspapers and major news websites. China Central Television also reported on Zeng's crimes.[81]

In addition to targeting specific influential NGOs, the Chinese party-state has also intensified general control over NGOs through new laws and regulations. In June 2015, the General Office of the CCP Central Committee announced the Provisional Regulation on Party Group Work (*zhongguo gongchandang dangzu gongzuo tiaoli, shixing*).[82] According to Article 5 of the regulation, the CCP can form a party group (*dangzu*)—a working group that aims to strengthen the CCP's leadership—in a social, cultural, or economic organization if that organization has more than three party members. This is the very first time in CCP's seventy-year history that it has issued a regulation regarding party groups. In September 2015, the CCP further issued the Opinion on the Work of Strengthening Party Building in Social Organizations (*guanyu jiaqiang shehui zuzhi dang de jianshe gongzuo de yijian, shixing*).[83] This opinion aims to give concrete instruction on how to enhance the party's leadership in social organizations. It stipulates that any social organization with more than three members should establish a party group. In addition, party groups in social organizations should promote and implement CCP policies and decisions, unify political identity of members, resist "improper tendencies," and police all kinds of illegal behavior. The formation of party groups in social organizations is apparently a measure to rein in and monitor NGOs daily, as well as to ensure that the emerging civil society remains subordinated to the party.

The Chinese state has also strengthened control over foreign NGOs. In April 2016, the National People's Congress passed the Foreign NGO Management Law (*jingwai fei zhengfu zuzhi jingnei huodong guanli fa*).[84] The Chinese state has been concerned that some foreign NGOs might conduct suspicious activities in China and undermine China's national security.[85] According to Professor Ma Huaide, one of the drafters of the National Security Law, the Foreign NGO Management Law, along with the National Security Law and

the Cybersecurity Law, aims to protect China's national security.[86] The Foreign
NGO Management Law sets behavioral guidelines for foreign NGOs. According to Article 5 of the law, foreign NGOs shall abide by Chinese laws; must
not endanger China's national unity, security, or ethnic unity; and must not
harm China's national interests, society's public interest, or other groups' and
citizens' lawful rights. In addition, foreign NGOs are barred from engaging in
political activism. The law authorizes the police, that is, public security organs, to govern and oversee foreign NGOs (Articles 6 and 7). In the past, the
Ministry of Civil Affairs was the main state agency in charge of foreign NGOs.
This shift reaffirms the Chinese state's concern about foreign NGOs' threats to
national security. The law further endows the police with far-reaching powers,
from summoning foreign NGOs for investigation to stopping their activities
and blacklisting them. In fact, since the Chinese state publicized the draft of
the Foreign NGO Management Law, the law has been perceived as hostile to
foreign countries and organizations by many countries and NGOs. The Chinese
state did make some compromise in the lawmaking process. Article 53 of the
law excludes certain forms of educational and academic exchange from the
application of the law, making sure that the law does not undermine scientific
and educational exchange.

TURNING THE GRAY ZONE RED

In addition to attacking the black zone, the Chinese state has also tried to turn
the gray zone red by cultivating voices to compete with the "black groups,"
boost the Chinese state's popularity, and further disseminate official discourse
and ideology. First, the Chinese state has been actively building two groups that
propaganda officials call "national teams." The first national team comprises
Weibo and WeChat public accounts operated by individual officials or party-
state agencies. Government agencies at various levels have set up Weibo and
WeChat accounts to reach the public. According to statistics publicized by Tencent, the number of official Weibo and WeChat accounts has significantly grown
since 2013. By the end of 2015, there were around 280,000 Weibo and more than
100,000 WeChat public accounts operated by the government.[87] Rather than
reacting to events passively, government agencies and officials now seek to get
ahead of issues by being the first to address events when they occur, hopefully
turning negative information into "positive energy."[88] The second national team
comprises Weibo, WeChat public accounts, and news apps operated by state-
controlled mainstream media. The two national teams interact regularly and
cooperate. For instance, when a local incident occurs, mainstream media use
Weibo and WeChat to disseminate information provided by local governments'
Weibo and WeChat public accounts. In so doing, the two national teams are
able to set agendas and amplify positive energy online.

Furthermore, the Chinese state under the Xi leadership has expanded the state's recruitment of "cyber-civilization volunteers" (*wangluo wenming zhiyuan-zhe*). Such practices have their roots in the Hu-Wen era. According to previous research, the Chinese state first began to use "Internet commentators" (*wanglou pinlun yuan*) in 2004 to guide online public opinion. Known as "fifty cents" (*wu mao*) or the "fifty-cent party" (*wu mao dang*), these commentators are either hired staff or volunteers who participate in online discussion and seek to channel it in certain directions (Yang 2009). In 2011, the CCP's Central Commission for Guiding Cultural and Ethical Progress formally institutionalized such practices. The commission instructed government agencies and SOEs to build teams of "cyber-civilization communication volunteers" (*wangluo wenming chuanbo zhiyuanzhe*). For example, according to the commission's instruction, in June 2011, Sichuan Province trained one thousand cyber-civilization communication volunteers, who were from twenty-one prefecture-level city governments: Sichuan Provincial Meteorological Bureau, Sichuan Electricity Company, Sichuan Surveying and Mapping Bureau, China Mobile Sichuan, and so forth.[89] The commission also came up with specific evaluation standards. Cyber-civilization communication volunteers are required to set up blogs, Weibo accounts, QQs, and online forum accounts to spread the core values of socialism and "positive voices," as well as to intervene in and guide online discussion.[90] Local governments usually give specific instructions on the number of cyber-civilization communication volunteers each government unit should contribute, the number of social media accounts each volunteer should sign up for, and the number of posts and articles each volunteer has to contribute per month.[91]

The Communist Youth League of China has scaled up this system. In 2015, echoing President Xi's call for building a clean online space, the Communist Youth League initiated a campaign to recruit ten million "youth cyber-civilization volunteers" (*qingnian wangluo wenming zhiyuanzhe*). The Communist Youth League announced that this initiative was its most important mission that year. It instructed each of its units to recruit no less than 20 percent of its members as youth cyber-civilization volunteers. Universities received instructions about how many volunteers they should recruit. These volunteers have two major responsibilities. The first is to amplify positive energy on Weibo and WeChat, actively spreading the core values of socialism and interacting with the Weibo and WeChat public accounts of the Communist Youth League and other party-state agencies. The second responsibility is to resist "negative energy," denouncing any information that contradicts the Four Cardinal Principles,[92] the core values of socialism, or ethnic unity. Many local governments and universities across China hosted ceremonies and events to celebrate the formation of their volunteer teams.

Finally, President Xi stated the need to enlist public opinion leaders to provide support for the realization of the "Chinese dream." At the Central

United Front Work Conference in May 2015, Xi pointed out that the government should strengthen its relationship with "well-known representatives of new media," set up regular contact and interaction with them both online and offline, and encourage them to "purify" cyberspace and amply the "main melody" and "positive energy" therein.[93] About two months before President Xi's talk, the CCP's United Front Work Department had already hosted a ten-day training session, in which one-third of the fifty-five trainees who took part were prominent new media professionals, CEOs of Internet companies, or Big Vs. This was the very first time the United Front Work Department had included new media people in its training. The training covered such issues as domestic and international affairs, economic problems and social transformation, the development of legal institutions in China, Internet governance, and big data science.[94] Xi's speech and this training reveal the Chinese state's effort to cultivate opinion leaders who are nationalistic and supportive of the Chinese state.

ASSERTING CYBER-SOVEREIGNTY

The Chinese state's effort to contain the contentious public sphere also includes asserting China's cyber-sovereignty and promoting the very concept of cyber-sovereignty. China has long been criticized for its censorship and repression. Rather than remaining silent on such criticism, Xi has been drawing on the concept of cyber-sovereignty to justify and defend the Chinese state's action. In July 2015, China passed the National Security Law (*guojia anquan fa*). According to Article 25 of the law, the Chinese state shall stop and punish unlawful and criminal activity on the Internet, such as cyberattacks, cybertheft, and dissemination of unlawful and harmful information; the state shall also maintain cyber-sovereignty, security, and the country's developmental interests.[95]

The Chinese state has also attempted to influence international norm making regarding Internet governance. In 2014, the Chinese state, specifically the Cyberspace Administration of China, established the World Internet Conference, also known as the Wuzhen Summit. At the second World Internet Conference, in 2015, President Xi gave a keynote speech in which he stated that China would undertake the mission to enhance global Internet governance because the current model not only failed to reflect the interests of most countries but also failed to address pressing global challenges such as terrorism and cyberattacks. Xi argued that in order to amend the global Internet governance system, one must follow the principle of respecting cyber-sovereignty. All countries should respect one another's right to choose its developmental path and models of Internet governance, as well as the right to participate in international policy making. No country should interfere in other country's domestic affairs; nor should a country support Internet activity that would undermine other countries' national security.[96] Essentially, Xi wanted to deliver the message that how the Chinese state regulates the Internet is its own business.

Uncertain Consequences

In some respects, the consolidated Chinese state has effectively tamed China's contentious public sphere. The Chinese state has forcefully cracked down on the most vocal and influential social networks in that sphere, that is, what the *People's Daily* called the "rights defense circle." Before 2014, rights defense lawyers, along with media professionals, public opinion leaders, outspoken newspapers, and public intellectuals, had been very successful in setting public agenda and turning events and litigations into nationwide public opinion incidents. These agendas and incidents tended to reflect social problems and reveal misconduct of state agencies. With the intensified crackdown, the influence of the rights defense networks on the formation of public opinion has clearly faded. Thus far, the leadership played by the key figures of the rights defense networks has not been taken up by other people. The absence of strong leadership suggests that the contentious public sphere in China is now less capable of thematizing problems and imposing pressure on the Chinese state.

To some extent, the Chinese state has also been able to control the contentious public sphere as it desires. Some evidence suggests that public attention to social conflicts and domestic problems has been usurped in recent years by issues related to international relations. The Public Opinion Monitoring Center of the People's Daily Online selects and analyzes the most widely discussed events every year based on the amount of articles and discussion in the news and social media. Comparing such events in 2014 and 2015, the report in 2015 finds that, among the mostly discussed events, the percentage of events related to social conflicts decreased by around 5 percent, while the percentage of events associated with China's foreign and military affair increased by around 5 percent.[97] This result is consistent with my own observations and recent research (Yang 2014). The top-down agenda of promoting the "Chinese dream" and the rise of popular nationalism go hand in hand, in the sense that popular nationalism does not lead to unmanageable nationalist protests. With China's rise on the global stage and its escalating tensions with other countries, issues related to international relations are likely to grab more public attention in the future. Such development, in general, works well for the Chinese state in terms of guiding the contentious public sphere, since the stance of the Chinese state and people tend to converge on issues related to China's international relations.

Nonetheless, the Chinese state is still limited in terms of the extent to which and how it can deal with the contentious public sphere. First, the Chinese state's effort to turn the gray zone into red had fairly limited success.

Although the number of Internet commentators and official Weibo accounts is huge, far from engaging with debates and controversial issues online, these accounts tend to produce posts that simply cheerlead for China, praise China's revolutionary history, or restate the regime's principles (Esarey 2015; King, Pan, and Roberts 2016), and the effects of such posts tend to be quite limited in terms of persuading Chinese citizens. In addition, the Communist Youth League's campaign to recruit ten million youth cyber-civilization volunteers was lambasted online. Many students posted that they were forced to sign up as volunteers. Facing widespread criticism, the Communist Youth League had to publish an article in the *China Youth Daily* to defend itself.[98] Furthermore, as I show in chapter 5, despite the crackdown on public opinion leaders, the majority of Weibo opinion leaders are political liberals. Although the Public Opinion Monitoring Center of the People's Daily Online finds that proliberal public opinion leaders lost significant influence after the crackdown in 2013, its own report shows that posts of proliberal public opinion leaders are still widely disseminated and read on Weibo and WeChat.[99]

Second, the Chinese state's upgrading techniques of surveillance and censorship have not led to better control of public opinion crises. The Chinese state has been enhancing its capacity to monitor, analyze, and respond to public opinion, but it still struggles with how to respond to public opinion crises. The 2015 Tianjin explosions, which led to the death of at least 165 people and injury of hundreds of others, demonstrate such weakness. Soon after the first explosion in Tianjin, information about and photos of the explosion were already being circulated widely via Weibo and WeChat, while the government and news media, particularly the media in Tianjin, provided little information. Chinese people were anxious and furious about the lack of transparency. Criticism of the media's collective silence and the government was everywhere online (Wei and Dai 2015; Wu and Liu 2015). But though the Chinese state was slow to provide information, it was fast to impose censorship. Soon after the explosions, the Department of Propaganda and the Cyberspace Administration of China instructed that news websites could only reprint news produced by the Xinhua News Agency and the *People's Daily* (Wei and Dai 2015). In two days, the Cyberspace Administration of China punished around fifty websites and about three hundred Weibo and WeChat users for spreading rumors.[100] Despite censorship, however, some marketized media outlets outside of Tianjin, particularly *Beijing News*, *Southern Metropolis Daily*, *Caijing*, and Caixin Media, as well as Internet portals like NetEase and Tencent, still managed to provide readers with investigative reports, although some of these media outlets were already severely purged or restructured by the Chinese state. The Tianjin explosions reveal the state's limited capacity to guide public opinion and impose complete censorship, as well as the resilience of marketized media.

But the most visible outcome of the state's intensified crackdown on the contentious public sphere was that rights defense lawyers did not organize to provide legal aid in the Tianjin explosion event as they had for similar such events in the past. The Chinese state had already arrested a group of rights defense lawyers just one month before the explosions. The middle-class residents whose housing was damaged in the explosions kneeled down in the streets, begging the party and the government to protect their property rights.[101] Online discussion pointed out that the explosions revealed the cruel fact that the middle class was not too different from "the disadvantaged" or petitioners in terms of their vulnerability in front of the state.[102] The absence of rights defense lawyers in the Tianjin explosions made the compensation a less salient issue in the contentious public sphere.

Third, the Chinese state's attack on the black zone has failed to silence critical voices, including direct criticism of the government's crackdowns. For example, *Legal Daily*, a newspaper affiliated with the CCP's Central Commission for Political and Legal Affairs, published an article criticizing the government's crackdown on Big Vs and other Internet users in 2013. The article argues that rather than combating crime, the state's harsh punishment and abuse of criminal law has undermined the state's credibility and made the public feel sympathetic toward the people punished.[103] Also, three days after the Chinese state arrested a group of rights defense lawyers and their assistants in July 2015, Caixin Media published an article on its website and on Weibo that called for protection of lawyers' rights. The article covered the speeches of three prominent law professors—Jiang Ping, Gao Mingxuan, and Chen Guangzhong—all of whom criticized the state's attacks on lawyers and asserted the need to respect, support, and protect lawyers. Although this article was finally removed from Caixin's webpage under censorship, it was widely forwarded and gained much support from netizens.[104] In addition, after the Chinese state arrested several labor NGO activists in December 2015, *Caijing* magazine immediately published an article to challenge such practices and released the article on Weibo, which was eventually censored. The article argues that because labor NGOs can help workers negotiate with their employers, they actually mitigate rather than contribute to social conflicts. The article further calls for the government to better balance the realization of workers' constitutional rights and the maintenance of social order.[105]

Furthermore, Caixin Media and the *Beijing Times* used the timing before the opening of the annual plenary sessions of the National People's Congress and the National Committee of the Chinese People's Political Consultative Conference (CPPCC) in 2016 to criticize the state's crackdowns. On March 1, 2016, Caixin Media and the *Beijing Times* directly censured China Central Television's practice of televising confessions. The two media both interviewed Wei Zhengfu, the deputy chairman of the All China Lawyers Association and a member of the CPPCC. Wei emphasized that televised confession does not equal a judicial conviction. Wei further called for an end to televised confession because the practice infringes on human dignity, leads to wrongful conviction, and undermines judiciary independence.[106] Wei's speech was widely praised by netizens online. On March 3, 2016, Caixin Media published an article titled "Jiang Hong: Citizens' Right to Freedom of Speech Must Be Protected." As previously discussed, the Cyberspace Administration of China closed Ren Zhiqiang's Weibo in late February after the influential opinion leader criticized Xi's view on media. Reacting to this, Caixin Media interviewed Jiang Hong, a professor in Shanghai and a member of the CPPCC. Reflecting on the tightening of speech, Jiang said, "I am not a CCP member, so I don't want to say anything about the CCP. But as a citizen, I think citizens' right to freedom of speech must be protected." This article was censored. Caixin Media published another article based on Jiang Hong's reaction to the censorship. Jiang said that he felt terrible that his speech was considered "illegal" because he had only stated a constitutional right. The article was censored again. To counteract the censorship, Caixin published an article on its English website and wrote, "An article based on the interview was posted on the news websites, but on March 5 it was deleted by the Cyberspace Administration of China, a government censorship organ, because it contained 'illegal content.'"[107] The statement was an extremely unusual challenge of state censorship. Unsurprisingly, the article was deleted once again.

The above examples of criticism of the Chinese state's crackdown reveal that the Chinese state's efforts to contain the contentious public sphere have encountered resistance from legal and media professionals. These examples might also indicate power struggles within the party-state, despite or *because of* President Xi's effort to restructure the party-state and consolidate power. As shown in chapter 4, the media is a critical part of China's political system. Different media often represent interests of different factions within the party-state. It is highly unlikely that direct criticism of the Cyberspace Administration of China would be voiced if it did not have the support of other high-level officials, who may well resent how much power the administration and its head have been granted by President Xi. And once again, the existence of friction within the party-state could open up space for the media to speak up and weaken the efficacy of the state's control.

Fourth, the state's crackdown does not eradicate the mobilizing capacity of certain social forces, particularly highly educated members of the middle class. For instance, the five feminist activists arrested in March 2015 for picking quarrels and provoking trouble were all released by the police in April 2015 after mobilization within and outside China. In China, the case was handled by several rights defense lawyers and supported by NGOs, lawyers, LGBT activists, and, importantly, many college students online and offline. Threats from the state did not stop them from speaking up or taking action. Many netizens posted images of themselves online, calling on the government to release the activists. Outside of China, the case was widely supported by transnational feminist networks, NGOs, international organizations, and foreign governments.[108] The mobilized effort shows the strength of society despite the intensified control.

The death of Lei Yang in 2016 also demonstrates the power of the country's highly educated middle class. Holding a master's degree in environmental science from the Renmin University, one of the most prestigious Chinese universities, Lei Yang worked for an environmental organization affiliated with the State Council in Beijing. One day, Lei Yang was detained by Beijing police for soliciting prostitution. He was then found dead in custody. Alumni of Renmin University released several statements. They argued that Lei Yang's case was not an accident but an orchestrated tragedy. They demanded the "highest power authority" to have an independent and just investigation into Lei Yang's death and to discipline China's public security organs. They also demanded basic personal safety and citizen rights.[109] Despite the effort to censor information about Lei Yang's death, mobilization through elite social networks put Lei Yang's case at the center of public attention. It also led to the Beijing Procuratorate's decision to investigate the illegal behavior of the Beijing police, although in the end, the Procuratorate did not indict the police officers involved.[110]

Nonetheless, not every social group is as resilient as the highly educated middle class under the state's crackdowns. I would argue that the disadvantaged, particularly peasants, workers, petitioners, and ethnic minorities, can still be seriously affected by the Chinese state's clampdown on the contentious public sphere. In the past, the disadvantaged were greatly aided by rights defense lawyers, NGOs, activists, media professionals, and public opinion leaders. Given that many of the above actors have been arrested and that the disadvantaged do not have impressive cultural and social capital, they now face even more difficulty addressing their grievances and restoring justice through the contentious public sphere.

Conclusion: Changing Dynamics of the Public Sphere

In this chapter, I have shown how the Chinese state, particularly the Xi leadership, has strategically responded to a rising contentious public sphere in China. By firmly tying this sphere to issues of social stability and national security, the Xi leadership has justified taking combative measures to cope with the contentious public sphere. Under the Hu-Wen administration, the Chinese state adopted a relatively more liberal approach, but this has been changing since 2013.

The Chinese state under the Xi leadership has developed comprehensive measures to contain the contentious public sphere. The state has consolidated its fragmented structure to enhance the efficacy of regulation. Law and technology have been used to strengthen censorship and surveillance, as manifested by the continued effort to legalize controversial practices and penalize undesirable behavior, as well as the promotion of big data science and cloud computing for the purpose of control. The Chinese state has also cast a wide net to attack key actors who have contributed to the rise of public opinion incidents and the contentious public sphere—public opinion leaders, the disadvantaged, rights defense and public interest lawyers, journalists, and activists—and staged national media trials to counteract these actors' publicity strategies. Meanwhile, the state has tightened up control of media, NGOs, and Internet companies. Effort has also been made by the state to promote official discourse and ideology and to assert China's cyber-sovereignty.

I argue that the Chinese state's effort to contain the contentious public sphere has yielded mixed and uncertain consequences. The state's action has dismantled or impeded the key social networks that enabled previous nationwide public opinion incidents. The targeting of such networks has greatly undermined the mobilization of social forces in producing public opinion incidents. Nonetheless, the state's crackdown has not completely silenced critical voices and mobilization. The state has encountered resistance from some legal and media professionals. Frictions within the party-state can still be exploited to enable the media to speak up and challenge censorship. In addition, a highly educated middle class has not been significantly influenced by the crackdown in terms of their capacity to unite themselves and make their voices heard. In contrast, the disadvantaged could encounter enormous difficulty in mobilizing public support without concerted support from rights defense and public interest lawyers, NGO activists, and journalists. The contentious public sphere may continue to survive and thematize some problems, but it is likely to become a space for the middle class if the disadvantaged do not receive support. Given no other outlet for expression or redress, the disadvantaged in China could develop a more extreme and radical response to their grievances. And if discussion of societal problems significantly decreases, the contentious public sphere could devolve into a venue dedicated primarily to the expression of nationalism.

8

Conclusion

I began to engage with the long tradition of scholarship concerning the public sphere after becoming intrigued by the lively political discussion I saw in the mid-2000s in China's online forums. The English translation of Jürgen Habermas's *The Structural Transformation of the Public Sphere* in 1989, along with a series landmark events between 1989 and 1991—the 1989 Tiananmen democratic movement in China, the fall of the Berlin Wall, and the collapse of the Communist regimes in Eastern Europe—sparked interest in and debates over the study of the public sphere in the Chinese context (Huang 1993). Several scholars employed Habermasian concepts to suggest the existence of a public sphere in China in the nineteenth century or the early republican period (Rankin 1986; Rowe 1990; Strand 1989), but such findings have been disputed (Wakeman 1993). Furthermore, some scholars cautioned against uncritical extensions of Habermas's intellectual agenda to the Chinese context, considering the enormous disparity between socioeconomic, political, and cultural conditions in the Chinese and European contexts (Calhoun 1993; Huang 1993; Wakeman 1993).

Yet, efforts to study the history of public opinion in the Chinese context were not without precedent. Chinese writer and linguist Lin Yutang published *A History of the Press and Public Opinion in China* in the United States in 1936. Like Habermas, Lin conceptualized public opinion as public discourse rather than as aggregated political attitudes or individual opinions. In addition, Lin's and Habermas's views on the normative role of public opinion in substantiating democracy were remarkably similar. Lin narrated the history of public opinion from the Han dynasty (206 BC to AD 220) to the republican era in the early twentieth century. He described the development of public opinion in China as a tug-of-war between the ruler and the people, given the tendency of rulers to suppress public criticism and the long-standing institution of censorship. His narrative portrayed a passive public that generally remained inactive except in unusual circumstances. As he put it, "It seems that the power of public opinion was always dormant in the nation, and if only placed under a good leadership or goaded by national danger, could and did it assert itself, fighting under great odds" (1936, 5). Lin showed that, even after the transition from imperial to republican rule, the antagonism between the state and public opinion endured. Rather than developing into a permanent sociopolitical force, public opinion returned instead to a more dormant state, partly due to continued state censorship in the republican era. Lin wrote, "We cannot ignore the contemporary censorship of books, magazines and newspapers in China, because it alone explains the retarding of the growth of public opinion" (1936, 168). He ended *A History on the Press and Public Opinion* with a call to awaken public opinion in China.

Censorship and authoritarian rule continue to exist in China, yet I have demonstrated and explained the rise of a nationwide contentious public sphere in PRC in the post-2005 period. The durability of such a contentious public sphere is precarious because of inadequate institutional protection against the aggression of the state. Nonetheless, the very existence of such a sphere reflects a fundamental social, cultural, and political transformation. Instead of existing as atomized individuals, many Chinese citizens are now able to coordinate and constitute a public that asserts nationwide influence. Rather than being obedient or indifferent, they have developed a contentious culture organized around the concept of law and rights. Through social and cultural practices, this public has uncovered societal problems and demanded responsiveness and accountability from the Chinese state, which now increasingly, if reluctantly, views public opinion as a force it must reckon with.

When I began this project in the late 2000s, I intended simply to explore how the Internet and information communication technologies (ICTs) had empowered and facilitated political communication in China—a subject very much on the minds of scholars in various contexts. But the story turned out to be much more complex than I had expected. I soon realized that I couldn't answer a number of questions—such as where public opinion leaders came from, why a specific group of media professionals took so many high-level positions in major Internet companies, and why so-called public opinion incidents were so highly associated with law and rights—without considering the marketization of media and the development of legal institutions in China, as well as the relationship between these institutional processes and their role in China's broader project of modernization. Throughout this book, I have sought to demonstrate that the rise of China's contentious public sphere has been an unintended consequence of the Chinese state's authoritarian modernization project, specifically the ways in which the Chinese state institutionalized and constrained the double-edged instruments of modern law, marketized media, and the Internet to pursue modernization. I have also suggested that the development of such a sphere continues to be subject to the authoritarian state's adaptive yet fragmented rule. Furthermore, I argue that examining the public sphere in China provides valuable insights that extend beyond the Chinese case alone; I discuss these insights in turn.

Modernization and Political Development

The development of the contentious public sphere in China is essentially a narrative about modernization, specifically, the unintended consequences of the Chinese state's modernization project. There have been long-standing, albeit often criticized, efforts to study and theorize the relationship between modernization and democratization (Inglehart and Welzel 2005).[1] Although the Chinese case is not one of transition to liberal democracy, the development of China's public sphere still provides some insights into the mechanisms through which modernization influences political development, particularly the rise of a more participatory and critical political culture.

The seminal argument in this respect is that offered by Seymour Martin Lipset (1959), who argued that economic development leads to democracy because it produces certain sociocultural changes that shape human actions. According to Lipset, various aspects of economic development—industrialization, urbanization, wealth, and education—enhance the conditions for democracy and contribute to a democratic culture. He argued that macro-level transformation, particularly education and communication, leads to individual transformation and more political participation. Subsequent studies, alternately critiquing or supporting Lipset, have examined the relationship between economic development and political regime. Despite the actual complexity of Lipset's writing, his statement that "the more well-to-do a nation, the greater the chances that it will sustain democracy" has often been singled out and used to fuel research examining the statistical association between per capita income and the probability that a country will transition to and sustain a liberal democracy (Epstein et al. 2006; Lipset 1959, 75; Przeworski and Limongi 1997). Other studies have investigated the links between political regime and the interaction between social classes in the process of modernization (Moore 1966; Rueschemeyer, Stephens, and Stephens 1992), or between political regime and levels of inequality (Acemoglu and Robinson 2001; Acemoglu 2006; Boix and Stokes 2003).

The literature in this area, however, does not adequately attend to how modernization can lead to a prodemocratic cultural change; it also tends to focus more on the strategic action of elites than the masses (Inglehart and Welzel 2010; Welzel and Inglehart 2008). To tackle these problems, Ronald

Inglehart and Christian Welzel (2005) proposed a revised version of modernization theory and analyzed several waves of cross-national survey data. For Inglehart and Welzel, democracy is not just about elite bargaining and constitutional engineering but depends on entrenched orientations among ordinary people that motivate them to demand freedom and government accountability. Rising levels of education, expanding mass communication, and increasingly knowledge-intensive work widen people's intellectual recourses, make people more cognitively autonomous, and lead to an emphasis on human autonomy. Finally, Inglehart and Welzel deal with the causal linkage between values and institutions. They ask, "Is a prodemocratic political culture among the public a precondition for the success of democratic institutions at the system level? Or are prodemocratic mass values simply a consequence of living under democratic institutions?" (Inglehart and Welzel 2005, 8). Inglehart and Welzel contend that the causal flow runs from values to institutions rather than the other way around, and they emphasize that such value change can occur under either democratic or authoritarian institutions.

In keeping with Inglehart and Welzel's theory, the rise of China's contentious public sphere is linked to the rise of expressive practices and increased demands for state accountability and responsiveness based on the concept of law and rights. Nonetheless, the Chinese case also challenges Inglehart and Welzel's theory in certain ways. First, in their original argument, Inglehart and Welzel contended that since mass demand for freedom already exceeded the institutional supply in China, they predicted in 1995 that China would make a transition to a liberal democracy within the next two decades (Inglehart and Welzel 2005, 191). They were correct to point out the increasing demand for state responsiveness and accountability in China, but importantly, demands do not equal or necessarily produce democratization. Formal institutional change (or lack thereof) is still influenced by a wide range of factors, such as geopolitics and the structure of the state and society (e.g., the level of fragmentation of the state) as well as the interaction of these factors. Inglehart and Welzel's theory does not adequately specify how and under which conditions demands for democracy will actually lead to a transition to liberal democracy.

Second, the Chinese case suggests the significance of institutions in shaping a more liberal and participatory political culture. Whereas Inglehart and Welzel stress the causal influence of values and culture on the building of democratic institutions, the Chinese case shows the influence of institutions, particularly modern legal institutions and the market, on the formation and dissemination of values and culture, even though the design and operation of these institutions remains subject to the control of an authoritarian state. Within a context characterized by market competition and the dissemination of the concept of rights, institutional processes in China created capable individuals, enhanced individual autonomy, and led to the overlap of multiple social networks. Both the media and legal professions became more diverse and relatively autonomous while the legal institution, legal service market, and news market were developing. Rising levels of educations and expanding mass communication certainly contributed, as Inglehart and Welzel would predict, but institutional processes also affected what *kinds* of values and culture were produced and transmitted.

It is worth reiterating that institutions do not emerge and exist in a vacuum. The specific ways in which the Chinese state built China's institutions and the ways in which certain key actors (e.g., legal and media professionals) interacted with institutions were deeply influenced and conditioned by China's active pursuit of modernization and selective adoption of globally hegemonic institutions originating from the West since the late Qing period.

Media, the Internet, the Law, and Political Liberalization

The institutionalization of modern law, marketized media, and the Internet was a critical part of the Chinese state's modernization project. The study of China's contentious public sphere also speaks to the relationships among media, the Internet, law, and political liberalization. The general insight gleaned from the Chinese case is that although marketized media, the Internet, and law have been used by the Chinese state as important instruments to pursue its authoritarian modernization project, they have also unequivocally empowered Chinese people in various ways. The level and scope of empowerment is drastic if we compare civic life in the post-2005 period with life before the reform and consider the accumulative and multiplying effects of institutional processes in both media and legal fields. I emphasize accumulative effects because the development of China's contentious public sphere is related to the convergence of media, the Internet, and law, rather than the operation of just one or the other. The limited emancipation and empowerment generated by marketized media was hugely magnified through network processes mediated by the Internet. Indeed, one of my central arguments is that we need to trace such complicated processes and map their connections to explain the development of China's contentious public sphere, rather than looking for any single explanation.

Of course, the existence of emancipatory and empowering effects does not mean that marketized media, the Internet, and law have generated nothing but benefits for the public sphere. Abundant problems exist, such as the infiltration of money into marketized media's news production, political polarization on the Internet, and citizens' misunderstanding of law. Ordinary citizens, media and legal professionals, media organizations, and business actors are not all innocent in or ignorant of these issues. But the most fundamental problem still comes from the Chinese state. Few, if any, institutional mechanisms restrict the Chinese state's ability—particularly at the highest level—to powerfully shape and delimit the role of media, the Internet, and the law. As a result, while these technologies and institutions have enabled and empowered Chinese people to some extent, the Chinese state continues to adapt to the situation, seeking to turn media, the Internet, and the law into better tools for propaganda, repression, and surveillance. Such state aggression threatens the durability of China's contentious public sphere.

Despite the uncertain future of China's contentious public sphere, it is still important to consider what its development means for relevant debates on the relationships among media, the Internet, the law, and politics. Extant studies tend to predict or point out unequivocal political consequences of media marketization in authoritarian contexts. Market mechanisms are expected to generate forces that counteract the monopolistic power of the authoritarian state (Curran 1991, 48; Keane 1991, 152–53). The acceleration of media marketization in China since 1992 has drawn several scholars to study its political implications, but the expected liberalizing effects have not been found—at least not in the form expected. The most common explanation for this has been to point to the state's updated control mechanisms, which effectively monitor news content, journalists, and media (Lee 2000; Lynch 1999; Zhao 1998, 2004). Scholars also argue that media marketization has, in fact, rendered media into even more effective propaganda organs for an authoritarian state, thus enhancing the state's legitimacy (Stockmann and Gallagher 2011; Stockmann 2013). Another argument is that media marketization has led to the triumph of political and capitalist market power, as well as the exclusion of disadvantaged groups (Zhao 2004).

This book contributes to the debate in two ways. First, rather than seeing media marketization as a process with a homogeneous impact in China, my analysis in chapter 4 provides a more nuanced understanding of this process and highlights the significance of political fragmentation in moderating the effect of media marketization. In localities where journalist communities were paired with a competitive newspaper market and less unified state agencies, the fragmented environment allowed journalists to produce critical news reports. Specifically, journalists were able to develop social networks across media and legal fields and collaborate with liberal-leaning legal professionals in ways that resisted political pressure and facilitated critical news reporting. The production and circulation of news was, simultaneously, a process of coalition building among professionals in different fields, a process of establishing civil society networks, a process of culture making and diffusing, and a process of resistance. Conversely, in localities without this conjunction of conditions, such coalition building and critical news reporting did not develop to the same degree. My analysis shows that, although media is often described as depoliticized in various contexts, media organizations in authoritarian contexts can act as de facto social movement organizations under certain conditions. Second, as noted in chapter 5, I attend more explicitly to the connection between the traditional press and the Internet news market by tracing the connection between the two sectors. I find that liberalization effects in the press, albeit limited, played a significant role in shaping the operation of online news services and social media, as well as the growth of the contentious public sphere.

My findings also help us rethink the debate over the political consequences of the rise of the Internet. Conventional wisdom understands ICTs as conducive to democracy. There are two main rationales. First, technology can spread liberty and democracy. Technology is believed to contribute to a participatory citizenry and culture, both of which are essential for democracy. Scholars continue to debate this relationship between technology and democracy, with some praising the democratic potential of technology, and others viewing the conventional wisdom as unrealistically romantic (Barber 1998, 2000; Barney 2000; Benkler 2006; Sunstein 2007). In the Chinese context, some argue that the Internet has had democratic consequences (Lei 2011; Tai 2006, 289; Tang 2005, 87, 98; Yang 2009; Zheng 2008). Others contend there has been no real democratizing effect because the Internet remains primarily a playground for entertainment that is well within the state's control (Kluver et al. 2010; Peters 2002; Yang 2009, 10). Middle-ground arguments are more ambivalent about the development (Zhao 2008; Zhou 2006).

The Chinese case does support the notion of the Internet having liberalizing effects, partly owing to its technological properties (Benkler 2006). The Internet has significantly undermined the role of the state and the state-controlled media as gatekeepers of news and information, despite the continuing existence of censorship. It is true that people's chances of being heard remain far from equal in the networked public sphere, but the situation is, nonetheless, vastly improved compared to when there was only the mass media. The Chinese case also clearly shows that the Internet has enhanced individuals' capabilities and helped them not only pursue their personal interests but also build associational life through establishing connections (however loose) and organizations. Compared with the mass media, the Internet is far more effective at facilitating social connection. Through enabling the overlap of multiple social networks, the Internet has helped to break social and spatial boundaries and connect various social groups previously unable or unlikely to communicate, particularly elites and nonelites. The Internet's technological properties have thus weakened the Chinese state's technique of "divide and rule," which aims to prevent interaction between various social groups to avoid the formation of competitive social forces (Perry 2007).

The Chinese case also reminds us that the political effects of technology are context dependent. Before elaborating on this point, I should clarify what we can and cannot glean from the Chinese situation. The Chinese case is about incremental political change—how an influential contentious public sphere capable of regularly holding the government accountable was able to emerge in an authoritarian context. It is not an example of revolution and regime transition as in the events composing the Arab Spring. In the Chinese case, technology was a catalyst to consolidate a series of historical processes. On the one hand, had it not been for ICTs, an influential contentious public sphere could have taken much longer to arise in China, as ICTs did help to produce and spread critical political culture across social groups. ICTs are especially important in extending critical culture and practices from politicized elites to ordinary citizens. On the other hand, had it not been for the previous development and institution building in the media and legal fields, the effect of ICTs would have been very limited. ICTs do not automatically spread democracy or lead to critical culture and practices. Sociocultural foundations that support the production of critical culture and capable agents need to exist. In essence, technology is critical and operative but not deterministic.

The study of China's contentious public sphere also contributes to discussion of a global trend—states' use of the Internet and ICTs for hypersurveillance around the world in the name of national security. In chapter 7, I describe how the Chinese state under the Xi leadership has come to see the Internet as a battlefield for national security and has been accelerating efforts to repurpose ICTs, cloud computing, and big data science for censorship and surveillance. In China, the fact that most Internet users use the same platform, particularly WeChat, to deal with many aspects of life (e.g., public discussion, private messaging, group interaction, traffic arrangement, payment, etc.) makes surveillance even easier and the scope of surveillance enormous. But it is not only authoritarian states that are deeply implicated in surveillance abuses using ICTs. In 2013, Edward Snowden's disclosure of global surveillance programs run by the U.S. National Security Agency revealed the extent to which even liberal-democratic states work with one another and with telecommunication companies to conduct surveillance of citizens. The difference between the situation in China and that in liberal democracies is that, in the latter, people have more freedom to criticize surveillance, seek redress through a system of checks and balances, and oversee (at least in theory) the state's actions. Moving forward, how liberal democracies, especially the United States, handle the question of state misuse of ICTs will be an issue watched closely by the Chinese state, which is always looking for ways to debunk liberal democracy.

Finally, I turn to the relation between law and political development. The notion of the rule of law is often connected to liberal democracy in public and academic discourse. The rule of law reflects the notion of self-determination. The lawmaking process requires democratic procedures to ensure that the law reflects the will of citizens. Law can bind the state and citizens because the law derives its validity from the consent of citizens (Habermas 1996). In other words, consent from the governed justifies and counterbalances the law's oppressive characteristics. Nonetheless, many authoritarian states, including the Chinese party-state, embrace law as well, although they have different understandings of the "rule of law." As legal scholar Brian Tamanaha (2004) states and Jothie Rajah's (2012) study of Singapore show, authoritarian states' adoption of a thin formulation of the rule of law is beneficial for capitalist development, while still being compatible with authoritarian rule. According to this formulation of the rule of law, or what scholars have variously called "authoritarian rule of law" (Rajah 2012), "a thin theory of rule of law" (Peerenboom 2002, 3), or most commonly "rule by law" (Ginsburg and Moustafa 2008), law is an instrument for government action. Rule by law can be said to exist as long as the government uses law to conduct its affairs. This formulation puts few legal limitations on the government (Tamanaha 2004, 92). As such, when an authoritarian state espouses rule by law, the strategy can actually strengthen the authoritarian state's domination (Lee 2007, 10; O'Brien and Li 2006; Tamanaha 2004, 111). As I show in chapter 3, China also adopted rule by law. Intent on installing law as a critical instrument of governance, the Chinese state used media to disseminate legal knowledge and transform Chinese people into legal subjects. Although the Chinese state defends rule by law by invoking the concept of "rule of law with Chinese characteristics," scholars and commentators contend that the situation in China is undemocratic and lacks the true quality of rule of law (Diamond 2003; Tamanaha 2004; Zhao 2003).

Nonetheless, the development of China's contentious public sphere suggests that even rule by law can bring about significant social and cultural changes. As David Clark (1999, 34) argues, "The risk to political rulers of using the rhetoric of legal rule and legal equality is that these terms will be deployed to press for real political accountability by political rulers." In E. P. Thompson's study of legal history in England, he found that although English liberal law reinforced social inequalities and benefited the ruling class, the ideology of law—the thinking that rulers ought to be bound by law—enabled the transformation of rhetoric to reality. As the ideology of law spread, it became a culture that shaped the behavior of both the rulers and the ruled (Tamanaha 2004; Thompson 1975). Indeed, when rhetoric is taken for granted and deeply rooted in culture, it can become a sociocultural force with self-fulfilling properties.

Studies of the legal profession in China have shown that the Chinese state's establishment of rule by law has led to the emergence of lawyers who have, in contrast, developed a liberal ideology of the rule of law and pushed for a thicker version of it. For instance, Terence C. Halliday and Sida Liu (2007) find that some Chinese lawyers have developed a liberal ideology of the rule of law, while also challenging the state's discourse of the rule by law and pointing out the illiberal aspects of China's legal institutions. Furthermore, Liu and Halliday (2011) identify variation among Chinese criminal lawyers in terms of their political and legal ideology. A group of politically liberal lawyers Halliday and Liu term "notable activists" rely on the media and the Internet to protect themselves and to influence public opinion. The research of rights defense (*weiquan*) and public interest lawyers has also reached similar findings (Fu and Cullen 2008; Fu and Cullen 2011). Such viewpoints of liberal and public-minded lawyers compete with official legal discourse through the mediation of the media. These lawyers have also mobilized law to push for legal, political, and social changes.

Existing literature also finds that not only legal professionals but also ordinary citizens mobilize law to demand accountability from the state. Studies in the Chinese context of labor and peasant protests have already pointed out that the Chinese state is pressured by Chinese people to live up to its promises under the law and that failure to deliver on those promises can lead to rightful resistance—resistance that aims to restore interests or rights in accordance with the law (Lee 2007, 261; O'Brien and Li 2006). Research also suggests that disputants share their experiences with journalists or on the Internet as a strategy to fight for their rights. He Xin, Wang Lungang, and Su Yang's (2013) study of migrant wage claimants finds that migrant workers who feel alienated by formal legal institutions have appealed to the court of public opinion to address their grievances. In a similar vein, Guobin Yang's (2009) research on the Internet finds disputants often discuss their frustrations regarding legal and political institutions online to mobilize public support and restore justice.

Adding to the above literature, I have demonstrated that law serves as a medium connecting individuals to the Chinese state and to other Chinese people. As my analysis in chapter 6 shows, various kinds of issues, contentions, and incidents as well as different social groups have been connected through the concept of law and rights. The results have led to both antagonism and social integration. Law has given Chinese people a legal status as citizens, allowing them to demand that the state itself follow the law and fulfill their rights. As laws and rights have become the major cultural framework used by citizens to make sense of social problems and make moral judgments, the state's continuing inaction to enforce the law and protect rights has created tension between the Chinese state and the people, leading some citizens to point out the structural roots of many societal problems in China. Whereas previous studies on law and resistance in China have found that Chinese people blame only their local party-state for ignoring rights or violating the law (Lee 2007, 261; O'Brien and Li 2006), my findings in chapter 6 demonstrate that some Chinese people have directed their contestation to the central party-state and the very nature of the political regime. In addition to affecting the vertical relationship between individuals and the state, the law has also aided social interaction, reshaping the horizontal relations among Chinese people. Previous studies have focused primarily on how individuals with personal grievances engage with the law (He, Wang, and Su 2013; He 2014; Lee 2007, 261; O'Brien and Li 2006), whereas I have demonstrated how various actors in the public sphere without personal grievances came to constitute a public through the mediation of media, collectively invoking legal claims to challenge the Chinese state. Legal and media professionals, NGOs, activists, grievants, and netizens came together in this sphere, united by a common citizen identity and an understanding that citizens' rights should be respected and protected.

I have also shown that China's rule by law has led to contestation about the very meaning of the rule of law and the relationship between the rule of law and the political regime. The Chinese party-state sees law as its instrument and embraces a top-down, paternalistic legal order. Echoing liberal-leaning media and legal professionals who advocate a thicker version of the rule of law, some Chinese netizens have begun to reflect on the normative meanings of law and question the "rule of law with Chinese characteristics." They have developed a conception of the rule of law that is similar to the common conception of the rule of law in liberal democracies (Tamanaha 2004), while even challenging law on the books itself when it deviates from their substantive, normative understanding of law.

It is meaningful to situate my findings regarding law in relation to Habermas's account of the rise of the classic bourgeois public sphere in Europe. In Habermas's study, private law secured the individual autonomy so that private people were able to pursue their affairs with one another, free from impositions by the state (Habermas 1989, 76). In the Chinese case, although law does not secure autonomy for individuals or society, the authoritarian rule by law in China has paradoxically led to a relatively democratic and participatory political culture and more organized citizenry. The Chinese situation suggests that three conditions were important for the rule by law to have such social and cultural effects. The first condition is that modern Chinese law *acknowledges* similar basic civil, political, and socioeconomic rights as their counterparts in liberal democracies, even though these rights are not realized and may even be suppressed by the state. Even when confined to a largely rhetorical existence, these rights empower citizens and give them grounds to make demands on the state. The second condition is that law became a shared cultural medium, providing a common language for citizens to discuss problems and develop a common identity. The Chinese state is one of the very few authoritarian states willing and able to disseminate law widely. The third condition is that experts, especially legal and media professionals, provided citizens with interpretations of laws and rights that competed with the official interpretation, thus raising citizens' expectations about the rule of law and democracy. Under these conditions, the authoritarian rule by law—however flawed—has generated sociocultural forces that aim to hold the government accountable and enhance citizen rights.

Institutions, Individuals, Networks, and Civil Power

The study of China's contentious public sphere is also relevant to what John Padgett and Walter Powell call "the problem of emergence" (Padgett and Powell 2012a). Unlike Poland under communism, China does not have an independent trade union or a strong religious organization like the Catholic Church. Given the CCP's penetration of Chinese society (Zhao 2001, 41), it is reasonable to ask how civil power could emerge in the first place, let alone consolidate. Padgett and Powell argue that new organizational forms or inventions often emerge through spillover across multiple intertwined social networks. In addition, movement of a practice from one domain to another (i.e., what they call "transposition") as well as feedback among multiple social networks constitute sources of novelty. Furthermore, transformation at the individual level co-occurs with the evolution of networks. In order words, Padgett and Powell contend that the coevolution of individuals and multiple networks leads to the emergence of novelty.

Padgett and Powell's argument is borne out by the developments in China. As I argue, the overlapping of multiple social networks involved in uncovering and addressing societal problems, as well as the constitutive relationship between such network processes and individual transformation, gave rise to civil power in China. In the beginning, the key social networks were networks of journalists. These networks intersected with networks of lawyers and intellectuals through law dissemination programs, provision of legal aid, and critical news reporting. Growing BBS forums incubated activist networks, which then led to the creation of some NGOs. These activist networks further intersected with the networks of journalists, lawyers, and intellectuals through two mechanisms. First, some journalists were simultaneously activists and key players in NGOs. Second, activists and NGOs working on various issues from public health to antidiscrimination, environment, food safety, and labor came together to provide legal aid and/or disseminate legal knowledge to related social groups. As a result, these activists and NGOs connected themselves to lawyers. The activist networks associated with BBS forums also included grievants who were using the new medium to voice their problems, as well as ordinary citizens who participated in discussion or served as donors or volunteers. Moreover, the above networks extended to major Internet companies and an enormous number of netizens through the labor market of media professionals and social media, particularly Weibo. In short, continuous expansion and overlapping of social networks—a process aided by market mechanisms and ICTs—contributed to the connection of various social groups and the rise of civil power. Accordingly, although existing literature emphasizes the importance of associational life to the development of a public sphere (Calhoun 1993; Eley 1992), the Chinese case reveals the importance of not only associational life but also processes of network overlap.

Innovative and contentious practices emerged and spread through these network overlap processes. As I demonstrate in chapter 4, the commingling of media and legal professionals contributed to innovative critical news reports that overcame certain aspects of censorship and highlighted public dimensions of the law and rights—particularly those aspects of the law and rights related to the relationship between individuals and the state and the communal relationship among individuals. The practices of using law and rights to uncover problems and demand state responsiveness and accountability soon spread across multiple networks. My empirical analysis also demonstrates individual transformation, especially empowerment, in this process. For instance, media professionals became more capable and felt empowered by their collaboration with lawyers, while netizens became politicized in the process of discussing societal problems and discerning the structural connections between only-seemingly individual issues. In essence, one of the reasons that the Chinese state did not have absolute control of its authoritarian modernization project was this unexpected emergence of overlapping network processes, as well as the growth of key actors' creativity and capability in the process.

Nonetheless, as much as I agree with Padgett and Powell (2012a, 2012b) that spillover across multiple networks provides a powerful answer to "the problem of emergence," I don't think their answer gives enough credit to the role of institutions. As the development of China's contentious public sphere shows, individuals and networks coevolve in institutional contexts. Actors are empowered, enabled, and constrained by institutions. Institutions also influence what kinds of social networks actors form, as well as how likely it is that multiple networks will overlap. In the case of China's contentious public sphere, the Chinese state's emphasis on rule by law and its dissemination of legal knowledge and the concept of rights rendered legal professionals key players in relevant social networks and made the cultural medium of law and rights critical to the formation of a contentious political culture. The institutional structure, such as the fragmentation of the state, also affects whether and how multiple networks intersect with one another. Therefore, I argue that the coevolution of not only individuals and networks but also institutions plays a critical role in the emergence of civil power.

Fragmentation and Adaptability of the State

The study of China's contentious public sphere also sheds light on the relationship between the state's fragmentation and adaptability and the public sphere. As I demonstrate in chapter 4, fragmentation of the state structure, interacting with market competition, opened up space for public-spirited journalists to collaborate with lawyers. In other words, media and legal networks would not have overlapped and facilitated the emergence of innovative practices had it not been for the state's fragmentation. Therefore, the state's fragmented structure, especially when paired with market competition, is a key factor explaining the Chinese state's inability to fully control how its authoritarian modernization project unfolded and why the state's action led to unintended consequences.

There is a striking parallel between this finding that political fragmentation in China opened up space for political mobilization and what Paul Starr describes as the emergence of de facto public spheres in Western Europe and North America. By a de facto public sphere, Starr means a public sphere that is not constitutionally protected. The contentious public sphere in China belongs to this category. In *The Creation of the Media*, Starr (2004, 47) finds that the development of public spheres in Western Europe and North America varied, but an embryonic, or de facto, public sphere generally emerged "once communications networks developed if and when there were significant political cleavages and competition among printers." Such de facto public spheres helped to create the experiences that laid a critical foundation for later constitutionally protected public spheres.

In the English case, a vigorous de facto public sphere emerged in the 1690s owing to the division in parliament—the competition between two parties, Whigs and Tories. Both parties used party-sponsored, market-oriented newspapers to mobilize political support in order to win elections. Such competition led to the growth of the press and the emergence of a space for public discussion and debate. In the case of the Netherlands, an independent press developed by the eighteenth century owing to the absence of a strong central government capable of ensuring censorship. As political power resided at the city level, printers moved from one location to another to evade censorship. Such fragmented conditions cultivated relatively independent newspapers. In British North America, competition and divisions among local elites contributed to the outbreak of public controversy in Boston, New York, and Philadelphia during the 1700s. The commonality between the above cases and the Chinese case indicates the critical significance of political fragmentation to the emergence of a de facto public sphere.

In addition to fragmentation, which is a weakness of the state, my analysis also shows the importance of the Chinese state's adaptability—something that has long been considered by scholars of Chinese studies as a strength of the Chinese state and a key to explaining the CCP's endurance (Heilmann and Perry 2011; Nathan 2003; Tsai 2006). As I show in chapter 7, the Chinese state under President Xi Jinping has also clearly recognized this fragmentation as weakening the state's regulatory capacity and as a factor that contributed to the rise of China's contentious public sphere. The state under Xi has thus moved to consolidate administrative and regulatory power, and has cracked down on key actors to cease the expansion and overlap of social networks. These measures might work in the short term but could have uncertain effects in the long term.

Various examples discussed in the empirical chapters suggest this possibility for unintended long-term consequences. For example, after the 1989 Tiananmen incident, the Chinese state did not publicly repudiate the notion of "supervision by public opinion" proposed by the reformist leader Zhao Ziyang; instead, the state emphasized the need to guide and control public opinion. Since then, propaganda officials have been assessing the general climate of public opinion and adjusting the state's efforts to control it accordingly. When the general climate of public opinion is considered unruly and threatening to stability, propaganda officials tighten the leash. Conversely, when the general climate of public opinion is not seen as threatening, propaganda officials loosen their grip. Such adaptability enabled the Chinese state to take public opinion into consideration in its decision making without risking instability—but only for a limited period. By the mid-2000s, the notion of "supervision by public opinion" helped liberal-leaning journalists and lawyers to produce critical news reports and provided justification for Chinese citizens to voice their problems. The Chinese state's flexible adjustment of its "leash" on public opinion did not forestall the rise of public opinion in the post-2005 period.

The state's adaptability has also led to ideological fragmentation, which undermines the state's ability to win "ideological battles" in China's contentious public sphere as well as to gain legitimacy based on ideology (Zhao 2001). As I point out in chapter 7, the Xi leadership considers the management of public opinion a question of not only social stability but also ideological struggle and national security. This concern is very real. To achieve their respective images of modernity, Chinese leaders after Mao have come up with contradictory policies, theories, and practices and adopted institutional arrangements associated with capitalism and liberal democracy. Deng Xiaoping shifted away from Communist ideology under Mao. At the Twelfth National Congress of the CCP in 1982, Deng used the term "socialism with Chinese characteristics." Based on Deng's talk during his Southern Tour in 1992, President Jiang Zemin employed the notion of "socialist market economy" in the Fourteenth National Congress the same year. President Jiang further announced the building of a "socialist legal system with Chinese characteristics" in the Fifteenth National Congress in 1996.

Although this adaptability on the part of Chinese leaders has contributed to China's economic success, it has triggered backlash as well. On the one hand, the shift away from Mao alienated those who had supported him and his version of communism. This then manifested among some Chinese people as support for Bo Xilai, who endeavored to develop an alternative socioeconomic development model that hewed more closely to Mao's thinking. On the other hand, as I demonstrate in chapter 6, many Chinese citizens use institutions and ideologies in liberal democracies to criticize the Chinese "versions" that are then developed. For instance, they claim that "rule of law with Chinese characteristics" is essentially the absence of rule of law and an opposition to justice, citizens' rights, and conscience. In addition, although the notion of "Chinese characteristics" provides the flexibility for Chinese leaders to adapt the state to new situations, what exactly "Chinese characteristics" are remains vague. President Xi Jinping has been promoting what he terms "socialist core values," which include prosperity, democracy, civility, harmony, freedom, equality, justice, the rule of law, patriotism, dedication, integrity, and friendship. But the efficacy of this strategy in terms of helping the CCP achieve ideological coherency and win ideological battles remains to be seen.

In short, the development of China's contentious public sphere reveals both the weakness and the strength of the Chinese state, as well the contingency of its governance in general. As Bröckling, Krasmann, and Lemke (2011, 49) write, "Government is always a precarious affair: it must always take into account the unforeseen and crises of governability. It thus realizes itself as crisis prevention and management, performs continual reinterpretations, produces unintended effects, and necessarily falls short of its goals."

Looking Back and Looking Forward

The goal of this book is to describe and explain the development of China's contentious public sphere. Back in the late 2000s, when China's contentious public sphere was on the rise, many media and legal professionals, netizens, public opinion leaders, activists, scholars, and observers, including me, saw a rosy picture of political and civil life in China. Despite the state's continued control and suppression, people were nonetheless thrilled by the rising power of public opinion as social and political forces disciplining the authoritarian state and holding the state accountable. The very responsiveness of the Chinese state in meeting certain demands of the public strengthened confidence in the power of public opinion. Scholars have thus begun to emphasize the responsive side of China's "responsive authoritarianism" (Hassid 2015; Reilly 2012). But developments have not stood still. The last couple years have witnessed severe crackdowns on China's contentious public sphere. The ruthless crackdowns and escalating control and surveillance have muted perceptions of the state's responsiveness and shown the authoritarian and precarious side of China's "responsive authoritarianism." Despite the crackdowns, however, looking back to the late Qing period and China's prereform years, the development of China's contentious public sphere remains a truly significant social, political, and cultural transformation. I still believe that the common measurements that social scientists have been using to determine level of liberty and regime types do not fully capture the dynamics of political and civil life in China. In addition,

I still think we should not underestimate or simply disregard the relatively democratic aspects of life under so-called authoritarian rule, even though these democratic aspects are subject to the state's discipline and aggression.

Looking forward, how political and social forces align will greatly influence the development of China's contentious public sphere. The Xi leadership's effort to consolidate power and crack down on corruption may have alienated some within the party-state. This could create opportunities for political mobilization. If the media and intermediary actors can continue to speak for the disadvantaged, promote public interests, and mobilize public support, there remains hope for a contentious public sphere with a better capacity to address societal problems. A less promising outcome would see the state and the middle class form an alliance, affording those in the middle class some room for contention, while foreclosing it for all others. Whether the Chinese state can positively and meaningfully engage with public opinion will largely influence whether China's contentious public sphere will lead to more social tension or serve as a platform for consensus building and social integration.

The continuously evolving process of globalization is another factor that will influence the development of China's contentious public sphere. As Nettl and Robertson argue, societies often compare themselves with one another, selecting among various versions of modernity and picking and choosing particular elements therein. Such comparisons are often intertwined with issues related to national identity (Nettl and Robertson 1966; Robertson 1992). Since the late Qing period, Chinese states and people have perceived China as a "latecomer" and looked to normative images of modernity associated with the West. As I describe in chapters 4 through 6, many media and legal professionals, public opinion leaders, and a proportion of Chinese netizens admire the idea of liberal democracy and see it as a superior and more just political model. With the increasing economic and social development in China and China's rise in global power, how the Chinese state, Chinese people, and even foreign actors perceive China in relation to other countries and societies has changed and will continue to change over time. In addition, scholars have been warning about the decay of liberal democracies (Fukuyama 2012). Indeed, the rising support for antisystem populist-nationalists in Europe and in the United States seems to indicate the decline of liberal democracy and its decreasing moral appeal as a political model in the West. These recent developments in the West have been surprising for many Chinese people, particularly intermediary actors in China's public sphere, while also prompting them to rethink and compare different political and developmental models. The changing phase of globalization and the shifting perceptions of various political and developmental models, in turn, may affect the Chinese state's constitutive choices in the future about institutions and technologies, the participation of various actors in China's institutional process, and the development of China's contentious public sphere.

APPENDIX

Chapter 2

NOTE ON CONTENT ANALYSIS

I collected articles with titles containing "public opinion" (*yulun, yuqing,* or *minyi*) between 1949 and 2015. According to my interviewees, using the occurrence of "public opinion" within titles instead of full texts as the selection criteria would help to identify articles explicitly addressing public opinion. I excluded articles that only disseminated policies without describing public opinion.

TABLE A2.1. Interviews with informants

Interviewee	Interview date	Interview location
Editor at *People's Daily*	July 2011	Beijing
Journalist at *People's Daily*	July 2011	Beijing
Journalist at *People's Daily*	July 2011	Beijing
Editor at *People's Daily*	July 2014	Beijing
Journalist at *People's Daily*	July 2015	Beijing
Propaganda official	July 2011	Beijing
Propaganda official	July 2014	Beijing
Editor at NetEase	June 2011	Beijing

Note: Face-to-face interviews took place in Beijing between 2011 and 2015. Each interview lasted about one to one and half hours.

Chapter 4

1. CASE SELECTION

To investigate how local market and political environment influenced critical news reporting, I selected comparable newspaper organizations situated in different local conditions. Case selection was based on analysis of secondary literature and thirty-eight preliminary interviews with journalists and scholars knowledgeable about the Chinese press. I conducted these preliminary interviews between 2009 and 2010 in China and in the United States. There were three stages to the case selection process. I first selected the region to study, then chose specific localities within the region, and finally chose newspaper organizations from the selected localities.

First, I chose to study China's coastal urban region. China is a huge country with spatially heterogeneous economies. The geographic inequality of coastal versus inland provinces and the urban-rural divide is well documented (Xie and Hannum 1996). As the level of economic development in the coastal urban region is relatively homogeneous, I decided to focus on this region to control for this element. Readers in areas with different levels of economic development could arguably have distinct demands with regard to news content that would, in turn, further influence news production. Focusing on newspaper organizations in areas with relatively comparable economic development makes the task of comparison more viable.

Second, I selected the three coastal region cities of Beijing, Shanghai, and Guangzhou because the local market and political environment varies across these three sites. Guangzhou has a much more competitive local newspaper market than Beijing and Shanghai (Huang and Zeng 2011; Liu 2010). State agencies in Guangzhou and Beijing are also more structurally fragmented than their counterparts in Shanghai because of the coexistence of multilevel party-state agencies (Huang and Zeng 2011; Lee, He, and Huang 2007). As such, how the media field is situated in relation to state agencies and the newspaper market varies across the three sites. In Guangzhou, the media field is situated in relation to less unified state agencies and a highly competitive newspaper market. In Beijing, the media field is positioned in tandem with less unified state agencies and a less competitive newspaper market. In Shanghai, the media field is situated alongside a more unified state apparatus and a less competitive newspaper market. These variations allow me to tease out the relationships between local market and political environment of the media field and critical news reporting.

Third and finally, I selected six comparable newspaper organizations. To do this, I focused on local, commercially oriented, nonspecialized newspapers that attempt to attract urban readers in the three cities (i.e., *dushibao* and *wanbo*). I first excluded noncomparable newspaper organizations from the selection pool, specifically, local newspapers with cross-regional backgrounds. The Chinese state generally prohibits cross-regional collaboration between newspaper organizations in order to contain their political influence, but the government has allowed a few newspapers to engage in cross-regional collaboration—for example, *Beijing News* (*xinjingbao*) and the *Oriental Morning Post* (*dongfang zaobao*). Unlike ordinary local newspapers, local newspapers with a cross-regional background are operated by newspaper organizations in two localities and thus supervised by local governments in two places. As local newspapers with cross-regional backgrounds are embedded in an exceptionally complicated field environment, they are not comparable to ordinary local newspapers. After excluding noncomparable newspapers, I randomly chose two newspapers from the pool in each city. Each of the three cities has around four to six comparable local newspapers. Because of limited resources in terms of data collection and analysis, I decided to select two local newspapers for each city. The selection process was also restricted by the availability of data, as not every local newspaper was included in WiseNews, a professional digital news archive.

2. MARKET COMPETITION

I examined market competition according to previous literature and interviews with informants. Very few empirical studies compare the level of competition across regions in newspaper markets. Previous studies based on interviews with journalists point out that competition is highest in Guangdong, as it has the largest number of newspaper conglomerates (four) in China as of 2007 (Huang and Zeng 2011). In comparison, Beijing and Shanghai had three and two newspaper conglomerates, respectively, in 2007. Such an approach, however, does not take into consideration variations on the demand side. Therefore, I took both production and demand sides into account when evaluating market competition. Based on the indices calculated by one Chinese scholar on the factor of production and demand in local newspaper markets at the subnational level (Liu 2010), I plotted the factor of production index against the demand index in figure A4.1. The factor of production index takes into consideration circulation and revenues

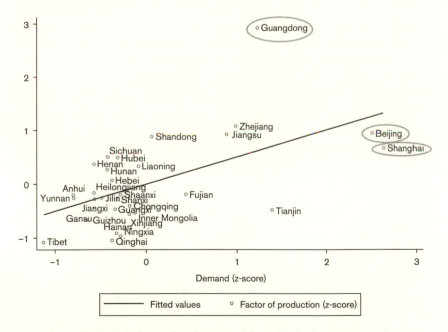

A4.1. Relationship between factor of production and demand in local newspaper markets.

of newspapers, as well as the ratio of employees in the cultural industry in each province. The demand index considers GDP per capita, the ratio of expenditure in cultural industry (per capita), and readership of the daily newspaper. Figure A4.1 shows that Guangdong is an extreme outlier as the factor of production is so high, even after taking demand into consideration. In comparison, the factor of production index is commensurate with the demand levels in Beijing and Shanghai. This result is consistent with journalists' observations regarding market competition across regions based on their experiences.

3. DEFINING "CRITICAL NEWS REPORTS"

To determine what constitutes a critical news report, I asked fifty-eight journalists I interviewed to name five important societal problems and solutions to these problems that journalists should report given a context of no governmental censorship or pressure. My research assistant and I combined similar responses into categories as presented in table A4.1. We decided to consider "judicial independence" and "general judicial reform" as two separate categories, as many interviewees emphasized that judicial independence is a distinct issue from general judicial reform. According to interviewees, the Chinese state is more permissive regarding discussion of the latter, but less so with the former. We also saw "crony capitalism" and "corruption" as two separate categories. Interviewees stressed that the former concerns the collusion of power and money in general, whereas the latter refers more specifically to the wrongdoing of government officials.

For each category, we calculated the percentage of journalists who considered the category critical (see table A4.1). We then selected the categories

TABLE A4.1. Topics covered in critical news reports

Category	Percentage (%)
Civil society and political participation	55.36
The state's infringement of rights	53.57
Judicial independence	48.21
Unconstitutionality	44.64
Rights of disadvantaged groups	42.86
Crony capitalism	41.07
Inequality	32.14
Corruption	32.14
Problems in healthcare institutions	30.35
Problems in educational institutions	28.57
Environmental pollution	26.79
General judicial reform	23.21
Others	32.14

that were mentioned by at least 40 percent of the subjects. We decided to set 40 percent as the threshold because it reflects a high level of consensus. In the process of conducting content analysis, we also tried different thresholds—for example, 50 percent and 30 percent—but the pattern of variation across newspapers in the three cities in terms of critical news reporting remained the same.

4. PRELIMINARY SELECTION OF NEWS REPORTS USING KEYWORDS

I used the keywords listed in table 4.2 or the preliminary selection of news reports. I employed two methods to decrease the potential bias that results from using keywords for preliminary selection. First, I continually improved the list in response to feedback from my interviewees, who are familiar with how journalists across news organizations report relevant issues. Second, I used synonyms of the keywords for selection. One powerful feature of WiseNews is its integrated thesaurus, which allows for a comprehensive search by keywords. Table A4.2 presents the numbers of articles based on keyword selection.

TABLE A4.2. Number of articles based on keyword selection (2003–2006)

	Guangzhou		Beijing		Shanghai		National
	Southern Metropolis Daily	Yangcheng Evening News	Beijing Times	Beijing Evening News	Shanghai Morning Post	Xinmin Evening News	People's Daily
Unconstitutionality	170	95	75	47	42	85	67
The state's infringement of rights	78	42	31	23	21	21	124
Judicial independence	621	340	246	201	176	248	386
Civil society and political participation	419	175	83	92	42	121	467
Rights of disadvantaged groups	250	100	33	38	21	68	90
Crony capitalism	521	243	161	125	76	221	168

5. CONTENT ANALYSIS

My research assistant and I read through each article that passed the preliminary selection. Following a protocol, we independently identified which of the six dimensions was the most important theme of the article in the domestic context. The six dimensions are mutually exclusive. Many articles were excluded because they discussed issues in foreign contexts. I calculated Cohen's kappa (Cohen 1960) to assess the interrater reliability. The agreement score (0.87) suggests excellent agreement. We deliberated and made a collective decision on the rare occasions when we had different opinions.

6. RESULTS OF CONTENT ANALYSIS

TABLE A4.3. Number of articles, by dimension and newspaper (2003–2006)

	Guangzhou		Beijing		Shanghai		National
	Southern Metropolis Daily	Yangcheng Evening News	Beijing Times	Beijing Evening News	Shanghai Morning Post	Xinmin Evening News	People's Daily
Unconstitutionality	51	28	29	5	2	4	8
The state's infringement of rights	45	12	17	3	3	1	8
Judicial independence	86	27	29	9	3	5	18
Civil society and political participation	72	23	14	1	1	1	19
Rights of disadvantaged groups	142	56	23	20	5	26	36
Crony capitalism	131	34	47	16	4	17	28
Total critical news reports	527	180	159	154	18	54	117
Total news reports	207,678	142,860	111,648	123,995	104,993	185,186	152,083

TABLE A4.4. Percentage of critical news reports, by dimension and newspaper (2003–2006)

	Guangzhou		Beijing		Shanghai		National
	Southern Metropolis Daily (%)	Yangcheng Evening News (%)	Beijing Times (%)	Beijing Evening News (%)	Shanghai Morning Post (%)	Xinmin Evening News (%)	People's Daily (%)
Unconstitutionality	0.025	0.020	0.026	0.004	0.002	0.002	0.005
The state's infringement of rights	0.022	0.008	0.015	0.002	0.003	0.001	0.005
Judicial independence	0.041	0.019	0.026	0.007	0.003	0.010	0.012
Civil society and political participation	0.035	0.016	0.013	0.001	0.001	0.001	0.012
Rights of disadvantaged groups	0.068	0.039	0.021	0.016	0.005	0.014	0.024
Crony capitalism	0.063	0.024	0.040	0.013	0.004	0.009	0.018
Total critical news reports	0.254	0.126	0.141	0.043	0.018	0.037	0.076

TABLE A4.5. Percentage of critical news reports, by city (2003–2006)

	Two Guangzhou newspapers	Two Beijing newspapers	Two Shanghai newspapers	People's Daily
Percentage	0.202	0.090	0.025	0.077

TABLE A4.6. Critical news reports suggesting the responsibility of the central government (2003–2006)

	Guangzhou		Beijing		Shanghai		National
	Southern Metropolis Daily	Yangcheng Evening News	Beijing Times	Beijing Evening News	Shanghai Morning Post	Xinmin Evening News	People's Daily
Number	85	29	25	2	0	1	2
Percentage of total reports (%)	0.0409	0.0203	0.0224	0.0016	0.0000	0.0005	0.0013

TABLE A4.7. Critical news reports suggesting the responsibility of the central government, by city (2003–2006)

	Two Guangzhou newspapers	Two Beijing newspapers	Two Shanghai newspapers	*People's Daily*
Number	114	27	1	2
Percentage of total reports (%)	0.033	0.011	0.000	0.001

7. INTERVIEWS

In addition to content analysis, this chapter also draws on analysis of ninety-one in-depth interviews. I conducted two waves of interviews. The first wave consisted of thirty-eight preliminary interviews with twenty-eight journalists and ten scholars knowledgeable about the Chinese press between 2009 and 2010. I conducted face-to-face interviews in China and in the United States. Each first-wave interview lasted about two hours. After I selected specific newspaper organizations, I conducted the second-wave interviews between 2011 and 2014 with four groups: Chinese journalists who work or have worked in the selected newspaper organizations; lawyers and legal scholars; communication studies scholars; and propaganda officials. The distribution of these subjects is provided in table A4.8. I conducted face-to-face interviews in Guangzhou, Beijing, and Shanghai. I also conducted phone interviews with some journalists working in Shanghai. Each second-wave interview lasted about two to two and half hours. E-mails were exchanged when further information was required.

TABLE A4.8. Distribution of interview subjects in second-wave interviews

Interview subjects	Numbers
Southern Metropolis Daily journalists	8
Yangcheng Evening News journalists	4
Beijing Times journalists	4
Beijing Evening News journalists	2
Shanghai Morning Post journalists	4
Xinmin Evening News journalists	2
People's Daily journalists	4
Lawyers and legal scholars	13
Communication studies scholars	5
Propaganda officials	7
Total	53

Chapter 5

TABLE A5.1. Interviews with informants

Interviewee	Interview date	Interview location
Editor at *People's Daily*	July 2011	Beijing
Journalist at *People's Daily*	July 2011	Beijing
Propaganda official	July 2011	Beijing
Communication studies scholar	July 2011	Beijing
Communication studies scholar	July 2014	Beijing
Official at the General Administration of Press and Publication	July 2014	Beijing
Former Official at the General Administration of Press and Publication	July 2014	Beijing
Official at the State Internet Information Office	July 2014	Beijing
Formal official at the Ministry of Industry and Information Technology	July 2014	Beijing
Former editor at *Southern Weekly*	June 2011	Guangzhou
Former journalist at *Southern Metropolis Daily*	July 2011	Beijing
Scholar of WTO laws	July 2011	Beijing
Employee at NetEase	July 2011	Beijing
Employee at NetEase	July 2011	Beijing
Employee at NetEase	July 2014	Beijing
Employee at Sina	July 2011	Beijing
Employee at Sina	July 2014	Beijing
Employee at Tencent	June 2011	Guangzhou
Employee at Tencent	June 2014	Beijing
Employee at Sohu	July 2011	Beijing

Chapter 6

TABLE A6.1. Daily interaction and New Year greeting on social networks

Type of interaction and social network	One-on-one interaction on an average day[a]	Proportion of nonfamily members in everyday interaction	Number of kin in New Year greeting social network[b]	Number of nonkin in New Year greeting social network[b]
Newspaper	0.419***	0.217**	0.365***	0.581***
	(0.0992)	(0.0922)	(0.0973)	(0.102)
TV	0.0221	−0.0162	−0.0962	−0.0468
	(0.127)	(0.135)	(0.148)	(0.144)
Internet	0.351**	0.622***	0.0896	0.789***
	(0.153)	(0.147)	(0.147)	(0.154)
Female	−0.486***	−0.236***	−0.0335	−0.290***
	(0.0808)	(0.0812)	(0.0809)	(0.0864)
Age	−0.0162***	0.00274	−0.0116***	−0.0138***
	(0.00311)	(0.00319)	(0.00287)	(0.00313)
Elementary school	0.249*	0.375***	0.627***	0.525***
	(0.132)	(0.126)	(0.129)	(0.147)
Middle school	0.440***	0.403***	0.771***	0.685***
	(0.137)	(0.133)	(0.131)	(0.154)
High school	0.546***	0.640***	0.702***	0.572***
	(0.169)	(0.161)	(0.162)	(0.184)
College	0.537**	0.675***	0.994***	1.025***
	(0.253)	(0.246)	(0.225)	(0.248)
Subjective class	0.0329	0.00337	0.0669***	0.0705***
	(0.0241)	(0.0232)	(0.0232)	(0.0240)
Life satisfaction	0.0412**	−0.00747	0.0693***	0.0499***
	(0.0176)	(0.0181)	(0.0185)	(0.0178)
Party member	0.344**	0.0212	0.410***	0.384**
	(0.152)	(0.150)	(0.147)	(0.174)
Interest in politics	0.0970*	−0.0264	0.0258	0.0282
	(0.0495)	(0.0470)	(0.0497)	(0.0516)
N	3,321	3,417	3,230	3,065

Source: 2008 China Survey.
Note: Standard errors in parentheses. Control variables also include geographic location and urban/rural division.
*$p < .05$
**$p < .01$
***$p < .001$
[a]"One-on-one interaction on an average day" measures the number of people a respondent interacted with daily.
[b]"New Year greeting social network" measures the number of people a respondent sent a "Happy New Year" message to during the Chinese New Year festival.

TABLE A6.2. Experience of contacting party leaders, lawyers, and journalists in social networks

Contact	Party-state leaders	Lawyers	Journalists
Newspaper	0.506***	0.570**	0.360
	(0.130)	(0.255)	(0.341)
TV	0.194	0.569	0.171
	(0.252)	(0.494)	(0.568)
Internet	0.498***	0.991***	0.672*
	(0.187)	(0.282)	(0.355)
Female	0.00882	−0.292	−0.200
	(0.122)	(0.254)	(0.323)
Age	0.0116***	0.0162*	0.00453
	(0.00431)	(0.00858)	(0.00960)
Elementary school	0.527**	−0.101	−0.153
	(0.217)	(0.604)	(0.645)
Middle school	0.649***	0.909	0.0163
	(0.215)	(0.601)	(0.624)
High school	1.061***	0.805	0.702
	(0.242)	(0.631)	(0.659)
College	1.424***	1.513**	1.718**
	(0.302)	(0.619)	(0.684)
Subjective class	−0.0343	0.0340	−0.122
	(0.0330)	(0.0751)	(0.0782)
Life satisfaction	0.0422*	0.0599	0.0744
	(0.0255)	(0.0629)	(0.0631)
Party member	0.927***	0.323	0.322
	(0.173)	(0.310)	(0.366)
Interest in politics	0.130*	−0.126	−0.000587
	(0.0732)	(0.138)	(0.186)
N	3,552	3,552	3,552

Source: 2008 China Survey.

Note: Standard errors in parentheses. Control variables also include geographic location and urban/rural division.

*p < .05
**p < .01
***p < .001

TABLE A6.3. Whether respondents trust government officials

Respondent characteristics	Trust in provincial government officials	Trust in central government officials
Newspaper	−0.0480	−0.0385
	(0.0762)	(0.0771)
TV	0.0169	0.145
	(0.110)	(0.110)
Internet	−0.125	−0.253**
	(0.117)	(0.117)
Female	0.0132	0.00592
	(0.0643)	(0.0650)
Age	0.00525**	0.00802***
	(0.00239)	(0.00241)
Elementary school	0.0373	0.0469
	(0.0956)	(0.0973)
Middle school	−0.0741	−0.130
	(0.104)	(0.105)
High school	−0.0545	0.0426
	(0.128)	(0.128)
College	−0.141	−0.0695
	(0.182)	(0.182)
Subjective class	0.0377**	0.0435**
	(0.0167)	(0.0169)
Life satisfaction	0.0699***	0.0542***
	(0.0139)	(0.0140)
Party member	0.0759	0.0414
	(0.121)	(0.124)
Interests in politics	0.369***	0.390***
	(0.0376)	(0.0380)
N	3,552	3,552

Source: The 2008 China Survey.
Note: Standard errors in parentheses. Control variables also include geographic location and urban/rural division.
*$p < .05$
**$p < .01$
***$p < .001$

TABLE A6.4. Political attitudes

Respondent characteristics	Demonstration should not be forbidden	One-party system is not the best for China		Citizens should oversee the government	
Newspaper	0.0126	0.0793	0.0770	−0.234**	−0.251**
	(0.0950)	(0.0931)	(0.0922)	(0.102)	(0.101)
TV	−0.0241	−0.257**	−0.259**	0.310*	0.303*
	(0.101)	(0.114)	(0.114)	(0.161)	(0.162)
Internet	0.436***	0.145		0.101	
	(0.162)	(0.156)		(0.171)	
Using social media to read political issues			0.489**		0.562***
			(0.244)		(0.208)
Female	−0.106	0.281***	0.281***	0.113	0.113
	(0.0785)	(0.0800)	(0.0801)	(0.0834)	(0.0836)
Age	−0.00932***	−0.00517*	−0.00497*	0.00711**	0.00780**
	(0.00269)	(0.00268)	(0.00264)	(0.00310)	(0.00305)
Elementary school	−0.311***	−0.462***	−0.460***	0.268*	0.272**
	(0.105)	(0.116)	(0.115)	(0.137)	(0.137)
Middle school	−0.638***	−0.569***	−0.568***	0.233	0.238*
	(0.115)	(0.126)	(0.125)	(0.142)	(0.142)
High school	−0.352**	−0.698***	−0.696***	0.186	0.179
	(0.155)	(0.159)	(0.157)	(0.167)	(0.166)
College	0.379	−0.383*	−0.403*	0.217	0.169
	(0.231)	(0.223)	(0.215)	(0.218)	(0.205)
Subjective class	0.00620	0.0211	0.0212	0.0350	0.0355
	(0.0212)	(0.0220)	(0.0221)	(0.0272)	(0.0272)
Life satisfaction	−0.0477***	−0.0774***	−0.0767***	−0.00813	−0.00749
	(0.0167)	(0.0174)	(0.0175)	(0.0210)	(0.0210)
Party member	−0.0759	−0.290*	−0.277*	0.310**	0.321**
	(0.169)	(0.159)	(0.158)	(0.133)	(0.134)
Interests in politics	−0.149***	−0.236***	−0.237***	0.176***	0.171***
	(0.0476)	(0.0484)	(0.0484)	(0.0548)	(0.0552)
N	3,552	3,552	3,552	2,914	2,914

Source: The 2008 China Survey.

Note: (1) Standard errors in parentheses. Control variables also include geographic location and urban/rural division. (2) Since "Internet" and "using social media to read political issues" are highly correlated, I include only one of them at a time to run a regression model. (3) Since "using social media to read political issues" is not a statistically significant predictor of "demonstration should not be forbidden," I do not include the result in the table. For "one-party system is not the best for China" and "citizens should oversee the government," I present the results of two models—one with "Internet" and the other with "using social media to read political issues."

$*p < .05$

$**p < .01$

$***p < .001$

TABLE A6.5. Whether respondents are concerned with current social or political problems

Respondent characteristics	Environmental protection	Social stability	Political democracy (1)	Political democracy (2)
Newspaper	0.510***	0.137	0.142	0.140
	(0.0895)	(0.0970)	(0.103)	(0.103)
TV	0.125	0.348**	0.278	0.273
	(0.135)	(0.154)	(0.175)	(0.175)
Internet	0.455***	0.0763	0.188	
	(0.149)	(0.143)	(0.145)	
Using social media to read political issues				0.404**
				(0.188)
Female	−0.0863	0.127	−0.0972	−0.101
	(0.0778)	(0.0825)	(0.0884)	(0.0884)
Age	−0.000542	−0.00630**	−0.00681**	−0.00688**
	(0.00290)	(0.00313)	(0.00341)	(0.00333)
Elementary school	0.503***	0.0528	0.355**	0.355**
	(0.118)	(0.128)	(0.152)	(0.152)
Middle school	0.727***	0.0781	0.588***	0.589***
	(0.126)	(0.136)	(0.157)	(0.157)
High school	0.914***	0.214	0.807***	0.821***
	(0.154)	(0.163)	(0.182)	(0.180)
College	1.213***	0.258	1.050***	1.066***
	(0.237)	(0.223)	(0.235)	(0.228)
Subjective class	−0.00286	0.0109	−0.0171	−0.0164
	(0.0197)	(0.0214)	(0.0230)	(0.0231)
Life satisfaction	−0.0149	0.0528***	0.0717***	0.0705***
	(0.0161)	(0.0176)	(0.0190)	(0.0190)
Party member	0.137	0.260*	0.151	0.162
	(0.146)	(0.149)	(0.154)	(0.154)
Interests in politics	−0.0230	−0.139***	0.0399	0.0381
	(0.0440)	(0.0482)	(0.0520)	(0.0520)
N	3,552	3,552	3,552	3,552

Source: The 2008 China Survey.

Note: (1) Standard errors in parentheses. Control variables also include geographic location and urban/rural division. (2) Since "Internet" and "using social media to read political issues" are highly correlated, I include only one of them at a time to run a regression model. (3) Since "using social media to read political issues" is not a statistically significant predictor of "environmental protection" and "social stability," I do not include the results in the table. For "political democracy," I present the results of two models—one with "Internet" and the other with "using social media to read political issues."

*$p < .05$

**$p < .01$

***$p < .001$

TABLE A6.6. Political behavior: Whether respondents have experience discussing political issues or contacting officials

Respondent characteristics	Discuss political issues		Contact officials	
Newspaper	0.310***	0.316***	0.450***	0.456***
	(0.117)	(0.116)	(0.152)	(0.151)
TV	0.462**	0.458**	−0.0257	−0.0343
	(0.194)	(0.194)	(0.294)	(0.293)
Internet	0.327*		0.373	
	(0.190)		(0.233)	
Using social media to read political issues		0.559**		0.604**
		(0.271)		(0.304)
Female	−0.243**	−0.247**	−0.0296	−0.0386
	(0.106)	(0.106)	(0.135)	(0.135)
Age	−0.0142***	−0.0148***	0.0260***	0.0254***
	(0.00385)	(0.00379)	(0.00497)	(0.00484)
Elementary school	−0.0520	−0.0556	0.286	0.280
	(0.171)	(0.171)	(0.214)	(0.214)
Middle school	0.177	0.175	0.531**	0.525**
	(0.177)	(0.177)	(0.232)	(0.232)
High school	0.377*	0.406**	0.874***	0.903***
	(0.208)	(0.206)	(0.262)	(0.261)
College	0.400	0.453*	1.491***	1.545***
	(0.279)	(0.271)	(0.340)	(0.324)
Subjective class	0.0486*	0.0488*	0.0310	0.0313
	(0.0273)	(0.0273)	(0.0377)	(0.0378)
Life satisfaction	0.0105	0.0123	0.0114	0.0132
	(0.0223)	(0.0223)	(0.0296)	(0.0299)
Party member	0.468***	0.483***	1.082***	1.106***
	(0.179)	(0.178)	(0.180)	(0.180)
Interests in politics	1.022***	1.023***	0.528***	0.525***
	(0.0700)	(0.0700)	(0.0783)	(0.0781)
N	3,552	3,552	3,552	3,552

Source: The 2008 China Survey.

Note: (1) Standard errors in parentheses. Control variables also include geographic location and urban/rural division. (2) Since "Internet" and "using social media to read political issues" are highly correlated, I include only one of them at a time to run a regression model. I present the results of two models for each dependent variable.

*p < .05
**p < .01
***p < .001

TABLE A6.7. Political behavior: Whether respondents have experience contacting media and NGOs as well as joining a petition

Respondent characteristics	Contact media		Contact NGOs	Petition
Newspaper	0.520	0.510	0.558**	0.526*
	(0.380)	(0.381)	(0.261)	(0.270)
TV	−0.362	−0.393	0.525	0.439
	(0.601)	(0.585)	(0.453)	(0.497)
Internet	1.137**		0.663*	0.785***
	(0.548)		(0.345)	(0.302)
Using social media to read political issues		1.747***		
		(0.523)		
Female	0.0948	0.0148	0.764***	0.117
	(0.339)	(0.346)	(0.220)	(0.227)
Age	0.0145	0.0144	0.0286***	−0.0223***
	(0.0149)	(0.0143)	(0.00895)	(0.00864)
Elementary school	−1.024*	−1.041*	0.247	−0.0207
	(0.548)	(0.552)	(0.342)	(0.417)
Middle school	−0.275	−0.301	0.436	0.348
	(0.463)	(0.464)	(0.370)	(0.408)
High school	−0.146	−0.0415	0.962**	0.502
	(0.634)	(0.609)	(0.419)	(0.461)
College	0.352	0.420	1.025*	0.587
	(0.685)	(0.655)	(0.559)	(0.574)
Subjective class	0.125	0.115	0.132**	−0.0100
	(0.120)	(0.120)	(0.0628)	(0.0529)
Life satisfaction	−0.0408	−0.0333	0.0146	0.0325
	(0.0887)	(0.0878)	(0.0526)	(0.0448)
Party member	0.0574	0.209	0.746***	0.807**
	(0.379)	(0.364)	(0.264)	(0.335)
Interests in politics	0.882***	0.848***	0.557***	0.580***
	(0.222)	(0.225)	(0.128)	(0.130)
N	3,343	3,343	3,530	3,552

Source: The 2008 China Survey.

Note: (1) Standard errors in parentheses. Control variables also include geographic location and urban/rural division. (2) Since "Internet" and "using social media to read political issues" are highly correlated, I include only one of them at a time to run a regression model. (3) Since "using social media to read political issues" is not a statistically significant predictor of "contacting NGOs" and "petition," I do not include the results in the table. For "contact media," I present the results of two models—one with "Internet" and the other with "using social media to read political issues."

$*p < .05$
$**p < .01$
$***p < .001$

TABLE A6.8. Selected survey items for political beliefs and the proportion and conditional probabilities of responses of each latent class

$N = 1,576$		Total (100%)	Type 1 the contentious (24.5%)	Type 2 the conformist (42.4%)	Type 3 the apathetic (33.1%)
ITEM 1:	1. good	0.231	0.287	0.295	0.107
Having a strong	2. DK	0.339	0.118	0.124	0.779
leader who does not	3. bad	0.430	0.595	0.581	0.114
have to bother with					
parliament					
and elections					
ITEM 2:	1. good	0.312	0.478	0.379	0.103
Having experts, not	2. DK	0.369	0.113	0.143	0.848
government, to	3. bad	0.319	0.409	0.478	0.049
make decisions					
ITEM 3:	1. good	0.220	0.165	0.376	0.061
Having the army rule	2. DK	0.371	0.131	0.129	0.860
	3. bad	0.409	0.704	0.495	0.080
ITEM 4:	1. bad	0.041	0.096	0.037	0.007
Having a democratic	2. DK	0.331	0.095	0.069	0.842
political system	3. good	0.628	0.808	0.895	0.151
ITEM 5:	1. no	0.069	0.102	0.073	0.038
Is choosing leaders	2. DK	0.162	0.023	0.028	0.439
in free elections	3. yes	0.769	0.876	0.899	0.523
an essential					
characteristic of					
democracy?					
ITEM 6:	1. no	0.055	0.085	0.047	0.044
Is civil rights	2. DK	0.234	0.050	0.065	0.587
protection against	3. yes	0.711	0.864	0.888	0.370
oppression an					
essential characteristic					
of democracy?					
ITEM 7:	1. not important	0.055	0.095	0.040	0.046
How important	2. DK	0.166	0.045	0.016	0.449
is it for you to live	3. important	0.779	0.860	0.945	0.505
in a country that					
is governed					
democratically?					
ITEM 8:	1. no	0.388	0.383	0.463	0.296
Should protecting	2. DK	0.200	0.047	0.065	0.486
freedom of speech	3. yes	0.412	0.570	0.472	0.218
be among the top					
aims of this country?					

(*continued*)

TABLE A6.8. (*continued*)

N = 1,576		Total (100%)	Type 1 the contentious (24.5%)	Type 2 the conformist (42.4%)	Type 3 the apathetic (33.1%)
ITEM 9: Do you trust in the press?	1. yes	0.619	0.319	0.864	0.528
	2. DK	0.150	0.085	0.016	0.368
	3. no	0.231	0.596	0.120	0.104
ITEM 10: Do you trust in TV?	1. yes	0.681	0.356	0.907	0.632
	2. DK	0.101	0.055	0.006	0.256
	3. no	0.218	0.589	0.087	0.111
ITEM 11: Do you trust in police?	1. yes	0.754	0.434	0.948	0.741
	2. DK	0.046	0.020	0.006	0.116
	3. no	0.201	0.546	0.046	0.143
ITEM 12: Do you trust in the courts?	1. yes	0.759	0.435	0.959	0.742
	2. DK	0.006	0.031	0.010	0.144
	3. no	0.181	0.534	0.029	0.114
ITEM13: Do you trust in your central government?	1. yes	0.883	0.747	1.000	0.834
	2. DK	0.046	0.028	0.000	0.119
	3. no	0.070	0.225	0.000	0.047
ITEM 14: Do you trust in political parties?	1. yes	0.756	0.529	0.967	0.652
	2. DK	0.133	0.105	0.023	0.296
	3. no	0.111	0.365	0.010	0.052
ITEM 15: Is China governed democratically today?	1. yes	0.584	0.525	0.834	0.307
	2. DK	0.223	0.051	0.059	0.559
	3. no	0.194	0.424	0.107	0.134
ITEM 16: Are human rights respected in China?	1. yes	0.690	0.645	0.903	0.450
	2. DK	0.188	0.052	0.046	0.470
	3. no	0.122	0.303	0.051	0.080
ITEM 17: Are you willing to sign a petition?	1. no	0.462	0.379	0.385	0.621
	2. DK	0.028	0.012	0.023	0.046
	3. yes	0.510	0.609	0.592	0.332
ITEM 18: Are you willing to join in boycotts?	1. no	0.510	0.430	0.443	0.656
	2. DK	0.027	0.012	0.020	0.048
	3. yes	0.463	0.558	0.538	0.296

Source: 2007 China World Value Survey.

TABLE A6.9. Coding scheme

	Coding	1	2	3
I	Normative standards (ITEMS 1–8)	Support the norms of democracy	DK	Do not support the norms of democracy
II	Evaluation of the status quo (ITEMS 9–16)	Positive evaluation	DK	Negative evaluation
III	Willingness to participate in collective action (ITEMS 17–18)	Lack willingness	DK	Demonstrate willingness

Source: 2007 China World Value Survey.

Note: Respondents who had experience in actual participation, and those who didn't have experience but expressed willingness to participate were both coded as willing to participate in collective action.

The dependent variable regarding political beliefs is a categorical variable indicated by 18 items as listed in table A6.8. The 18 items were selected to probe opinions on normative standards, evaluation of the status quo, and willingness to participate in collective action. The responses to each item are coded into three categories, as table A6.9 shows. "Don't know (DK)" responses are coded as a separate category. The remaining responses are classified into those that are supportive of the norms of democracy, satisfied with the status quo, or willing to participate in collective action, and those that are not. These items are *not* combined into indices. I applied latent class analysis (Blaydes and Linzer 2008; Yamaguchi 2000) to detect the underlying *discrete* patterns of political beliefs, that is, the latent class. Respondents with similar response patterns are grouped together and assigned the same latent class membership. In so doing, I was able to estimate the most probable latent class membership for each respondent and to analyze the relationship between independent variables and the latent class membership.

TABLE A6.10. Comparison of models with different numbers of latent class

	BIC	Sample size–adjusted BIC	AIC	Vuong-Lo-Mendell-Rubin test (*p*-value)	Lo-Mendell-Rubin–adjusted LRT test (*p*-value)	Parametric bootstrapped likelihood ratio test approximate (*p*-value)	Entropy
2 classes	41,750.509	41,518.604	41,359.036	0.0000 Ho: 1 class	0.0000 Ho: 1 class	0.0000 Ho: 1 class	0.921
3 classes	40,733.479	40,384.033	40,143.588	0.0000 Ho: 2 classes	0.0000 Ho: 2 classes	0.0000 Ho: 2 classes	0.886
4 classes	40,227.517	39,760.529	39,439.208	0.1165 Ho: 3 classes	0.1180 Ho: 3 classes	0.0000 Ho: 3 classes	0.875

Source: 2007 China World Value Survey.

Note: As lower BIC, sample size–adjusted BIC, and AIC indicate better fit, a four-class model seems to be a good choice. Nonetheless, in light of the *p*-values of the Vuong-Lo-Mendell-Rubin Test and Lo-Mendell-Rubin–adjusted LRT test, a four-class model is not significantly superior to a three-class model.

TABLE A6.11. Multinomial logit latent class regression model of political beliefs

Contrast of political beliefs	The contentious vs. the conformist	The contentious vs. the apathetic	The conformist vs. the apathetic
Media embeddedness			
Netizens vs. traditional media users	0.847***	1.134***	0.286
	(0.302)	(0.379)	(0.412)
Netizens vs. nonmedia users	0.626	1.227***	0.602
	(0.435)	(0.435)	(0.437)
Traditional media users vs. nonmedia users	−0.222	0.094	0.315
	(0.289)	(0.337)	(0.192)
Demographic factors			
Female	−0.513*	−0.835***	−0.322*
	(0.235)	(0.237)	(0.156)
Age	−0.017*	−0.019**	−0.002
	(0.007)	(0.007)	(0.007)
Education	0.081*	0.185***	0.104***
	(0.033)	(0.029)	(0.024)
Income	0.105	0.150**	0.045
	(0.055)	(0.058)	(0.048)
Unemployment	0.668	0.855	0.187
	(0.526)	(0.454)	(0.510)
Professional worker	−0.091	−0.008	0.082
	(0.347)	(0.435)	(0.422)
Agricultural worker	0.266	−0.189	0.077
	(0.286)	(0.272)	(0.229)
Manual worker	−0.587	0.296	0.883**
	(0.439)	(0.376)	(0.285)
Subjective class (vs. lowest class)			
Working class	−0.689**	−0.182	0.507*
	(0.242)	(0.239)	(0.204)
Lower middle class	−0.823**	−0.256	0.567**
	(0.288)	(0.285)	(0.214)
Upper middle class	−1.254**	−0.797	0.457
	(0.475)	(0.490)	(0.375)
Party member	−0.258	0.685	0.943***
	(0.320)	(0.387)	(0.296)
Importance of politics	−0.274***	−0.151	0.123
	(0.084)	(0.091)	(0.074)
Interest in politics	−0.372***	−0.039	0.332***
	(0.074)	(0.085)	(0.069)
Life satisfaction	−0.262**	−0.028	0.234***
	(0.085)	(0.083)	(0.072)
Happiness	−0.199*	−0.064	0.136
	(0.101)	(0.098)	(0.076)
Geographic area (vs. West)			
East	1.695***	1.000*	−0.695**
	(0.429)	(0.455)	(0.257)
Middle	1.368***	1.402***	0.034
	(0.424)	(0.406)	(0.276)
N	1,576	1,576	1,576

Source: 2007 China World Value Survey
Note: Standard errors in parentheses.
*p < .05   **p < .01   ***p < .001

TABLE A6.12. Logistic regression model of collective action

	Participation in collective action (1)[a]	Participation in collective action (2)[a]
Media embeddedness		
Netizens vs. traditional media users	0.517*	0.511*
	(0.259)	(0.263)
Netizens vs. nonmedia users	1.215**	1.135**
	(0.508)	(0.511)
Traditional media users vs. nonmedia users	0.697	0.624
	(0.449)	(0.450)
Demographic factors		
Female	0.0746	0.113
	(0.200)	(0.202)
Age	−0.00765	−0.00640
	(0.00812)	(0.00812)
Education	0.140***	0.128***
	(0.0324)	(0.0331)
Income	0.125	0.116
	(0.0669)	(0.0672)
Unemployment	0.968*	0.932*
	(0.400)	(0.402)
Professional worker	0.0321	0.0483
	(0.313)	(0.313)
Agricultural worker	−0.0428	−0.0472
	(0.307)	(0.307)
Manual worker	0.0113	−0.0463
	(0.290)	(0.291)
Subjective class (vs. lower class)		
Working class	0.135	0.109
	(0.326)	(0.328)
Lower middle class	0.122	0.0989
	(0.334)	(0.337)
Upper middle class	0.210	0.209
	(0.471)	(0.475)
Party member	0.743**	0.698**
	(0.230)	(0.230)
Importance of politics	−0.128	−0.137
	(0.0913)	(0.0917)
Interests in politics	0.113	0.0999
	(0.0880)	(0.0896)
Life satisfaction	0.0160	−0.00963
	(0.0986)	(0.100)
Happiness	0.0312	0.0325
	(0.117)	(0.118)
Geographic area (vs. West)		
East	−0.791*	−0.757*
	(0.337)	(0.342)
Middle	−0.837*	−0.852*
	(0.335)	(0.338)
Political belief (vs. the contentious)		
The conformist		0.0415
		(0.246)
The apathetic		−0.7332*
		(0.354)
N	1,576	1,576

Source: 2007 China World Value Survey
Note: Standard errors in parentheses.
[a]The difference between the two models is that I do not include political belief as an independent variable in "participation in collective action (1)."
*p < .05   **p < .01   ***p < .001

TABLE A6.13. Descriptive statistics of the 2008 Asian Barometer Survey

Variable	Definition	Mean	Min	Max	SD
Female	1=female	0.49	0	1	0.50
Age	Respondent's age in years	47.66	18	99	16.07
Education level					
Below primary	1=below primary	0.23	0	1	
Primary	1=primary	0.20	0	1	
Secondary	1=secondary	0.47	0	1	
Tertiary	1=tertiary	0.04	0	1	
No answer	1=no answer	0.06	0	1	
Local government could be corrupt	0=not very corrupt 1=others	0.69	0	1	0.46
Central government could be corrupt	0=not very corrupt 1=others	0.66	0	1	0.47
Government officials withhold information	1=government officials withhold important information at least occasionally 0=others	0.40	0	1	0.49
Central government does not always abide by the law	0=central government officials abide by the law most of the time 1=others	0.33	0	1	0.47
Trust in the central government	1=quite a lot of trust or a great deal of trust 0=others	0.88	0	1	0.33
Trust in local governments	1=quite a lot of trust or a great deal of trust 0=others	0.55	0	1	0.50
Trust in courts	1=quite a lot of trust or a great deal of trust 0=others	0.70	0	1	0.46
Our form of government is the best for us	1=agree 0=others	0.74	0	1	0.44
Main source of political information					
Internet	1=Internet	0.07	0	1	0.25
Newspaper	1=newspaper	0.21	0	1	0.41
Television	1=television	0.89	0	1	0.32
Radio	1=radio	0.12	0	1	0.32

TABLE A6.14. Logistic regression analysis of perception of the government's legality

	Government officials withhold information	National government does not always abide by the law	Local government could be corrupt	Central government could be corrupt
Main source of political information				
Internet	0.458**	0.457**	0.492**	0.141
	(0.165)	(0.173)	(0.179)	(0.163)
Newspaper	0.345***a	0.00352	0.0355	−0.197a
	(0.101)	(0.112)	(0.104)	(0.102)
Television	0.378**	−0.645***	−0.444**	−0.532***
	(0.142)	(0.124)	(0.149)	(0.146)
Radio	0.148	−0.305*	−0.209a	−0.182
	(0.119)	(0.132)	(0.120)	(0.115)
N	5,075	5,075	5,075	5,075

Source: 2008 Asian Barometer Survey.

Note: Standard errors in parentheses. Control variables include gender, age, education level, frequency of following political news, subjective class, perceived impact of politics on daily life, and media use.

a$< .1$

*$p < .05$

**$p < .01$

***$p < .001$

TABLE A6.15. Logistic regression of trust in institutions

	Trust in the central government	Trust in local governments	Trust in courts	Our form of government is the best for us
Local government could be corrupt	−0.439*	−0.663***	−0.465***	−0.413**
	(0.196)	(0.0972)	(0.112)	(0.137)
Central government could be corrupt	−0.962***	0.222*	−0.396***	−0.586***
	(0.185)	(0.0929)	(0.105)	(0.128)
Government officials withhold information	−0.312*	−0.491***	−0.551***	0.445***
	(0.128)	(0.0787)	(0.0861)	(0.103)
National government does not always abide by the law	−0.929***	−0.714***	−0.645***	−0.950***
	(0.120)	(0.0821)	(0.0860)	(0.0937)

Source: 2008 Asian Barometer Survey ($N = 5,075$).

Note: Standard errors in parentheses. Control variables include gender, age, education level, subjective class, frequency of following political news, and perceived impact of politics on daily life.

*$p < .05$

**$p < .01$

***$p < .001$

NOTE REGARDING THE STUDY OF
THE 2008 SANLU MILK SCANDAL

The first type of data I analyzed was texts produced by Tianya participants, *People's Daily*, and Xinhua News Agency. I extracted textual data from webpages of the Tianya Forum from September 2008 to December 2011. To examine official discourse, I also collected news written by *People's Daily* and Xinhua News Agency from September 2008 to 2011. News reports written by *People's Daily* and Xinhua News Agency represent and reflect the stance of the central government. They are the most widely distributed official news sources. I then selected discussion threads and news reports related to the Sanlu milk scandal for analysis. If the milk scandal was the main theme of an article or an initial post in a discussion thread, that article or thread was included in the data set. Accordingly, I generated two sets of texts used for content analysis: (1) *People's Daily* and Xinhua News Agency reports, and (2) Tianya discussion.

I qualitatively analyzed a 20 percent random sample of the Tianya texts, as well as all the texts representing the official discourse (161 articles). The 20 percent random sample comprised eighty-four discussion threads (including 2,323 posts) regarding the milk scandal. Computer scientist Daniel Xiaodan Zhou helped me to apply computer-assisted co-occurrence analysis to the two sets of texts without sampling in order to investigate the conceptions of law that emerged in official discourse and in the Tianya Forum. I conceptualized the semantic meaning of a term as its co-occurrence relations with other terms in the same context (Krippendorff 2004, 207). For instance, suppose the term "democracy" co-occurs frequently with "human rights," "election," and "freedom," as in the liberal tradition; its meaning would thus be quite different from the Maoist definition of "democracy," which co-occurs frequently with "class," "people," and so forth.

We conducted co-occurrence analysis via the following steps. We first used ICTCLAS (Institute of Computing Technology, Chinese Lexical Analysis System) to process word segmentation. Next, we used a synonym table to combine synonymous terms. A considerable proportion of the synonymous terms were created by Chinese netizens to circumvent censorship. Following convention in content analysis, we considered two terms as co-occurring when they were within fifty words' distance of one another (Krippendorff 2004). Finally, we identified the terms that co-occurred with the term "law" (*falu*) in the two sets of texts in turn.

I also conducted in-depth interviews with fifteen Tianya users who participated in the discussion in the Sanlu case. The distribution of the interviewees is provided in table A6.16. In addition, I also interviewed lawyers, media professionals, NGO participants, and parents of victims affected by the scandal. Despite censorship, these actors still endeavored to disseminate information and viewpoints that deviated from official discourse to elicit support from the public. The distribution of these interviewees is provided in table A6.17. Each interview lasted about one to one and a half hours.

TABLE A6.16. Interviews with Tianya participants

	Age	Gender	Education	Occupation	Interview date	Interview location
P-1	31	Male	College	Employee of a company	June 2011	Guangzhou
P-2	25	Male	Graduate school	Graduate student	June 2011	Guangzhou
P-3	34	Male	College	Employee of a government agency	June 2011	Guangzhou
P-4	29	Female	High school	Employee of a company	June 2011	Guangzhou
P-5	41	Female	College	Employee of a company	June 2011	Guangzhou
P-6	37	Male	High school	Manager of a company	June 2011	Guangzhou
P-7	32	Female	College	Employee of a company	June 2011	Beijing
P-8	28	Male	College	Employee of a government agency	July 2011	Beijing
P-9	27	Male	High school	Business owner	July 2011	Beijing
P-10	24	Male	Graduate school	Graduate student	July 2011	Beijing
P-11	22	Male	College	College student	July 2011	Beijing
P-12	29	Male	College	Business owner	July 2011	Chongqing
P-13	31	Female	College	Business owner	July 2011	Chongqing
P-14	35	Male	High school	Taxi driver	July 2011	Chongqing
P-15	26	Male	Graduate school	Graduate student	July 2011	Chongqing

TABLE A6.17. Interviews with informants

	Category of interviewees	Interview date	Interview location
I-1	Volunteer lawyer for consumer litigation	July 2011	Beijing
I-2	Volunteer lawyer for consumer litigation	July 2011	Beijing
I-3	Volunteer lawyer for consumer litigation	July 2011	Beijing
I-4	Journalist at *Southern Weekly*	July 2011	Guangzhou
I-5	Journalist at *Southern Weekly*	July 2011	Guangzhou
I-6	Journalist at *Oriental Morning Post*	July 2014	Shanghai
I-7	Journalist at *Oriental Morning Post*	July 2014	Shanghai
I-8	Volunteer at Open Constitution Initiative (*gongmeng*)	July 2011	Beijing
I-9	Employee at Open Constitution Initiative (*gongmeng*)	January 2015	Boston
I-10	Father of a victim	June 2011	Beijing
I-11	Father of a victim	July 2011	Beijing
I-12	Employee at NetEase	July 2011	Beijing
I-13	Employee at Sina	July 2011	Beijing
I-14	Employee at Tencent	June 2011	Guangzhou
I-15	Employee at Sohu	July 2011	Beijing
I-16	Employee at Tianya	June 2011	Phone interview
I-17	Moderator at Tianya	June 2011	Phone interview
I-18	Propaganda official	June 2011	Beijing

NOTES

Chapter 1: Introduction

1. Chinese people call Internet users "netizens" in China. When I use the term "netizens," I am simply referring to Internet users.

2. According to Reporters Without Borders, "China is the world's biggest prison for journalists, bloggers, and cyber-dissidents." Reporters Without Borders, *World Report—China*, January 5, 2010, available at *Refworld*, http://www.refworld.org/docid/4b7aa9bc28.html (accessed August 23, 2016).

3. Reporters Without Borders, "Enemies of the Internet 2014: Entities at the Heart of Censorship and Surveillance," *RSF*, March 11, 2014, https://rsf.org/en/news/enemies-internet-2014 -entities-heart-censorship-and-surveillance (accessed August 23, 2016).

4. *People's Daily*, October 25, 2011, and April 11, 2011.

5. Some scholars, for instance, Nancy Fraser (1990) and Margaret Somers (1993), contend that Habermas fails to examine how interaction in the public sphere can influence individuals' subjectivity and political practices.

6. The Asian Barometer Survey and AsiaBarometer Survey are two different surveys.

Chapter 2: The Rise of a Nationwide Contentious Public Sphere

1. In chapter 7 of *The Structural Transformation of the Public Sphere* (1989), Habermas describes how the concept of public opinion has changed over time and become an object of social-psychological research.

2. For example, *People's Daily*, August 14, 1950; March 10, 1952; September 6, 1953; and April 23, 1954.

3. For example, *People's Daily*, June 5, 1950; February 23, 1954; and April 3, 1954.

4. For example, *People's Daily*, July 4, 1954; August 20, 1954; and August 27, 1954.

5. *People's Daily*, April 13, 1954, and July 12, 1954.

6. *People's Daily*, May 27 and June 19, 1969; May 5, May 8, and June 13, 1976.

7. *People's Daily*, May 5, May 8, May 11, and May 30, 1976.

8. *People's Daily*, May 27 and June 19, 1969; May 5, May 8, and June 13, 1976.

9. *People's Daily*, October 19 and October 21, 1987.

10. *People's Daily*, March 4, 1988.

11. *People's Daily*, June 10, 13, 27, 29, and 30; July 1 and 7; August 6, 7, and 29; and September 3, 1989.

12. *People's Daily*, February 4, May 1, and June 14, 1994.

13. *People's Daily*, June 14, 1994.

14. *People's Daily*, December 16, 1998.

15. *People's Daily*, July 8, 1999.

16. For example, *People's Daily*, August 29, 2013; May 21, 2014; June 22, 2015; and July 19, 2015.

17. *People's Daily*, October 25, 2011.

Chapter 3: The Chinese State's Turn to Law and Rights

1. For example, *People's Daily*, August 29, 2013; May 21, 2014; June 22 and July 19, 2015.

2. *People's Daily*, July 5 and 24, 1979.

3. *People's Daily*, October 1, 1999.

4. The title of the document is "Resolution on Certain Questions in the History of Our Party since the Founding of the PRC"; it was adopted by the CCP's Sixth Plenary Session of the Eleventh Central Committee on June 27, 1981 (hereafter 1981 Resolution).

5. *People's Daily*, March 22, 1978.

6. 1981 Resolution.

7. *People's Daily*, December 25, 1978.

8. Although the CCP leaders discussed the Cultural Revolution in the Third Plenary Session of the Eleventh Central Committee and at the central working conference held prior to this session in 1978, they did not come up with a full narrative of the Cultural Revolution, particularly its causes, until 1981. It is noteworthy that since its founding, the CCP had adopted only two resolutions—one in 1945 and one in 1981—to address fundamental historical issues. This shows how critical the 1981 Resolution was in PRC's history.

9. Deng Xiaoping also mentioned this point at the New Year reception held in Beijing by the National Committee of the Chinese People's Political Consultative Conference on January 1, 1980; see *People's Daily*, January 2, 1980.

10. Jiang Hua, the president of the Supreme People's Court between 1975 and 1983, also advocated this view; see *People's Daily*, December 15, 1980.

11. Chen Jun interviewed Gao Xingjian in 2005, *China News Digest*, http://my.cnd.org/modules/wfsection/article.php?articleid=31018 (accessed June 15, 2016).

12. The Communique of the Third Plenary Session of the Eleventh Central Committee, *People's Daily*, October 25, 1977.

13. 1981 Resolution, n.p.

14. *Economic Observer Newspaper* (*jing ji guan cha bao*), May 26, 2008

15. *Procuratorial Daily*, August 20, 2009.

16. *People's Daily*, June 21, 1985.

17. *Procuratorial Daily*, August 13, 2009.

18. *People's Daily*, August 15, 1986.

19. *People's Daily*, October 19 and November 19, 1987.

20. Interview with a former government official working with Zhao Ziyang, August 2010, Hong Kong.

21. *People's Daily*, October 28, 1988.

22. *People's Daily*, February 17, 1989.

23. Interview, August 2010, Hong Kong.

24. *People's Daily*, October 28, 1988.

25. Interview, April 2014, Boston.

26. *People's Daily*, August 23, 1989.

27. *People's Daily*, October 25, 1989.

28. *People's Daily*, February 1 and April 21, 1990.

29. *People's Daily*, April 9, 1993.

30. *People's Daily*, June 29 and July 3, 1988.

31. Interview, June 2011, Beijing; interview, April 2014, Boston.

32. Interview, June 2011, Beijing.

33. Ibid.

34. The World Bank defines the adult literacy rate as "the percentage of people ages 15 and above who can, with understanding, read and write a short, simple statement on their everyday life." According to the World Bank, the adult literacy rate in China in 1982 was 66 percent. In 1990, 2000, and 2009, the adult literacy rate in China was 78, 91, and 94 percent, respectively; see "China," The World Bank, http://data.worldbank.org/country/china (accessed June 15, 2015).

35. *People's Daily*, October 6, 1979.

36. *People's Daily*, December 1, 1979.

37. *People's Daily*, December 1, 1988.

38. *People's Daily*, May 12, 1984.

39. *China Journalism Yearbook* (2004, 331).

40. According to Zhou Yu, the minister of justice from 1983 to 1988, Chinese central and local governments began to disseminate law actively in 1979; see *People's Daily*, June 17, 1985.

41. *People's Daily*, December 9, 1979.

42. *People's Daily*, May 28, 1978.

43. *People's Daily*, September 2, 1982.

44. *People's Daily*, December 9, 1979; and June 22, 1981. The strategy of "comprehensive governance" was later written as the "Decision of the Standing Committee of the National People's Congress on Intensifying the Improvement of Social Security by Taking Comprehensive Measures" in 1991.

45. *People's Daily*, June 7, 1984.

46. *People's Daily*, April 3, 1983.

47. A five-year plan of the Publicity Department of the CCP Central Committee and the Ministry of Justice announced the goal of acquainting citizens with basic knowledge of law (June 1985).

48. I used *quanli*, *qunyi*, and *weiquan* to search for articles with "rights" in titles and used *shoufa* to search for articles with "abiding by law" in titles.

49. Note that I did not include articles addressing nondomestic issues. As the Chinese government sometimes employed the discourse of rights to address international relation issues and criticize the status of rights protection in other countries, including those cases here would have wrongly inflated the visibility of such rights discourse vis-à-vis domestic issues.

50. *People's Daily*, August 26, 1985.

51. *People's Daily*, May 2, 1988.

52. *China Journalism Yearbook* (1994, 6).

53. For example, see *People's Daily*, August 14 and 18, 1955; February 22, 1953.

54. For example, see *People's Daily*, January 1 and December 17, 1949.

55. For example, *People's Daily*, March 15, 1995, and November 7, 2000.

56. For example, *People's Daily*, March 13, 1993.

57. For example, *People's Daily*, February 12, 2003, and February 28, 2005.

58. For example, *People's Daily*, February 29, 1998, and July 27, 2000.

59. For example, *People's Daily*, August 12, 2004, and July 7, 2008.

60. Interview, June 2011, Beijing.

61. See, for example, the *Court Today* episode description on *Baike.com*, a Chinese online encyclopedia, October 20, 2010, http://www.baike.com/wiki/%E3%80%8A%E4%BB%8A%E6%97%A5%E5%BC%80%E5%BA%AD%E3%80%8B (accessed 16 June 2016).

62. Gao Zhen also acknowledged the assistance and support from foreign and international organizations, such as the United Nations, the Ford Foundation, and the Asia Foundation, in helping to establish China's legal-aid institution.

Chapter 4: Critical News Reporting and Legal-Media Collaborative Networks

1. The news media are expected not only to uncover problems, but also to help the public analyze those problems and come up with solutions. These practices are broader than what is conventionally referred to as "watchdog journalism" and investigative reporting, which focus only on fact-finding, especially facts regarding illegal practices.

2. *Southern Metropolis Daily*, March 1, 2010.

3. *China Journalism Yearbook* (1982).

4. Liu Binyan was expelled by the CCP in the 1987 antirightist campaign. He then went to Harvard University in the fall of 1988 as a Nieman Fellow. Because of his criticism of the Chinese government's crackdown on the 1989 Tiananmen democratic movement, Liu was not allowed to return to China and remained in exile until his death in 2005. Bob Giles, "Statement on the Death of Liu Binyan From Nieman Foundation Curator Bob Giles," Nieman Foundation, December 5, 2005, http://nieman.harvard.edu/news/2005/12/statement-on-the-death-of-liu-binyan-from-nieman-foundation-curator-bob-giles/ (accessed July 1, 2016).

5. "How Xi Wenju established *Huaxi Metropolitan Daily*," *New Broad*, April 26, 2016, http://www.new-broad.com/index.php?m=content&c=index&a=show&catid=21&id=301 (accessed July 2, 2016).

6. The SEEC was established by nine prominent Chinese financial organizations in 1989 to build a treasury bond trading system in China. The SEEC is not affiliated with the Chinese government, although its establishment was supported by the government.

7. *China Journalism Yearbook* (1982, 1999).

8. I capitalize Department of Propaganda when referring to the department associated with the central government, rather than the lower-level propaganda departments.

9. Hassid argues that a minority group of Chinese journalists are "American-style" journalists. They commit to journalistic independence but not advocacy. These journalists stress the neutrality and objectiveness of their reporting. They tend not to confront power holders, and they are less likely to use emotional terms. I agree with Hassid that these journalists tend to emphasize objectiveness and avoid using emotion-laden language, but my interview data suggest that some of these journalists still commit to advocacy and aim to bring about social change. They just do it in less salient ways.

10. World Press Trends survey, http://www.wptdatabase.org (accessed April 3, 2017). The survey includes data about the press from more than seventy countries.

11. According to my interviewees, this problem-solving strategy was not borrowed from media in Hong Kong or elsewhere but developed endogenously.

Chapter 5: Extending Liberalization from the Press to the Internet

1. "Internet Freedom," Freedom House, https://freedomhouse.org/issues/internet-freedom #.VS7Nn_nF9UU (accessed April 19, 2015).

2. The Asian Barometer Survey and AsiaBarometer Survey are two different surveys.

3. See Articles 8 and 9 of the Provisions on the Administration of Newspaper Publication (2005).

4. President Bill Clinton, Address on Permanent Normal Trade Relations Status for China, March 8, 2000, available at *Tech Law Journal*, http://www.techlawjournal.com/cong106/pntr /20000308sp.htm (accessed July 18, 2016).

5. "The Internet Timeline of China 1986–2003," CNNIC, June 28, 2012, https://www.cnnic.cn/IDR/hlwfzdsj/201306/t20130628_40563.htm (accessed July 16, 2016).

6. "Management Provisions on Electronic Bulletin Services in Internet," Law of China, November 6, 2000, http://www.lawinfochina.com/display.aspx?lib=law&id=1664&CGid= (accessed July 19, 2016).

7. *China Journalism Yearbook* (2001, 55–58).

8. Regulation on Internet Information Service of the People's Republic of China (2000).

9. Articles 8, 9, and 22–25 of the Provisions for the Administration of Internet News Information Services.

10. *China Journalism Yearbook* (2002, 56).

11. China Websites Ranking, http://www.chinarank.org.cn (accessed May 11, 2015).

12. Reverse takeover (RTO) refers to "a type of merger used by private companies to become publicly traded without resorting to an initial public offering. Initially, the private company buys enough shares to control a publicly traded company." "Reverse Takeover—RTO," *Investopedia*, http://www.investopedia.com/terms/r/reversetakeover.asp#ixzz3Yz0QMAMG (accessed July 19, 2016).

13. Initial public offering (IPO) refers to the first sale of stock by a private company to the public. "IPOs are often issued by smaller, younger companies seeking the capital to expand, but they can also be done by large privately owned companies looking to become publicly traded." "Initial Public Offering—IPO," *Investopedia*, http://www.investopedia.com/terms/i/ipo.asp#ixzz3YyzpoTbM (accessed July 19, 2016).

14. CNNIC, *Statistical Report on Behavior of Social Media Users in China, 2014*, http://www.cnnic.cn/hlwfzyj/hlwxzbg/201408/P020140822379356612744.pdf (accessed May 11, 2015).

15. CNNIC, *Statistical Report on Internet Development in China, 2011*, http://www.cnnic.cn/hlwfzyj/hlwxzbg/201101/P020120709345289031187.pdf (accessed May 11, 2015); CNNIC, *Statistical Report on Internet Development in China, 2015*, http://www.cnnic.cn/hlwfzyj/hlwxzbg/201502/P020150203551802054676.pdf (accessed May 11, 2015).

16. CNNIC, *Statistical Report, 2014*.

17. I constructed a table that presented the fourteen editors in chief with detailed information about their employment history; however, after much consideration, I have decided not to include the table in the book to avoid disclosing too much personal information.

18. CNNIC, *Statistical Report, 2014*.

19. Generally speaking, a Big V has more than 100,000 followers. According to 2013 statistics, over 19,000 Weibo accounts had more than 100,000 followers; over 3,300 Weibo accounts had more than one million followers; and over 200 Weibo accounts had more than ten million followers. "Social Responsibility of Big Vs," *Xinhuanet*, August 12, 2013, http://news.xinhuanet.com/2013–08/12/c_132621768.htm (accessed April 4, 2017).

20. Shen Yang and Zhu Xuqi, "Weibo Opinion Leaders Top 100 Ranking," Tencent Weibo, January 2015, http://p.t.qq.com/longweibo/index.php?id=445939089524042 (accessed May 20, 2015).

21. The Global Times Forum is operated by the *Global Times*, which is under the auspices of the *People's Daily* and focuses on international issues.

22. Shen and Zhu, "Weibo Opinion Leaders."

23. "Undesirable Western Constitutionalism," *Qstheory*, December 4, 2014, http://www.qstheory.cn/zhuanqu/rdjj/2014–12/04/c_1113523690.htm (accessed April 4, 2017).

24. *Guangming Daily*, November 15, 2014; *Qiushi*, January 2, 2015; *Hongqi Wengao*, January 9, 2015; "Rule of Law in China and Western Constitutionalism are Different," *CPCNEWS*, April 1, 2015. http://dangjian.people.com.cn/n/2015/0401/c117092–26784957.html (accessed April 4, 2017).

25. I created a table of these top one hundred public opinion leaders, in which I documented their Weibo ID, political orientation, and connection with outspoken newspapers; however, after much consideration, I have decided not to include the table in this book to avoid disclosing too much personal information.

26. *Beijing News*, May 20, 2015.

Chapter 6: An Emerging Online Public

1. "Internet Development Research," CNNIC, http://www.cnnic.net.cn/hlwfzyj/ (accessed July 24, 2016).

2. "How Censorship Works in China: A Brief Overview," Human Rights Watch, August 2006, https://www.hrw.org/reports/2006/china0806/3.htm (accessed July 29, 2016).

3. *Los Angeles Times*, September 14, 2002.

4. "Top Ten Most Influential Lawsuits in 2006," *Legal Daily*, January 16, 2007, http://www
.legaldaily.com.cn/misc/2007-01/16/content_516410.htm (accessed April 2, 2017).

5. "Fujian 1721 People v. Chemical Plant Environmental Pollution Infringement Case Was Named the Top Ten Influencing Lawsuit in China in 2005," Center for Legal Assistance to Pollution Victims, January 23, 2006, http://www.clapv.org/NewsContent.asp?id=348&title=%D7
%EE%D0%C2%B6%AF%CC%AC&titlecontent=NewsList&lei1=106 (accessed August 5, 2016).

6. "Top Ten Most Influential Lawsuits in 2005," *Xinhuanet*, January 9, 2006, http://news
.xinhuanet.com/legal/2006-01/09/content_4026867.htm (accessed April 4, 2017).

7. "The Surrounding Gaze," China Media Project, January 2011, http://cmp.hku.hk/2011/01
/04/9399/ (accessed August 10, 2016).

8. "Influence of Big Vs on Public Opinion," Cyberspace Administration of China, July 21, 2016, http://www.cac.gov.cn/2016-07/21/c_1119257801.htm (accessed April 4, 2017).

9. CNNIC, *Statistical Report on Internet Development in China, 2009*, http://www.cnnic.cn
/hlwfzyj/hlwxzbg/200912/P020120709345307778361.pdf (accessed February 17, 2014).http://
www.cnnic.cn/hlwfzyj/hlwxzbg/200912/P020120709345307778361.pdf

10. Ibid.http://www.cnnic.net.cn/hlwfzyj/hlwxzbg/200907/P020120709345315706062
.pdf

11. Interviews: I-4, I-5, I-6, and I-7.

12. Interviews: I-4, I-5, I-6, and I-7.

13. Interviews: I-4, I-5, I-6, and I-7.

14. Interviews: I-4, I-5, I-6, I-7, I-12, I-13, I-14, I-15, and I-16.

15. *People's Daily*, October 1, 2008.

16. As I explain in further detail in the appendix, Daniel Xiaodan Zhou and I used ICTCLAS to process word segmentation. In this set of texts, we identified 1,413 nouns in total.

17. Interviews: I-10 and I-11.

18. Interviews: I-8 and I-9.

19. Interviews: I-12, I-13, I-14, and I-15.

20. CNNIC, *Statistical Report, 2009*.

21. *Southern Weekly*, September 18, 2008, and January 8, 2009; *China Economic Times*, September 18, 2008; *China Enterprise News*, December 4, 2008.

22. Interviews: I-4 and I-5.

23. Interviews: I-1, I-2, and I-3.

24. *Southern Weekly*, April 16, 2009.

25. *Southern Weekly*, January 15, 2009.

26. *Southern Weekly*, November 13, 2008, and March 5, 2009; *Henan Daily*, June 4, 2009.

27. *Southern Weekly*, December 30, 2009.

28. NetEase, December 30, 2009, http://focus.news.163.com/09/1230/11/5RPCUM4 D00011SM9.html (accessed February 10, 2015).

29. *Oriental Morning Post*, November 12, 2010.

30. *Southern Weekly*, July 23, 2009.

31. Interview: P-11

32. Interview: P-14.

33. ID: caprice, September 20, 2008. This is a quotation from a post in the Tianya Forum. I documented the user's ID in Tianya Forum and the date of the post for all quotations.

34. ID: 什么时候, October 8, 2008.

35. ID: 76huolong, September 12, 2008.

36. ID: richardgui, September 24, 2008.

37. ID: 文中思, September 19, 2008.

38. ID: kill2004, January 25, 2009.

39. ID:飞飞是头猪, October 8, 2010.

40. ID: heart, October 8, 2010.

41. Interviews: P7 and P8.

42. ID: 应先生, January 25, 2009.

43. I selected Chongqing for two reasons. First, it encompasses a rural area along with a core urban area. This made access to subjects with diverse backgrounds easier. Moreover, I had the assistance of a local collaborator in Chongqing, who helped me to recruit subjects and implement interviews.

Chapter 7: The Chinese State Strikes Back

1. *People's Daily*, March 7, 1997.

2. *People's Daily*, December 13, 2004.

3. For example, Yiping Jiang, a senior editor at *Southern Metropolis Daily*, was removed from her position in December 2008.

4. "Hu Jintao's Speech at the 17th National Congress of the Communist Party of China," *Xinhuanet*, October 24, 2007, http://news.xinhuanet.com/newscenter/2007–10/24/content _6938568_5.htm (accessed April 4, 2017).

5. *People's Daily*, November 27, 2013; "Xi Jinping: Ideology Work is a Critical Task," *China Daily*, August 20, 2013, http://www.chinadaily.com.cn/dfpd/shizheng/2013–08/20/content _16908782.htm (accessed April 4, 2017).

6. *People's Daily*, July 23, 2014.

7. *People's Daily*, April 21, 2016.

8. *People's Daily*, September 17, 2013.

9. *People's Daily*, September 4, 2013.

10. "Integrating Two Public Spheres," *Xinhuanet*, December 2, 2013, http://news .xinhuanet.com/zgjx/2013–12/02/c_132934361.htm; "Red, Gray, and Black Zones in Ideology," *Sina*, September 7, 2013, http://news.sina.com.cn/pl/2013–09–07/110428157069.shtml (accessed April 4, 2017).

11. "Xi Jinping Spoke at the Party School Work Conference," NetEase, May 1, 2016, http:// money.163.com/16/0501/17/BM0FH24V00253B0H.html (accessed May 14, 2016).

12. *People's Daily*, May 18, 2014.

13. *People's Daily*, November 16, 2013.

14. *People's Daily*, November 11, 2000.

15. *People's Daily*, May 5, 2011.

16. The sixteen organizations involved were Department of Propaganda; Ministry of Information Industry; the State Council Information Office; Ministry of Education; Ministry of Culture; Ministry of Health; Ministry of Public Security; Ministry of State Security; Ministry of Commerce; State Administration of Radio, Film and Television; General Administration of Press and Publication; the National Administration for the Protection of State Secrets; the State Administration for Industry and Commerce; the State Food and Drug Administration; the Chinese Academy of Sciences; and the People's Liberation Army General Staff Department. "Notice on the Issuance of the 'Coordinated Work Program for Internet Site Management,'" China Food and Drug Administration, February 17, 2006, http://www.sda.gov.cn/WS01/CL0056/10768.html (accessed May 22, 2016).

17. *People's Daily*, May 5, 2011.

18. "Notice on Carrying out Special Action against Crimes Committed to Cybercrime," State Administration for Industry and Commerce, July 7, 2011, http://www.saic.gov.cn/zwgk /zyfb/lhfw/lhfw/zxjgj/201107/t20110707_107557.html (accessed May 21, 2016).

19. *People's Daily*, February 28, 2014.

20. "Notice of Internet Information Content Management," State Council, August 26, 2014, http://www.gov.cn/zhengce/content/2014-08/28/content_9056.htm (accessed April 4, 2017).

21. *New York Times*, December 1, 2014.

22. "Internet Management," *Eastday*, October 19, 2014, http://pinglun.eastday.com/p /20141019/u1ai8398239.html (accessed May 17, 2016).

23. "Summary of Annual Report of People's Daily Online," Cninf.com, April 25, 2016, http://www.cninfo.com.cn/finalpage/2016-04-15/1202180638.PDF (accessed May 17, 2016).

24. Interview, July 2015, Beijing.

25. *Yangzi Evening News*, December 23, 2013.

26. "An Urgent Need for Public Opinion Analysts," *Xinhuanet*, August 27, 2014, http:// news.xinhuanet.com/yuqing/2014-08/27/c_126923720.htm (accessed May 17, 2016).

27. Interview, July 2015, Beijing.

28. "General Secretary Xi Jinping 's Speech at the Symposium on Cybersecurity and Information Work," Cyberspace Administration of China, April 25, 2016, http://www.cac.gov.cn /2016-04/25/c_1118731366.htm (accessed April 4, 2017).

29. "E-mail Security Ranking," *Seavia*, October 24, 2015, https://www.seavia.com/it/news /which-email-is-safe.html (accessed April 4, 2017).

30. *Global Times*, December 30, 2014.

31. "2 in 3 Chinese VPN Users Access Weekly," Global Web Index, January 31, 2017, https:// www.globalwebindex.net/blog/2-in-3-chinese-vpn-users-access-weekly (accessed April 4, 2017).

32. *Global Times*, January 23, 2015.

33. "Cybersecurity Law (Draft)," National People's Congress, July 6, 2015, http://www.npc .gov.cn/npc/xinwen/lfgz/flca/2015-07/06/content_1940614.htm (accessed April 4, 2017).

34. "Cybersecurity Law," National People's Congress, November 7, 2016, http://www.npc .gov.cn/npc/xinwen/2016-11/07/content_2001605.htm (accessed April 4, 2017).

35. "Xi: Without Cybersecurity, There Is No National security," *People's Daily Online*, November 20, 2014, http://cpc.people.com.cn/xuexi/n/2014/1120/c385475-26061137.html (accessed April 4, 2017).

36. "Commission Welcomes Agreement to Make EU Online Environment More Secure," European Commission, December 8, 2015, http://europa.eu/rapid/press-release_IP-15-6270 _en.htm (accessed April 5, 2017).

37. "Japan: Cybersecurity Basic Act Adopted," Library of Congress, December 10, 2014, http://www.loc.gov/law/foreign-news/article/japan-cybersecurity-basic-act-adopted/ (accessed April 5, 2017).

38. "To Improve Cybersecurity in the United States Through Enhanced Sharing of Information about Cybersecurity Threats, and for Other Purposes," Congress.gov, March 17, 2015, https://www.congress.gov/bill/114th-congress/senate-bill/754 (accessed April 5, 2017).

39. Generally speaking, a Big V has more than 100,000 followers. According to statistics in 2013, over 19,000 Weibo accounts have more than 100,000 followers; over 3,300 Weibo accounts have more than one million followers; and over 200 Weibo accounts have more than ten million followers. "Lu Wei and Big Vs talked about Social Responsibility," *Xinhuanet*, August 12, 2013, http://news.xinhuanet.com/2013–08/12/c_132621768.htm (accessed April 5, 2017).

40. *People's Daily*, November 17, 2013.

41. "Police Cracked Down on 100,000 Websites," *Tencent*, December 2, 2014, http://tech.qq.com/a/20141202/071886.htm (accessed April 5, 2017).

42. *People's Daily*, September 10, 2013.

43. The decision was made by the Fujian Shaoan County People's Court on July 13, 2015 (2015 *shao xin chu zi* #55).

44. The decision was made by the Anhui Fengtai County People's Court on September 15, 2015 (2015 *feng xin chu zi* #00303).

45. The decision was made by the Hubei Changyan Tujiazu Autonomous County People's Court on October 19, 2015 (2015 *e changyan xin chu zi* #00084).

46. The decision was made by the Guanxi Zhuanzu Autonomous District Tiane County People's Court on July 23, 2015 (2014 *e xin chu zi* #95).

47. Rights defense lawyers are lawyers who help Chinese citizens to assert their rights through litigation and legal activism. See Fu and Cullen (2008)

48. *People's Daily*, August 1, 2012.

49. "New Five Black Categories," *China Digital Space*, https://chinadigitaltimes.net/space/New_five_black_categories; "China's New 'Black Five' Categories," *Global Voices*, August 13, 2012, https://globalvoices.org/2012/08/13/chinas-new-black-five-categories-social-threat-or-core-strength/ (accessed April 5, 2017).

50. "China's Irrepressible Lawyers," *Washington Post*, July 19, 2015, https://www.washingtonpost.com/opinions/chinas-irrepressible-lawyers/2015/07/19/81d0a04e-2a7b-11e5-a250–42bd812efc09_story.html?utm_term=.5ac3279fb606 (accessed June 2, 2016).

51. *People's Daily*, July 11, 2015. This quotation was translated by the *New York Times*, http://cn.nytimes.com/china/20150714/c14sino-lawyers/en-us/ (accessed August 12, 2015).

52. "China Sentences Legal Activist to 4 Years for Role in Protests," *New York Times*, January 26, 2014, http://cn.nytimes.com/china/20140126/c26xuzhiyong/en-us/ (accessed April 5, 2017).

53. *Beijing News*, January 23, 2014.

54. "Lawyer Li Xungbing was Barred from Leaving China," *Radio Free Asia*, December 3, 2015, http://www.rfa.org/cantonese/news/lawyer-a-12032015073507.html (accessed April 5, 2017).

55. "Lawyer Li Fangping was Taken by the Police," *Radio Free Asia*, March 1, 2016, http://www.rfa.org/mandarin/Xinwen/3–03012016101012.htmll (accessed April 5, 2017).

56. "Villagers in Chongqing Hope Ren Zhiqian Can Return to his Job," *Tencent*, October 18, 2012, http://news.qq.com/a/20121018/001270.htm (accessed April 5, 2017).

57. *Southern Morning Post*, February 20, 2013; May 15, 2015.

58. "Activist Lawyer Pu Ziqiang was Put on Probation," *BBC Chinese*, December 22, 2015, http://www.bbc.com/zhongwen/simp/china/2015/12/151222_china_rights_lawyer_verdict (accessed April 5, 2017).

59. "Ten Important Things in the Chinese Newspaper Industry," *People's Daily Online*, February 5, 2006, http://media.people.com.cn/GB/40710/40715/4075938.html (accessed April 5, 2017).

60. *Guangmin Daily*, June 19, 2014.

61. "China Will Strengthen Its Regulation of Journalists," *Xinhuanet*, July 8, 2014, http://news.xinhuanet.com/politics/2014–07/08/c_1111508621.htm (accessed April 5, 2017).

62. *Zhejiang Daily*, February 26, 2016.

63. *People's Daily*, October 23, 1990.

64. "Hu Jintao's Speech at the People's Daily," *People's Daily Online*, June 20, 2008, http://media.people.com.cn/GB/40606/7409348.html (accessed April 5, 2017).

65. "The Cyberspace Administration of China Closed Ren Zhiqiang's Weibo," NetEase, February 28, 2016, http://tech.163.com/16/0228/16/BGU382UI000915BF.html (accessed April 5, 2017).

66. "Ren Zhiqiang's Was Put on One-Year Probation," *Sina*, May 2, 2016, http://news.sina.com.cn/c/nd/2016–05–02/doc-ifxrtzte9875772.shtml (accessed April 5, 2017).

67. *Shenzhen Special Zone Daily*, April 9, 2014.

68. Interview, July 2015, Beijing.

69. "Tou Zhen Was Appointed as the Deputy Head of the Department of Propaganda," *Caixin*, July 17, 2015, http://china.caixin.com/2015–07–17/100829972.html (accessed April 5, 2017).

70. *People's Daily*, February 4, 2015.

71. "The Cyberspace Administration of China Summoned the Executive Chiefs of NetEase," *People's Daily Online*, February 3, 2015, http://media.people.com.cn/n/2015/0203/c40606-26495916.html (accessed April 5, 2017).

72. "The Cyberspace Administration of China Summoned the Executive Chiefs of Sina," *People's Daily Online*, April 11, 2015, http://politics.people.com.cn/n/2015/0411/c1001–26828533.html (accessed April 5, 2017).

73. *People's Daily*, April 29, 2015.

74. For instance, in 2007, the Chinese state enacted the Employment Promotion Law, which stipulates that the hiring process cannot discriminate against people with infectious disease. In addition, several hepatitis B patients won discrimination-related lawsuits against employers. "1,611 Citizens Applied for Constitutional Review," *People's Daily Online*, November 26, 2003, http://www.people.com.cn/GB/shehui/1061/2212867.html (accessed April 5, 2017).

75. *Southern Weekly*, August 23, 2007; *Life Times*, June 21, 2013.

76. *Southern Weekly*, August 23, 2007.

77. *Henan Daily,* September 18, 2008.

78. "The Clampdown on the Beijing Yirenping Center," *Human Rights in China*, March 25, 2015, http://www.hrichina.org/en/node/15955 (accessed April 5, 2017).

79. "Member of the Beijing Yirenping Center were Arrested by Beijing Police," *NPOst.tw*, June 16, 2015, http://npost.tw/archives/19923 (accessed April 5, 2017).

80. "Chunfeng Labor Disputes Services Center Decided Not to Accept Foreign Funding," Zhang Zhiru's blog, *Sina*, December 31, 2014, http://blog.sina.com.cn/s/blog_4b79809f0102veq8.html (accessed April 5, 2017).

81. *People's Daily*, December 23, 2015.

82. *People's Daily*, June 17, 2015.

83. *People's Daily*, September 29, 2015; "The Opinion on the Work of Strengthening Party Building in Social Organizations," *CPC News*, September 29, 2015, http://dangjian.people.com.cn/n/2015/0929/c117092-27645046.html (accessed April 5, 2017).

84. "The Foreign NGO Management Law," *Xinhuanet*, April 28, 2016, http://news.xinhuanet.com/politics/2016–04/29/c_1118765888.htm (accessed April 5, 2017).

85. *Global Times*, June 3, 2015.

86. *People's Daily*, July 2, 2015. The National Security Law was enacted in July 2015.

87. "The Government Operated around 280,000 Weibo and More Than 100,000 WeChat Public Accounts," *People's Daily Online*, January 23, 2016, http://media.people.com.cn/n1/2016/0123/c40606-28078213.html (accessed April 5, 2017).

88. "Report and Trend of the Government's Weibo," Chinese Police, January 22, 2016, http://www.cpd.com.cn/n15737398/n26490099/c31812105/content.html (accessed April 5, 2017).

89. "Sichuan Province Trained One Thousand Cyber-Civilization Communication Volunteers," *Sichuan Wenming*, June 21, 2011, http://sc.wenming.cn/tt/201106/t20110621_219680.html (accessed April 5, 2017).

90. "Notice on How to Do Cyber-Civilization Volunteering," *Jinan Sunshine Sister*, February 22, 2013, http://www.jn-ygdj.com/ygdjxw/4261.jhtml (accessed April 5, 2017).

91. "Notice on How to Do Cyber-Civilization Volunteering," *Zhongguo Wenming*, May 27, 2016, http://nxwz.wenming.cn/wjzl/201605/t20160527_2583320.htm (accessed April 5, 2017).

92. The Four Cardinal Principles—the four issues not debatable in the PRC—were listed by Deng Xiaoping in 1979. They are upholding the socialist path, upholding the people's democratic dictatorship, upholding the leadership of the CCP, and upholding Mao Zedong's thought and Marxism-Leninism.

93. *People's Daily*, May 21, 2015.

94. *Beijing Youth Daily*, May 22, 2015; "The CCP's United Front Work Department Offers Training Courses for Big Vs," *People's Daily Online*, May 22, 2015, http://politics.people.com.cn/n/2015/0522/c1001-27039108.html(accessed April 5, 2017).

95. "National Security Law," Ministry of National Defense, July 1, 2015, http://news.mod.gov.cn/headlines/2015-07/01/content_4592594_2.htm(accessed April 5, 2017).

96. "Xi Jinping's Speech at the Second World Internet Conference," *Xinhuanet*, December 16, 2015, http://news.xinhuanet.com/politics/2015-12/16/c_1117481089.htm(accessed April 5, 2017).

97. "Analysis of Public Opinion in 2015," *People's Daily Online*, December 24, 2015, http://yuqing.people.com.cn/n1/2015/1224/c401685-27972434.html(accessed April 5, 2017).

98. "Calls for Responsibility of Youth in Cyberspace," *People's Daily Online*, June 24, 2015, http://theory.people.com.cn/n/2015/0624/c40531-27198282.html (accessed April 5, 2017).

99. "Analysis of Public Opinion in 2015," *Caijing*, January 20, 2016, http://comments.caijing.com.cn/20160120/4057441.shtml (accessed April 5, 2017).

100. "Hundreds of Weibo Accounts Were Investigated," *Beijing News*, August 14, 2015, http://www.bjnews.com.cn/news/2015/08/14/374356.html; "Fifty Websites were Investigated for Spreading Rumors in the Tianjin explosion," China News, August 15, 2015, http://www.chinanews.com/sh/2015/08-15/7469724.shtml (accessed April 5, 2017).

101. "Residents Near the Tianjin Explosion Petitioned Again," *Zhaobao*, August 17, 2015, http://www.zaobao.com.sg/media/photo/story20150817-515680 (accessed April 5, 2017).

102. "The Tianjin Explosion Turned Residents into Petitioners," *Initium*, September 8, 2015, https://theinitium.com/article/20150907-mainland-tianjin-explosion/; "Petitions after the Tianjin Explosion," *Caijing*, August 17, 2015, http://weibo.com/1642088277/CwdED4Pcl?ref=&type=comment#_rnd1464696581238 (accessed April 5, 2017).

103. *Legal Daily*, December 8, 2013.

104. "Protecting the Rights of Lawyers," *Caixin*, July 13, 2015, http://weibo.com/1663937380/CqWkw4mgn?type=comment (accessed April 5, 2017).

105. "Reflection on Detention of Labor NGO members," *Caixin*, December 11, 2015, http://weibo.com/1684012053/D7T9Fvd7s?type=comment#_rnd1464719200781 (accessed April 5, 2017).

106. "Television Confession Should Be Cautious," *Caixin*, March 1, 2016, http://china.caixin.com/2016-03-01/100914547.html; "Television Confession Does Not Equate to a Judicial Conviction," *Beijing News*, March 2, 2016, http://epaper.bjnews.com.cn/html/2016-03/02/content_624607.htm(accessed April 5, 2017).

107. "Article Denouncing Censorship Removed from Chinese Magazine *Caixin*'s Website," *Hong Kong Free Press*, March 9, 2016, https://twitter.com/HongKongFP/status/707175487492128768/photo/1 (accessed April 5, 2017).

108. "Wang Zheng: The Five Sisters Incident and the Future of Feminism in China," *University of Michigan News*, May 14, 2015, http://www.ns.umich.edu/new/chinese-translations/22891-2015-05-14-14-19-56-wang-zheng (accessed May 31, 2016).

109. "Statement of Renmin University Alumni on Lei Yang Incident," Elections and Governance, May 11, 2016, http://www.chinaelections.org/article/587/242147.html (accessed May 31, 2016).

110. "The Beijing Police Was Under Investigation," *Caixin*, June 1, 2016, http://china.caixin.com/2016-06-01/100950007.html (accessed January 11, 2017); "No Trial for Beijing Officers Over Death of Environmentalist," *New York Times*, December 23, 2016, https://www.nytimes.com/2016/12/23/world/asia/china-lei-yang-police.html (accessed January 11, 2017).

Chapter 8: Conclusion

1. Criticism of modernization theory is often associated with the theory's assumption about a trajectory of human progress.

REFERENCES

Acemoglu, Daron. 2006. *Economic Origins of Dictatorship and Democracy*. New York: Cambridge University Press.

Acemoglu, Daron, and James A. Robinson. 2001. "A Theory of Political Transitions." *American Economic Review* 91 (4): 938–63.

Alford, William P. 1990. "'Seek Truth from Facts'—Especially When They Are Unpleasant: America's Understanding of China's Efforts at Law Reform." *UCLA Pacific Basin Law Journal* 8 (1–2): 177–96.

———. 1997. "Law, Law, What Law?: Why Western Scholars of Chinese History and Society Have Not Had More to Say About Its Law." *Modern China* 23 (4): 398–419.

———. 1999. "A Second Great Wall? China's Post-Cultural Revolution Project of Legal Construction." *Cultural Dynamics* 11 (2): 193–213.

Atabaki, Touraj, and Erik Jan Zürcher. 2004. "Introduction." In *Men of Order: Authoritarian Modernization under Atatürk and Reza Shah*, edited by T. Atabaki and E. J. Zürcher, 1–12. New York: Palgrave Macmillan.

Baker, Beverly G. 1981. "Chinese Law in the Eighties: The Lawyer and the Criminal Process." *Albany Law Review* 46 (3): 751–75.

Balkin, Jack M. 2009. "Critical Legal Theory Today." In *On Philosophy in American Law*, edited by F. J. Mootz, 64–72. New York: Cambridge University Press.

Barber, Benjamin R. 1998. "Three Scenarios for the Future of Technology and Strong Democracy." *Political Science Quarterly* 113 (4): 573–89.

———. 2000. "Electronic Democracy: Which Technology for Which Democracy? Which Democracy for Which Technology?" *International Journal of Communications Law and Policy* 6:1–8.

Barney, Darin. 2000. *Prometheus Wired: The Hope for Democracy in the Age of Network Technology*. Chicago: University of Chicago Press.

Baum, Richard. 1986. "Modernization and Legal Reform in Post-Mao China: The Rebirth of Socialist Legality." *Studies in Comparative Communism* 19 (2): 69–103.

Benkler, Yochai. 2006. *The Wealth of Networks: How Social Production Transforms Markets and Freedom*. New Haven, CT: Yale University Press.

Bhattasali, Deepak, Shantong Li, and Will Martin. 2004. *China and the WTO: Accession, Policy Reform, and Poverty Reduction Strategies*. Washington, DC: World Bank and Oxford University Press.

Blaydes, Lisa, and Drew A. Linzer. 2008. "The Political Economy of Women's Support for Fundamentalist Islam." *World Politics* 60 (4): 576–609.

Boggs, Carl. 2000. *The End of Politics: Corporate Power and the Decline of the Public Sphere*. New York: Guilford Press.

Boix, Carles, and Susan C Stokes. 2003. "Endogenous Democratization." *World Politics* 55 (4): 517–49.

Bourdieu, Pierre. 1987. "Force of Law: Toward a Sociology of the Juridical Field." *Hastings Law Journal* 38 (5): 805–53.

———. 1994. "Rethinking the State: Genesis and Structure of the Bureaucratic Field." *Sociological Theory* 12 (1): 1–18.

———. 2001. "Television." *European Review* 9 (3): 245–56.

Bourdieu, Pierre, and Loïc J. D. Wacquant. 1992. *An Invitation to Reflexive Sociology*. Chicago: University of Chicago Press.

Bröckling, Ulrich, Susanne Krasmann, and Thomas Lemke. 2011. "From Foucault's Lectures at the Collège De France to Studies of Governmentality: An Introduction." In *Governmentality: Current Issues and Future Challenges*, edited by U. Bröckling, S. Krasmann, and T. Lemke, 1–33. New York: Routledge.

Cai, Yongshun. 2010. *Collective Resistance in China: Why Popular Protests Succeed or Fail*. Stanford, CA: Stanford University Press.

Calhoun, Craig 1992. "Introduction." In *Habermas and the Public Sphere*, edited by C. Calhoun, 1–48. Cambridge, MA: MIT Press.

———. 1993. "Civil Society and the Public Sphere." *Public Culture* 5 (2): 267–80.

Calhoun, Craig, and Guobin Yang. 2007. "Media, Civil Society, and the Rise of a Green Public Sphere in China." *China Information* 21 (2): 211–36.

Chang P'eng-yuan. 1989. "Constitutionalism in the Late Qing—Conception and Practice." *Chinese Studies in History* 23 (1): 3–22.

Chen Chih-Jou Jay. 2015. "Popular Protest in an Authoritarian Regime: A Wildcat Strike in Southern China." *Taiwanese Sociology* 30 (1): 1–53.

Chen Hui-Xin. 1993. "Ru Jia Fa Jia Si Xiang Zai Zhong Guo Chuan Tong Fa Zhi De Rong He Guo Cheng" (The integration of Confucian and legalist thoughts in the Chinese traditional legal system). In *Zhong Guo Fa Zhi Xian Dai Hua Zhi Hui Gu Yu Qian Zhan* (The past and future of the modernization of the Chinese legal system), edited by Dai D. X., 1–22. Taipei: School of Law of the National Taiwan University.

Chen Jianfu. 2008. *Chinese Law: Context and Transformation*. Boston: Martinus Nijhoff.

Chen Meijian. 2013. "Dou Shi Bao Fa Zhi Xin Wen De Gu Shi Hua Ce Lue Tan Xi" [Analysis of strategies of story telling in metropolis daily newspapers]. *Xin Wen Shi Jian* [Practical journalism] 3:48–49.

Cheng Chen and Wei Zhang. 1988. "Pu Fa Jiao Yu Ying Xiang Na Xie Fang Mian Shen Hua: Pu Fa Diao Yan Hou De Si Kao" (How to deepen dissemination of law: Reflection after investigation of law dissemination campaigns). *Fa Xue* (Jurisprudence) 3:42–44.

Cheng Zhongyuan, Wang Yuxiang, and Li Zhenghua. 2008. *Zhuan She Nian Dai: 1976–1981 Nian De Zhong Guo* [The era of transition: China between 1976 and 1981]. Beijing: Zhong Yang Wen Xian Chu Ban She [Central Party Literature Press].

China Journalism Yearbook. 1982–2004. Beijing: China Society Science Publishing House.

Clark, David. 1999. "The Many Meanings of the Rule of Law." In *Law, Capitalism and Power in Asia: The Rule of Law and Legal Institutions*, edited by K. Jayasuriya, 24–37. New York: Routledge.

Cohen, Jacob. 1960. "A Coefficient of Agreement for Nominal Scales." *Educational and Psychological Measurement* 20 (1): 37–46.

Curran, James. 1991. "Rethinking the Media as a Public Sphere." In *Communication and Citizenship: Journalism and the Public Sphere*, edited by P. Dahlgren and C. Sparks, 27–57. London: Routledge.

Dahlgren, Peter. 1995. *Television and the Public Sphere: Citizenship, Democracy and the Media*. London: Sage Publications.

———2000. "The Internet and the Democratization of Civic Culture." *Political Communication* 17 (4): 335–40.

———. 2005. "The Internet, Public Spheres, and Political Communication: Dispersion and Deliberation." *Political Communication* 22 (2): 147–62.

Deng Xiaoping. 1993. *Deng Xiao Ping Wen Xuan* [Deng Xiaoping anthology]. Vol. 3. Beijing: Ren Min Chu Ban She [People's Publishing House].

———. 1994. *Deng Xiaoping Wen Xuan* [Deng Xiaoping anthology]. Vol. 2. Beijing: Ren Min Chu Ban She [People's Publishing House].

DeWoskin, Kenneth J. 2001. "The WTO and the Telecommunications Sector in China." *China Quarterly* 167:630–54.

Diamond, Larry. 2002. "Thinking About Hybrid Regimes." *Journal of Democracy* 13 (2): 21–35.

———. 2003. "The Rule of Law as Transition to Democracy in China." *Journal of Contemporary China* 12 (35): 319–31.

Dittmer, Lowell, and Guoli Liu. 2006. *China's Deep Reform: Domestic Politics in Transition*. Lanham, MD: Rowman and Littlefield.

Downey, John, and Natalie Fenton. 2003. "New Media, Counter Publicity and the Public Sphere." *New Media and Society* 5 (2): 185–202.

Eley, Geoff. 1992. "Nations, Publics, and Political Cultures: Placing Habermas in the Nineteenth Century." In *Habermas and the Public Sphere*, edited by C. Calhoun, 18–31. Cambridge, MA: MIT Press.

Epstein, David L., Robert Bates, Jack Goldstone, Ida Kristensen, and Sharyn O'Halloran. 2006. "Democratic Transitions." *American Journal of Political Science* 50 (3): 551–69.

Esarey, Ashley. 2005. "Cornering the Market: State Strategies for Controlling China's Commercial Media." *Asian Perspective* 29 (4): 37–83.

———. 2015. "Winning Hearts and Minds? Cadres as Microbloggers in China." *Journal of Current Chinese Affairs* 44 (2): 69–103.

Fraser, Nancy. 1990. "Rethinking the Public Sphere: A Contribution to the Critique of Actually Existing Democracy." *Social Text* (25–26): 56–80.

Fu, Hualing, and Richard Cullen. 2008. "Weiquan (Rights Protection) Lawyering in an Authoritarian State: Building a Culture of Public-Interest Lawyering." *China Journal* 59:111–27.

———. 2011. "Climbing the Weiquan Ladder: A Radicalizing Process for Rights-Protection Lawyers." *China Quarterly* 205 (1): 40–59.

Fukuyama, Francis. 2012. "The Future of History: Can Liberal Democracy Survive the Decline of the Middle Class?" *Foreign Affairs* 91 (1): 53–61.

Gallagher, Mary E. 2005a. *Contagious Capitalism: Globalization and the Politics of Labor in China*. Princeton, NJ: Princeton University Press.

———. 2005b. "'Use the Law as Your Weapon!': The Rule of Law and Labor Conflict in China." In *Engaging the Law in China: State, Society, and Possibilities for Justice*, edited by N. J. Diamant, S. B. Lubman, and K. J. O'Brien, 54–83. Stanford, CA: Stanford University Press.

———. 2006. "Mobilizing the Law in China: Informed Disenchantment and the Development of Legal Consciousness." *Law and Society Review* 40 (4): 783–816.

Gamson, William A. 1992. *Talking Politics*. New York: Cambridge University Press.

Gao Guanqi and Liu Yu. 2012. "Ti Sheng Fa Zhi Lei Jie Mu Bao Dao Li Du De Tan Suo Yu Si Kao" [Exploring and thinking about how to raise the power of legal program]. *Xin Wen Cai Bian* [Cover and edit news] 5:9–11.

Gao Zhen. 2004. "Foundation and Development of Chinese Legal System." *China Law* 12:115–18.

Gao Zhen and Wuguan Jia. 2008. "The Practice and Exploration of the Legal Aid Works in Rural Areas." *China Law* 4:80–82.

Gel'man, Vladimir. 2016. *Authoritarian Modernization in Russia: Ideas, Institutions, and Policies.* New York: Routledge.

Ginsburg, Tom, and Tamir Moustafa. 2008. *Rule by Law: The Politics of Courts in Authoritarian Regimes.* New York: Cambridge University Press.

Goldman, Merle. 2005. *From Comrade to Citizen: The Struggle for Political Rights in China.* Cambridge, MA: Harvard University Press.

Gong Ting. 1993. "Corruption and Reform in China: An Analysis of Unintended Consequences." *Crime, Law and Social Change* 19 (4): 311–27.

Guo Sujian and Guo Baogang. 2008. "Introduction: China in Search of a Harmonious Society." In *China in Search of a Harmonious Society*, edited by Guo S. and Guo B., 1–12. Lanham, MD: Lexington Books.

Gurevitch, Michael, and Jay G. Blumler. 1990. "Political Communication Systems and Democratic Values." In *Democracy and the Mass Media: A Collection of Essays*, edited by J. Lichtenberg, 269–89. New York: Cambridge University Press.

Habermas, Jürgen. 1989. *The Structural Transformation of the Public Sphere: An Inquiry into a Category of Bourgeois Society.* Cambridge, MA: MIT Press.

———. 1996. *Between Facts and Norms.* Cambridge, MA: MIT Press.

———. 2006. "Political Communication in Media Society: Does Democracy Still Enjoy an Epistemic Dimension? The Impact of Normative Theory on Empirical Research." *Communication Theory* 16 (4): 411–26.

Halliday, Terence C., and Sida Liu. 2007. "Birth of a Liberal Moment? Looking through a One-Way Mirror at Lawyers' Defense of Criminal Defendants in China." In *Fighting for Political Freedom: Comparative Studies of the Legal Complex and Political Liberalism*, edited by T. C. Halliday, L. Karpik, and M. Feeley, 65–108. Portland, OR: Hart.

Han Dayuan. 2009. "Ji Ben Quan Li Gai Nian Zai Zhong Guo De Qi Yuan Yu Zhuan Bian" [The origin and evolution of the concept of fundamental rights in China]. *Zhong Guo Fa Xue* [China legal science] 6:19–25.

Harwit, Eric, and Duncan Clark. 2001. "Shaping the Internet in China: Evolution of Political Control over Network Infrastructure and Content." *Asian Survey* 41 (3): 377–408.

Hassid, Jonathan. 2008. "Controlling the Chinese Media: An Uncertain Business." *Asian Survey* 48 (3): 414–30.

———. 2011. "Four Models of the Fourth Estate: A Typology of Contemporary Chinese Journalists." *China Quarterly* 208:813–32.

———. 2015. "China's Responsiveness to Internet Opinion: A Double-Edged Sword." *Journal of Current Chinese Affairs* 44 (2): 39–68.

Hay, Colin. 1999. "Crisis and the Structural Transformation of the State: Interrogating the Process of Change." *British Journal of Politics and International Relations* 1 (3): 317–44.

He Xin. 2014. "Maintaining Stability by Law: Protest-Supported Housing Demolition Litigation and Social Change in China." *Law and Social Inquiry* 39 (4): 849–73.

He Xin, Wang Lungang, and Su Yang. 2013. "Above the Roof, Beneath the Law: Perceived Justice Behind Disruptive Tactics of Migrant Wage Claimants in China." *Law and Society Review* 47 (4): 703–38.

Heilmann, Sebastian, and Elizabeth J. Perry. 2011. "Embracing Uncertainty: Guerrilla Policy Style and Adaptive Governance in China " In *Mao's Invisible Hand: The Political Foundations of Adaptive Governance in China,* edited by S. Heilmann and E. J. Perry, 1–29. Cambridge, MA: Harvard University Press.

Howard, Pat. 1988. *Breaking the Iron Rice Bowl: Prospects for Socialism in China's Countryside.* Armonk, NY: M. E. Sharpe.

Hsueh, R. 2011. *China's Regulatory State: A New Strategy for Globalization.* Ithaca, NY: Cornell University Press.

Hu Qiaomu. 1999. *Hu Qiaomu Tan Zhong Gong Dang Shi* [Hu Qiaomu's talk on the history of the Chinese Communist Party]. Beijing: Ren Min Chu Ban She [People's Publishing House].

Hu Shuli. 2008. "Cai Jing Shi Nian" [Ten years at Caijing magazine]. In *Zhong Guo Chuan Mei Feng Yun Lu* [A record of change in China's media], edited by Chen W. and Qian G., 83–110. Hong Kong: Cosmos Books.

Huang Haixing. 1999. "'She Hui Jing Wei' Gai Ban Hou Fa Zhi Zhuan Ti Jie Mu De Ding Wei" [The situation of legal programs after the revision of "social longitude and latitude"] *Dian Shi Yan Jiu* [TV research] 3:64.

Huang, Philip C. 1993. "'Public Sphere'/'Civil Society' in China?: The Third Realm Between State and Society." *Modern China* 19 (2): 216–40.

Huang Yu and Zeng Fanxu. 2011. "From 'Not in My Back Yard' to Policy Advocacy: The Co-Empowerment Model between Media and Protests in China." *Mass Communication Research* 109:168–201.

Hughes, Christopher R. 2007. "Chinese Cyber Nationalism: Evolution, Characteristics and Implications." *International Journal of Communication* 1:174–75.

Hung Chin-Fu. 2003. "Public Discourse and 'Virtual' Political Participation in the PRC: The Impact of the Internet." *Issues and Studies* 39 (4): 1–38.

Inglehart, Ronald, and Christian Welzel. 2005. *Modernization, Cultural Change, and Democracy: The Human Development Sequence.* Cambridge: Cambridge University Press

———. 2010. "Changing Mass Priorities: The Link between Modernization and Democracy." *Perspectives on Politics* 8 (2): 551–67.

Ji Weidong. 2005. "Shang Fang Chao Yu Shen Su Zhi Du De Chu Lu" [Burst of Shangfang and future of the institution of petition]. *Jing Ji Guan Li Wen Zhai* [Economy and management digest] 15:8–10.

Jia Xijin. 2011. "The Development and Institutional Environment of Non-Governmental Think Tanks in China." In *NGOs in China and Europe: Comparisons and Contrasts*, edited by Li Y., 53–70. Farnham, UK: Burlington Ashgate.

Jin Guantao and Liu Qingfeng. 1999. "Evolution of the Concept of 'Quanli' (Rights) in Modern China: From Late Qing to La Jeunesse." *Bulletin of the Institute of Modern History Academia Sinica* 32:209–60.

Keane, John. 1991. *The Media and Democracy.* Cambridge: Blackwell.

King, Gary, Jennifer Pan, and Margaret E. Roberts. 2013. "How Censorship in China Allows Government Criticism but Silences Collective Expression." *American Political Science Review* 107 (2): 326–43.

———. 2016. "How the Chinese Government Fabricates Social Media Posts for Strategic Distraction, Not Engaged Argument." *American Political Science Review.* http://gking.harvard.edu/50c.

Kluver, Randy, Xu Wu, Evgeny Morozov, Juntao Wang, David Bachman, and Guobin Yang. 2010. "Book Review Roundtable: The Power of the Internet in China." *Asia Policy* 10:163–88.

Krippendorff, Klaus. 2004. *Content Analysis: An Introduction to Its Methodology.* Thousand Oaks, CA: Sage.

Lagerkvist, Johan. 2005. "The Rise of Online Public Opinion in the People's Republic of China." *China: An International Journal* 3 (1): 119–30.

Lee Chin-Chuan. 2000. "Chinese Communication: Prisms, Trajectories, and Modes of Understanding." In *Power, Money, and Media: Communication Patterns and Bureaucratic Control in Cultural China*, edited by Lee C.-C., 3–44. Evanston, IL: Northwestern University Press.

———. 2003. "The Global and the National of the Chinese Media." In *Chinese Media, Global Contexts*, 1–31. New York: Routledge.

Lee Chin-Chuan, He Zhou, and Huang Yu. 2007. "Party-Market Corporatism, Clientelism, and Media in Shanghai." *Harvard International Journal of Press/Politics* 12 (3): 21–42.

Lee Ching Kwan. 2007. *Against the Law: Labor Protests in China's Rustbelt and Sunbelt*. Berkeley: University of California Press.

Lei, Ya-Wen. 2011. "The Political Consequences of the Rise of the Internet: Political Beliefs and Practices of Chinese Netizens." *Political Communication* 28 (3): 291–322.

Lei, Ya-Wen, and Daniel Xiaodan Zhou. 2015. "Contesting Legality in Authoritarian Contexts: Food Safety, Rule of Law and China's Networked Public Sphere." *Law and Society Review* 49 (3): 557–93.

Leung, Parry P. 2015. *Labor Activists and the New Working Class in China: Strike Leaders' Struggles*. New York: Palgrave Macmillan.

Li Biao. 2011. "Study on Spatial Communication Structure of Network Events: An Analysis of 40 Network Events in Recent Years." *Journalism and Communication* 3:90–99.

———. 2012. "Portraits of Weibo Public Opinion Leaders." *Journalism Review* 9:19–25.

Li Fan. 2011. *Dang Dai Zhong Guo De Zi You Min Quan Yun Dong* [Rise of civil rights movement in contemporary China]. Gaoxiong: Chulu Publisher.

Li Jing. 2007. "Dian Shi Fa Zhi Jie Mu Zai Zhong Guo Fa Zhi Hua Jin Cheng Zhong De Jiao Se: Dian Shi Fa Zhi Jie Mu Xian Zhuang Yu Fa Zhan Fen Xi" [The role of legal TV programs in China's legalization: Analysis of the development of legal TV programs]. *Xhong Guo Guang Bo Dian Shi Xue Kan* [China radio and TV academic journal] 3:62–64.

Li Kangning. 2014. "Quan Li Zai Zhong Guo De Dan Sheng Cheng Zhang Yu Cheng Xing" [The birth, growth and development of rights in China]. *Gan Su Zheng Fa Xue Yuan Xue Bao* [Journal of Gansu Political Science and Law Institute] 1:1–15.

Li Lianjiang. 2004. "Political Trust in Rural China." *Modern China* 30 (2): 228–58.

Li Peilin, Chen Guangjin, and Chang Yi. 2014. *Society of China Analysis and Forecast 2014*. Beijing: She Hui Ke Xue Wen Xian Chu Ban She [Social Science Academic Press].

———. 2015. *Society of China Analysis and Forecast 2015*. Beijing: She Hui Ke Xue Wen Xian Chu Ban She [Social Science Academic Press].

Li Wei. 2002. "Corruption During the Economic Transition in China." In *Corrupt Exchanges: Empirical Themes in the Politics and Political Economy of Corruption*, edited by D. Della Porta and S. Rose-Ackerman, 160–77. Baden-Baden, Germany: Nomos.

Liao Zhixiong. 2015. "Implications of China's Latest Statute on Internet and the Forthcoming Real-Name Registration Scheme." *International Journal of Technology Policy and Law* 2 (1): 55–70.

Lieberthal, Kenneth. 1992. "Introduction: The 'Fragmented Authoritarianism' Model and Its Limitation." In *Bureaucracy, Politics, and Decision Making in Post-Mao China*, edited by K. Lieberthal and D. M. Lampton, 1–30. Berkeley: University of California Press.

Liebman, Benjamin L. 1999. "Legal Aid and Public Interest Law in China." *Texas International Law Journal* 34:211–86.

———. 2005. "Watchdog or Demagogue? The Media in the Chinese Legal System." *Columbia Law Review* 105 (1): 1–157.

———. 2011. "A Populist Threat to China's Courts?" In *Chinese Justice: Civil Dispute Resolution in Contemporary China*, edited by M. Y. K. Woo and M. E. Gallagher, 169–203. New York: Cambridge University Press.

Lin Fen. 2008. "Turning Gray: Transition of Political Communication in China, 1978–2008." PhD diss., University of Chicago.

Lin Han. 2012. "The Role of NGOs in Maintaining Social Stability in China—Based on the Perspective of Public Security Service Delivery." In *Building Service-Oriented Government: Lessons, Challenges and Prospects*, edited by Wu W., 99–118. Singapore: World Scientific Publishing.

Lin Mu. 2004. "Changes and Consistency: China's Media Market after WTO Entry." *Journal of Media Economics* 17 (3): 177–92.

Lin Yutang. 1936. *A History of the Press and Public Opinion in China*. Chicago: University of Chicago Press.

Lipset, Seymour M. 1959. "Some Social Requisites of Democracy: Economic Development and Political Legitimacy." *American Political Science Review* 53 (1): 69–105.

Liu, Alan P. L. 1996. *Mass Politics in the People's Republic: State and Society in Contemporary China*. Boulder, CO: Westview Press.

Liu Bing. 2014. "Dian Shi Fa Zhi Jie Mu De Fa Zhan" [The development of TV legal programs]. *Xi Bu Guang Bo Dian Shi* [Western broadcast TV] 14:52.

Liu Fuzhi. 1998. "Nan Wang De Tan Hua" [Unforgettable Talks]. In *Hui Yi Deng Xiaoping* [In commemoration of Deng Xiaoping], edited by C. P. L. R. Group, 177–82. Peking: Central Party Literature Press

Liu Guangjin. 1994. "Explorative Analysis of Human Rights in Late Qing." *New History Journal* 5 (3): 1–23.

Liu Sida and Terence C. Halliday. 2011. "Political Liberalism and Political Embeddedness: Understanding Politics in the Work of Chinese Criminal Defense Lawyers." *Law and Society Review* 45 (4): 831–66.

Liu Yi. 2010. "Research and Evaluation on Media Competitiveness across Provinces." *Modern Audio-Video Art* 2:24–29.

Lorentzen, Peter. 2014. "China's Strategic Censorship." *American Journal of Political Science* 58 (2): 402–14.

Lorentzen, Peter, and Suzanne Scoggins. 2015. "Understanding China's Rising Rights Consciousness." *China Quarterly* 223:1–20.

Lynch, Daniel C. 1999. *After the Propaganda State: Media, Politics, and "Thought Work" in Reformed China*. Stanford, CA: Stanford University Press.

MacKinnon, Rebecca. 2012. *Consent of the Networked : The Worldwide Struggle for Internet Freedom*. New York: Basic Books.

Man, Joyce Y. 2011. "Local Public Finance in China: An Overview." In *China's Local Public Finance in Transition*, edited by J. Y. Man and Y.-h. Hong, 3–20. Cambridge, MA: Lincoln Institute of Land Policy.

McCormick, Barrett L., and Qing Liu. 2003. "Globalization and the Chinese Media: Technologies, Content, Commerce and the Prospects for the Public Sphere." In *Chinese Media, Global Contexts*, edited by C.-C. Li, 136–55. New York: Routledge.

Menefee, Trey, and Bjorn Harald Nordtveit. 2012. "Disaster, Civil Society and Education in China: A Case Study of an Independent Non-Government Organization Working in the Aftermath of the Wenchuan Earthquake." *International Journal of Educational Development* 32 (4): 600–607.

Meng Bingchun. 2011. "From Steamed Bun to Grass Mud Horse: E Gao as Alternative Political Discourse on the Chinese Internet." *Global Media and Communication* 7 (1): 33–51.

Mertha, Andrew. 2009. "'Fragmented Authoritarianism 2.0': Political Pluralization in the Chinese Policy Process." *China Quarterly* 200:995–1012.

Merton, Robert. K. 1959. "Notes on Problem-Finding in Sociology." In *Sociology Today: Problems and Prospects*, edited by R. Merton, L. Broom, and L. S. Cottrell, ix–xxxiv. New York: Basic Books.

Moore, B. 1966. *Social Origins of Dictatorship and Democracy: Lord and Peasant in the Making of the Modern World*. Boston: Beacon.

Moustafa, Tamir. 2007. *The Struggle for Constitutional Power: Law, Politics, and Economic Development in Egypt*. New York: Cambridge University Press.

Nasser, Osama, Shamis AlThuhli, Morshed Mohammed, Rashed AlMamari, and Faizal Hajamohideen. 2015. "An Investigation of Backdoors Implication to Avoid Regional Security Impediment." In *Communication Technologies (GCCT), 2015 Global Conference IEEE*, 409–12. Piscataway, NJ: IEEE.

Nathan, Andrew J. 2003. "China's Changing of the Guard: Authoritarian Resilience." *Journal of Democracy* 14 (1): 6–17.

Nettl, J. P., and Roland Robertson. 1966. "Industrialization, Development or Modernization." *British Journal of Sociology* 17 (3): 274–91.

Niu Anqi. 2012. "Lun 'Jin Ri Shuo Fa' De Chuang Xin Ce Lue" [The innovation strategies of legal report and practical significance]. *Chang Chun Jin Rong Gao Deng Zhuan Ke Xue Xiao Xue Bao* [Journal of Changchun Finance College] 2:90–91.

Nordin, Astrid, and Lisa Richaud. 2014. "Subverting Official Language and Discourse in China? Type River Crab for Harmony." *China Information* 28 (1): 47–67.

O'Brien, Kevin J. 1996. "Rightful Resistance." *World Politics* 49:31–55.

O'Brien, Kevin J., and Li Lianjiang. 2006. *Rightful Resistance in Rural China*. Cambridge: Cambridge University Press.

Owen-Smith, Jason, and Walter W. Powell. 2008. "Networks and Institutions " In *The Sage Handbook of Organizational Institutionalism*, edited by R. Greenwood, 596–623. Los Angeles: SAGE.

Padgett, John Frederick, and Walter W. Powell. 2012a. "Coda: Reflections on the Study of Multiple Networks." In *The Emergence of Organizations and Markets*, edited by J. F. Padgett and W. W. Powell, 566–70. Princeton, NJ: Princeton University Press.

———. 2012b. "The Problem of Emergence " In *The Emergence of Organizations and Markets*, edited by J. F. Padgett and W. W. Powell, 1–29. Princeton, NJ: Princeton University Press.

Pan Zhongdang. 2010. "Bounded Innovation in the Media." In *Reclaiming Chinese Society: The New Social Activism*, edited by Y.-t. Hsing and C. K. Lee, 184–206. New York: Routledge.

Pan Zhondang and Joseph Man Chan. 2003. "Shifting Journalistic Paradigms: How China's Journalists Assess 'Media Exemplars'." *Communication Research* 30 (6): 649–82.

Pangestu, Mari, and Debbie Mrongowius. 2004. "Telecommunications Services in China: Facing the Challenges of WTO Accession." In *China and the WTO: Accession, Policy Reform, and Poverty Reduction Strategies*, edited by D. Bhattasali, S. Li, and W. Martin, 157–80. Washington, DC: Oxford University Press.

Papacharissi, Zizi. 2002. "The Virtual Sphere: The Internet as a Public Sphere." *New Media and Society* 4 (1): 9–27.

Peerenboom, Randall. 2002. *China's Long March toward Rule of Law*. New York: Cambridge University Press.

Pei Minxin. 1997. "Citizens v. Mandarins: Administrative Litigation in China." *China Quarterly* 152:832–62.

Peng Gaoqin. 2008. "Jia Qiang Pu Fa Xuan Chuan Zuo Hao Fa Zhi Bao Dao" [Enhance law dissemination and legal reports]. *Xin Wen Chuan* [News window] 4:55.

Peng Lan. 2005. *Zhongguo Wang Luo Mei Ti De Di Yi Ge Shi Nian* [The first decade of the Chinese Internet media]. Beijing: Tsinghua University Press.

Perry, Elizabeth J. 2007. "Studying Chinese Politics: Farewell to Revolution?" *China Journal* 57:1–22.

————. 2008. "Chinese Conceptions of 'Rights': From Mencius to Mao—and Now." *Perspectives on Politics* 6 (1): 37–50.

Peters, Bernhard. 2008. "Law, State and the Political Public Sphere as Forms of Social Self-Organization." In *Public Deliberation and Public Culture: The Writings of Bernhard Peters, 1993–2005*, edited by H. Wessler, 17–32. New York: Palgrave Macmillan.

Peters, Robert. 2002. "China, Democracy and the Internet." In *Information Technology and World Politics*, edited by M. J. Mazarr, 101–13. New York: Palgrave Macmillan.

Price, Vincent. 1992. *Public Opinion*. Newbury Park, CA: SAGE.

Przeworski, Adam, and Fernando Limongi. 1997. "Modernization: Theories and Facts." *World Politics* 49 (2): 155–83.

Qian Gang. 2008. "Zheng Zhi Gai Ge Feng Yu Zhong De Zhong Guo Chuan Mei" [Chinese media in the storm of political reform]. In *Zhong Guo Chuan Mei Feng Yun Lu* [A record of change in China's media], edited by Chen W. and Qian G., 137–55. Hong Kong: Cosmos Books.

Qian Gang and David Bandurski. 2010. "China's Emerging Public Sphere: The Impact of Media, Commercialization, Professionalism, and the Internet in an Era of Transition." In *Changing Media, Changing China*, edited by S. L. Shirk, 38–76. New York: Oxford University Press.

Rajah, Jothie. 2012. *Authoritarian Rule of Law: Legislation, Discourse, and Legitimacy in Singapore*. New York: Cambridge University Press.

Rankin, Mary Backus. 1986. *Elite Activism and Political Transformation in China: Zhejiang Province, 1865–1911*. Stanford, CA: Stanford University Press.

Reed, Kristina M. 1999. "From the Great Firewall of China to the Berlin Firewall: The Cost of Content Regulation on Internet Commerce." *Transnational Lawyer* 12 (2): 543–68.

Reilly, James. 2012. *Strong Society, Smart State: The Rise of Public Opinion in China's Japan Policy*. New York: Columbia University Press.

Robertson, Roland. 1992. *Globalization: Social Theory and Global Culture*. Newbury Park, CA: SAGE.

Rosen, Stanley. 2010. "Is the Internet a Positive Force in the Development of Civil Society, a Public Sphere, and Democratization in China?" *International Journal of Communication* 10:509–16.

Rowe, William T. 1990. "The Public Sphere in Modern China." *Modern China* 16 (3): 309–29.

Ru Xin, Lu Peiyi, and Li Peilin. 2011. *Society of China Analysis and Forecast (2011)*. Beijing: She Hui Ke Xue Wen Xian Chu Ban She [Social Science Academic Press].

Ruan Pei. 2014. "Fa Zhi Ji Zhe De Min Sheng Yi Shi" [The consciousness of legal reporters]. *Shi Ting Jie* [Broadcasting realm] 3:106–7.

Rueschemeyer, Dietrich, Evelyne Huber Stephens, and John D. Stephens. 1992. *Capitalist Development and Democracy*. New York: Polity.

Schudson, Michael. 1994. "Public Sphere and Its Problems: Bringing the State (Back) In." *Notre Dame Journal of Law, Ethics and Public Policy* 8:529–46.

Sen, Amartya. 2008. "Development as Capability Expansion." In *The Community Development Reader*, edited by J. DeFilippis and S. Saegert, 319–27. New York: Routledge.

Shen Fei, Wang Ning, Guo Zhongshi, and Guo Liang. 2009. "Online Network Size, Efficacy, and Opinion Expression: Assessing the Impacts of Internet Use in China." *International Journal of Public Opinion Research* 21 (4): 451–76.

Shen Yang and Wu Jingji. 2014. "Analysis of Opinion Leaders." *Caijing* 393:30–37.

Shi Yunqing. 2015. *Zai Zao Chng Min* [Becoming citizens]. Beijing: She Hui Ke Xue Wen Xian Chu Ban She [Social Science Academic Press].

Shirky, Clay. 2011. "The Political Power of Social Media: Technology, the Public Sphere, and Political Change." *Foreign Affairs* 90 (1): 28–41.

Somers, Margaret R. 1993. "Citizenship and the Place of the Public Sphere: Law, Community, and Political Culture in the Transition to Democracy." *American Sociological Review* 58 (5): 587–620.

Song Lianlian. 2009. "Fu Wu Xing: Rang Fa Zhi Bao Dao Cheng Pu Fa Zhu Zhen Di" [Service: Let legal reports become the battle front of law dissemination]. *Zhong Guo Ji Zhe* [Chinese journalist] 9:45.

Spires, Anthony J. 2011. "Contingent Symbiosis and Civil Society in an Authoritarian State: Understanding the Survival of China's Grassroots NGOs." *American Journal of Sociology* 117 (1): 1–45.

———. 2012. "Lessons from Abroad: Foreign Influences on China's Emerging Civil Society." *China Journal* 68:125–46.

Starr, Paul. 2004. *The Creation of the Media: Political Origins of Modern Communications*. New York: Basic Books.

Stern, Rachel E. 2011. "From Dispute to Decision: Suing Polluters in China." *China Quarterly* 206:294–312.

Stockmann, Daniela. 2013. *Media Commercialization and Authoritarian Rule in China*. New York: Cambridge University Press.

Stockmann, Daniela, and Mary E. Gallagher. 2011. "Remote Control: How the Media Sustains Authoritarian Rule in China." *Comparative Political Studies* 43 (4): 436–67.

Strand, David. 1989. *Rickshaw Beijing: City People and Politics in the 1920s*. Berkeley: University of California Press.

Sunstein, Cass R. 2007. *Republic.Com 2.0*. Princeton, NJ: Princeton University Press.

Swidler, Ann. 1986. "Culture in Action: Symbols and Strategies." *American Sociological Review* 51 (2): 273–86.

Tai Zixue. 2006. *The Internet in China: Cyberspace and Civil Society*. New York: Routledge.

Tamanaha, Brian Z. 2004. *On the Rule of Law: History, Politics, Theory*. New York: Cambridge University Press.

Tang Lijun and Yang Peidong. 2011. "Symbolic Power and the Internet: The Power of a 'Horse.'" *Media, Culture, and Society* 33 (5): 675–91.

Tang, Min, Laia Jorba, and Michael J. Jensen. 2012. "Digital Media and Political Attitudes in China." In *Digital Media and Political Engagement Worldwide: A Comparative Study*, edited by E. Anduiza Perea, M. J. Jensen, and L. Jorba, 221–52. New York: Cambridge University Press.

Tang Qiaoying. 2015. "The Study of Network Public Opinions—Based on an Analysis of Internet Events (2003–2014)." *New Media and Society* 3:207–27.

Tang Wenfang. 2005. *Public Opinion and Political Change in China*. Stanford, CA: Stanford University Press.

Teng Biao. 2012. "Rights Defence (Weiquan), Microblogs (Weibo), and the Surrounding Gaze (Weiguan): The Rights Defence Movement Online and Offline." *China Perspectives* 3:29–41.

Thompson, E. P. 1975. *Whigs and Hunters: The Origin of the Black Act*. New York: Pantheon Books.

Thornton, Patricia M. 2011. "Retrofitting the Steel Frame: From Mobilizing the Masses to Surveying the Public." In *Mao's Invisible Hand: The Political Foundations of Adaptive Governance in China*, edited by S. Heilmann and E. J. Perry, 237–68. Cambridge, MA: Harvard University Press,

Tian, Robert G., and Yan Wu. 2007. "Crafting Self Identity in a Virtual Community: Chinese Internet Users and Their Political Sense Form." *Multicultural Education and Technology Journal* 1 (4): 238–58.

Tong Jingrong. 2007. "Guerrilla Tactics of Investigative Journalists in China." *Journalism* 8 (5): 530–35.

Tong Yanqi and Lei Shaohua. 2014. *Social Protest in Contemporary China, 2003–2010: Transitional Pains and Regime Legitimacy*. Vol. 35. New York: Routledge.

Tsai, Kellee S. 2006. "Adaptive Informal Institutions and Endogenous Institutional Change in China." *World Politics* 59 (1): 116–41.

Tsai Wen-Hsuan. 2016. "How 'Networked Authoritarianism' Was Operationalized in China: Methods and Procedures of Public Opinion Control." *Journal of Contemporary China* 25 (101): 1–14.

Tsui Lokman. 2003. "The Panopticon as the Antithesis of a Space of Freedom: Control and Regulation of the Internet in China." *China Information* 17 (2): 65–82.

Wagner, Rudolf G. 1986. "Liu Binyan and the Texie." *Modern Chinese Literature* 2 (1): 63–98.

Wakeman Jr, F. 1993. "The Civil Society and Public Sphere Debate: Western Reflections on Chinese Political Culture." *Modern China* 19 (2): 108–38.

Wang Chenguang. 2010. "From the Rule of Man to the Rule of Law." In *China's Journey Toward the Rule of Law: Legal Reform, 1978–2008*, vol. 1, edited by Cai D. and Wang C., 1–50. Leiden: Brill

Wang Ping and Xie Yun. 2012. "Empirical Analysis of the Role of Weibo Opinion Leaders in Public Opinion Incidents." *Contemporary Communications* 3:82–88.

Wang Ping, Bao Xianzhi, and Dong Xiaowen. 2015. "Nong Min Jie Chu Dian Shi Fa Zhi Xin Xi Chuan Bo De Zhuang Kuang Diao Cha Fen Xi: Yi Jiang Su Sui Ning Nong Cun Wei Li" [Investigation and analysis of how peasants are exposed to TV legal information: Using a village in Jiansu Suining as an example]. *Sheng Ping Shi Jie* [Voice and screen world] 1:29–32.

Wang Shaoguang. 1997. "China's 1994 Fiscal Reform: An Initial Assessment." *Asian Survey* 37 (9): 801–17.

Wang Shaojung S. 2012. "China's Internet Lexicon: Symbolic Meaning and Commoditization of Grass Mud Horse in the Harmonious Society." *First Monday* 17 (1). http://firstmonday.org /article/view/3758/3134.

Wang Wei. 2001. "China's Access to WTO: Impact on Telecommunications and Internet Information Services." In *China's Integration with the World Economy: Repercussions of China's Accession to the WTO*, edited by K. T. Lee, J. Y. Lin, and S. J. Kim, 288–310. Seoul: Korea Institute for International Economic Policy.

Wang Zheng. 2014. "The Chinese Dream: Concept and Context." *Journal of Chinese Political Science* 19 (1): 1–13.

Wang Zhongyuan. 2011. "Min Gong Wei Quan: She Hui Huan Jing Ri Yi Guan Zhu Ruo Zhe" [Migrant workers' rights defense: Social environment increasingly attends to the disadvantaged]. *Zhong Guo Zhi Liang Wan Li Hang* [China quality long march] 4:20–32.

Wei Yongzheng and Dai Yajing. 2015. "Changing Modes of Information Dissemination About Emergencies in the Era of Integrated Media." *News Field* 18:19–25.

Welzel, Christian. 2006. "Democratization as an Emancipative Process: The Neglected Role of Mass Motivations." *European Journal of Political Research* 45 (6): 871–96.

Welzel, Christian, and Ronald Inglehart. 2008. "The Role of Ordinary People in Democratization." *Journal of Democracy* 19 (1): 126–40.

Wu Guoguang. 1994. "Command Communication: The Politics of Editorial Formulation in the *People's Daily*." *China Quarterly* 137 (1): 194–211.

Wu Guoguang. 2000. "One Head, Many Mouths: Diversifying Press Structures in Reform China." In *Power, Money, and Media: Communication Patterns and Bureaucratic Control in Cultural China*, edited by C.-C. Lee, 45–67. Evanston, IL: Northwestern University Press.

Wu Sen. 2012. "Cheng Shi Dian Shi Tai Fa Zhi Jie Mu Chuang Xin Tan Xi: Yi Nan Jing Dian Shi Tai Jiao Ke Pin Dao 'Fa Zhi Xian Chang' Wei Li" [Exploring innovation of city televisions' legal programs: Using "Legal Scene" as an example]. *Jv Ying Yue Bao* [Drama and film journal] 5:54–56.

Wu Wenjuan. 2008. "Nong Min Bao Fa Zhi Bao Dao De Bian Ji Si Xiang" [Editorial thinking on legal reports in peasant newspapers]. *Xin Wen Qian Shao* [Press outpost] 2:47.

Wu Xu. 2007. *Chinese Cyber Nationalism: Evolution, Characteristics, and Implications.* Lanham, MD: Lexington Books.

Wu Xueyao and Liu Shixin. 2015. "Evaluating the Chinese Government's Credibility from the Tianjin Explosion Incident." *Legal Institution and Society* 10:221–22.

Wu Yingnu, Shen Yang, and Zhou Qin. 2014. "Online Behavior of Weibo Public Opinion Leaders." *News Journalists* 1:29–35.

Xiao Qiang. 2010. "The Rise of Online Public Opinion and Its Political Impact." In *Changing Media, Changing China,* edited by S. L. Shirk, 202–24. New York: Oxford University Press.

———. 2011. "The Battle for the Chinese Internet." *Journal of Democracy* 22 (2): 47–61.

Xie Yu and Emily Hannum. 1996. "Regional Variation in Earnings Inequality in Reform-Era Urban China." *American Journal of Sociology* 101 (4): 950–92.

Xin Xin. 2006. "A Developing Market in News: Xinhua News Agency and Chinese Newspapers." *Media, Culture and Society* 28 (1): 45–66.

Xung Guangqing. 2012. "The Evolving Logics of Internet Public Incidents in China." *EAI Working Papers* 91:1–23.

Yamaguchi, Kazuo. 2000. "Multinomial Logit Latent-Class Regression Models: An Analysis of the Predictors of Gender-Role Attitudes among Japanese Women 1." *American Journal of Sociology* 105 (6): 1702–40.

Yang, Dali L. 2004. *Remaking the Chinese Leviathan: Market Transition and the Politics of Governance in China.* Stanford, CA: Stanford University Press.

Yang, Guobin. 2009. *The Power of the Internet in China: Citizen Activism Online.* New York: Columbia University Press.

———. 2013. "Contesting Food Safety in the Chinese Media: Between Hegemony and Counter-Hegemony." *China Quarterly* 214:337–55.

———. 2014. "The Return of Ideology and the Future of Chinese Internet Policy." *Critical Studies in Media Communication* 31 (2): 109–13.

Yang Jun. 2006. "'Nin Zui Guan Xin De Jiu Shi Wo Men Zui Guan Zhu De': Cong Gong Ren Ri Bao 'Wei Quan Zhou Kan' Kan Bao Zhi Zhuan Fu Kan De Du Zhe Ding Wei" [What you care about the most is what we care about the most: Situating newspapers' special issue from the experience of Worker Daily's Weiquan Weekly]. *Xin Wen Zhan Xian* [The press] a:12.

Yang Xiaoqing. 2013. "Comparative Study of Constitutionalism and People's Democracy." *Hongqi Wengao* 10:4–10.

Yang Yuguan and Chen Zinan. 2015. "Wan Shan Wo Guo Fa Lu Yuan Zhu Zhi Du Ruo Gan Wen Ti Yan Jiu" [Research on problems related to how to enhance legal aid institution in China]. *Li Lun Xue Kan* [Theory journal] 1:102–7.

Yu Haiqing. 2012. "Governing and Representing HIV/AIDS in China: A Review and an Introduction." *International Journal of Asia Pacific Studies* 8 (1): 1–33.

Yu Jianrong. 2011. *Di Ceng Li Chang [The perspective of the lower class].* Shanghai: Shanghai San Lian Shu Dian [Shanghai Joint Publishing Company].

Yuen, Samson. 2015. "Becoming a Cyber Power: China's Cybersecurity Upgrade and Its Consequences." *China Perspectives* 2:53–58.

Zarrow, Peter. 2016. "Felling a Dynasty, Founding a Republic " In *The Oxford Illustrated History of Modern China,* edited by J. N. Wasserstrom, 91–117. Oxford: Oxford University Press.

Zhao Decheng. 2006. "A Report on the Legal Consciousness of Businessmen in Rural Areas." *Journal of Hunan Public Security College* 6:5–15.

Zhao Dingxin. 2000. "State-Society Relations and the Discourses and Activities of the 1989 Beijing Student Movement." *American Journal of Sociology* 105 (6): 1592–632.

———. 2001. *The Power of Tiananmen: State-Society Relations and the 1989 Beijing Student Movement*. Chicago: University of Chicago Press.

Zhao Suisheng. 2003. "Political Liberalization without Democratization: Pan Wei's Proposal for Political Reform." *Journal of Contemporary China* 12 (35): 333–55.

Zhao Yuezhi. 1998. *Media, Market, and Democracy in China: Between the Party Line and the Bottom Line*. Chicago: University of Illinois Press.

———. 2000. "From Commercialization to Conglomeration: The Transformation of the Chinese Press within the Orbit of the Party State." *Journal of Communication* 50 (2): 3–26.

———. 2004. "Underdogs, Lapdogs and Watchdogs: Journalists and the Public Sphere Problematic in China." In *Chinese Intellectuals between State and Market*, edited by E. X. Gu and M. Goldman, 43–74. New York: Routledge.

———. 2008. *Communication in China: Political Economy, Power, and Conflict*. Lanham, MD: Rowman and Littlefield.

Zhao, Ziyang, Pu Bao, Renee Chiang, Adi Ignatius, and Roderick MacFarquhar. 2009. *Prisoner of the State: The Secret Journal of Zhao Ziyang*. New York: Simon and Schuster.

Zheng Bowang. 2007. "The Channels through Which Chinese Citizens Develop Their Legal Consciousness and the Implications." *Journal of Huainan Vocational and Technical College* 4:103–7.

Zheng Y. and Wu Guoguang. 2005. "Information Technology, Public Space, and Collective Action in China." *Comparative Political Studies* 38 (5): 507–36.

Zheng Yongnian. 2008. *Technological Empowerment: The Internet, State, and Society in China*. Stanford, CA: Stanford University Press.

Zhong Ying and Yu Xiucai. 2010. "1998–2009 Zhong Da Wang Luo Yu Lun Shi Jian Ji Qi Chuan Bo Te Zheng Tan Xi" [An analysis of some key network public opinion cases and their dissemination characteristics]. *Xin Wen Chuan Bo Yu Yan Jiu* [Journalism and communication] 4:45–52.

Zhou Jiaxiang. 1999. "Zeng Qiang He Duan Zheng Gong Min De Fa Ding Quan Li Guan—Yi Ge Zai Pu Fa Jiao Yu Zhong Zhi De Zhong Shi De Wen Ti" [Enhancing and correcting citizen's concept of rights: A noteworthy problem in education to disseminate law]. *Xian Ning Shi Zhuan Xue Bao* [Journal of Xianning Teachers College] 2:86–89.

Zhou Yongming. 2006. *Historicizing Online Politics: Telegraphy, the Internet, and Political Participation in China*. Stanford, CA: Stanford University Press.

Zuo Fang. 2008. "Chuang Ban Nan Fang Zhou Mo" [Launching southern weekend]. In *Zhong Guo Chuan Mei Feng Yun Lu* [A record of change in China's media], edited by Qian G. and Chen W., 49–78. Hong Kong: Cosmos Books.

INDEX

NOTE: Page numbers followed by *f* indicate a figure; those with *t* indicate a table.

A NOTE ON THE TYPE

This book has been composed in Adobe Text and Gotham. Adobe Text, designed by Robert Slimbach for Adobe, bridges the gap between fifteenth- and sixteenth-century calligraphic and eighteenth-century Modern styles. Gotham, inspired by New York street signs, was designed by Tobias Frere-Jones for Hoefler & Co.